Umbanda

Umbanda
Religion and Politics in Urban Brazil

by
Diana DeG. Brown

COLUMBIA UNIVERSITY PRESS
NEW YORK

Columbia University Press Morningside Edition
Columbia University Press
New York   Chichester, West Susex

Morningside Edition with new preface
Copyright © 1994 Columbia University Press
Copyright © 1986 Diana DeGroat Brown

Library of Congress Cataloging-in-Publication Data

Brown, Diana DeG. (Diana DeGroat), 1938–
Umbanda : religion and politics in urban Brazil / by Diana DeG. Brown.
p. cm.
Originally published: Ann Arbor, Mich. : Umi Research Press,
© 1986, in series: Studies in cultural anthropology ; no. 7.
A revision of author's Ph.D. thesis, Columbia University, 1974.
Includes bibliographical references and index.
ISBN 0-231-10005-1 (pbk.)
1. Umbanda (Cult)—Brazil. 2. Brazil—Politics and
government—1930–1954. 3. Brazil—Politics and
government—1954–1964. 4. Brazil—Religious life and customs.
I. Title.
[BL2592.U513B75 1994]
299'.67—dc20
94-1721(
CIP

∞

Printed in the United States of America

p 10 9 8 7 6 5 4 3 2 1

To my parents
Elliot W. Brown
and
Christine Q. Brown
for their unwavering
love and support.
My husband Mario Bick
and my son Alexander Brown Bick.

All of them have given me their
love and companionship and have
supported this project. They
have, in one way or another, made
great contributions to this project.

Contents

Figures

Tables

Acknowledgments

This book is a product of many years of researching, discussing and mulling over in my own mind various facets of Umbanda. A great many people have aided me in this task. I owe special thanks to Robert Murphy and Charles Wagley for intellectual stimulus and encouragement of my research, and for introducing me to the field of Brazilian studies. Anthony Leeds also provided helpful suggestions in my initial fieldwork on patronage and informal networks. Donald Warren's mutual interest in Spiritism and his friendship and support of my research have aided me both in Brazil and New York.

For special critical assistance and moral support in the preparation of this text, I thank Judith Shapiro, with whom I have shared many years of anthropological study and discussion, and who assisted me in bringing my dissertation to term; Joyce Riegelhaupt, who in addition to her friendship and generously offered critical readings of both the dissertation and this text, has provided me with a model of high standards of critical thought; and Mario Bick, friend, intellectual companion and husband, whose creative insights and uncompromising critical eye, together with his encouragement, have made an invaluable contribution to all of my work.

I thank the faculty and students of the Conjunto de Antropologia at the Universidade Estadual de Campinas for inviting me to teach there and for their hospitality to me during 1975-76, and 1978-79. My understanding of Brazil and of Umbanda was honed during intense late evening discussions with Peter Fry, Maria Manuela Carneiro da Cunha, Verena Stolcke, Mariza Côrrea, Plínio Denizen, Michael Hall, Rubem Cesar Fernandes, Carlos Brandão, and many others. Lícia Valladares, a close friend since my early days in Rio, has deepened my knowledge of Brazil, and contributed greatly to the strong continuing ties I feel with Rio.

For their hospitality and insights during earlier phases of my research, I thank Florestan Fernandes and Cândido Mendes de Almeida. Anthony Knopp and Bela Bianco greatly assisted me with their knowledge of Brazil and of the finer details of the Portuguese language.

I owe very special thanks as well to the many Umbandistas who shared with me their experiences and their time. Armando Cavalcanti Bandeira not only served as my chief mentor in the world of Umbanda in Rio, but has remained a close friend. I thank as well Henrique Landi, Jr., Mauro Porto, Maria das Dores Lima, Dra. Massena, Nogueira Aranha, Pedro McGregor, Moab Caldas, Labanca, and many others too numerous to mention here. I thank as well the students from the Fundação Getúlio Vargas with particular appreciation to Louis César Queiroz Ribeiro and the students of Universidade Federal do Estado do Rio de Janeiro in Niteroi, who cheerfully helped me to surmount the many difficulties involved in administering the questionnaire.

I received financial assistance for my research from many sources. A Metropolitan Summer Field Training Program grant from the Ford Foundation in 1966, a Fulbright-Hays Doctoral Research Grant for 1968–70, and funds from the Institute for Latin American Studies at Columbia University both in the field and for writing up the dissertation, all helped to make this research possible. Subsequent funding was provided by a Schuster Fellowship from Herbert H. Lehman College in 1975, and a research grant from the City University of New York, in 1977–78.

To all of these, and to many others whose friendship and encouragement have contributed to this book and to my own intellectual development, I thank you all.

Preface to the Morningside Edition

On New Year's Eve 1993, from the window of a Rio de Janeiro apartment overlooking Copacabana beach, I waited expectantly for the worshippers of Yemanjá to arrive, dressed for their ceremonies, the women resplendent in their long, white lace-trimmed outfits or in brightly colored full satin skirts. I wanted to see them loaded down with flowers, candles, food and drink; to watch them set up these offerings in the sand and begin their ceremonies; to go down and join them. In 1970, the last New Year's Eve I had spent in Rio doing research for this book, the evening had begun with a religious procession much like those for Catholic saints days except that it was the Afro-Brazilian sea deity Yemanjá whose image was carried aloft to the edge of the beach, accompanied by thousands of Umbanda worshippers carrying lighted candles and singing Umbanda hymns and, at the head of the procession, the Umbandista politicians who were the secular patrons of this public event. Then this famous beach, a long crescent of white sand framed by the lights of the buildings along the shore, had become so densely crowded with Umbanda rituals that I could hardly move among them. Circles of onlookers formed human walls around the religious activities within: the drummers pounding out the beat and the initiates singing, dancing, becoming possessed by their spirits, and even offering spiritual consultations to the onlookers. The sea, too, had been awash with flowers and other offerings sent off into the waves to praise and petition the sea goddess, even tiny boats bearing her image—a beautiful young woman with pale skin and long straight dark hair, in a blue gown—and filled with offerings to her female vanity; perfumes, scented soaps, combs, mirrors. Worshippers and initiates possessed by their spirits waded out into the waves fully clothed, their hair loosed for the spirit to enter to pay homage to her.

But this year there was little evidence of Umbanda. When I finally went down to the beach sometime before midnight I counted only some ten Umbanda ceremonies which were hardly visible among the groups of Brazilians and foreign tourists milling about and waiting for the fireworks promised for midnight. This display, over 20 tons of fireworks that lit up the night sky, was followed by live entertainment in front of a large tourist hotel. This was broadcast along the length of the beach by loudspeakers, and put an end to the Umbanda ceremonies. Copacabana Beach on New Year's Eve now belongs to secular entertainment, and, as I learned later, the worshippers of Yemanja without benefit of religious processions now make their separate ways to other beaches at the farther edges of the city.

The contrastive images of these two moments on Copacabana Beach provide a point of departure for exploring changes in Umbanda and in Brazilian society since the period covered in this book (1930–1970). I want to extend my interpretation of that period and speculate about Umbanda in the early 1990s within the changing political economic, and religious landscape of Brazil. This requires somewhat of an oblique approach for after almost two decades in which Umbanda dominated research on Brazilian religions (see Chapter 12 below for a review of the literature on Umbanda for the period 1970–85), the past few years have produced fewer studies. More important, these new studies portray Umbanda rather differently from the earlier literature without attempting to either unravel the sources of the differences or the historical processes through which they have come about. This will be my task. I will begin by situating Umbanda within the period covered in this book and will then explore linkages between recent views of Umbanda and earlier interpretations in three specific areas. First, I will examine the political economic changes that lie behind its recent disappearance from Copacabana Beach on New Year's Eve. Next, I will consider changes in Afro-Brazilian religious identity and the "Africanization" of Afro-Brazilian religious culture. Finally, I will view Umbanda as a social movement and an arena for class politics among the urban poor.

This book captures the explosion of a "new" Afro-Brazilian religion onto the Brazilian public cultural scene in Rio and other southeastern cities in the period from 1930 to 1970. In 1970, when Umbanda dominated Copacabana Beach on New Year's Eve, this Afro-Brazilian religion was at a high point in its public visibility. Widely acclaimed as the most rapidly growing religion in Brazil and viewed as the major challenger to Brazilian Catholicism, Umbanda had a national following estimated to be as high as 20 million, drawn from all sectors of the urban population. Rio alone had an estimated 20,000 centers of worship.

Umbanda's growth during this period testifies to the continuing vitality of Afro-Brazilian religious traditions in Brazil since the slave period, but it also reveals the persistent efforts of those in power to use these religions as a basis for influencing the cultural practices and mobilizing the political behavior of their practitioners. In the colonial period such efforts were authored mainly by the Catholic Church; in 20th century urban Brazil it was members of the largely white, urban middle sectors who sought to transform Afro-Brazilian religious practices long popular among the urban poor. Its middle class organizers gave Umbanda a European Spiritist orientation, sought to impose their own "deAfri-canized," or "whitened" form of cosmology and rituals, and attempted to bring an extremely varied and eclectic range of rituals and practices under their own organization, direction and control. Much of the book deals with the ideology of this "whitening" process, its expression through changes in ritual and cos-mology, and the efforts of its middle class leaders to organize and influence all Afro-Brazilian practices under the rubric of Umbanda.

These middle class leaders were involved in politics. They used Um-banda's syncretic background and cosmology, in which African deities and Catholic saints mingle with the spirits of Brazilian Indians and African slaves, to promote its image as a major national symbol of Brazilian religious and cultural unity and of racial harmony. And, they built vertically structured politi-cal clienteles linked to the individual Umbanda centros through which politi-cians could gain access to Umbanda voters. Umbanda was courted and sup-ported by politicians as a religious interest group. The mass public religious ceremonies organized in Rio and other major southern cities were central to these populist appeals and were often sponsored by local and state govern-ments. Umbanda's visibility in urban Brazilian public life was thus inseparable from its romance with populist politics and the publicity and the cachet with this romance conferred upon its activities and its public image. Thus, as I argue in this book, it was through such a project, involving political connections, clientele politics, and the symbolic importance of such mass festivities during the heyday of populism that Umbandistas gained access to and dominated a major public symbolic space, Copacabana Beach, on what was a major secular national holiday as well as the most important celebration in the Umbanda religious calendar.

I link Umbanda's rising star to major transformations of Brazilian society during this period (the 1930s–1970) involving urbanization, the shift to an in-dustrial economy, and the consolidation of a national state. Although dictator-ships alternated with periods of democratic politics, the enduring structures of this new society and state were the vertical linkages established by the state and dominant groups within Brazilian society with the expanding numbers of the urban lower sectors whom they sought to mobilize and control. Umbanda expressed this vertical orientation, while its cultural emphasis on the themes of "whitening" and nationalism articulated the hegemonic racial ideology of Bra-zilian society's dominant sectors, blended with the state's enterprise of creating a sense of national unity among diverse regions, populations and cultures. Though my research predates the publication of Hobsbawm and Ranger's *In-*

vention of Tradition (1983), my interpretation of the rise of Umbanda exemplifies their model of the 'invention' or transformation of ongoing traditions as a process through which groups in power seek to employ, invent, or transform cultural traditions as a means of legitimizing their own national projects.

Today, Umbanda is established as a major Brazilian religion with a following currently estimated at some 30 million people (Brumana and Martinez 1991). However its major ceremonies no longer take place in such prestigious public spaces as Copacabana Beach and it has less public visibility in the city's cultural and political life. Copacabana Beach has also changed. Increased numbers of new tourist hotels have intensified this area's image of affluence but, in recent years, it has become a politically contested space, a symbol to the increasing numbers of the city's poor of the affluence which they do not share and of the luxuries of a white society to which *negros* (a term preferred in Brazil over the term "preto" or "black")[1] are increasingly denied access. Copacabana Beach has become a politically and racially contested arena to which predominantly male, predominantly *negro,* and uniformly poor youth have journeyed from other parts of the city to both express their anger at the society that has excluded them and to acquire some of its benefits for themselves. Intervention by city authorities has been utilized to stem the tide of this protest and to repossess the beach for the affluent. It has lost its innocence as a locus of mass appeal and has become a more self-consciously and an exclusively class segmented space of the affluent and white sectors of Carioca society which has become increasingly polarized in terms of both class and race following recent class and racial contestations.

Umbanda's declining public visibility and the changing character of Copacabana Beach both form part of the continuing narrative of post-Abertura, post-Economic Miracle Brazil. An initial optimism and exuberance that began in the mid 1970s with the Abertura or "political opening," a period of intense political organizing and widespread popular movements that ushered out the military dictatorship and initiated the process of redemocratization, has now given way to a deep pessimism in the face of the continuing precipitous decline of the economy and disillusion with the process of redemocratization.

In 1970, under the final years of military dictatorship, Brazil was in the midst of its Economic Miracle, the years from 1968–74 when the country averaged over 10% yearly economic growth rate in its GNP. Since that time, its economy has steadily declined (a result among other causes of the oil crisis, inflation, declining world prices for its products, and spiraling foreign debt). The decade of the 1980s is now referred to as the "Lost Decade," (Silva 1992), and during the early 1990s the economy has declined even more precipitously. Significantly, the gap between rich and poor has widened steadily since 1960 giving Brazil today one of the most extreme levels of inequality in the world (Burns 1993; Moreira Alves 1985).[2] High inflation rates, declining real income, and increasing un- and underemployment which are exacerbated by continuing urban migration and growth have produced an increase in poverty and in the numbers of the urban poor, decreasing levels of education and health care, and increasing infant mortality and malnutrition (Moreira Alves 1985). This has led to escalating marginalization of the urban poor which is expressed through the growing numbers of the homeless, most visibly among them streetchildren, and increasing levels of urban violence. This general decline in the quality of urban life has become a Brazilian national trauma.

On the Brazilian political scene the waning of military power, the transition to civilian government, and the process of redemocratization opened a vast new political arena for the activities of political parties, labor unions, and a wide assortment of local grass roots popular movements, both secular and religious. This transition has produced some significant changes in Brazilian political culture; some transfer of power from the elites to the popular classes, visible particularly in the growth of the PT (Partido dos Trabalhadores, or Workers Party); the increased strength of labor unions; and a large and varied number of locally organized social movements articulating their own interests and increasingly critical of traditional forms of political graft. But deteriorating economic conditions, while they have fueled the voicing of local demands and popular protest, have also stimulated new fears on the part of political elites and led to new efforts at political repression and control (Moreira Alves 1985). There appears to be a retreat from the new forms of political organizing during the Abertura among grass roots local groups, labor unions, and political parties and from the democratic promises of the New Republic (1985) and the new constitution (1988). Brazil appears once again to be succumbing to elite control (Moreira Alves 1985; 1989; Campello de Souza 1989).

Umbanda's disappearance from Copacabana Beach on New Year's Eve and its decreased public visibility may be seen as related to changes in political style and practice. In an atmosphere of increased political liberalization, Umbanda centros now share and compete for political space and support with a vast number of other organizations and interest groups, both secular and religious. Clientelism remains an important feature of Brazilian political and social life, but local groups have taken more initiative in pressing for responses to their own local demands (Alvarez 1990; Escobar and Alvarez 1992; Gay 1994), and thus the form of vague mass appeals launched at the voters from above by politicians, which produced such mass spectacles as the New Year's Eve festivals of Yemanja on Copacabana Beach, have become politically outdated. In fact, one of the few remaining Umbanda clienteles in Rio dates from the time of my research and is associated with the old style populism of "Chaguismo."[3] Umbanda's involvement in these complex new styles of political negotiating remains to be investigated.[4]

Moreover, the increasing marginalization of the urban poor has resulted in a more overtly political tenor to many of the mass gatherings of recent years, which have included both organized protests against social injustices such as the cost of living, hunger, and urban violence and the apparently more spontaneous invasions of Copacabana Beach by busloads of poor black youths. Given Umbanda's large following among the urban poor and Brazilians of African descent, it is not difficult to imagine that city authorities might wish to keep such large mass gatherings as the Umbanda festivities away from the most visible and obvious centers of affluence and tourism.

So the political style that supported Umbanda's high public visibility and its mass festivities has passed, and the tone of public gatherings themselves with redemocratization has shifted to a more explicitly and self conscious political tone. While Umbanda remains popular, it is less visible to the changed conditions of Brazilian public life and politics.

The Africanization of Afro-Brazilian Religious Culture and Identity

Turning now to Afro-Brazilian religious culture, the most dramatic new trend is the increasing popularity of Candomblé in southeastern Brazil. Long famous and much studied in its original home in the most African of Brazilian cities, Salvador, in the northeastern state of Bahia, Candomblé represents the most Afro-centric of Afro-Brazilian religions—the most concerned with asserting purity and authenticity in its African rituals and cosmology. It thus occupies the opposite pole from Umbanda, which in the past has emphasized eclecticism, syncretism with other religions, and the "whitening" of its African forms. Bahian Candomblé leaders of the influential Yoruba tradition have in recent years intensified their insistence on African authenticity in ritual observance by urging initiates to study Yoruba language and rituals with African specialists and some have taken the extreme position of advocating the rejection of all Afro-Catholic syncretisms, that is accommodations made by these religions in their Brazilian context which have long been accepted as integral parts of Afro-Brazilian religious practice (Birman 1984; Fry 1984; Prandi and Gonçalves 1989; see also Carvalho and Segato 1992).

In the period around 1970, when Umbanda was still expanding northward into the territory of Candomblé, Candomblé began to spread southward and, during the past 20 years, has become increasingly popular in Rio and São Paulo. In the latter city, where in the mid 1960s there was a single Candomblé center, there were 2,500 centers by the end of the 1980s (Prandi 1991:22). While this figure is still far less than the 17,000 Umbanda centros registered at that same time, Candomblé is now said to be growing faster than Umbanda, and the great majority of new converts to Candomblé reportedly come from Umbanda (Concone and Negrão 1985; Prandi and Gonçalves 1989; Prandi

1991). (The significance of this is not entirely clear since this research gives no indication as to whether Umbanda also recruits new members from Candomblé, as had been common in the past.) Researchers report the conversion to Candomblé not only of individual Umbandistas but of entire Umbanda centros whose leaders now attempt to "clear away all traces of Umbanda," and conduct ceremonies of spiritual farewell, dispatching major Umbanda spirits of Brazilian Indians and old African ex-slaves permanently to the spirit world. Their places are relinquished to the African deities of Candomblé (Prandi and Gonçalves 1989; Prandi 1991). Other Umbanda centros in the process of "Africanizing" are also reportedly purging their rituals and cosmology of European (Spiritist and Catholic) influences and beginning to desyncretize Umbanda pantheons. Accounts of the travels and activities of major Candomblé leaders (Prandi 1991) also offer fascinating documentation of the manner through which this ritual form is spreading. The evidence of their leaders' high levels of geographic mobility, patterns of migration and visiting, is reminiscent of the spread of Umbanda in earlier years as documented in my own work.[5]

The prospect that Candomblé may be displacing Umbanda in southern Brazil presents the fascinating possibility of the reversal of the process with which I am concerned in this book, and which involves the "whitening," the syncretizing, and the Brazilianizing (and deAfricanizing) of Afro-Brazilian practices that have characterized the popular spread of Umbanda. Candomble's growth suggests that a reverse process may now be occurring, an "Africanizing" and desyncretism of Afro-Brazilian religious culture. The major supporter of this position (Prandi 1991) attributes this new enthusiasm for Candomblé, ironically, to the intellectualized rediscovery of Africa by the white middle classes of southern cities in search of their real Brazilian origins and of a "legitimate Brazilianness," assisted by the popularization of Candomblé in Brazilian popular music and the media. Prandi claims that it is this rediscovery of Africa that has drawn the white middle class into Candomblé as clients which has in turn acted to legitimize and popularize participation in Candomblé among the poor who form the main source of its membership.

This interpretation, which parallels my own account of the role of the white middle class in "whitening" Umbanda some 40 years earlier raises many questions as to why the same sectors of the population should in this brief time span change the direction of their cultural taste in Afro-Brazilian religions and reverse their earlier preference for a "whitened," de-Africanized form of "Brazilian" religion in favor of an explicitly Afro-centric one. I link the former process, the emphasis on whitening, to racial as well as cultural issues in Brazil, to the dominant ideological concerns of both the middle sectors and the Brazilian state during this period with "whitening" Afro-Brazilians and their cultures as an ideological expression of racial hegemony, and to the use of

Afro-Brazilian culture in symbolic constructions of cultural nationalism. Prandi, however, insists that the current process of Africanization represented in the popularization of Candomblé is a purely cultural matter related to the search for "authenticity," and is not connected in any way to racial issues. He bases his argument on the observation that Candomblé is attracting not only Brazilians of African descent, but many whites as well.

His claim that the popularity of Candomblé is not linked to racial partici-pation or identity supports an argument made earlier by Fry (1982; see also Hanchard 1993) that as a result of hegemonic appropriations, many areas of Afro-Brazilian culture have become "deracinated", that is they have lost their racial identities and their connections to the histories of Afro-Brazilian popula-tions from whom they originated and have become part of mainstream Brazilian national culture. For some Brazilian Candomblé may have become deracinated in just this way. What Prandi has noted as the increasing preference for Can-domblé over Umbanda among sectors of the Brazilian middle class may lie, as he suggests, in the greater appeal of its claims for religious purity and African authenticity over the more openly syncretic Umbanda, and in the reputedly greater powers of its African deities over the spirits of Umbanda (see also Dantas 1988). However there are compelling reasons to question how widely this deracinated view of Afro-Brazilian religions may be held, and by whom. This question is a particularly important one in light of the timing of Candom-blé's expansion. For the beginnings of Candomblé's southward expansion, in the period around 1970, coincided with the intensification of cultural and politi-cal ferment and new interests in an African identity among Brazilians of Afri-can descent. Racial discrimination within Brazilian society, though still denied by many Brazilians, has greatly restricted social mobility for Brazilians of Afri-can descent and kept them among the ranks of the poor (Andrews 1991; Lovell 1991; Silva and Hasenbalg 1992). The increasing impoverishment and margin-alization of the urban poor intensified this discrimination and resulted in in-creasing racial as well as class polarization (Andrews 1991; Hasenbalg 1985; Silva 1985; Skidmore 1993). This situation heightened racial consciousness among Brazilians of African ancestry and increased their receptivity to racial consciousness movements, African identities, and racial activism stimulated by a variety of transnational sources: Negritude, Black Power, Pan-Africanism, and African liberation movements, all of which found expression in Brazil be-ginning in the late 1960s. These currents have both stimulated new forms of Afro-Brazilian cultural expression, and have influenced established forms (see Hanchard 1993). They have resulted in a burgeoning expression of black con-sciousness and African cultural pride, often linked explicitly to racial themes, racial protest, and at times to expressions of racial separatism (see for example Cavalcanti 1990; Risério 1981). These new interests have acted not only to "Africanize" many areas of Afro-Brazilian culture but also to strengthen awareness and expressions among Brazilians of African ancestry of their cultural traditions and to reconnect them with an overt, positive, and politicized African identity.

Given the intensity of this ferment and its timing, it seems inconceivable that the expansion of so explicitly Afro-centric a cultural tradition as Candomblé is an unrelated phenomenon. In fact, although this matter has not been directly investigated, such links are implied in passing by several authors (see for example Birman 1984; Vogel 1993; 162). It seems far more likely that this ferment and the energies and activities it has spawned has been a major stimulus to the "Africanization" of Afro-Brazilian religious practice in southeastern Brazil for many sectors of its new practitioners (see also Negrão 1979). Thus, while the white middle classes in these southern cities may relate to it primarily as a "deracinated" aspect of Brazilian national culture, this certainly does not imply that it is similarly deracinated for all of its participants. It seems to me highly unlikely that initiates, mostly poor and many of them Afro-Brazilians, identify with Candomblé in the same way as its mainly middle class white clientele. Brazilians of African ancestry are clearly turning to a variety of Afro-Brazilian cultural forms, old and new, as means of recreating their African identities and reclaiming their history. I question whether Candomblé, with its strong and continuing popularity within the Bahian Afro-Brazilian community and its affirmation of African pride, has ever become deracinated among these sectors in Bahia (see Soares 1992). And, in the light of recent events, I think it likely that its very marked Afro-centric identity holds a new interest and a special meaning for Afro-Brazilians, provides them with an African identity, and a means of reconnecting with their African history. In other words, an alternative interpretation of Candomblé's growth in southeastern Brazil, particularly within the context of increased racial consciousness, takes its appeal to individuals of different classes and racial categories, its multi-class, multi-racial composition, not as the basis for a denial of its connections to racial issues and identity, but rather as the basis for an exploration of these issues in all their complexity.

And this same dictum may be applied to Umbanda which, despite its "whitened" image, has also retained its capacity to provide an Afro-Brazilian identity. A recent study of religious preferences in a working class Rio suburb finds that many Afro-Brazilians choose Umbanda over other churches because it affirms an African identity and provides "a counter discourse to racism" (Burdick 1993:160). Significantly, with respect to Prandi's argument above, Burdick notes that Afro-Brazilians' special identification with Umbanda is not evident from the composition of Umbanda centros, which are racially mixed, but emerges only from personal interviews and from the wider perspective of religious preferences within the community, which reveals that a high proportion of Afro-Brazilians choose Umbanda.[6] This study notes that while discourses of "whitening" may exist within Umbanda, in this working class suburb there is also another, alternative discourse of color. Burdick does not investigate how these preferences and identifications may have been influenced by contemporary racial and cultural politics. My own work suggests that they date back at least to the 1950s, and I believe that they have been strengthened by recent African consciousness raising in the Brazilian urban south.

Explicit references to Afro-Brazilians' identifications with racial egalitarianism in Umbanda raise another problematic issue concerning the referential ambiguity of statements in both discourse and ritual of racial and class equality in Umbanda. Many researchers, myself included, have read these statements frequently made in Umbanda centros, that "in Umbanda there is neither race nor class, all are equal" as hegemonic affirmations of equality that deny the marked hierarchy, class inequalities and racial discrimination that are present in Brazilian society and are represented as well in the secular structures of many Umbanda centros. Burdick's research indicates, however, that such statements may also serve to affirm ideals of racial and class egalitarianism and provide a sense of personal worth and empowerment among subordinated groups. These ambiguities signal the need for research that approaches these issues from the perspective of the participants themselves.

What are the implications of this recent racial ferment and the Africanization of Afro-Brazilian culture for Umbanda? One extreme possibility that might be inferred from the statistics on Candomblé's recent growth is that within this heightened climate of "Africanization," Umbanda, which downplays African identities by emphasizing a syncretic and national identity, will decrease in popularity and become absorbed by Candomblé. This seems highly unlikely. Current studies indicate that Umbanda is still enormously popular and in many areas still growing (see Burdick 1993) on an industrial suburb of Rio de Janeiro, and Segato (1994) on Porto Alegre, in the southern state of Rio Grande do Sul). So while its numbers may diminish, it's unlikely to disappear. A far more likely probability is that within this new context and given the development of multiple understandings of it, Umbanda will undergo its own internal changes in rituals, identity, and cosmology as it has in the past.

In fact, such a direction is suggested in current research by Hale (1993), who finds that the new climate of racial consciousness is exerting an influence over the identities and personae of central spirits in the Umbanda pantheon, the Pretos Velhos, or "Old Blacks". While many of these spirits retain their identities and characters as elderly ex-slaves from Bahia, humble, patient, and long suffering, others, when speaking through the mediums who receive these spirits during spirit possession, are identifying themselves as "personalities rather different from the kindly . . . norm," exploring "themes of racism and slavery from explicitly critical perspectives." One spirit, for example, claimed that he was never a slave in Brazil, but "escaped from the slave hunters in Angola . . .

(and) gathered around him a band of other runaways who waged guerrilla war-fare against the Portuguese colonists and slave traders. . . ." These themes suggest that the Afro-Brazilian figure of the Preto Velho may well serve as a focal point for change in Umbanda, for incorporating transnational cultural influences and identities from the black consciousness movement into Umbanda, and for introducing new levels of explicitness in discussing issues of racial consciousness and awareness within Umbanda centros. It is important to remember in this context the importance of spirit possession in Umbanda: the spirits descend directly to earth and through the mediums they possess are able to communicate directly with members of the congregation. Thus the messages of the spirits are conveyed directly to those who consult with them, allowing both for constant changes in spirit personae and for the communication of these to adherents. Another example of recent transformations in Umbanda cosmology is suggested by the incorporation into its pantheon of Zumbi, a historical and mythical hero of slave resistance, as spiritual mentor of the Pretos Velhos (Burdick 1992) and a similar incorporation might be predicted for a recently popular slave heroine Anastacia (see Sheriff 1993).[7]

Moving from ways in which Umbanda and Candomblé may represent creative responses to wider changes in Afro-Brazilian racial consciousness and identity, I now want to reverse the issue and consider the possible impact of these religions on developing processes of racial consciousness and activism. Hanchard classifies both Candomblé and Umbanda as examples of "culturalism" in which Afro-Brazilian social and political processes are relegated to the realm of culture (1993:59), rather than of racial activism, though he acknowledges the capacity of such "culturalist" forms to serve as vehicles for expressions of deepening racial awareness and African identity. To date, neither Candomblé nor Umbanda have become politically activist religions, and both have in the past been viewed as politically conservative. Yet current research suggests that both may have important political roles in strengthening racial and political consciousness. It seems crucial to further explore both the recent growth of Candomblé and recent changes in Umbanda within the broader context of developing racial polarization, popular political activism, and the cultural politics of identity among Afro-Brazilians, who are found mainly among Brazil's poor.

Social Movements and Social Class Relations

Studies of popular religions as vehicles for local level political mobilization, protest, and resistance have formed an important part of the recent literature on Brazilian social movements. Interest has been centered on the CEBs (Ecclesial Base Communities), Bible study groups promoted by Progressive Catholics to expand interest in Catholicism and stimulate political consciousness among the poor (see Mainwaring 1989; Burdick 1992) and on Pentecostalism, which has experienced recent growth of almost vertiginous proportions (see Stoll 1990; Fernandes 1992).[8] Umbanda has moved somewhat to the periphery of recent research, but the current tendency to place studies of individual religions within a broader religious field affords many glimpses of it (Burdick 1993; Prandi 1991:61–74; Soares, 1993; see also Brumana and Martinez 1991). These studies deal with Umbanda, Pentecostalism, the CEBs, Candomblé and Spiritism with varying degrees of emphasis.

The view of Umbanda that emerges in this new literature differs from my own portrayal of it in this book. In contrast to my emphasis on its multi-class composition and the hierarchical orientation permeating its social structural, ritual and cosmological relations, an interpretation widely shared by other researchers (see Chapter 12 below), recent literature portrays Umbanda as emphasizing horizontal, egalitarian relationships and solidarities, and rejecting hierarchy. There is a significant discrepancy between these two interpretations. Since recent studies have shown little inclination to address it, I will do so here after discussing some of this literature.

One intriguing view of Umbanda emerges in Burdick's (1993) recent study of the different religions in a working class suburb of Rio from the perspective of the participants. This study highlights their different social and religious concerns and the differing capacities of various churches to respond to them. It reveals the fluidity of the boundaries between the different religions and against more rigid notions of conversion as a unidirectional process. Burdick demonstrates the ease with which individuals move among religions according to their current problems and interests. Although his analysis focuses on the CEBs, Umbanda emerges clearly as countering prevailing gender and racial hierarchies more effectively than the CEBs, though the latter offer a greater degree of political consciousness raising. Noting that this political paradox contradicts previous interpretations of Umbanda, Burdick suggests that different categories of Brazilians may have different understandings of Umbanda, a theme to which I will return.

A second line of interpretation in this new literature (Brumana and Martinez 1991; Soares 1993) emphasizes a shared cultural universe among these religions, whose cornerstones are spiritual curing, the belief in the powers of sorcery, and moral definitions of Good and Evil. Umbanda and Pentecostalism are portrayed as participating in a common discourse of magic and sorcery and struggling for control over its definition and its powers. While Umbandistas view the deities and spirits that wield these supernatural powers as the providers of cures and protection, Pentecostalists regard them as the quintessence of evil, work to exterminate them, and label Umbanda's followers as "slaves of the Devil" (Brumana and Martinez 1991:438). The battle against these spirits, and thus against Umbanda, provides the raison d'etre for Pentecostal preachers, who are said to devote a major part of their activities to combatting it, particularly during public conversions, when potential converts are encouraged to become possessed by their Umbanda spirits, which are then publically exorcised (Brumana and Martinez 1991; Soares 1993). This struggle of Pentecostalism against Umbanda is interpreted not as an example of the conflict between these two religions but as evidence of their shared belief in sorcery, a shared discourse between *equals*, which is viewed as forming the core of a single cultural universe of belief and a common "web of alliances and conflicts" which is shared also by Candomblé and Spiritism (Brumana and Martinez 1991). In this view, these processes are interpreted as the evidence for increasing horizontal solidarities and egalitarian relations among these religions and, more generally, among the urban poor. Crucially, these religions are viewed as the central form of political expression available to these marginal groups, symbolic protests against the society that has marginalized them.

The Catholic Church, representative of the hierarchical structures, values, and practices associated with the dominant sectors of Brazilian society, is seen as the primary target of this symbolic protest, and one of the explicit forms of protest is the rejection of Afro-Catholic syncretisms. In this analysis, the concepts of syncretism and desyncretism take on an explicitly political and class symbolism, with syncretism signifying dialogue between classes and accommodation to the hierarchical and moral values of the dominant society, while desyncretism is viewed as a rejection of that cultural dominance and dialogue. This interpretation of desyncretism is explicitly extended to racial politics by one analyst of Candomblé (Vogel 1993) through linguistic references to syncretism as a form of national integration (Brazilian racial democracy), while desyncretism is seen as a move toward "separatism." Thus these subaltern religions, including Umbanda, are identified as rejecting the influence of, and the dialogue with the dominant sectors of society, turning to each other instead, in a closed discursive universe.

These deconstructivist interpretations use the medium of religion to address issues of autonomy and creativity among the urban poor and to provide an internal view of ideology and social relations within this sector. Their conclusions concerning increasing solidarities among the poor are politically tempting and plausible, given the evidence that this same process has been occurring among other local social movements in these same sectors. The role of sorcery beliefs and conflicts in defining group identities and boundaries, as represented in the battle between Pentecostalism and Umbanda, is not entirely new since it already existed at the time of my research, but may now have become more powerful, more open, and more important in promoting social solidarities.

The idea that these intra-class disputes may be subsumed within a more fundamental opposition between these "marginal" religions and the structures and culture of Brazil's dominant classes, as represented in Catholicism, is equally interesting but considerably more problematic. By drawing a closed boundary between the poor and the rest of Brazilian society, it posits a culturally and structurally bounded universe of the urban poor. This model seems to be most applicable, and may even in part derive from Pentecostalism, which in both its unambiguous rejection of Catholicism and predominant appeal to the urban poor, does seem to possess some potential as an independent form of cultural, and political expression. But it seems dangerous to generalize from this model to assumptions of a broader, more inclusive world view of the urban poor. The model does not take into account the popularity of the CEBs among the urban poor, which suggests that Catholic identity does not necessarily signify support for the dominant society. Moreover, since most of the Brazilian population including the urban poor and most adherents of Umbanda and Candomblé remain at the same time Catholic, it is hard to posit such a boundary between opposition to Catholicism, and the practice of it. There is the additional question of whether the belief in magic and sorcery constitutes a universe specific to the poor. Maggie (1991) argues convincingly that the belief in witchcraft and sorcery has been generalized throughout the Brazilian population since colonial times and that the very legal apparatus through which the Brazilian state has sought to control its practice reveals an underlying belief in its powers. I argue in a similar vein in this book that Umbanda's rapid spread among the educated, affluent sectors of Brazilian society was facilitated by the fact that many of them were (and continue to be) Spiritists who had already accepted such "magical" notions as the intervention of spirits in everyday life and the manifestation of the spirit world through spirit possession. The Catholic Church's own occasional participation in the exorcism of the Devil demonstrates that such beliefs are also held among Catholics, though discouraged by most Church leaders. These examples imply that a "magical" world view is not the unique province of the poor, and argue against the reification of class centered cultural categories, since such cultural exclusivities are far less easily established than these authors suggest.

For Umbanda, this intra-class interpretation is extremely problematic. In fact, it directly contradicts previous research and interpretations. Whereas I and others demonstrated the importance of middle class participation in Umbanda and its vertical hierarchical structure reinforcing the structures of secular Brazilian society, this interpretation characterizes Umbanda as a religion of the poor in which middle class participation is at best "marginal," and which rejects hierarchy and expresses symbolic resistance to dominant structures. This recent literature generally discounts or ignores Umbanda's history and its character as described in earlier interpretations.

Let me now address the issue of this discrepancy. On the one hand, it might indicate that Umbanda has changed significantly in the past 20 years, that middle class participation and efforts to control it have declined, and that its formerly vertical, hierarchical emphasis has weakened and given way to emerging solidarities among the poor. This would substantiate broader claims concerning the influence of redemocratization in Brazil in stimulating locally organized expressions of autonomy and resistance (see for example Alvarez 1990; Gay 1994), or it might suggest that by increasing marginalizing the poor, the upper sectors of Brazilian society have themselves acted to weaken these vertical linkages. On the other hand, this discrepancy might be seen as primarily the result of changes in research perspectives and strategies. In this case, my interpretation was influenced by the dominant concern with models of authoritarian, corporatist, clientelist states, spawned by a period of military dictatorship, all of which focussed on the exercise of power from above, and explored the vertical articulation of individuals and social groups through which it was exercised. These research priorities gave primacy to the investigation of the vertical orientations in Umbanda and efforts of the emergent middle classes to influence and control the Afro-Brazilian religious groups ubiquitous among the urban poor. The recent process of redemocratization has produced a different research emphasis which focuses on the empowerment of subordinate groups and on forms of organization among the urban lower sectors as autonomous expressions of such empowerment. This seems in turn to have led to an interpretation of Umbanda that seeks out forms of autonomy, solidarity, and action in this class sector. In this case, the discrepancy between the two interpretations of Umbanda would appear to be the result of research concerns, rather than necessarily of changes in Umbanda.

I believe that both of these positions produce insights into the politics and the nature of Umbanda. Its historical development embraces its dual heritage: on the one hand, it originated among Afro-Brazilian populations and the urban poor, and there is evidence (see below), though little empirical research, to suggest a continuing hierarchical tradition of racial and class identities and forms of cultural resistance among these groups; at the same time, Umbanda and other Afro-Brazilian religions such as Candomblé also show evidence of continuing efforts on the part of dominant sectors of the society to coopt and transform them. Thus it is possible to posit a continuing historical dialectical relationship of appropriation and resistance within Umbanda and other Afro-Brazilian religions between efforts of the dominant classes to appropriate them and efforts among their largely poor participants and members to resist this. It may well be that the relative strength of these efforts (and the emphasis of the researchers who have studied them) has varied historically between increased emphasis on hegemonic control in times of authoritarian regimes and increased autonomy in times of more democratic regimes. This view is reinforced by the extraordinary resemblance of recent interpretations of Umbanda under democratization to earlier interpretations of it made during the 1950s and early 1960s, a period of industrial growth and democratic regimes. At that time, both Willems (1966) and Bastide (1960) represented Umbanda as a new mass movement that rejected hierarchy and expressed horizontal solidarities. But in fact, the two perspectives, while similar in their class structural arguments, provide rather different understandings of Brazil; while this earlier literature spoke a language of inclusion, of classes in formation being integrated into an industrializing, democratic society; these new interpretations speak a language of exclusion, of horizontal solidarities resulting from the marginalization of the urban poor. Both tendencies—toward appropriation and toward resistance—have been present in Umbanda's history, and thus these research perspectives complement each other in the effort to assess Umbanda's changing historical reality.

While current analyses of Umbanda, which stress its egalitarian aspects, may reflect real changes in emphasis and a new strength in this intra-class identification, I believe that this picture has now become considerably overdrawn. It is implausible that the vertical ties that have for so long linked different class sectors, partially through Umbanda, and which continue to operate in the wider Brazilian society have entirely disappeared. I do think that they are there and that it would be interesting to see what has happened to them. They need to be investigated, not ignored. While strengthening the understanding of Umbanda's role and meaning in the lower sectors, a more complex and plausible view of Brazilian society and an understanding of the continuity of vertical linkages, has been lost. Umbanda may have become more a religion of resistance and opposition, rather than of accommodation; of new solidarities, a locus for a more militant racial consciousness, but I think it likely that this represents only one of its multiple facets, a new refraction. This may be stronger today than in the past, but I have seen no evidence that the shift has resulted in the elimination or full replacement of Umbanda's capacity to keep open the dialogue and exchange between classes in the increasingly hierarchical realities of Brazilian society.

Conclusions

The past 20 years in Brazil are marked by two major developments: the process of democratization has fostered increased empowerment of local grassroots groups and has produced some shift of power from elites to the working classes and the urban poor. This has occurred within the context of a declining economy, worsening economic inequality, and increasing levels of class and racial polarization. The poor have gained greater levels of political autonomy, threatened always by elite cooptation during a period of increasing economic marginalization involving absolute deprivation and a lowering of living standards. Among the groups that have mobilized in response to these developments, religious movements have been prominent and have taken an active and central role among proliferating social movements. Researchers are now struggling to interpret their significance and their political potential.

Where does Umbanda stand in relation to other religions in this historical moment? It seems to contrast with those religions whose appeal to particular sectors of the population and whose social and political orientation and identity can be somewhat more narrowly defined. Pentecostalism, the fastest growing of these religions, appeals predominantly to the poorest, unskilled, and marginally employed urban sectors within Brazilian society including many Afro-Brazilians, which indicates that religious choices among Afro-Brazilians are not all made on the basis of symbols of an African identity. Pentecostalism in Brazil offers an independent, non-Catholic religious identity, a less conservative political stance than has been associated with Pentecostal groups elsewhere in Latin America, particularly in Central America,[9] and the potential for articulating a class based political position, though this has not yet been realized. The CEBs are the most political, action oriented of these religions, but appeal more narrowly to the skilled working class, and apparently hold less appeal for Afro-Brazilians. Though Catholic, CEB adherents are both politically and structurally opposed to mainstream Catholicism.

Umbanda and Candomblé both combine long and continuous historical strength and appeal among the urban poor with specific links to an African identity, features that have made them targets for cultural appropriation and patronage by elite sectors of the urban population. In both cases, this has resulted in their Brazilianization and incorporation into mainstream Brazilian culture, though as I have argued, I believe that many of their practitioners may have resisted appropriation and retained earlier class and racial identifications and that this resistance is increasing. But at the moment, both of these religions seem to me to differ significantly from Pentecostalism and the CEBs in that they remain multi-class as well as multi-racial with significant levels of participation from the middle classes, which militates against their coalescence as class based religions of the poor though such currents may form within them. While Candomblé, taking cultural pride and political consciousness in its long and now even more emphatic Afro-centric identity, has become more militantly African, Umbanda seems to be moving in another direction. In this current atmosphere of class and racial polarization, when African cultural and racial themes have become particularly politicized and contested, Umbanda, with its diverse forms and participants, seems particularly prone to remaining an arena for efforts at hegemonic appropriation and resistance. That racial themes can easily become contested battlegrounds in Brazilian society is exemplified in a dramatic way in the recent events involving the celebration of the Centennial of Abolition in 1988. Government efforts to define and celebrate 100 years of the abolition of slavery became a contest over the right to speak of and to define the African experience and African identity in Brazil (see Hanchard 1992; Maggie 1989).

Umbanda remains singular among these religions in that its previous history of multiclass membership, strong vertical orientation, and appropriation and transformation of the Afro-Brazilian heritage through "whitening" embodies the very structures and identities of the past decades that are presently directly under challenge from popular movements. It is for this reason, because of its previous history, that the portrayal of Umbanda as simply a "culture of resistance", which denies that history, similarly empoverishes its interpretation. Of all of the religions discussed here, Umbanda seems to provide the most interesting testing ground for recent directions of social change and mobilization around the linked issues of emerging class and racial solidarities and identities. Exploration of the ways in which it has changed and of multiple identities that have emerged within it offers the opportunity to assess the degree to which Brazilian society itself has been transformed by these wider changes. Umbanda's changing rituals, its vast and varied cosmology, and the structures of its individual centros hold clues to these changes, to whether these vertical and appropriative orientations have weakened or changed, and to the degree to which Umbanda has itself become an autonomous form of expression.

Umbanda has been and continues to be a "protean" religion, that is fluid; flexible; able to transform and to take on many roles, meanings and appearances; eclectic; and continually absorbing and responding to new ideas and social and political currents. Its approximately 30 million adherents make it a force in Brazilian society and culture, which is responsive, reflexive, constructive and creative. For these same reasons, it is interesting to follow it beyond Brazil's borders to the areas where it has traveled with emigrating Brazilians, and has continued to evolve within its new environments. These include Argentina (see Frigerio 1989; Carozzi 1991), Uruguay (Segato 1991) and the United States, where it has been popular in New Jersey and in New York among the large Brazilian community (see Margolis 1994) and among other Latin American immigrants. My own fascination with Umbanda continues. Although I have done no recent research on it in Brazil, I have studied it in Newark (Brown 1991), and, even as I write this, am preparing to attend an Umbanda session in the New York City borough of Queens.

Endnotes

Acknowledgments: My thanks to friends in Brazil who provided such generous hospitality during my January 1994 trip, and gave me invaluable suggestions, guiding me to recent publications and research sources, and helping me to interpret changes in Umbanda and Brazil (though they cannot be held responsible for what I have written here): Licia Valladares, for her friendship, support, and assistance, and Patricia Birman, Marilena Chauí, Peter Fry, Michael Hall, and Yvonne Maggie, all of them friends and colleagues over the years whose ideas have contributed much to shaping my own. And to Mario Bick, who has given unlimited loving, creative, intellectual, and moral support to my work on Umbanda, and in the process has become as much a specialist on Umbanda as I.

1. Burdick (1992) indicates that this is the prevailing self-referential term among Brazilians of color. Maggie (1989b) discussing the preference of Brazilians for the term "negro" over "preto", claims that it is a way of avoiding association with the polarized black–white racial categories used in the United States which have been equated with the terms preto and branco; and, more controversially, she suggests that "negro" in Brazil is a term that connotes cultural categories of color and ethnicity, and not social inequalities.

2. The percentage of the national income held by the wealthiest 10% of the Brazilian population which in 1960 was at 40%, had by 1990 increased to 53%, while that held by the poorest 50% of the population, only 17% in 1960, had by 1990 declined to 11% (Burns 1993:471).

3. "Chaguismo" was so named after the Rio politician Carlos Chagas whose career and political style epitomized the form of populism based on personal loyalty, without political agenda or ideology (see Gay 1994:21–22).

4. New styles of political negotiating involve not only links to elected politicians, but also to the many Non-Governmental Organization (NGO) networks that provide various social services. Valladares and Impelizieri (1992) indicate that Umbanda centros are among the local NGOs that provide social welfare services for homeless children, though it is not clear how these services articulate with political structures.

5. The rise of Candomblé addresses another major issue in the sociology of religion concerning directions of religious change in modernizing societies. If the growth in modern Brazilian cities of a religion such as Umbanda, based on rituals that evoke an African slave past and

including spirit possession, challenges modernization theories' predictions of the disappearance of such "traditional" cultural forms in modern industrial settings, the growth of Candomblé in these same settings intensifies this challenge (see Prandi 1991). Candomblé is at once more highly ritualized, more demanding of time and resources, and less flexible in the demands it places on initiates than Umbanda. The popularity of both of these religions adds as well to the mounting evidence against a simple Weberian model of secularization in modern life.

6. Burdick (1993) compares the CEBs, which are his main focus of attention, with Umbanda and Pentecostalism, and finds that Afro-Brazilian members of the community find more racial equality in both Umbanda and Pentecostalism than they do in the CEBs.

7. Zumbi, leader of the 17th century quilombo of Palmares, has become a major symbol of slave resistance (see Burdick 1992; Hanchard 1992). Anastácia, who perhaps might be viewed as his female counterpart, heroically resisted slavery Brazil's northeast during the 18th century, and is now often viewed popularly as a saint, and endowed with miraculous powers (Sheriff 1993).

8. Recent figures (Stoll 1990) put the total Evengelical (very predominantly Pentecostal) population in Brazil in 1986 at some 18% of the total Brazilian population. Comparative figures from 1960 (when the total number stood at 4.4%) to 1985 show an average annual growth factor of 3.6%, and if this continues, the Brazilian population will by the year 2011 be 57.4% Protestant (Stoll 1990:337), a dramatic, though improbable change in a country that has until recently been over 90% Catholic.

9. Current observations suggest that, especially in Brazil, Pentecostal politics may not be as linked to the conservative ideologies of these religions' original American founders as has been formerly portrayed in the literature (see Stoll 1990; Burdick 1993; Eckstein 1989).

Bibliography

Alvarez, Sonia
    1990   Engendering Democracy in Brazil: Women's Movements in Transition Politics. Princeton: Princeton University Press.

Andrews, G. Reid
    1991   Blacks and Whites in São Paulo Brazil 1888–1988. Madison: University of Wisconsin Press.

Bastide, Roger
    1978   The African Religions of Brazil. (orig. pub. 1960) Tr. by Helen Sebba. Baltimore: The Johns Hopkins University Press.

Birman, Patrícia
    1984   Comentários à propósito da II Conferência Mundial da Tradição dos Orixás. Comunicações do ISER 3(8): 47–54.

Brown, Diana
    1991   Religion and Ethnic/Racial Identity: The Transformation of Afro-Brazilian Religions in Greater New York. Paper presented at the Meetings of the American Anthropological Association, Chicago, November 20–24.

Burdick, John
    1992   Rethinking the Study of Social Movements: The Case of Christian Base Communities in Urban Brazil. In The Making of Social Movements in Latin America, A. Escobar and S. Alvarez, eds. Boulder CO: Westview Press; pp. 171–184.
    1993   Looking for God in Brazil: The Progressive Catholic Church in Urban Brazil's Religious Arena. Berkeley: University of California Press.

Brumana, Fernando and Elda Martinez
    1991   Marginália Sagrada. Campinas SP: Editora da UNICAMP.

Burns, E. Bradford
    1993   A History of Brazil. Third Edition. New York: Columbia University Press.

Campello de Souza, Maria do Carmo
    1989   The Brazilian "New Republic": Under the "Sword of Damocles". In Democratizing Brazil: Problems of Transition and Consolidation. Alfred Stepan, ed. New York: Oxford University Press, pp. 351–394.

Carozzi, Maria Julia
    1991   Religiões afro-americanas: reencantamento em Buenos Aires. Comminicações do ISER 41:68–74.

Carvalho, Jorge de and Rita Laura Segato
1992   Shango Cult in Recife, Brazil. Caracas, Venezuela: CONAC/INIDEF/OAS.
Cavalcanti, Maria Laura Vivieros de Castro
1990   A temática racial no Carnaval carioca: algumas reflexões. Estudos Afro-Asiáticos 18:27–44.
Concone, Maria Helena e Lisias Negrão
1985   Umbanda: da repressão a cooptação. In Umbanda e Política. Cadernos do ISER 18. Rio de Janeiro: ISER e Marco Zero, pp. 43–79.
Cunha, Carlos, and Reginaldo Teixeira Perez
1992–93   The Political Party System in Brazil. Camões Center Quarterly 4(3–4):42–48.
Dantas, Beatriz Góis
1988   Vovó Nagôe Papai Branco: Usos e Abusos da África no Brasil, Rio de Janeiro: Edições Graal Ltda.
Eckstein, Susan
1989   Power and Popular Protest in Latin America. In Power and Popular Protest: Latin American Social Movements, Susan Eckstein, ed. Berkeley: University of California Press, pp. 1–10.
Escobar, Arturo, and Sonia Alvarez, eds.
1992   The Making of Social Movements in Latin America: Identity, Strategy and Democracy. Boulder CO: Westview Press.
Fernandes, Rubem Cesar
1992   Censo Institutional Evangélico CIN 1992: lo Comentários. Rio de Janeiro: ISER, Núcleo de Pesquisa.
Floriano, Maria da Graça and Regina Novaes
1985   Relacões Racíais no Protestantismo Brasileiro. Communicações do ISER, Ano 4, Edição Especial. Rio: ISER.
Fontaine, Pierre-Michel
1981   Transnational Relations and Racial Mobilization: Emerging Black Movements in Brazil. In Ethnic Identities in a Transnational World. John F. Stack, ed. Westport CT: Greenwood Press, pp. 141–162.
Frigério, Alejandro
1989   With the Banner of Oxala: Social Construction and Maintenance of Reality in Afro-Brazilian Religions in Argentina. Ph.D. dissertation, Department of Anthropology, UCLA.
Fry, Peter
1982   Para Ingles Ver. Rio de Janeiro: Zahar.
1984   Reflexoes sobre a II Conferência Mundial da Tradicão dos Oriẍas e Cultura. De um observador não participante. Comunicações do ISER 3(8):37–45.
Gay, Robert
1994   Popular Organization and Democracy in Rio de Janeiro: A Tale of Two Favelas. Philadelphia: Temple University Press.
Hale, Lindsay
1993   Personal Communication. See also forthcoming Ph.D. dissertation: Hot Breath, Cold Spirits: The Poetics of the Sacred in a Brazilian Spirit Religion. Department of Anthropology, University of Texas, Austin.
Hanchard, Michael
1992   Raça, hegemonia e subordinação na cultura popular. Estudos Afro-Asiáticos 21:5–26.
1993   Culturalism vs. Cultural Politics: Movimento Negro in Rio de Janeiro and São Paulo, Brazil. In The Violence Within. Kay Warren, ed. Boulder CO: Westview Press, pp. 57–86.

Hobsbawn, Eric, and Terence Ranger, eds.
1983 The Invention of Tradition. Cambridge: Oxford University Press.

Landim, Leilah, ed.
1989 Sinais dos Tempos: Diversidade Religiosa No Brasil. Rio de Janeiro: ISER.

Lovell, Peggy, ed.
1991 Desigualdade racial no Brasil contemporáneo. Belo Horizonte: UFMG/CEDEPLAR.

Maggie, Yvonne
1989a Cultos Afro-Brasileiros: Concenso e Diversidade. In Sinais dos Tempos: Igrejas e Seitas no Brasil. Leila Landim, ed. Cadernos do ISER, No. 21:77–82.
1989b Cor, Hierarquia e Sistema de Classificação: A Diferença Fora do Lugar. In Catálogo: Centenário de Abolição. Yvonne Velho, ed. Rio de Janeiro: UFRJ, pp. 1–27.
1991 Medo do feitiço: relaçõés entre magia e poder no Brasil. Rio de Janeiro: Arquivo Nacional de Pesquisa.

Mainwaring, Scott
1989 Grassroots Popular Movements and the Struggle for Democracy: Nova Iguacu. In Democratizing Brazil: Problems of Transition and Consolidation. Alfred Stepan, Ed. New York: Oxford University Press, pp. 168–204.

Margolis, Maxine
1994 Little Brazil: An Ethnography of Brazilian Immigrants in New York City. Princeton: Princeton University Press.

Meyer, Marlyse
1993 Maria Padilha e Toda a Sua Quadrilha. São Paulo: Duas Cidades.

Moises, José Álvaro
1993 Elections, Political Parties and Political Culture in Brazil: Changes and Continuities. Journal of Latin American Studies 25:575–611.

Negrão, Lisias
1979 A Umbanda como espressão de religiosidade popular. Religião e Sociedade 4:171–180.

Peixoto, Maria Solange, et al
1990 Movimento Popular: a escola communitária e a cidadania. Bahia: Universidade Federal da Bahia.

Prandi, Reginaldo
1991 Os Candomblés de São Paulo. São Paulo: HUCITEC/Editora da USP.
———, and Vagner Gonçalves
1989 Axé São Paulo. In Meu Sinal está no Seu Corpo. Carlos Eugenio Marcondes de Moura, ed. São Paulo: EDICON/USP, pp. 220–241.

Risério, Antonio
1981 Carnaval Ijexá. Salvador: Corrúpio.

Segato, Rita Laura
1991 Uma Vocação de Minoria: A Expansão dos Cultos Afro-Brasileiros na Argentina como Processo de Reetnicização. Dados 34(2)249-278.

Sheriff, Robin
1993 Woman/Slave/Saint: Parable of Race, Resistance and Resignation from Rio de Janeiro, Brazil. Paper presented at the Annual Meetings of the American Anthropological Association, Washington, D.C., November 17–21.

Silva, Luiz Carlos Eichenberg da
1992 O Que Mostram os Indicadores Sobre a Pobreza na Decada Perdida. Texto para discussao # 274. Brasilia: Serviço Editorial, Instituto de Pesquisa Economica Aplicada, Ministério da Economia, Fazenda e Planejamento.

Silva, Nelson do Valle
1985 Updating the Cost of Not Being White in Brazil. In Race Class and Power in Brazil,

Pierre-Michele Fontaine, ed. Los Angeles: Center for Afro-American Studies, U.C.L.A., pp. 42–55.

——— and Carlos Hasenbalg

1992 Relacões Raciais no Brasil Contemporaneo. Rio de Janeiro: Rio Fundo Editora/IUPERJ.

Skidmore, Thomas

1993 Bi-racial USA vs. Multi-racial Brazil: is the Contrast Still Valid? Journal of Latin American Studies 25(2):373–386.

Soares, Cecília Moreira

1992 Resistência negra e religião: a repressão as candomblé de Paramerim, 1853. Estudos Afro-Asiáticos 23:133–142.

Soares, Luiz Eduardo

1993 Dimensões Democráticas do Conflito Religioso no Brasil: A Guerra dos Pentecostais Contra o Afro-Brasileiro. In Os Dois Corpos do Presidente. Rio de Janeiro: Relume-Dumará, pp. 203–216.

Stoll, David

1990 Is Latin America Turning Protestant? Berkeley: University of California Press.

Valladares, Licia and Flavia Impelizieri

1992 Invisible Action: A Guide to Non-Governmental Assistance for Underprivileged and Street Children of Rio de Janeiro. Rio de Janeiro: IUPERJ.

Vogel, Arno, et al

1993 A Galinha d'Angola: Iniciação e Identidade na Cultura Afro-Brasileira. Rio de Janeiro: FLACSO/EDUFF.

Willems, Emilio

1966 Religious Mass Movements and Social Change in Brazil. In New Perspectives of Brazil. Eric Baklanoff, ed. Nashville: Vanderbilt University Press.

1

Introduction

Umbanda is an Afro-Brazilian religion now practiced by millions throughout Brazil. This study explores its history and development, from its beginnings in Rio de Janeiro in the period just prior to 1930 to 1970, and portrays the changing spectrum of its practices and beliefs. My main focus, however, is on Umbanda practitioners from the urban middle sectors,[1] and on their efforts to redefine and codify Umbanda ritual and belief in conformity with their own class interests. Their participation transformed Afro-Brazilian religious practices previously centered in the lower sectors into a more sedate, bureaucratic, nationalistic, and above all, a de-Africanized form of religious practice. I will examine this process of transformation within Umbanda and set it within the context of contemporary Brazilian urban political economic transformation. I will give particular attention to its involvements with patronage systems and clientele politics. My data are derived from research in Rio de Janeiro and other Brazilian cities in 1966 and 1968-69, as well as more recent material gathered on subsequent visits to Brazil and studies by other researchers.

Historically, the label "Umbanda" refers to an extremely varied and eclectic range of beliefs and practices, and it remains a deceptively simple term in current usage as well. At one extreme lie Umbanda groups that draw heavily on Kardecism (*Kardecismo,* also known as *Espiritismo* or "Spiritism"), a form of Spiritualism introduced into Brazil from France in the mid-nineteenth century. Some of these groups even consider Umbanda to be a form of Kardecism. At the other extreme, many groups emphasize Umbanda's historical ties and continuing identification with Afro-Brazilian religious traditions such as *Candomblé* and *cultos de nação* (religions of African "nations," the ethnic subgroups that developed among African slave populations in Brazil). For the majority of Umbanda groups that fall between these extremes, Umbanda's defining features are an eclectic blend of Catholic belief and practice, Kardecism, Afro-Brazilian practices, and aspects of Hinduism, Buddhism, and other currents of mysticism. Practitioners may variously locate the origins of Umbanda in the Far East, Africa, or Brazil

Some more nationalistic Umbandistas identify it as the only true *Brazilian* religion, an embodiment and synthesis of the main elements of the Brazilian historical experience—African, indigenous Indian, and Iberian—a stance reminiscent of, and ultimately derived from, the writings of Gilberto Freyre. These differences in belief and identity notwithstanding, all forms of Umbanda share with their Afro-Brazilian and Kardecist progenitors two basic features: a belief in the active intervention of spiritual entities in the lives of humankind, and the practice of spirit possession as the central means by which these entities communicate with and help or hinder humans.

Since its inception in the 1920s, Umbanda has undergone dramatic changes. The proliferation of ritual forms described above is only a part of a far more fundamental transformation: an exponential increase in the numbers of its practitioners, especially those from the middle sectors; its geographic expansion throughout Brazil; and the elevation of its status from a position of extreme marginality to one of legitimacy and greatly increased social acceptability. In the 1920s, the term "Umbanda" was found in many Afro-Brazilian religious groups within the lower sectors of Rio's burgeoning urban populace. Members of the dominant sectors referred to these groups (although often secretly attending their rituals) under the generic term "Macumba,"[2] a pejorative designation that is still used today in both the social science literature and the media. During this period, all forms of Afro-Brazilian religious practice and, to a lesser degree, of Kardecism, had a precarious existence. In strict legal terms, their practice constituted an offense against public morality. The press and popular literature of the period painted lurid pictures of these religions, labelling them barbaric, depraved, pathological, and routinely naming them as causes of crime, violence, immoral acts, and mental illness. Afro-Brazilian religious groups, because they were located primarily within the lower sectors, were particularly vulnerable to attack. During the frequent periods of political repression practiced against the lower classes in major cities during the 1920s and 1930s, Afro-Brazilian ritual centers were often invaded by the police, their sacred objects confiscated, and their leaders jailed and harassed. Such tactics did not succeed in suppressing these religious activities, but they did drive many groups to secrecy and underground practice.

By the 1970s, however, Umbanda had been transformed into a legitimate national religion, with an estimated 10 to 20 million adherents, that is, as much as 10 percent of the Brazilian population. From its early beginnings in Rio, it rapidly expanded throughout Brazil in the years after World War II. While remaining concentrated in the major cities of the south, above all in Rio, it diffused throughout the country, from Amazonas to Rio Grande do Sul, and from major cities into the small towns of the interior. It has traveled with Brazilian immigrants to their new communities in the United States—to

California, Washington, New York, New Jersey—and to other Latin American countries such as Uruguay (Moro and Ramirez 1981). Perhaps most striking is its changed status within Brazilian society. As of 1965, its places of worship (known as *centros* or *terreiros*) could be legalized by a simple process of civil registration. Some centers have further qualified for tax-exempt status as nonprofit, charitable institutions and gained access to local and state funds. At the same time, Umbanda has gained official recognition and acquired its own independent category in the annual national religious census. Its major festivals have now taken their place in local and state festival calendars, along with those of the Catholic Church, and have become important attractions for the expanding tourist industry. Large and varied enterprises have grown up around the production and sale of Umbanda literature and ritual objects.

Today, Umbanda counts many vocal defenders among its large number of middle and dominant sector participants: high-ranking military officers and members of the professions, journalists, radio announcers, and politicians. Myriad Umbanda federations now provide protection, legitimacy, and social services to affiliated centros and their members, and elected politicians and public officials address the interests of Umbanda clienteles. Despite continuing negative publicity and social disapproval, and often overt expressions of class and racial prejudice—Umbanda leaders' battles against discrimination have gained them legality, state protection, and a considerable degree of public visibility as well. Umbanda has emerged during a period of rapid urban change as a legitimate Brazilian religion, and as one of the few contemporary instances of endogenous religious formation in Latin America.

At the time of my first fieldwork, however, in 1966, Umbanda's newly won legitimacy had had little impact on the social science literature dealing with Afro-Brazilian religions. Despite its growing popularity, Umbanda had attracted very little notice. Attention remained riveted on religions of the northeast, and particularly on Bahian *Candomblé,* which had a magnetic attraction for both Brazilian and foreign intellectuals and social scientists. The few existing descriptions of Umbanda,[3] which frequently employed the term "Macumba," described it as an inferior stepsister to its "purer," more African relatives in the northeast, and as unworthy of independent study. At best, it was treated as only one more regional variant among the panoply of traditions categorized together as "Afro-Brazilian cults." Neither Umbanda's eclecticism, with its wealth of varied and complex forms and practices, nor its increased size and legitimacy excited the interest of investigators.

The literature on Afro-Brazilian religions was by this time quite extensive, and constituted a legitimate speciality within Brazilian social science. Thus the reasons for Umbanda's persistent invisibility and the biases against it in the literature merit a brief discussion. Studies of Afro-Brazilian religions had begun at the end of the nineteenth century with the research of Raymundo Nina Rodrigues and his followers, who dominated the field from 1896, the publication date of Nina Rodrigues' *O Animismo Fetichista dos Negros Baianos (The Fetichistic Animism of the Bahian Negroes)*, the first extensive ethnographic treatment of Afro-Brazilian religions. During the 1930s and 1940s, Artur Ramos emerged as a second major influence in this field.[4] Both of these researchers were medical doctors with specialities in forensic medicine and psychiatry, and their interest in Afro-Brazilian religions stemmed from a deeper concern with the physical and mental capabilities of Brazil's African populations. They were steeped in the evolutionism of Comte and Spencer, and the phrenological studies of the Italian medical specialist Lombroso, and their investigations were designed to provide information on the origins and cultural level of the Afro-Brazilian populations in various areas. They treated religious groups as laboratories for investigations of the intellectual, psychological and moral capabilities of persons of African ancestry. Their primary concern with the problems that Africans' "inferior capabilities" might present for their adaptation within Brazilian society, which extended so far as to question their mental capacity to incur liability under the Brazilian legal system, reveals the depth of the racist assumptions underlying their work (see Côrrea 1982).

In the 1930s, a third generation of researchers also emerged. Brazilian and American scholars, under the dominating intellectual influence of Melville Herskovits, pursued the study of these same Afro-Brazilian religions, this time using them as another kind of laboratory for the retrieval and study of African cultural survivals in the New World. This generation included such scholars as Edison Carneiro, Octavio da Costa Eduardo, Donald Peirson, Ruth Landes and René Ribeiro, and it produced much of what is still the best known literature on Afro-Brazilian religions.[5] Their work forms a major part of the English literature available on this subject. Despite the many contributions of these researchers, however, their focus on cultural survivals, together with an often explicit acculturation model, projected a strangely distorted view of Afro-Brazilian religions. Through their research lens, religions that deviated from an ideal of African purity were seen as "tainted," "adulterated," and greatly inferior to the purer forms.[6] Their bias led them to equate cultural purity with moral and aesthetic superiority and to rank less pure, more syncretic forms as inferior. This ranking system, in turn, resulted in a set of research priorities that focused on the "purer," more African of these religions and virtually ignored their more eclectic relatives. It had a particularly pernicious effect on the study of Umbanda, since the very eclecticism which was its hallmark demoted it in the eyes of these scholars to the level of a "degenerated," "tainted" practice. It was judged unworthy of study, and after a few cavalier remarks, dismissed.

This distorted lens produced a widespread regional imbalance in the study of Afro-Brazilian religions, directing attention almost exclusively to Afro-Brazilian religions of the urban north and northeast: the famed Bahian *Candomblé, Xangô* in Recife, the *Casa das Minas* in São Luis, Maranhão. With the exception of Porto Alegre (Herskovits 1943), southern Brazil was ignored. But the distortion went far beyond this. Even in cities like Salvador and Recife, where, for historical and demographic reasons, the "purest" African-oriented groups were principally found, these groups, which became the focus of so much study and the source for the general image of all Afro-Brazilian religions, formed only a small fraction among the many more eclectic or "syncretic" groups. Like those in the southern cities, these more eclectic groups in the north and northeast also tended to receive much criticism and little study. In celebrating the "purer," more African-oriented traditions, then, this biased research selected the north and northeast over the south, raising to fame a small and in many respects an unrepresentative minority of Afro-Brazilian religions. In the process, the great majority of these religions were relegated to social illegitimacy, marginality, and obscurity, although their growing tendencies toward eclecticism represented the principal directions of change among these religions as a whole.

Because the interests of the scholars who focused on African survivals in Brazil converged in a subtle but significant (and still poorly researched) way with emerging Brazilian nationalist concerns, their findings and their biases gained wide public attention and influence, rather than remaining arcane and isolated scholarly concerns. Since the nineteenth century, Brazilian intellectuals had explored the contributions of Brazil's non-European populations to the creation of Brazilian identity. During the 1930s, these intellectual interests came to coincide with the larger political agenda of the Vargas dictatorship, and of the liberal governments that followed it, in promoting a national cultural identity that would provide the basis for overriding differences and conflicts between classes and regions. Within this intense nationalist climate, some Afro-Brazilian religions quickly came to serve as important symbols for Brazil's national cultural identity. But because of the persisting bias, it was the "purer," more African religions such as Candomblé, rather than Umbanda, which were raised to the level of national symbols of Brazilian identity.

In the process of becoming symbols for national unity, however, all of these religions suffered demotions in their status as religions. This process had already begun under the scholars discussed above, whose interest in culture, combined with the nonliterate and pagan origins of the religions they studied, had resulted in the definite, though subtle, demotion of these religions to the status of cults, in contrast to religions such as Catholicism.[7] Similarly, the tendency to trivialize the contextual significance of African culture in favor of a simplistic emphasis on its survival, as noted by Bastide (1974), perpetuated, in attenuated form, the racism of an earlier generation of researchers. Within the climate of interest in cultural nationalism, these "cults" underwent further secularization as they were translated by scholars and the public into cornerstones of a secular national folklore. Viable and integrated social phenomena were thus reduced to exotic fragments for touristic and popular consumption.

The literature of this period did not totally neglect Umbanda; but the brief descriptions, often under the opprobrious term "Macumba," were couched in the derogatory language reserved for the less pure, "tainted" African traditions.[8] These descriptions in turn provided the basis for its popular image and carried the same negative stereotypes over into the mass media and public opinion. Today, they still remain an important source of the negative image against which Umbanda leaders and defenders must battle. I frequently encountered this negative opinion of Umbanda from educated Brazilians, who laughed at my intention to study Umbanda, or "Macumba." Few people understood my interest in studying it as an example of religious change within a dynamic urban environment. "If you are really seriously interested in these religions you should go to Bahia and study Candomblé," they would tell me. "That's where the *real* Afro-Brazilian religion is. Umbanda? Macumba? That's just ignorance. You don't want to study that."

But in addition to these folklorist objections to my study of Umbanda, Brazilian intellectuals from both the left and the right criticized it on more serious social and political grounds. Brazilian Marxists at that time (though less today) considered the study of religion in general, and such an obvious magical opiate as Umbanda in particular, to be both trivial and irrelevant to the study of political and class struggle. Conservative Brazilian scholars also shared this general opinion, though for quite different reasons. Inspired by the ideals of modernization, and ambitious for their country to develop as rapidly as possible along the lines of Europe and the United States, they saw Afro-Brazilian religions as impediments to development, blots on Brazil's image as a developing nation, embarrassing, even shameful evidence of her continuing state of backwardness, ignorance, and primitivism. Some went so far as to plead with me not to study Umbanda, not to "publicize our national shame," not to study a religion that is "a symbol of our underdevelopment."

The Catholic Church added its own voice to the climate of negativism surrounding Umbanda. By the early 1950s Catholic leaders had recognized that the explosive expansion of Umbanda, Kardecism, and Pentecostal forms of Protestantism in post-World War II urban Brazil represented a direct challenge and threat to centuries of Catholic hegemony. They responded by mounting a major campaign. From the pulpit, in the media, and in their published literature, Catholic leaders sought to denigrate these new religions as throwbacks to a primitive mentality, and to portray their places of worship as dens of depravity visited only by the ignorant. While this campaign officially ended in 1962 with the policy changes instituted by the Second Vatican Council, its impact on educated sectors of Brazilian society was still fresh in the late 1960s.

Thus as I first set to work on Umbanda, I confronted its pervasive negative image. In choosing to research Umbanda, it seemed as if I had somehow unwittingly selected a topic that was the object of a general conspiracy of major sectors of the educated elite: intellectuals of the left and right, many scholars of Afro-Brazilian religions, and the Catholic clergy. While Candomblé had been given a legitimate, even a hallowed place within Brazilian national culture and folklore, Umbanda, in its efforts to gain legitimacy and acceptance as a serious modern, urban religion, was protected by no such romantic, folkloric image. As an example of religious innovation from within the modern sectors of Brazil, it was viewed, rather, as threatening to Brazil's image.

One of the few sources of interest in Umbanda and support for my own approach to studying it came from a group of sociologists at the University of São Paulo. In the early 1960s this group had produced the first sociological analyses of Umbanda, and although I came shortly to diverge from many of their interpretations, their approach provided intellectual support and direction for my work. This group, now known as the "São Paulo School," included Florestan Fernandes, Otávio Ianni, Fernando Henrique Cardoso, and Roger Bastide. During the 1950s, they had begun to study the growth of urban industrial capitalism in Brazil and its effects upon class structure, race relations, social mobility, and ethnicity among the growing populations of southern Brazilian cities.[9] The French scholar Roger Bastide, a charter member of this school, was a pivotal figure in bringing this new orientation to bear on Umbanda. A leading scholar of Afro-Brazilian religious phenomena and author of the monumental *The African Religions of Brazil* (1978; originally published in French in 1960),[10] he treated Candomblé and "Macumba" in ways that largely reflected the biases and value judgements favoring African "purity" mentioned above (see also Bastide 1958; 1959; 1960). However, in his treatment of Umbanda, Bastide broke with this earlier model. He viewed Umbanda as a new phenomenon, a product of postwar industrial capitalism distinct from "Macumba," and interpreted it as expressing changes in class and racial relations. He thus reoriented the focus of inquiry to a concern with Umbanda as an expression of urban industrial change, and raised questions concerning both its role in change and its capacity to express change. Bastide's brief treatment of Umbanda in *African Religions in Brazil,* together with another study of Umbanda and Kardecism by Camargo (1961), formed the basis for the first sociological treatment of Umbanda in English, by Willems (1966), which appeared just before I first left for the field.

These initial treatments of Umbanda provided support for my own interests, yet the conclusions these authors drew concerning Umbanda's class origins, and consequently its significance as a social movement, were far from what I was to encounter in my initial fieldwork. These Paulista scholars portrayed Umbanda as a religion that was essentially lower class in both membership and origin. On this basis, they analyzed its rituals, belief system, and forms of organization as social indicators of current changes taking place within the lower sectors with respect to the formation of class and racial solidarities and the emergence of political consciousness. Bastide (1960), followed by Willems (1966), portrayed Umbanda as a spontaneous expression from within the lower classes of new forms of egalitarian social relations signaling new social class solidarities consonant with the emergence of an urban proletariat. To this, Bastide added the factor of racial solidarity, interpreting Umbanda as heralding the rise of a mulatto proletariat (1960). Willems reported that Umbanda expressed a rejection of "the paternalistic tutelage of the upper strata" (Willems 1966:225). Camargo (1961) interpreted Umbanda in functionalist terms as serving to integrate and adapt formerly rural populations into a new urban milieu. Based on these early interpretations, Lanternari, in his influential book on religious movements, cited Umbanda as an example of what he called religions of the oppressed (1963).

In retrospect, this interpretation can be seen to rest on two false premises, both of which involved the application of modernization models of development. The first was that Umbanda was lower class. Granted that there were many lower class participants in Umbanda—and probably a greater proportion in São Paulo, where these researchers were based, than in Rio, where I worked—it is still hard to understand why the increasing visibility and influence of middle sector religious and media leaders, ideologues, and politicians in this religion were so consistently overlooked. I would suggest that these assumptions concerning the class locus of Umbanda stemmed in part from prevailing Weberian-derived models which associated highly ritualized, emotionalized religious behavior with the lower classes and presumed middle class religious practice to be associated with far more restrained and sedate forms (see Brown 1979).

The second false premise was the assumption that the Brazilian lower sectors were evolving toward greater levels of autonomy and solidarity, and that Brazilian society as a whole was at that time moving in the direction of a democratic model along the lines of those developed in Euro-America. These scholars did not anticipate the 1964 military coup, which destroyed the democratizing process in Brazilian politics and derailed the movement toward lower class solidarity and autonomy.[11]

These interpretations were my only guidelines when I arrived in Brazil in 1966 on my first field trip. They prepared me to find a lower class religion whose adherents would be disproportionately of rural origin, would have low levels of education, and would be significantly, if not predominantly, of African descent. I expected to encounter small, closely-knit, perhaps even secretive groups, whose social structures, cultural forms of expression, and political significance I would investigate in relation to transformations within the larger urban society.

In accord with my original research plan, I selected a research site in what I assumed to be Umbanda's natural and logical habitat, a *favela* (shantytown). Within a few days of my arrival I moved in with a family living in a large favela in the industrial North Zone of the city, and I immediately began visiting the various Umbanda centros located within the favela. I was thus astonished, at the end of my first week of research in the favela, to find myself traveling to a distant and solidly middle sector neighborhood to interview a retired general who was the president of an important Umbanda federation to which several of the favela centros belonged and to which they, in turn, had directed me.

This was to become the familiar pattern—the visit to an Umbanda centro where, in addition to lower sector participants, I would discover the middle sectors, as participants, as religious leaders, as federation presidents, and as politicians identified with Umbanda interests. What I was finding was not at all the uniformly lower sector religious milieu I had been led to expect. Instead, I was confronting a complex religion marked by the active participation and reflecting a clear intellectual influence of the middle sectors.

These findings confounded the interpretations of Umbanda provided in earlier accounts. It was neither a religion exclusive to the lower sectors nor one in which middle sector participation was of marginal importance. On the contrary, my growing contacts with middle sector Umbanda leaders and adherents, together with the historical materials I was gathering, soon convinced me that, although fewer in number than those of the lower sectors, they had exerted a disproportionate influence over Umbanda ritual and belief, its organization, and its growth and increasing legitimacy. This seemed to hold true not only for Rio but on a national scale as well. I began to suspect that often Umbanda expressed the attitudes and values of the middle sectors far more that it did those of the lower sectors.

I ultimately concluded that the history of Umbanda, as I observed it and elicited it from Rio informants, represented an extremely important though not entirely successful effort by middle sector whites, dating back to the period just before 1930, to exert cultural and political dominance over a lower sector popular religion and to redefine the Afro-Brazilian cultural identity. It appeared as well that Umbanda, as an endogenous contemporary urban Brazilian religion, was tending to reproduce class relations of domination present in the larger society, rather than rejecting them as Willems had suggested.

Within a relatively short time, my own field data led me to radically alter my research plans. Assuming Umbanda to be a lower sector form of religious expression, I had intended to select a reasonably representative religious center in the favela as the focus for my research and to conduct a traditional ethnographic study, emphasizing social and political relations and religious behavior and meaning in a small group. However, within the vastly varied and complex social and ritual canvas presented by Umbanda in Rio, such representativeness was not only out of my reach, it was irrelevant to the questions confronting me. The variety within Umbanda itself represented the ongoing dynamic process of urban class and cultural change that I wished to understand. Accordingly, when I returned in 1968-69 for my doctoral research, I resolved to take Rio as my social universe and to focus on the crucial and unstudied role of the middle sectors in Umbanda. I wanted to understand their influence over its rituals, beliefs, and organizations and the historical process through which this influence had come about. While precedents for such broad-scale research on religion already existed in the anthropological literature, for example in Geertz's *Religion in Java* (1960), my own interests were closer to those of Peter Worsley in *The Trumpet Shall Sound* (1957), which stressed the dynamic aspects of class formation and the political role of religion both in bringing about and in expressing changes.

My research strategies were related to my two main interests: first, to present an empirical study of Umbanda as practiced in Rio in 1970 (and as it still is today); and second, to provide an account of the historical process through which it had developed—a history of Umbanda in Rio and an interpretation of its significance within wider processes of transformation of Brazilian society. To interpret its current practice, I visited Umbanda centros and attended their ritual performances on as wide a basis as possible, seeking to establish the range and parameters of variation in ritual, organization, size, location, and social composition. In 22 months of fieldwork, I visited over 200 centros, where I observed rituals and had them interpreted for me by leaders and participants. In addition, I inquired about the organization of the centros and their class membership and leadership. From an initial impression of enormous variation, I began to observe patterns and to form a clearer idea of the principal currents within Umbanda, the constellations of ritual and cosmological practices, and the sectoral, racial, and political interests that they represented.

In order to document the social background of the participants and the history of their involvement in Umbanda, I arranged to conduct formal interviews with the participants in selected Umbanda centros during the final months of my research. I enlisted the help of a team of Brazilian university students, and together we interviewed leaders and mediums (the most active and committed sector of participants) in 14 different centros chosen to represent the widest possible range in variation in Umbanda. This process produced a total of 403 interviews, which provided detailed material on the background of the mediums and leaders as well as on their practice of Umbanda. These interviews also yielded important data on the socio-economic and class composition of individual centros and on members' socio-economic status in relation to their ritual status.

In order to understand the historical process of Umbanda's development in Rio, I sought out leaders at all levels of Umbanda and obtained personal recollections of how Umbanda had changed. I interviewed leaders of centros and Umbanda federations, major writers of Umbanda literature, and politicians and local officials, both within and outside of Umbanda, who supported it and courted its voters. I was able to delineate information networks within which information tended to circulate very rapidly and within which the same individuals, organizations, and events tended to be known and discussed. The local networks that emerged, many of which overlapped and indicated that certain individuals and organizations were widely known in the city, allowed me to map out different factions within Umbanda. The rivalry among these factions provided a means of crosschecking the data given by informants. Older participants and leaders, some of whom had been involved in Umbanda since its beginnings, furnished me with oral histories of their own perspective on their participation in Umbanda, and I supplemented these with a careful reading of Umbanda newspapers and the many columns on Umbanda in diverse major daily newspapers dating back to the 1940s. I also read the extensive Umbanda literature that attempted to define, codify, and divulge its practices and beliefs.

Finally, in order to trace Umbanda's growth elsewhere in Brazil, and to verify that Rio was the origin point for its national development, I spent several weeks each in the cities of São Paulo and Porto Alegre (Rio Grande do Sul) and made shorter visits to many smaller cities to attend ceremonies and interview leaders.

Throughout my research, Umbandistas' enthusiastic reception of my proposed study was the exact opposite of the reaction of educated non-Umbandistas. Umbandistas of all social sectors treated me with great warmth and strongly supported my study of their religion. In fact, the social disapproval of Umbanda among educated sectors in the wider society probably helped me among Umbandistas, who regarded the interest of a foreign academic as a mark of prestige for their religion. My presence and my interest in Umbanda were seen as helping to legitimize it. Even beyond this, many Umbanda leaders expressed the conviction that Umbanda would become the next world religion and cast me in the role of its unwitting missionary. I was the traveler who would carry the message across the seas to the United States.

Unlike the secrecy which practitioners had sought to maintain during an earlier period, and which I had also expected to encounter, I found Umbanda centros wide open to me, as they were to the general public. In fact, attracting new visitors to public rituals was a major source both of prestige to the centro and of the recruitment of new members. I was invited, encouraged, pressed, sometimes almost coerced into attending rituals. Once there, I received special treatment, was often publicly introduced, and sometimes asked to speak. I was also subjected to repeated efforts by religious leaders to induce the spirits to possess me, both to demonstrate my own mediumic aptitudes, and, I believe, to prove the leaders' own spiritual powers. Finally, very late in my research, and among Umbandista friends whom I trusted, I had the extraordinary experience of going into trance.

I was escorted to public ceremonies and constantly invited to people's homes, where I was treated with great friendliness and generosity and to very frank discussions—except when talk headed toward the subject of the contemporary national political scene. At this, a deadly silence would fall. Such was the climate created by the most repressive years of the Brazilian dictatorship. Because of the nature of my interest in Umbanda, I was of course very interested in Umbandistas' political views and attitudes. However, while national politics was a taboo topic, local clientele politics, which became of central interest to me, seemed to be distant enough from the national scene to be less threatening. Umbanda leaders hotly denied their own political ambitions, invoking the need to separate religion from politics, but they loved to gossip about their rivals. In this way I learned much about local political matters.

This material has been fashioned into the first in-depth, empirical study of Umbanda. My discoveries, particularly with respect to the important influence of the middle sectors, have led me to a reinterpretation of Umbanda's social and political significance that diverges sharply from the conclusions reached by my predecessors, Bastide and Willems. I interpret Umbanda as emphasizing vertical dyadic ties and patronage, rather than rejecting them, and reproducing the relations of class domination, rather than denying them. But if my findings diverge from earlier interpretations of Umbanda, they will be seen to converge in important ways with new models of urban Brazilian society which were appearing at the time of my study and which also emphasized the dominance of vertical structures, patronage, and dependency in labor, in politics, in the state, and in international relations. If during the 1950s and 1960s Umbanda had displayed the emergent egalitarian class solidarities previously attributed to it, it would have emerged as an unusual example of a vanguard organization fostering the formation of working class solidarity. Such a reading is not borne out either by my own or by subsequent analyses.

The chapters that follow present the results of my research. I have made some revisions in the original form of its presentation (see Brown 1974) involving the reorganization of material in some of the chapters. The major addition is an Epilogue reviewing the Umbanda literature published since my study was completed. Chapter 2 provides a brief discussion of Umbanda's progenitors, Kardecism and Afro-Brazilian religions, emphasizing the class, as well as cultural contrasts between them.[12] In chapter 3 I discuss the emergence of Umbanda within the middle sectors in the period just before 1930 and describe their efforts to transform and codify it according to their own values and interests: to rationalize and bureaucratize it, to give it a strongly nationalistic orientation, and, above all, to present a whitened, de-Africanized version of its Afro-Brazilian heritage. I also treat the reaction to this effort by lower sector, predominantly black practitioners of Afro-Brazilian forms of Umbanda.

Chapters 4 and 5 respectively present and analyze aspects of Umbanda ritual and cosmology as new interpretations of the Afro-Brazilian heritage. I give particular attention to the process of Umbanda's codification and discuss its focus on curing and on charity, or *caridade,* which includes both spiritual healing and material donations and exchanges of resources in Umbanda centros.

I turn next to the socio-economic and political aspects of Umbanda, beginning in chapter 7 with the ritual and administrative organization of Umbanda centros and their social class composition. Chapter 8 presents and analyzes data from my questionnaire on the social and economic background of participants, their religious background, and the nature of their beliefs and activities in Umbanda centros. Chapters 9 and 10 take up issues in the history of Umbanda and its significance within the wider context of social, political, and religious change in Brazilian society. Chapter 9 presents the history of Umbanda in Rio with a focus on its involvement in the political process. Chapter 10 presents an analysis of patronage in Umbanda as an overarching model for organizational forms and political activities, its social relations, cosmology, and rituals. Here I contrast forms of urban patronage in Umbanda with rural forms of patronage in Popular Catholicism.

The conclusions (chapter 11) briefly summarize my findings, and discuss their wider implications for studies of Afro-Brazilian religions and for broader areas of the social science literature at the time of my research.

Finally, I have provided an Epilogue in which I discuss my study's contemporary relevance and review current research on Umbanda, outlining some present problems and debates in the field and suggesting promising areas for further research.

2

Umbanda's Progenitors:
Kardecism and "Macumba"

This chapter sets out the major characteristics of the two traditions out of which Umbanda developed. My interest in exploring this topic, however, goes beyond simply presenting a prehistory of the cultural traditions out of which Umbanda evolved. In addition to a treatment of their rituals and beliefs, I will also be concerned with the class composition of these religions, and insofar as possible, with the class-related values, interests, social relations, and activities that they express. These aspects of Kardecism and "Macumba" have been little analyzed, yet they are integral to an understanding of the development of Umbanda. Its two progenitors, located in two distinct sectors of the urban population—Kardecism in the middle and professional sectors, "Macumba" in the lower sectors—bring to Umbanda elements of class-associated beliefs and practices that become significant for its subsequent social and political development. They also provide a backdrop against which to view the ways in which Umbanda resembles and diverges from its parent traditions.

Kardecism

In 1855, after attending Spiritualist seances, Léon Rivail, a Parisian schoolteacher and translator of science books, began to receive messages from a spirit who identified himself as a Druid named Allan Kardec.[1] The psychographed communications which this spirit delivered over the next 15 years formed the basis of the philosophy/science/religion known in France as *Spiritisme,* and in Brazil as *Espiritismo* or *Kardecismo.* Kardec's first book, *Le Livre des Esprits* (1855), reached Brazil in 1857 in the luggage of a returning Brazilian traveler, and within 30 years, all of Kardec's major works had been translated into Portuguese.[2] Rio had become the national capital of Kardecism in Brazil and the hub of a dense network of Kardecist federations and publications that stretched throughout the country.

In 1950, a century after Kardecism's arrival in Brazil, census figures located the majority of Kardecists in major urban centers (Camargo 1961:90), with the heaviest concentrations in the more highly urbanized and industrialized southern states. Brazil's two largest cities, São Paulo and Rio de Janeiro, accounted for over 26 percent of the country's total official Spiritist population (Ibid.:115). [3] At the end of the 1960s, estimates of the movement's size placed its active national membership at between two and three million people (Warren 1968b; Renshaw 1969:110), although official census figures were considerably lower. [4] Kardecist leaders and more recent census data suggest that Kardecism may have been declining in recent years. [5] It is quite possible that this decline may in part be the result of loss of members to Umbanda, whose ranks include many former Kardecists.

Social Composition

Since its arrival in Brazil over 100 years ago, Kardecism has appealed mainly to the educated sectors of Brazilian society. As Renshaw has noted, more than simple literacy, it requires "an interest in study and in the intellectualization of beliefs... being a Spiritist is one way of being an intellectual (1969:119-25). Kardecism was first introduced into the professional sectors among medical doctors, with whom it has always been especially popular, lawyers, politicians, and military officers (Amorim 1965:170-76; McGregor 1967:88). These, and other members of the literati gave it a certain amount of legitimacy and prestige. One journalist, writing of Kardecism in Rio in 1904, observed that "the Navy, the Army, law, medicine, professors, the *grande mundo* (social elite, high society), the press, and commerce have thousands of Spiritists in their ranks (Rio 1951:89). However, after Kardec's works began to appear in Portuguese, Kardecism appeared among a wider spectrum of literate Brazilians. By the end of the nineteenth century, the individuals most frequently mentioned in Rio's Spiritist newspapers as the founders and directors of Kardecist centers and federations, and as spokesmen in the hotly debated issues of doctrine, were from commerce, the government bureaucracy and civil service, and the lower ranks of the military officer corps.

   Kardecism's social composition appears to have changed little during the twentieth century. The occupations reported in recent studies to be most prevalent among Kardecists include teachers, members of the liberal professions, the police and the military, the civil service, commerce, and other white collar workers (Camargo 1961:166; Renshaw 1969:216).

   Despite this consistent evidence of solidly middle and professional sector membership, treatments of Kardecism often characterize it, like Umbanda, as a lower class religion (Bastide 1960:426; Willems 1967:213). These echo the social image given it in the early 1940s by a leading Brazilian intellectual who characterized it as a religion found only at "the lowest levels of society" among individuals of "low mental capabilities" (F. Azevedo 1943; quoted in Amorim 1965:164).[6] The Catholic Church, too, has attacked it as a den of ignorance, magic, sorcery, and superstition (see for example, Kloppenburg 1961:22-24). These attitudes, so reminiscent of those towards Umbanda, reflect both popular and scientific prejudices against spirit possession and the same patriotic reluctance on the part of the dominant sectors to acknowledge the existence of such practices within the educated sectors of Brazilian society.

Many researchers have also observed that Kardecism seems to be predominantly a religion of the white educated sectors (Renshaw 1969:122; Bastide 1960:437-38; Warren: personal communication). It is not clear whether this reflects the racial composition of the upper sectors of Brazilian society, in which continuing discrimination has denied upward mobility to the great majority of persons of Afro-Brazilian descent, or whether racial discrimination within Kardecism has also been a factor. Early Kardecists also appear to have been very predominantly men. It is not surprising that this was true of Kardecism's founders and early leaders given the almost exclusively male professional circles into which it was introduced. Contemporary Kardecist leadership continues to be dominated by men, however women now participate in direct proportion to their representation in the general population (Renshaw 1969:119). This undoubtedly reflects the greater educational possibilities for women over those a century ago.

Cosmology and Ritual

Kardecist beliefs reflect the eclecticism characteristic of much of nineteenth-century French intellectual thought. Spiritualist beliefs in the communication between disincarnate spirits and the living combine with the social evolutionism and Positivism of Auguste Comte, with Hindu concepts of reincarnation and the Law of Karma, or Divine Fate, and with Christian ethics. Comtean Positivism provided a rationalistic, scientistic framework for Kardecist philosophy, and served as the basis for a marriage of science and Spiritualism. Kardec viewed the study of spiritual phenomena as an extension of positivistically, "empirically" oriented studies, rather than as a retreat from them. He considered spiritual phenomena to be scientific facts capable of being apprehended by the senses and proven by empirical testing. "Spiritism is presented as a science because . . . it proceeds in exactly the same way as the positive sciences, applying the experimental method . . . to metaphysical subjects" (Pires 1964a:155).

However, while French Kardecism retained a primary orientation toward science and rational philosophy and was only secondarily, if at all, a religion, Kardecism in its Brazilian environment was quickly transformed into a mystical religion (Kloppenburg 1961b:63; Renshaw 1969:74; Warren 1968b:397). Kardec had declared, "in Spiritism there are absolutely no mysteries, only a rational faith which is based in fact, strives toward enlightenment, and reaches for clarity" (1890:201). But for most Kardecists in Brazil faith soon came to be based not on reason, but on the interpretation of spiritual cures of the sick and the suffering as miracles (Renshaw 1969:152–53). Parallel to this, what Kardec viewed as primarily a doctrine, with minimal emphasis and attention to ritual, gained in Brazil increased emphasis on its ritual aspects, particularly those of spiritual healing. Kardec considered rituals to be mainly for the discussion of doctrine and for the reception of messages from the spirits, and recommended that they remain closed to all but initiates (Ibid.:103), but in Brazil they were quickly opened to those who wished to be healed or helped by the spirits. Charity, a moral precept in French Kardecism, was transformed into a humanitarian goal implemented by the provision of material assistance to the needy.

What Renshaw describes as the current directions of Brazilian Kardecism, its transformation into a practical, instrumental religion (Ibid.:154), and the increasing emphasis on healing, sentimental mysticism and on works of charity (Ibid.:135), are not a recent innovation. Rather, they are part of a historical process of adaptation that began at the moment when Kardecism first began to flower in its Brazilian environment. Moreover, it is clear from a reading of nineteenth-century Kardecist newspapers that this shift in emphasis had taken place and gained wide approval and ascendancy within the enormously powerful Brazilian Spiritist Federation *(Federação Espírita Brasileira)* by the end of the nineteenth century.[7] This same combination of religious mysticism and pragmatism will reappear in Umbanda.

Only a small, though very articulate, minority of the more intellectually oriented Kardecists coming mainly from the professional sectors has resisted this mystical religious direction and continued to espouse a more philosophical and scientific form of Kardecism. This branch of Kardecists has turned to the study of parapsychology and other extrasensory phenomena and has also explored relationships between Spiritist philosophy and various social issues, such as the educational system, criminal law, and politics.[8] But while highly respected within Kardecism, its leaders represent a countercurrent to the major direction of this religion's development.

If the ideas of Positivism can be seen as the linchpin of Kardecian rationalism and scientism, Brazilian Catholicism has undoubtedly served as the principal source of its mysticism. Formal, orthodox Roman Catholic dogma has always had a very limited range of influence in Brazil, while the great majority of Brazilians have practiced a far more relaxed form of

"Popular" or "Folk" Catholicism (Azevedo 1968; Bastide 1951). This has been characterized by a reduced doctrinal and ethical emphasis and an increased focus on rituals and beliefs pertaining to the worship and propitiation of the saints, who are seen as miraculous, benevolent beings. Rituals are performed to please the saints, "inclining them to reply favorably to the appeals of their 'devotees' in cases of difficulty and crisis" (Azevedo 1968:177). Illness, unhappiness, and bad luck are seen to result from the displeasure of these supernaturals or from other, obscure causes out of reach of their victims (Ibid.:177–78). Most importantly, eschatological ends are subordinated to therapeutic objectives, thus creating exactly the kind of emphasis on healing that was to develop within Brazilian Kardecism. This form of Catholicism, whose historical roots lie in Portugal,[9] is still prevalent in Brazil today in urban as well as rural areas. It is not limited to the lower social sectors but is found as well in the upper sectors of the population, as indicated by research in the city of Salvador, Bahia (Ibid.:177–78). Despite an active battle waged by the Catholic Church against the Spiritist heresy, many Kardecists are also Catholics and feel no conflict between the two religions.

Unlike Popular Catholicism, however, in which illness, suffering and hardship may be attributed to distant and often supernatural causes, Kardecism attributes them to an individual's own past lives, or to the actions of "suffering" or "ignorant" spirits who wander in a limbo close to the earth and may return to perturb its inhabitants, causing a variety of difficulties. If one lives immorally, one has little moral strength with which to resist such harmful influences, and immorality may even attract difficulties. All illnesses and difficulties are at least partially the result of spiritual ignorance (Renshaw 1969:77–79).

The concept of evolution also introduces into Kardecism many ideas that are alien to Catholicism. In Kardecist terminology, evolution refers to the moral and intellectual progress of individual spirits from a state of ignorance to one of enlightenment, which comes about through the study of Kardecist doctrine, through its promulgation to others, and through performing acts of Christian charity. Spirits are considered to be *evoluido* (evolved) or *baixo, ignorante, sem luz* (low, ignorant, without light) on the basis of their performance in these activities. Earthly incarnations provide spirits with a succession of opportunities to further their own spiritual progress through study and good works. By the law of Karma, according to which every act has its inevitable consequences, a worthy life leads to reincarnation in a more spiritually evolved human form, while an immoral or wasteful life retards the process and necessitates expiation, usually through reincarnation as a sufferer from the very immoralities and ignorance that were formerly perpetrated against others. Spirits that have passed beyond the stage of reincarnating in earthly lives continue their upward progress by returning to earth to enter and possess the bodies of specially trained mediums and provide moral instruction and spiritual healing to those who attend Kardecist rituals.

The spiritual entities who inhabit the Kardecist cosmos and possess Kardecist mediums include famous figures from both ancient and recent history, a multitude of lesser personages from various epochs and cultures, spirits from astral spaces, and the spirits of the recently dead, including friends and relatives of the living. This spirit pantheon is hierarchically ranked, with the spirits of men, and occasionally of women, whom history has distinguished for their learning and other notable achievements, such as Confucius, John the Baptist, Abraham Lincoln, and Getúlio Vargas, standing high on the evolutionary scale, while less eminent and accomplished figures receive correspondingly lower status. Spirits are also ranked according to nineteenth-century evolutionist concepts of levels of cultural development. Chinese, Egyptian, Aztec, Inca and other spirit representatives of what are deemed "high" civilizations are considered to be highly evolved, while spirits of Africans and of Brazilian Indians are often categorically considered to be ignorant and inferior on the basis of the imputed inferiority of their culture. This evaluation serves to express common Brazilian prejudices concerning the cultural achievements of these latter groups.

Kardecist rituals, called *sessões* (sessions),[10] take place several times a week in the evening. Specially trained mediums seated around a table become possessed by a variety of spirits who descend from the astral spaces to communicate through these mediums with those who attend the session. Customarily there is an area with seats where other members and visitors, many of whom have come to receive spiritual healing, may sit and watch and wait their turn. The spirits deliver messages from beyond the grave, give *passes* (the laying on of hands),and *vibrações* (spiritual vibrations), both of which are forms of spiritual healing derived from Mesmerism and serving to conduct beneficial fluids and forces into the individual and to draw out negative forces. The spirits also offer moral instruction to mortals and to suffering spirits *(espíritos sofredores)*, who through their ignorance or low level of evolution may persecute mortals, often unintentionally, and cause them illness and harm.

The treatment that African and indigenous Brazilian Indian spirits receive at Kardecist public rituals often differs greatly from their reception in Umbanda, where these same figures invariably occupy center stage. In Kardecism, their humble social origins and reputedly uncouth and violent behavior (Renshaw 1969:90), i.e., their lack of "culture," is socially disapproved, and they may be forbidden entry to Kardecist rituals. Due to a further tendency to associate the level of evolution of a spirit with that of the medium who receives it,[11] this same unfriendly attitude may extend to the mediums who receive such spirits and act to discourage them from further participation. Kardecists have reported to me that mediums who receive "low spirits," such as Africans or Indians, may be asked to leave the centro (see also Bastide 1960:442). Such attitudes on the part of Kardecists may have influenced the racial composition of Kardecism as a whole. Levels of "spiritual evolution," with their clear references to education and "culture" in its popular sense, also serve to express class and racial prejudices.

In this context, it is worth mentioning Kardecists' insistence upon maintaining sharp boundaries between themselves and groups that have shown admixtures of Afro-Brazilian influences. During the late nineteenth century, such blends were frequently part of what came to be known as "Low Spiritism" *(baixo espiritismo)*, found within the lower sectors (see for example Rio 1951:199–206). I think it quite possible that this demeaning label was invented and popularized by the Kardecists themselves, as a way of excluding and distancing individuals and groups whose practices, and the spirits received, did not meet with their approval.

I would note that Kardecists tend to extend these same prejudices more generally to Afro-Brazilian religions and Umbanda, which they also regard as less evolved, as animistic and folkloristic (Amorim 1947:23), or as "inferior religions which work with inferior spirits" (see Camargo 1961:87). One Kardecist explained to me that Umbanda, with its emphasis on African and Indian spirits, was "good for humble people, but not for those with any education." In fact, Kardecists' view of these religions is expressed in the same terms used to describe the Kardecists by the Brazilian intellectual elite and the Catholic Church.

Charity

Charity *(caridade)* is one of the cornerstones of Kardecism. In rituals of the type I described, it takes the principal form of the *passe* (the laying on of hands), which gives a kind of spiritual cleansing, and consultations, at which visitors and members may discuss their problems and receive spiritual advice. Such activities may also take place on a far larger scale. Already, at the turn of the century, the Rio headquarters of the Brazilian Spiritist Federation (FEB) were described as a "charity bank," with multitudes of the sick and troubled awaiting consultation and spiritual curing, all provided free of charge. Officials of the federation claimed that their organization, supported by several hundred affiliated Kardecist centers and individual members, was providing spiritual curing and counseling to the needy at a rate of some 48,000 individuals per year, or approximately 1,000 individuals per week (Rio 1951:189–99). Such activities have now become standardized among both Spiritist federations and the larger individual centros. For example, the São

Paulo branch of the FEB was by the 1950s reported to be offering these services to 10,000 persons per week (Camargo 1961:27–28). Since Kardecist federations have customarily offered religious healing within the context of religious rituals, they must have provided a tremendous avenue for the diffusion of Kardecism to members of the lower sectors, who were the prime recipients of its charity.

Spiritual healing has also been further popularized in the activities of individual "curing mediums" who have gained national and even international reputations for their successful treatments of all manner of reportedly incurable diseases. These mediums may combine spiritual healing with homeopathy, or even with sophsticated new allopathic medicines. The most famous of these mediums was the late Jose Arigó, a minor civil servant who, under the alleged spiritual direction of a nineteenth-century German physician named Dr. Fritz, used such instruments as rusty table knives to perform successful eye operations and restore sight to the blind.[12] Arigó's clients have numbered in the thousands, and his former treatment center in Congonhas, in the state of Minas Gerais, houses crowded testimonial rooms resembling those at Catholic pilgrimage centers (see for example, Gross 1971), where his former patients have left remembrances of their cures.

By the end of the nineteenth century, Kardecist charity had begun to take on important material as well as spiritual dimensions and to develop the many forms of medical and other welfare services for which Kardecists have become so well known during the present century. These material forms of charity were certainly modeled to some degree on the charitable activities of the Catholic Church. In addition, Kardecists may have emulated homeopathy,[13] which had been introduced into Brazil from Europe early in the nineteenth century. The homeopathists were deeply imbued with a social conscience toward *os pobres* (the poor) and as early as the 1840s had opened clinics in Rio to treat the poor free of charge, in the name of "God, Christ, and Charity" (McGregor 1967:88). Many prominent nineteenth century Kardecists were also homeopathists. By the end of the late nineteenth century some of the larger and more prosperous of Rio's individual Kardecist centers had begun to open clinics for medical treatment and social welfare centers that provided shelter for orphans, the elderly, and the destitute. Today medical, dental, and psychiatric treatment—some of it homeopathic and some allopathic—orphanages, and distributions of food and clothing are common in Kardecist centers. They are provided free of charge or at nominal cost financed by contributions of members, and staffed by volunteers.

Kardecism has come to assume a major role in providing charity to the lower sectors, adding significantly to the grossly inadequate health and social welfare services available in Brazil. According to the 1958 census, Kardecists in the state of São Paulo, who represented only a fraction of the population

(1.5 percent nationally, somewhat higher in São Paulo), maintained more such services than the Catholic Church (representing 93.4 percent of the national population) and serviced almost as many people (Carmargo 1961:131-37). Such figures served to dramatize to the Catholic Church, perhaps even more than the rise in the numbers of Kardecists, the seriousness of the competition it faced from Kardecism.

Kardecism in Brazilian Society

Kardecism arose within the middle and professional sectors during the latter part of the nineteenth century, the period during which these sectors began to emerge as significant socio-economic and political forces and to articulate their own distinctive interests. They began to diverge from traditional ideas and values held by the elite, espousing new ideologies that the Catholic Church, a traditional cornerstone of Brazilian cultural identity, often viewed as heretical. Kardecism is the least known of these urban middle sector ideologies, which included Protestantism, Masonry, Positivism, and Republicanism. All were derived from Europe, mainly from France, which was the intellectual Mecca for Brazilians during the nineteenth century, and all were markedly anticlerical. They expressed in ideological terms opposition to the economic and political hegemony traditionally exercised by the rural agrarian elite and supported by the Catholic Church. Kardecism may thus be seen as part of the far larger social phenomenon of the emergence and expansion of new urban social groupings.

    Kardecism's contribution to the history of ideas in Brazil still awaits in-depth treatment by an intellectual historian, comparable for example to Robert Darnton's treatment of Mesmerism (1968). Kardecism, because it both provides a Brazilian interpretation of imported intellectual currents and is in itself a synthesis of them, offers a good opportunity to examine the history of ideas within the Brazilian middle sectors. I am convinced that such a treatment would also verify important links between Kardecism and Positivism.[14] Not only did Comtean Positivism directly enter into Kardec's philosophical scheme; Positivism itself was introduced directly into Brazil at the same time as Kardecism, and it underwent a similar mysticalization in its Brazilian environment.[15] I believe that a comparison of these two ideologies would reveal a reciprocal relationship: that the infusion of Positivist ideas into the dominant sectors of the population laid a foundation there for the acceptance of Kardecist cosmology and philosophy, and that Kardecism served as a vehicle for introducing a somewhat popularized version of Positivist ideology into a wider spectrum of the middle sectors, where Positivism per se had not, and might never have, penetrated.

    Such a study might also reveal much about Brazilian Catholicism as it has been understood and practiced in the daily life of educated urban Brazilians, rather than as portrayed in Catholic dogma. It would provide additional evidence as well on the relationship of Kardecism to homeopathy, whose acceptance and legitimacy within medical circles helped to legitimize Kardecism, and particularly its curative powers. Such a study would undoubtedly also indicate Kardecism's debt to myriad other currents of European scientism, including Mesmerism.

Most importantly, this brief analysis of Brazilian Kardecism provides a background for understanding the development of Umbanda, which was deeply influenced by Kardecism but at the same time diverged from it in many important ways. Kardecism's popularity in the educated upper and middle sectors of the urban population assured that spirit possession, spirit communication, and spiritual healing were accepted and practiced within these sectors by the latter half of the nineteenth century. The popularity and acceptance of Umbanda within these same sectors years later, then, did not necessitate or did it herald any sudden conversion or radical shift to spirit beliefs or spirit possession. It built upon an already existing stratum of such beliefs and practices, which had been laid down by Kardecism a half century before. However, Umbandistas' treatment of African slave and indigenous Indian spirits, which were elevated to central positions in ritual and cosmology, diverges sharply from Kardecist views of these same spirits.

From the mid-nineteenth century to the present, it is possible to identify a vertically ordered series of linked beliefs among the educated sectors of the Brazilian population which show a decreasing influence of Europe and an increasing influence of the Brazilian environment: Positivism, the most prestigious of them, acts to legitimize and influence Kardecism; and Kardecism in turn acts to legitimize and influence Umbanda. While all mingle science with mysticism, they show a decreasing emphasis on science and philosophy and an increasingly mystical orientation which, I have suggested, is in part a result of the Brazilian Catholic environment.

Kardecism emerged as an urban phenomenon representing specific sectoral interests, and it quickly developed a strong commitment to providing charity to the urban poor. However, the form in which this charity was offered clearly indicated it was not intended as a mechanism either to recruit the lower sectors into Kardecist religious practice or to bridge the gap between the better off and the poor. On the contrary, Kardecism's large-scale charitable activities are structured in the form of distributions that clearly establish the superiority of the givers and permanently separate them from the receivers. Its rituals celebrate class values related to education and culture and act to discourage the participation of those who lack them. Kardecist charity acts to reinforce class boundaries between givers and receivers, between middle and professional sectors, on the one hand, and the urban poor, on the other.

This same position is expressed internally within Kardecist ritual and belief: less educated and cultured spirits who clearly symbolize the lower sectors of the population are rejected rather than incorporated into rituals, and beliefs stress class standards of intellect, education, and culture. Kardecism, through its rigid insistence on the maintenance of class identifications and boundaries, resisted development as a multiclass religion, although it is clear that it possessed the potential to be one. Charity acted as a conduit for Kardecism into the lower sectors; however, class interests were too strong to permit it to open its doors to wide-scale lower sector participation. "Low Spiritism" and Afro-Kardecist syncretisms were intentionally and successfully kept outside the pale of Kardecism. Many of those rebuffed from joining its ranks have turned to Umbanda.

Umbanda has reached out exactly where Kardecism has resisted, responding to syncretic tendencies and embracing charity in a form that draws in and recruits the needy rather than excluding them. Umbandista leaders have actively sought out the participation of the lower sectors, and Umbanda has become a multiclass religion.

Kardecism, then, both helps to account for Umbanda's successful spread within the middle and professional sectors, and at the same time serves to provide a contrastive class strategy and thus to illuminate the process of Umbanda's dynamic growth.

"Macumba"

So much less is known of "Macumba," in contrast to the information available on Kardecism, that it is even difficult to place interpretations of these two progenitors of Umbanda side by side. My use of quotation marks with the term "Macumba" is intended to indicate that although widely used, this term lacks any clearly established referent. It is not clear whether it was ever closely identified with a specific set of practices by those who practiced them; whether, like "Umbanda" today, it acquired meaning as a generic reference to diverse practices; or whether, like the term "Low Spiritism," discussed in the preceding section on Kardecism, it may also have acquired its generic usage as well as its pejorative implications at the hands of upper sector nonpractitioners.

The persisting confusion concerning "Macumba" is partly a result of the folklorist bias against eclectic Afro-Brazilian religions. Researchers' brief and impoverished treatments of what they labeled "Macumba" during the period of the 1930s through the 1950s were almost invariably accompanied by disparaging comments. Ramos, for example, stated that "the Macumba of the Rio de Janeiro Negroes is the least interesting of [the] Afro-Brazilian religious survivals, so great is its degree of inter-mixture and adulteration in contact with an elaborate and complicated urban civilization" (1939:92–94). Bastide identified Macumba in Rio as constituting the "disintegrative" phase of African culture at the hands of modern capitalism (1960:297), and Pierson, a student of Bahian Candomblé, compared the practitioners of "Macumba" unfavorably with the "genuinely wholesome character of the Bahian Africanos," and stated that Macumba "is now in such a state of disintegration that many unwholesome and even vicious practices have crept into its rituals" (1942:305).

Although these comments make concrete references to "Macumba," it is hard to know whether the brief accompanying descriptions are in fact of a distinct set of practices of this name, or whether they are in reality early descriptions of Umbanda or of practices influenced by it. The failure of these researchers to mention Umbanda as a separate religion raises doubts as to whether they were even aware of it. Yet it had begun in the late 1920s, and these descriptions range from the early 1930s to the late 1950s. Had these scholars interested themselves in the development of eclectic Afro-Brazilian religions, they might have provided both important material on Umbanda's formative phase and more detailed and reliable descriptions of the Afro-Brazilian religious practices that remained distinct from it.

However, this is only part of the problem. The crucial period for understanding "Macumba" and its contribution to Umbanda is the period *before* Umbanda began, from around 1900 to the mid 1920s. Yet I found only one easily accessible source on Afro-Brazilian religions in Rio during this period: a survey of the Rio religious scene in 1904 by a journalist (Rio 1951), in which brief descriptions of a variety of Afro-Brazilian religious practices form only a part, though a fascinating and suggestive one. Additional material must certainly lie buried in archives: descriptions by researchers or by folklorists; materials that practitioners of "Macumba" may themselves have produced; accounts in contemporary newspapers (the survey mentioned above is a collection of articles originally published in a large Rio daily newspaper). Given the apparent frequency with which these religions were harassed by police officials, police files and court records for the period should also constitute a major source of further data.[16]

The contrast between the scarcity of information on "Macumba" and the extensive materials available on Kardecism is clearly also a product of the differences between a largely nonliterate, popular, lower sector tradition and a highly literate middle and upper sector one. Kardecism has always emphasized intellectual pursuits and has generated a flood of its own literature since the day of its arrival in Brazil. Afro-Brazilian religions, on the other hand, have been part of a largely oral tradition whose origins lie in preliterate African religions and which has been practiced within a social environment marked by extremely high levels of illiteracy. Thus a major portion of the social history of the urban lower sectors during this period, including the history of their religious practices, lacks written documentation. Reconstructing the history of their daily life and of cultural practices involves all the difficulties associated with the historiographical approach that has become known as history from the bottom up.

Faced with these limitations, I will discuss very briefly areas of Afro-Brazilian religious experience that seem to me especially relevant for understanding Umbanda: the underlying historical factors that have contributed to the generally high level of vitality of Afro-Brazilian religions; the conditions in Rio that appear to underlie the religious eclecticism invariably attributed to both "Macumba" and Umbanda; and evidence of the nature and extent of this eclecticism in the period just after 1900. Finally, I will note some of the problems in interpreting the relationship between the ritual and organizational features of these Afro-Brazilian religions in various southern Brazilian cities, and the subsequent development of Umbanda.

Afro-Brazilian Religious Vitality

The vitality of Afro-Brazilian religions in twentieth-century Brazil cannot be understood without reference to patterns of Brazilian slavery.

Unquestionably, this vitality reflects a desire on the part of Afro-Brazilian populations both to preserve traditional forms of worship, and to express their own religious identities and resistance to the dominant religion of the society which oppressed them. However, the possibilities for realizing these desires depended as well on the socio-political and demographic contexts of slavery.

Unlike the pattern in countries such as the U.S., where initially high levels of slave importation rapidly gave way to an increasing reliance on a native-born slave population, levels of slave importation in Brazil showed an opposite pattern. Slave importation continued to increase throughout the colonial period and until 1851, when the slave trade was finally suppressed. Of the three to five million African slaves who entered Brazil in over 300 years of the slave trade (1530–1851), it is estimated that just under one-half million entered in the last 20 years (1831–50), and estimates of rates of importation during the final five years of the trade run as high as one-quarter of a million (Conrad 1967:24–25). Until 1850, thousands of Africans per year were still arriving in Brazil, bringing with them fresh infusions of the cultures of their African homelands, including, of course, their religious practices. This provided for a continual replenishing of religious knowledge and skills among Brazil's African and African-descended populations. These populations were most densely concentrated in the large coastal cities, which served as centers of slave importation: Rio, Recife, Salvador, Porto Alegre. The numbers and density of Afro-Brazilian populations provided favorable conditions for the maintenance of their cultural traditions; in addition, these large cities offered to these groups a relatively greater degree of free time and movement than was true, for example, of rural plantation life. Not surprisingly, it was these cities in which the various regional Afro-Brazilian religions first developed.

The Catholic Church also played an important role in the continuing vitality of Afro-Brazilian religious traditions. In fact, throughout the New World African religions have shown a generally higher rate of survival in Catholic areas than in Protestant ones (Bastide 1971:153). The Church was weaker in Brazil than in Spanish areas of the New World (Vallier 1967:194), and its influence upon African religions was a contradictory one. Although it wished to convert Africans to Catholicism and to eradicate slave religions, the Church's increasing loss of power and resources, particularly during the nineteenth century, greatly reduced its ability to do so. Moreover, the institutions through which it attempted to exercise control over the religious life of slaves seem to have contributed to the survival of Afro-Brazilian religious traditions.

In the major urban centers the Church exercised its control principally through the *irmandades* (Catholic lay Brotherhoods), voluntary associations that, in addition to their religious activities, functioned as social clubs and mutual aid societies, and were popular at all levels of the population. Brotherhood memberships reflected social stratification along socioeconomic, occupational, racial, and ethnic lines: whites and nonwhites, slaves and free, all had their own irmandades. Slave brotherhoods were further segregated: into *criollos* (Brazilian-born slaves) and the various "nations" into which African-born slaves were divided (Cardozo 1947:25). These *nações* (nations) were ethnic categories representing major cultural and linguistic groupings among the slave populations. Some bore the names of African tribal units, some of the colonies, or even the ports from which the slaves had embarked for Brazil.[17] These ethnic distinctions were reinforced by the colonial government and were the basis of its "Divide-and-Rule" policy toward African-born slave populations (Bastide 1960:220).

The brotherhoods provided the Church with institutional access to the slave populations and with the opportunity to influence their religious behavior. Through this means, it succeeded in imposing what is often referred to as a veneer of Catholicism over slaves' religious practices. The brotherhoods have been accepted as a major source of the Afro-Catholic religious syncretisms found throughout Brazil and elsewhere in the New World (see for example Bastide 1971:152–62; Herskovits 1937; Pierson 1942). On the other hand, the brotherhoods helped to sustain and to preserve the organization of the slaves into groups that represented a degree of ethnic unity; in addition they reportedly took a permissive attitude toward the slaves' continued practice of their own religious traditions. This has led them to be viewed as providing a crucial institutional framework which enabled African religious practices to survive in urban areas throughout the colonial period (Bastide 1971:93).

Reports of the emergence of Afro-Brazilian religious centers as independent institutions date from the time of Brazilian independence from Portugal (1822), and coincided as well with a sharp decline in popularity and membership among the Catholic brotherhoods. This decline was part of a more general weakening of the Catholic Church in Brazil caused by internal dissension and growing anticlericalism. The presence of autonomous Afro-Brazilian religious centers is first reported in Salvador, Bahia around 1830 (Bastide 1960); in 1850 in Recife (Ribeiro 1952:34–35); in 1870 in São Luis, Maranhão (Costa Eduardo 1948:47), and in the late nineteenth century in Porto Alegre, Rio Grande do Sul (Herskovits 1943; Bastide 1959). In Rio, they were in full bloom in 1904 at the time of João do Rio's survey, (Rio 1951) and must certainly go back considerably earlier.

These cities were all major centers of slave importation, and most had maintained continuously high densities of African and African-descended populations throughout the colonial period. These environments, with their large numbers of relatively more independent and less impoverished *negros de ganho* (wage slaves), together with freed and escaped slaves, apparently afforded sufficient density of Afro-Brazilian population, the economic resources, and the relative freedom and anonymity which have been considered necessary preconditions for the development of independent religious centers (Carneiro 1961:17; Bastide 1960:69–74; Ribeiro 1952:29). These early centers survived, though often precariously, and served as bases for the development of ongoing local traditions, despite strong official disapproval and frequent police harassment. In some cities, these original centers are still functioning today.

These local practices have now become established as regional traditions, known by different names: *Candomblé* in Bahia, *Xangô* in Pernambuco and Alagoas, *Casa das Minas* in Maranhão, *Batuque* in Porto Alegre and in Belém, and *"Macumba"* in Rio. The characters of these various religions are attributed to the dominance of particular African cultural groupings in particular areas, for example, the Yoruba dominance in Salvador and that of the Dahomeans in São Luis; to the influence of local cultural traditions, such as indigenous Brazilian influences in the Amazon; and to variations in rates of urbanization and industrialization.

As these Afro-Brazilian religions have continued to expand through the twentieth century, they appear, with the exception of Umbanda, to have remained primarily located within the urban lower sectors.[18] In some areas these sects have retained an ethnic identification and locus among Brazilians of African descent. This is especially true of northeastern cities such as Bahia, Recife, and São Luis, whose social structures were until recently less affected by internal migrations and industrialization; and the far south, in Porto Alegre, where the same conditions combine with marked racial segregation. In areas to which these religions are not indigenous, such as Belém, or where high rates of internal migration and industrialization have blended the ethnic traditions among the lower sectors, such as in Rio, these religions have spead far beyond their original ethnic locus and have become generalized within the lower sectors (Leacock and Leacock 1972:108–11; Costa Pinto (1952:241).

Religious Eclectism in Rio

The principal characteristic usually associated with "Macumba" is its eclecticism, which has been attributed both to the predominance of "Bantu" slaves and to what are vaguely referred to as the "disintegrative" forces of urbanization and industrial capitalist development.

My own analysis of eclecticism in Rio "Macumba" will stress two somewhat different factors: the socio-economic and demographic aspects of change which influenced the social life of the lower sectors in Rio; and the evidence of widespread religious eclecticism and sorcery and its commercialization found among different cultural traditions and throughout all sectors of the Rio population. I do not wish to deny the significance in the development of Afro-Brazilian religions of African ethnic factors, which have unquestionably influenced the character of all Afro-Brazilian religious practices, in Rio and elsewhere. However, unraveling exactly what their significance has been is a complex problem to begin with, and it has been further complicated by researchers' use of vague and often biased concepts. In addition to the well-known difficulties in establishing the provenience of slaves,[19] the categories "Bantu" and "Sudanese" are in themselves both excessively broad and problematic. "Bantu" has been used to refer collectively to all slaves imported from the coast south of the Equator, including the Congo, Angola, and Mozambique, and "Sudanese" to refer to the entire coast of West Africa north of the Equator, between present-day Portuguese Guinea and Cameroon.[20] The suggestion that Sudanese traditions favored strongly collective religious traditions, and thus the retention of African religious practices, while Bantu traditions were more individualistically oriented, and thus inclined toward syncretism represents a dangerous overgeneralization, and the reliability of this view is further weakened by overt or implicit references to the cultural, religious, and moral superiority of "Sudanese" over "Bantu" slaves.[21]

Moreover, the picture I will paint of the variety and evanescence of turn-of-the-century Rio religious traditions raises further questions concerning the relative importance of an established ethnic predominance among Rio's resident slave population, as compared with the wealth of ethnic variety introduced by migrants from other areas of Brazil. I have thus left the matter of ethnic influences in abeyance. I would argue that eclecticism is characteristic of all sectors of the population, crossing both class and ethnic boundaries.

The highly eclectic nature of the Afro-Brazilian religions in Rio that has so troubled twentieth-century researchers seems both logical and inevitable in light of the economic and demographic changes that occurred in this city during the latter half of the nineteenth century. In 1822, Rio, formerly the political center of the Brazilian colony, became the new national capital. In the course of the nineteenth century it also became the financial and economic center of Brazil, as the Brazilian economy shifted southward from its former base in the agriculture of the northeast and mining in Minas Gerais, to coffee production in the states of Rio and São Paulo. The city of Rio served at this time as the chief port for coffee export, and as a result, it became the economic hub of Brazil.

These economic changes produced considerable shifts in population, as increasing numbers of northeastern slaves were sold south to work in coffee production. Rio was the main receiving area for this internal migration and also acted as a magnet for ex-slaves, freedmen, and more generally for diverse numbers of rural and urban poor in search of work. Thus, to the already large resident Afro-Brazilian population, both slave and free, that had been prominent in Rio as in other major slave ports throughout the colonial period was now added a new and highly mobile migrant population.

The image of cosmopolitan Rio as a hive of activity and a potpourri of highly diverse populations is borne out in João do Rio's turn-of-the-century survey of the Rio religious scene. *As Religiões no Rio,* a collection of journalistic pieces originally published in Rio's large daily newspaper the *Gazeta de Notícias,* consists of the author's excursions through the city of Rio with assorted knowledgeable companions to visit and interview various religious specialists. His accounts, though brief, are full of detail, including long lists of the names and addresses of individuals and groups visited. While he often criticizes what he describes, his data are both rich and concrete enough to suggest the extent of religious variety in the city among Afro-Brazilian and various other religious practitioners. In addition, they provide insights into the social milieu within which these practices were set.

Of the various Afro-Brazilian practices visited, the *Candomblé dos Orixás* (Orixá is the Yoruba term for deity) is reportedly the most popular. Its cult houses are described as "full of Bahian migrants," mainly "Minas" (Africans from Nigeria and Dahomey (Rio 1951:19)). This evidence of what seems from the description to resemble closely Bahian Candomblé, practiced and very possibly imported by Bahian migrants, suggests the connections between the demographic shifts just mentioned and the diffusion and variety of Afro-Brazilian religions in Rio.

A promising candidate for a forerunner of "Macumba" (perhaps even an early description of it) is a form of practice known alternatively as *Candomblé das Cambindas* (Cambinda was the name of a principal slave port in the Congo as well as of a large "Bantu" slave nation) and as *Macumba* (Rio 1951:27). The resemblance of its rituals to a syncretic variant of nineteenth-century Bahian Candomblé, known as *Candomblé de Nação* (see Nina Rodrigues 1945), raises the possibility that it, too, may represent a diffusion from Bahia rather than a locally developed form of religious practice. The sketchy but tantalizing description provided by Rio (1951:26–33) contains many features resembling those later found in Umbanda. It is portrayed as a form of group spirit possession accompanied by songs, which are reportedly mainly in Portuguese and include snatches of descriptions of everyday life and nonsense rhymes. Rio gives the following example:

Maria Muçangué	Maria Muçangué
Lava roupa de sinhá	Washes the mistress's clothes
Lava camisa de chitá	Washes the cotton shirt
Nao é dela, e de iáiá	Its not hers, it belongs
	to her mistress
	(Rio 1951:27)

This shift into vernacular language and subject matter represents a major departure from the more orthodox Afro-Brazilian forms such as Bahian Candomblé, where songs are said to be traditional African ones, sung in their original languages. The song quoted above clearly marks a shift toward Brazilianization, toward greater accessibility to the Brazilian population and a greater reflection of the Brazilian experience. This particular song has additional political overtones in its expression of the slave's resentment at her state of servitude.

The use of the vernacular, together with the fact that the Orixás (Yoruba deities) and Catholic saints were addressed and worshipped by their "Bantu" names, distressed João do Rio's guide and led him to comment, in a vein similar to that of later researchers I have quoted, that he considered this form of Candomblé to be "very much inferior" to the Candomblé dos Orixás both because of its degree of syncretism and because of its loss of African traditions (Rio:1951:27).

Two other religions described by Rio, the religion of the *Alufás* (African Moslems), which he reported to be the second most popular religion at the time of his visits, and the *Casas das Almas* (houses of Dead Souls) were on the wane or had disappeared entirely by the 1930s (Ramos 1934). In any case they appear unrelated to Umbanda. However, they provide another example of the evanescence and variability and the rapidity with which religious traditions in Rio could wax or wane.

One of the most striking features of João do Rio's account is its wealth of references to an immense range of individual magico-religious specialists, generally referred to as *feitiçeiros* (sorcerers) and found among the lower sectors of the Rio population. Almost all of them seem to have many wealthy, even famous clients, including politicians and other well-known public figures. He reports numerous encounters with men and women from the upper sectors waiting for or receiving treatment for which they pay considerable sums of money. "We all believe in sorcery . . . it is our vice," he comments, "and we are most terrified of African sorcery" (1951:35). He then describes his visits to myriad African sorcerers, most of whom appear to be African-born and who (he comments) "are as omnipresent in Rio as ants" (Ibid). He reports on the activities of these sorcerers, their work with various evil and devil spirits (including Exú, a popular category of devil figure in Umbanda). He describes their activities in preparing and administering their countless spells, using *cachaça* (cane alcohol), vultures, toads, parrot feathers, animal sacrifices, feces, blood, herbs, offerings of food, and many other items.

These African sorcerers have their non-African counterparts in the many practitioners of Satanism, who make devil pacts, practice vampirism, and hold black masses. Although Rio attributed the origins of all these to seventeenth-century Europe, it is clear that they include African syncretisms as well. One client of Satanism, lamenting the growing syncretism among satanists, comments that the *"malefícios satánicas"* (satanic spells) have been steeped in *dende* oil (from Africa) and *hervas de caboclo* (indigenous Indian herbs) (Rio 1951:143). Even more syncretistic is the *culto do mar* (cult of the sea) practiced by groups of Portuguese, Italian, and Brazilian fishermen. This cult combines Catholic worship of the saints, worship and propitiation of natural forces—a water mother, the rainbow, the moon—with what are clearly African-derived sacrifices of chickens and other animals, which are prepared by African sorcerers (Ibid. 84-85). Eclecticism appears as well in Rio's investigations of magical/religious practices among more affluent sectors of the urban population, where he encounters a great variety of seers, fortunetellers, cartomancers, clairvoyants, crystal gazers, tarot card readers, telepathists, and Zoroastrians.

Ironically, syncretism is not reported in the many forms of "Low Spiritism," which Rio considers to be particularly fraudulent. He provides lurid accounts of possession scenes and conversations with dead relatives held by individual mediums in their homes, but these descriptions give no indication of the syncretism between Kardecism and Afro-Brazilian religions which so roused Kardecists during this period.

Certain members of the Catholic clergy had taken on the tremendous task of counteracting the influences of this array of sorcerers and evil spirits and their spells. Rio describes visits to a convent where an Italian priest spends a full day each week performing exorcisms for those who have been ensorcelled, mainly lower class clients. Contrary, perhaps, to the intentions of the Church, these exorcisms must have helped greatly to validate beliefs in the existence of sorcery.

From this welter of information, even with the limitations of biased comments and brevity, it is possible to make a number of inferences. First, the variety and heterogeneity of religious practices in Rio are dramatically evident, as is the widespread development of eclectic forms of religious practice based on syncretism among African traditions, and between these and diverse and also eclectic European traditions. Brief mentions of *caboclo* and *pagé* curers and of *hervas de caboclos* suggest the presence as well of elements of indigenous Indian traditions, though it is not clear through what means these had been introduced.

Certainly the picture Rio presents of the high degree of elaboration of sorcery among all levels of the population is a very convincing one. Even granting certain excesses of popular journalism, the variety of sorcerers, the range of techniques mentioned, and the profusion of clients involved in consulting with them are impressive. Moreover, it is clear that these beliefs and practices had penetrated deeply into all levels of the Rio population, crosscutting various racial, ethnic, and social class divisions and bringing individuals from diverse groups into contact with each other. It is evident as well that sorcery in Rio had become a form of commerce. Money, often in large sums, was reportedly paid out to sorcerers, and rich clients from the upper classes were clearly an important source of their income.

It is not known whether this profusion of sorcery and its high level of commoditization were distinctive to Rio, a unique product of its dynamic growth and mobile populations, or whether it also occurred in other cities, perhaps with a lesser intensity.[22] Certainly, however, it has been accepted as distinctive to Rio and has formed an integral part of the "unwholesome practices" said to taint Rio's Afro-Brazilian religious scene.

The particular class configuration of Rio sorcery as a lower sector skill catering in part to an upper sector clientele indicates the existence of vertically structured economic exchanges between different socio-economic sectors of the urban population. Yet these occur in a manner quite opposite to Kardecism, in which the upper sectors bestow charity upon the poor in a socially approved manner, but one which maintains class boundaries and avoids reciprocity. What João do Rio portrays is also a redistribution of wealth downward from the upper sectors to the urban poor, but it is an exchange in which the lower sectors exact payment for services provided on the basis of a shared belief in the dangers of sorcery and the need for protection from them. This exchange, moreover, takes place in a socially disapproved manner. Umbanda, as will shortly be seen, effects a blending between these two quite contradictory forms of power.

Afro-Brazilian Religions and Umbanda

Following upon this rich moment of description in 1904, there is a 30-year gap in the information available on Afro-Brazilian religions in Rio, until Ramos' (1934) description of "Macumba," which was followed by other descriptions of this religion in other southern cities (Bastide 1959; Teixeira Monteiro 1954). It has been generally supposed that these brief descriptions refer to an earlier substratum of Afro-Brazilian practices which formed the basis for the later development of Umbanda. However, since they postdate the founding of Umbanda—with the one interesting exception of a nineteenth-century account of practices in the state of Espírito Santo, adjacent to Rio (quoted in Ramos 1934:89–94)—this cannot be clearly established. For example, the description of "Macumba" that Ramos presents (1934:94–103) is of a public ritual in a religious center in Niteroi (across the bay from Rio), the same, at that time small, city where the man I identify as the founder of Umbanda lived and began his first Umbanda centro. Thus, it is quite possible that this description shows the influence of Umbanda on "Macumba," rather than representing a description of Umbanda's predecessor.

Furthermore, the histories of these religions, the links among them, and their connections to the practices described by João do Rio 30 years earlier remain unclear. To what extent did the "Macumba" visited by Ramos in 1931 represent a major local tradition that had emerged out of the welter of varied practices he described? What was the relation of "Macumba" to the *Cabula*, apparently similar in its rituals to "Macumba," which was described in Espírito Santo in the 1880s by a visiting bishop? Evidence provided by studies of "Macumba" in São Paulo and Vitória during the 1950s (Bastide 1959; Teixeira Monteiro 1954) describes it as of nonlocal origin and as coming there from Rio.

I should add here that while these descriptions reveal local differences, the various traditions probably evolved through a high level of exchange among themselves rather than developing independently and in isolation. The high degree of mobility in and out of Rio, the evidence there of a thoroughgoing spirit of innovation and syncretism, together with my own admittedly much later observations in Umbanda of the extreme rapidity with which new ritual elements and innovations traveled between centros, makes me skeptical of theories of independent innovation.

The descriptions of these various forms of "Macumba" and the Cabula indicate that all are blends of African, Catholic, and Kardecist practice, which resemble each other in many aspects of ritual and include among them the major elements of ritual practice and garb, linguistic terms, and spirits also found in Umbanda. For example, Ramos' description of Rio "Macumba" (1934:94–103) is of a physical layout and ritual form very similar to Umbanda. Leader and initiates, dressed in white outfits, dance to the accompaniment of drums and singing. Even the sacred songs, like those quoted by Rio from the Candomblé das Cambindas, are in Portuguese, though their subject matter has lost the immediacy with which it evoked its participants' daily activities and refers more to activities in the spirit world. This is a characteristic as well of the sacred songs in Umbanda. The terms used for the various categories of leaders and helpers, and many terms used in the ritual items, closely resemble those found in Umbanda; this is also true of the organization of the spirit world into "lines." Most striking is the identity of the spirit received by the leader, *"Pai Joaquim"* (Father Joaquim), the spirit of a deceased African slave, who appears to be a *Preto Velho* (Old Black) spirit, one of the chief lines of spirit workers in Umbanda. This is the first mention I know of this category of spirit in Rio. As in Umbanda, this spirit gives consultations during the public ritual to initiates and members of the congregation.

This ritual description does not mention the *Caboclos,* the Brazilian Indian spirits who form the other main category of spirits in Umbanda. However, they figure prominently, more prominently in fact than the African deities and Pretos Velhos, in descriptions of the forms of Umbanda in São Paulo and Vitória.

If I had wanted to focus this study of Umbanda on cultural syncretism and to devote my efforts to classifying and identifying the origins of its rituals and beliefs and their patterns of diffusion, this lack of data on "Macumba," Umbanda's supposed substratum, would pose a serious problem. Umbanda, like the descriptions of "Macumba" and the Cabula, is also a blend of African, Catholic, and Kardecist practices and, since it contains many of the same cultural items, might be hard to distinguish from these other religions. It might also be hard to establish a beginning point for it out of the continuing stream of similar and ongoing Afro-Brazilian syncretic religions. However, in examining Umbanda and discussing its beginnings, I will not be concerned either with the moment in which a particular ritual syncretism occurred or with the origins and diffusion of its particular cultural elements. I will focus, rather, on a particular historical moment when a group of middle sector Kardecists turned to Afro-Brazilian religions as the basis for establishing a religion which they called Umbanda and which they worked to define, codify, organize, and build into a form, social and political as well as ritual, that had not existed before.

3

The Founding of Umbanda:
Identities and Ideologies

In turning from Umbanda's progenitors to the formation of Umbanda itself, I leave behind the dubious security of secondary source materials and rely on my own research and my attempts to grapple with the complex and confusing historiographic problems involved in reconstructing Umbanda's beginnings as a self-conscious religion. I will take as my point of departure the efforts of a group of middle sector Kardecists to construct a blend of Kardecism and Afro-Brazilian religions that would express their own religious preferences, and along with them their own class values, interests, and ideologies. This resulted in the creation of a particular form of Umbanda, which its founders referred to as *Umbanda Pura* (Pure Umbanda) or *Umbanda Branca* (White Umbanda). I will use the term Umbanda Pura to refer to this form of Umbanda, which has greatly influenced Umbanda as a whole. However, there is no single form of Umbanda today, and there may never have been one. Umbanda has developed as a heterodox religion through a dialectic process that has expressed the contradictions and competitions among the different interest groups identifying with it, each seeking to secure its own position and to increase its influence over other, competing groups. The history of Umbanda is the history of Umbandistas fighting for power, control, validation, and the expansion of their own position. In this, Umbanda is no different from the universal religions, whose early histories have been similarly marked by high levels of controversy over competing versions of myth and ideology grounded in different and competing sectors among their participants.

Given this heterodoxy, I will not attempt to construct a coherent, linear history of Umbanda's internal ideological development, but will instead portray the development of Umbanda Pura in relation to various other ideological positions and their related rituals and cosmologies, which have distinguished other class, racial, and political interests within Umbanda. These positions have generated the continuing controversies which are a major source of Umbanda's dynamism.

I will examine the establishment of three ideological positions within Umbanda: Umbanda Pura, or de-Africanized Umbanda; Africanized Umbanda; and nationalistic interpretations of this religion. All of these positions represent efforts at the construction of a distinctive identity for Umbanda, and each in its own way deals with two clearly identifiable major themes: first, the establishment of Umbanda's historical origins. The profound disagreements on this issue extend to questions of which historical period and even what continent these origins should be assigned to. Did Umbanda originate in contemporary, colonial, or ancient history? In Brazil, Africa, or the Far East? The second theme concerns the establishment of Umbanda's relationship to the African cultural heritage, and again, the positions range from a warm embrace to an almost total rejection.

I will focus first on Umbanda Pura and will analyze a myth of Umbanda's founding that I find both plausible and symbolically suggestive, one that represented the first major effort by Umbanda's middle sector leadership to codify this religion and to dissociate Umbanda from an African identity. This will involve a discussion of "Quimbanda," Umbanda's polar opposite. I will then sketch out an opposing position that emerged somewhat later and represented a protest by lower sector Afro-Brazilian leaders against the de-Africanization of Umbanda. The third position I will examine is the nationalist position within Umbanda. Finally, I will evaluate the relative status of these various ideological positions at the time of my own research and contemporary variations on some of these themes.

Umbanda Pura: An Origin Myth

My research has led me to link the beginnings of Umbanda Pura to a particular individual, Zélio de Moraes, and his activities in Niteroi in the 1920s. His account of his illness, his revelation, and his subsequent founding of the first Umbanda centros was verified by several of the older Umbanda leaders in Rio, some of whom had been his associates for many years and had belonged to what he listed as the earliest centros. It was they who introduced me to Zélio. However, I cannot be sure that Zélio was *the* founder of Umbanda, or even that Umbanda had a single founder, although Zélio's centro and those founded by his associates were the earliest I found that had self-consciously identified themselves as Umbanda. Umbanda historiography is unclear on this matter. Outside of this network, his story is not widely known, nor has it gained general acceptance, particularly among younger leaders.

Whether or not this account represents the "real" historical moment of Umbanda's founding, it is certainly a legitimate origin myth and a convincing version of how Umbanda is likely to have been founded, in both real and symbolic terms. Moreover, the myth concerning Zélio's revelation blends into the reality of actual early Umbanda centros and identifiable personnel. It thus provides a good point of departure for examining the origins of Umbanda Pura.

According to the story told to me by Zélio de Moraes,[1] Umbanda began with an illness and a prophecy. Around 1920, Zélio, then in his early twenties, became paralyzed. His father, a civil servant and real estate agent in the city of Niteroi across the bay from Rio, was a Kardecist. After medical treatment failed to improve Zélio's condition, his father took him for a consultation at the Brazilian Spiritist Federation in Rio. While there, Zélio was visited by the spirit of a Jesuit priest, who revealed to him that his illness was spiritual and was the sign of a special mission. He was to be the founder of a new religion, a true Brazilian religion dedicated to the worship and propitiation of Brazilian spirits: *Caboclos* (spirits of Brazilian Indians) and *Pretos Velhos* (spirits of Africans enslaved in Brazil). This new religion would restore these spirits to the positions of respect and veneration denied them by Kardecists. The Jesuit spirit also revealed to Zélio that he would shortly receive a visitation from his own special spiritual mentor, who would give him further instructions and direct his future activities.

Zélio returned home and was soon cured. He then received the prophesied visit from his mentor, a spirit who identified himself as *O Caboclo das Sete Encruzilhadas* (the Caboclo of the Seven Crossroads) and who revealed to Zélio his mission to found a religion to be called Umbanda. Zélio was directed to organize the first Umbanda *centro* (religious center) and to have his followers found seven more centros, which would serve as the nuclei of the new religion. The Caboclo announced that he would serve as guiding spirit to the founding church, the Casa Mater, and would gradually reveal the rituals and doctrine to be followed.

The *Centro Espírita Nossa Senhora da Piedade* (Spiritist Center of Our Lady of Piety), which Zélio, then a man in his early 70s, identified to me as the first Umbanda centro, began in the mid-1920s in a rented backyard on the outskirts of Niteroi. After a series of moves, it settled in 1938 into a substantial building in the downtown area of central Rio, where it still flourishes today. Zélio himself remained its director until his retirement in 1967, when he transferred leadership to his daughter. In the course of Umbanda's first twenty years, the seven affiliated centros, and many others as well, were duly founded by initiates of the Casa Mater. They, too, have continued to flourish and today form the core of the largest, best known, best endowed Umbanda centros in Rio.

Zélio and his associates, the group of "founders" whose activities I have just recounted, came predominantly from the middle sectors. They worked in commerce, the government bureaucracy, the military officer corps, and the group included as well a few professionals, journalists, teachers, lawyers, and a few skilled laborers. All of these individuals were men, and almost all of them were whites. Of the 17 men portrayed in a 1941 official photograph of Umbanda's founders and major leaders, my informants identified 15 as whites and only two as mulattos. None was black.[2]

Many of this group of founders were, like Zélio, former Kardecists who had become disaffected with Kardecism and had taken to visiting various "Macumba" centers in the favelas around Rio and Niteroi. As I indicated in the previous chapter, middle and upper sector participation in Afro-Brazilian religions had been quite common since at least the late nineteenth century. Zélio and other of his associates whom I was able to interview reported that they had become tired of the highly evolved Kardecist spirits, with their long lessons in doctrine and the limited range of their spiritual curing and advice. They had come to prefer the African and Indian spirits and deities found in "Macumba," whom they considered far more competent in curing and treating a wider range of diseases and other problems. Moreover, they found "Macumba" rituals to be far more exciting and dramatic than those of Kardecism, which seemed static and dull by comparison.

Certain aspects of "Macumba," however, greatly disturbed these middle sector Kardecist visitors. They considered rituals involving animal sacrifices and devil spirits, together with the *ambiente* ("atmosphere" or "surroundings"), which often included drinking and rough behavior, to be repugnant. Furthermore, the location of "Macumba" *terreiros* (religious centers) in *favelas* (hillside shantytowns), and in other lower class neighborhoods generally considered to be dangerous and socially unacceptable, made these Kardecists somewhat reluctant to attend. Those who dared to do so tended to keep their participation clandestine, for fear of social criticism and disapprobation. Thus, while they were attracted to particular aspects of ritual and to the powers attributed to certain spirits, they were at the same time repelled and distressed by other aspects of Afro-Brazilian rituals and by the social setting in which they occurred. Not surprisingly, Umbanda, as it developed under the guidance of the Caboclo of the Seven Crossroads, came to express the preferences and dislikes of these founders.

This account of Umbanda's founding captures in symbolic form many of what have become essential elements of Umbanda. Zélio's paralysis and subsequent healing provide a starting point for this new religion in an illness not resolvable through medical treatment but cured through efficacious spiritual powers. The spiritual message subsequently delivered by the benevolent figure of the Jesuit priest recalls the historical role of the Jesuits as protectors of the Indians and of other oppressed populations in early colonial times. Yet, in a more universal sense, the priest's role in recognizing Africans and Amerindians, symbolized by the spirits with these identities, suggests that the Catholic Church itself is portrayed as sanctioning the creation of Umbanda. However the Church may have viewed Umbanda, Umbandistas have always recognized strong ties with Catholicism and hoped for its blessing.

The myth directs the Kardecist to leave the security of his class position to create a religion that celebrates oppressed, non-European components of Brazilian society. This particular blending of Kardecism and Afro-Brazilian tradition thus represents a self-conscious linking of different religions and social sectors. Moreover, it further suggests an important paradox of class relations: in spiritual terms, the middle sector does not see itself as powerful enough to resolve its own problems, so it turns to the greater vitality of the religions of the poor and, by implication, the vitality of the masses. The African and Indian spirits, the Pretos Velhos and Caboclos, are multiplex symbols, dense with racial, class, and nationalistic significance. The confluence in Umbanda of the Catholic (Iberian), African, and Brazilian Indian traditions brings together symbols of a Brazilian national identity, and this myth clearly characterizes Umbanda as a new and autochthonous Brazilian religion. This symbolic union has provided the basis for explicit nationalist interpretations of Umbanda.

The rationale given by this group of "founders" for the selective syncretism between Kardecism and Afro-Brazilian practices, although not part of the myth itself, suggests that if Kardecism was too refined, "Macumba" was seen as badly in need of refinement. This rationale foreshadows fundamental aspects of Umbanda class and racial ideology. All of the early efforts of middle sector leaders to define Umbanda reveal a preoccupation with propriety and a self-conscious effort to impose a class vision upon their new religion.

Umbanda de-Africanized

The gradual multiplication of this original network of Umbanda centros during the 1930s was followed in 1941 by a more ambitious organizational effort, the *Primero Congresso do Espiritismo de Umbanda* (First Congress of the Spiritism of Umbanda), held in Rio. This represented the earliest and one of the few major collective efforts to codify Umbanda. The proceedings of this Congress, which were published the following year (Anon. 1942), provide an invaluable record of the themes that preoccupied these early Umbanda leaders.

The participants, who came mainly from Rio, included many of the same individuals who had participated with Zélio de Moraes in the organizing of early Umbanda centros. They now met to set the parameters of ritual and belief in their new religion and to establish its identity as a separate religion.

These leaders revealed their doctrinal debt to Kardecism: Kardec's works and teachings were viewed as "the fundamental basis of Umbanda, and of all forms of Brazilian Spiritism" (Anon. 1942:21). These leaders also acknowledged a debt to the theosophists and Rosecrucians (Ibid.:101). Discussions of ritual, as will be shortly seen, revealed an extreme underlying preoccupation with dissociating themselves from "Macumba" and Afro-Brazilian religions and implicitly from the African heritage. However, at the same time, their religion was focused on Afro-Brazilian and Brazilian Indian spirits, and they showed a central concern with rehabilitating the Caboclos and Pretos Velhos from the lowly status given them by Kardecists:

> Although they are taken for simple Caboclos or Pretos Velhos, and because of this are scorned and despised by some ... Kardecists, these [spirits] show a degree of cultural and spiritual evolution superior to that of Western civilization, acquired evidently in previous incarnations.... The entities who direct Umbanda could have been Caboclos (actual Brazilian Indians) or Pretos Velhos (actual African slaves) in remote ages ... but beneath their appearances of humility and simplicity ... burn highly evolved spirits engaged in the noble mission of awakening in us (mortals) the desire to overcome the miseries of our lives. (Anon. 1942:39–40)

Their new status is justified here by introducing Christian humility as the true meausure of spiritual evolution. Umbandistas quite often comment that the Kardecists have been misled by social appearance to misjudge these spirits' true worth.

Even more interesting and revealing than the proposed cosmological and ritual directions were the efforts of participants to create a social identity for Umbanda: to establish its historical origins, and to give it an identity separate from Afro-Brazilian religions with which they clearly feared that it might be associated. Two central themes emerge in the Congress proceedings: the de-Africanization of Umbanda's origins, and the purification and whitening of its practices.

As an initial strategy in the effort to downplay Umbanda's African connection, Congress participants denied the term "Umbanda" an African origin. As I have indicated in the previous chapter, the term "Umbanda" had been mentioned in the literature on Afro-Brazilian religions, at that time and it was clearly identified as an African term from a "Bantu" language. This literature and Umbanda's clear associations with Africa and with Afro-Brazilian religions certainly must have been known to participants.[3] However, they rejected such an African origin point. Instead, they sought its origins in ancient Indo-European or even more remote etymological sources. One conference paper derived the term "Umbanda" from Sanskrit, from "Aum + Bhanda," interpreted as meaning "the limit in the unlimited," the "Divine Principle, radiant light, the source of life and constant evolution" (Anon. 1942:23). Another participant, going back even further, asserted that the term was "Adamic" (i.e., a word from man's original language) (Ibid.).

These leaders subjected Umbanda's origin as a religion to the same de-Africanization process. It was traced alternately to ancient India or to Egypt. Umbanda was hailed by one source as "a continuation of the mystical tradition found among the ancient Hindus, Egyptians, Greeks, Aztecs and Incas" (Anon. 1942:46). From its origins in ancient India, Umbanda was said to have diffused to the now lost continent of Lemuria, located in the Indian Ocean.[4] From Lemuria Umbanda spread to Africa, where under the influence of the *embruticimento* (brutishness) of African populations it degenerated to the level of fetichism, in which form it came to Brazil, disguised under the (African) rituals which were "degradations of its ancient forms" (Ibid. 1942: 46). One Umbandista pointed out that since African slaves lacked even rudimentary culture, Umbanda could not possibly have originated in Africa (Ibid.). Thus, these leaders resorted to nineteenth-century diffusionist and evolutionist theories and subjected them to theosophical reinterpretation involving cataclysms, lost continents, and cyclical periods of progress and degeneration in order to create an ancient history for their religion. They wished to locate it in the respectability of the world's great mystical traditions and to rescue it from the perceived social catastrophe of an African origin.

The passion with which Congress participants denied Umbanda's African origins suggests the extent to which they must have felt threatened by them and reveals much about the racist ideology prevailing in this social sector. The efforts to derive Umbanda's origins from the great world religions contradicted, or ignored, the origin myth just discussed, which stressed Umbanda's autochthonous development. The level of concern with denying Umbanda's African origins may well explain why this myth was not referred to at the Congress.

The effort to purge Umbanda of its African associations extended as well into the area of ritual practice. Early leaders expressed the need "to *purify* Umbanda from its essentially African rites practiced since the first wave of slaves brought to Brazil by the Portuguese" (quoted in McGregor 1967:169; italics mine). In the interests of stressing the distinction between Umbanda and those Afro-Brazilian religions associated with African rituals and evil sorcery, participants at the First Congress employed various qualifiers to refer to their religion. The proceedings reverberate with references to Umbanda as *Umbanda Pura* (Pure Umbanda), *Umbanda Limpa* (Clean Umbanda), *Umbanda Branca* (White Umbanda), or *Umbanda da linha Branca* (Umbanda of the White line). Some argued that these terms referred only to the kind of magic practiced—good or "white" magic in Umbanda, as opposed to the evil or black magic practiced elsewhere. However, the racial overtones of these terms were so obvious that they even aroused comment among the Congress participants themselves. One speaker, for example, protested the use of the qualifier *branca* (white) on the basis of his "impression that less informed members of the congregations may interpret this to mean redeeming the whites and condemning the blacks" (Anon. 1942:267). The use of these whitening, purifying qualifiers in references to Umbanda suggests that even its definition as a descendent of great world religions was not sufficient to detach Umbanda from its African connections. Additional qualifiers were necessary. Clearly, the particular ones chosen made use of the full range of ambiguity of color terminology, allowing the moral symbolism of black and white to convey racial implications.

Leaders of the Congress stressed that Umbanda's moral raison d'etre and its mission was to practice charity—to employ benevolent spirits to help humankind and to combat evil. All of its benevolent intentions are summed up in its dedication to the practice of *caridade* (charity), which means "good acts" in the more general sense.

All the evils against which these Umbandistas declared battle came to be epitomized in the term *Quimbanda*. This term provided a crucial negative mirror image against which to define Umbanda. Quimbanda was introduced into the discussion and was juxtaposed against Umbanda as its polar opposite. It was defined at this Congress as *magia negra* (black magic), and *a prática do mal*, (the practice of evil) and was associated with immoral spirits, with evil sorcery, and with "barbaric" African rituals. Quimbanda was Umbanda's underground double, peopled by *Exús*, which were associated in Brazil with the devil and had been identified in earlier descriptions of Afro-Brazilian religions in Rio as chief perpetrators of fraudulent and exploitative forms of sorcery. They were linked with various evil schemes involving the ritual use of toads, lizards, bats, animal sacrifices, and such. While many of these practices may have derived from European witchcraft practices via Portugal (though animal sacrifices were clearly African), they all tended to be associated with Africa, and with its reputedly fetichistic, barbaric religions.

The opposition between Umbanda and Quimbanda that emerges from the Congress proceedings may be organized as follows:

Umbanda	*Quimbanda*
Umbanda Limpa (Clean Umbanda)	
Umbanda Pura (Pure Umbanda)	
Umbanda Branca (White Umbanda)	
Umbanda da linha Branca	*Linha negra, preta, isquerda*
(Umbanda of the White line)	(the black line, the left line)
magia branca (white magic)	*magia negra* (black magic)
caridade sem cobrança	*exploração*
(charity without charge)	(exploitation)
a prática do bem	*a prática do mal*
(the practice of good)	(the practice of evil)

The meaning of the qualifiers attached to Umbanda emerges more clearly in this comparison with Quimbanda. This latter term apparently did not require qualifiers, perhaps because its African identity and negative associations were already basic aspects of its total identity, whereas in Umbanda these had to be denied.

Quimbanda thus came to embody notions of black magic, evil, immorality, and by implication, pollution. It became the ideological vehicle for expressing prejudices against the African religious heritage and against popular images of lower class religious behavior in general. It linked Africa, the lower classes, and evil.

The polar opposition between Umbanda and Quimbanda, white, pure, and good magic against black magic and evil, God against the devil, drew upon a Catholic model, the Manichean division of the world into Good and Evil, a battleground between God and the devil. The exorcisms practiced by members of the Catholic clergy had helped to keep alive beliefs in the existence of evil sorcery and black magic and the powers of devil spirits.

Suggestively, the practices these leaders associated with Quimbanda were those associated by researchers and the upper sectors of society with Afro-Brazilian religions in general, and with "Macumba" in particular. The discussions at this Congress suggest that the Afro-Brazilian religions known popularly as "Macumba" may have been undergoing a division: the positive elements purified, cleansed, and transformed into Umbanda, the negative elements concentrated within its polar opposite, Quimbanda.

The sociological and linguistic origins of Quimbanda and the practices associated with it are even murkier than those of Umbanda. If the sources can be trusted, the term as cited and defined in late nineteenth century sources and by Ramos (1934:87–89) seems to have had the same "Bantu" origins and the same meaning as the term Umbanda.[5] Just as I found no mention of the qualifers "white," "pure," or "good" in connection with Umbanda prior to its use by these early Umbanda leaders, I also found no prior evidence of Quimbanda's specific association with evil or exploitation. It appears likely that both the terms Quimbanda and Umbanda may have acquired their moral and racial overtones, and their opposed meanings, at the hands of these early Umbandista leaders. In other words, these early leaders may have "created" Quimbanda in the same sense that they "created" Umbanda. At the very least, they gave a special emphasis to the term Quimbanda that has had lasting influence. At the time of my research, in the late 1960s, the mere mention of Quimbanda was enough to cause shudders.

Early Umbandistas, then, espoused an ideological position that sought to whiten Umbanda, and they acknowledged an African influence only as a degenerative, negative one, with only one important exception: the Pretos Velhos, African slave spirits, which were derived from Afro-Brazilian religions. The Pretos Velhos, as slaves, not only escaped the purge of African influences in Umbanda but became central figures in Umbanda ritual and cosmology. It seems significant, however, that the Pretos Velhos were slaves. They were tamed, acculturated to Brazilian life, while the practices which these Umbandistas sought to expunge bore associations with precontact Africa, "primitive" and "barbaric" as these men thought it to be.

One crucial dimension of the ideas presented at this Congress sets them apart from the Umbanda origin myth discussed previously. The latter, however fascinating to the anthropologist, has never gained popularity outside of a limited circle of middle sector Umbandistas, though it did provide the basis for the nationalist interpretation of Umbanda. The ideology of whitening and the dichotomy between Umbanda and Quimbanda, however, have become enduring parts of Umbanda Pura, and have had wide influence throughout Umbanda. They have formed the basis for the elaboration of Umbanda cosmology and its ritual practice, directly influencing the particular selection of rituals and beliefs, and creating ritual codes of what must and must *never* be done. In other words, rather than remaining on the level of an esoteric accompaniment to Umbanda practice, this ideology has instead come to define it. As I will suggest in the next chapter, the ideals of whitening and de-Africanizing, and the racial attitudes that these imply, have become encoded within Umbanda. They have contributed to Umbanda's postion of increasing respectability in Brazilian society and have helped to ensure its acceptance and popularity within the better educated sectors.

Umbanda Africanized: Afro-Brazilian Leaders Respond

I want now to move beyond this early period into the 1950s and to indicate the reaction to Umbanda Pura by another sector of the Rio population. By this time, the form of Umbanda defined by these early leaders had achieved considerable publicity and visibility in Rio, through the publication of Umbanda literature and especially through the first Umbanda radio program, which began in 1947. The publicity achieved by Umbanda Pura may actually have helped to consolidate positions of opposition to it. In any case, it provoked strong statements of opposition and the definition of a counter position.

The reaction came from lower sector, predominantly black religious leaders who claimed that Umbanda was African. Their claim raises again the presently unanswered question of whether Umbanda already constituted a name and possibly a set of practices which had emerged out of the milieu of "Macumba" prior to the creation of Umbanda Pura, or whether these groups embraced the name later as it gained visibility and public acceptance. Although these Afro-Brazilian groups identified themselves with Umbanda, it is clear that they were referring to a different set of ideas and practices than those of Umbanda Pura. The literature that now began to emerge from this Afro-Brazilian milieu, while devoted principally to its own manuals of ritual practice, also contained brief editorial comments showing both a clear awareness and a deep resentment of the intentions represented in Umbanda Pura.

The dimensions of their disagreement can be illustrated in the following brief excerpts: "There is great controversy over the origin of Umbanda," stated one of their publications:

> Some who think themselves to be versed in religious matters in reality know nothing of our religion, and others do not even bother to hide their contempt for it because it was brought [to Brazil] by slaves. (Freitas and Pinto 1956:18)
>
> It is very amusing to hear them [the founders of Umbanda] say that "Umbanda suffered an African influence." No, my good comrades, Umbanda *is* African, it is the cultural heritage of the black race, and it is very different from... Kardecism (Ibid.:56).

One leader commented upon the statutes of a recently formed Umbanda federation which had adopted the ritual style of Umbanda Pura and which prohibited its member centros from using drums, singing pontos in the style of the *"Gêgê, Nàgó, Bantu, Queto, Angola* or *Omolocô"* nations, sacrificing animals, and offering ritual food to the deities. "An Umbanda terreiro which does not use drums and other ritual instruments, which does not sing pontos in the African style, which does not offer sacrifices [of animals] or food to the deities can be anything," he replied, "but it is *not* a terreiro of Umbanda" (quoted in Kloppenburg 1961a:56–57).

Afro-Brazilian leaders expressed their anger at "White Umbanda" in terms that stressed both social class and racial antagonism:

> Today...a great wave of mystification has invaded Umbanda. The intruders have created a white Umbanda.... They have modified the sacred ritual and worse, from the spiritual point of view, they have introduced commercialism into our religion.... People who know nothing of Umbanda, who were never initiated, let alone trained as religious leaders, open centros equipped with luxurious consulting rooms, where clients are attended according to numbered tokens. In these centros, the real Umbandistas are not admitted, but are turned away at the door with these words: "This is not Macumba, it is Umbanda. You are accustomed to low Spiritism."...
>
> Many times the truth resides in a poor, humble and unpretentious terreiro, while mystification masks itself in a luxurious centro, which appears well-organized, with excellent furnishings, a magnificent altar, an indexed file of its members, and a well dressed and well-spoken board of directors. (Freitas and Pinto 1956:19)

Afro-Brazilian leaders referred contemptuously to practitioners of Umbanda Pura as "mere Kardecists [who] call themselves Umbandistas without understanding anything about Umbanda" (Freitas and Pinto 1956:15).

Leaders of Umbanda Pura retorted in their own principal news organ, the *Jornal de Umbanda,* by labelling Afro-Brazilian practitioners "pseudo-Umbandistas who really practice Quimbanda and Candomblé" (9/56). The religious labels employed in the name-calling had come to signify more than simply differences in religious and ritual orientation. They had come to symbolize different social and racial sectors of the population.

Oppositions between Umbanda Pura and more African-oriented forms of Umbanda continue into the present and contribute to Umbanda's ongoing heterodoxy. However, for reasons to be explored further, they are not as antagonistic as during this earlier period but rather maintain a peaceful coexistence.

The Nationalist Position

The emphasis in Zélio's myth on Umbanda's autochthonous Brazilian origins and its dedication to Brazil's indigenous and oppressed minority populations under the patronage of Brazilian Catholicism suggest its incipient nationalist orientation. Although nationalist themes were not mentioned or explored at the First Congress, they emerged in clear form from within this same network of middle sector leadership during this same period. At least two early books on Umbanda published in the mid-1940s contain explicit nationalist interpretations of this religion in a form that quickly became and has remained extremely popular.

This early nationalist orientation appears to have been inspired directly by the form of cultural nationalism popularized by the Brazilian sociologist Gilberto Freyre, whose monumental best seller, *The Masters and the Slaves,* had appeared only a few years before, in 1933. This enormously influential book developed the theme that Brazil's distinctive identity consisted in its historical blending of three races and their cultures—the Portuguese, the African, and the Indian—into a unique form of culture and way of life.

Umbanda, by the very nature of its syncretic composition and by its thematic form, was ideally suited to this kind of nationalist interpretation. Its combination of (Iberian) Catholicism, together with African and Brazilian Indian spirits, suggested the exact racial and cultural blend celebrated by Freyre. What early Umbanda writers did was to extend Freyre's ideas into the realm of religious syncretism.

Uma Religião Genuimente Brasileira (A Genuinely Brazilian Religion), a book published in the early 1940s by an important early Umbanda leader, declared:

> Son of three races: the White, the Negro, the Indian, to the Brazilian must be destined an eclectic religion, whose principal characteristics are charity, humility, and tolerance for the immense ignorance of mankind, and which will unify the experience of the White, the tradition of the Indian, and the magic of the Negro. Anyone who knows Brazilian folklore

knows that just as the Negro is convinced that the waters, the forests, the rocky outcroppings *(pedreiras)* are governed by supernaturals, the Indian, too, has the same belief... (quoted in *Macaia* 10/68)

This same theme is found as well in another early work of this period:

> Given the racial background of our people, whose psychic substratum is formed of the totemism of the indigenous [Indian populations], the fetichism of the Africans, and Iberian medievalism, we must realize that religious miscibility obeyed the same laws as ethnic miscibility. (Anon. 1944:22)

Thus, early in its development Umbanda acquired an explicit nationalist interpretation. Nationalist themes have, in the course of Umbanda's development, served multiple purposes for different groups. They have been used by publicists of Umbanda to gain legitimacy for this genuinely Brazilian religion. In addition, the popularity of nationalism as a literary theme among educated Brazilians has helped to give Umbanda more appeal among educated sectors of the Brazilian public. This form of nationalism has also permitted the incorporation of the African heritage into Umbanda in a manner now considered respectable. Nationalism has also served as an extremely useful tool in politics, where it has helped to create the basis of an appeal to unity and to embue diverse social sectors with a common, all-embracing identity. Nationalist interpretations of Umbanda were widely used during this intensely nationalistic period in Brazilian history by politicians both inside and outside Umbanda, to appeal to Umbanda voters.

This form of nationalism incorporates the African heritage into Umbanda, and symbolically into the Brazilian identity, yet avoids the divisive ideological controversies generated by a more explicit focus on that heritage. Nationalism offers an interpretation of Umbanda's African heritage that values that heritage yet at the same time defines it as only one of several important influences within this religion. This has become both a respectable and a noncontroversial solution to the middle sector's dilemma concerning Umbanda's ties to Africa.

The Contemporary Status of These Ideas

Together with an origin myth that provides a charter for the founding of Umbanda, I have outlined different ideological stances taken by early middle sector leaders and by their lower sector opponents. I have described their efforts to define Umbanda's origins and identity and, through these, to create and construct it in the image of their own class, racial, and political interests. All of these ideas continued to be current at the time of my research, though none of them had succeeded in gaining ascendency over the movement as a whole. The Umbanda origin myth continues to be little known, although it is cited in one interpretation of Umbanda by a highly educated Umbandista, who, however, chose to publish his book only in English (McGregor 1967). The insistence on Umbanda's remote origins in the ancient Far East can still be found in current books on Umbanda by Umbandistas, though this interpretation is restricted principally to the more esoterically oriented literature aimed at middle sector readers.[6] I also frequently encountered this same position among Umbandistas in these circles. The idea of Umbanda's African origins, on the other hand, has now gained far greater acceptability and is popular among not only the many Afro-Brazilian groups who now define themselves as Umbandistas but among the middle sector Umbanda leadership as well. At a later Umbanda Congress held in 1961, for example, the official historian of the Congress returned to an African derivation for the word "Umbanda," referring to a dictionary of the *Kimbundu* (Bantu) language of Angola, which defined its meaning as "the art of curing..." (Bandeira 1961:39–40).

As Umbanda has achieved greater legitimacy and recognition as a religion, its middle sector practitioners may feel themselves less threatened by what they once perceived as the social catastrophe of African origins. More relaxed attitudes concerning the African connection have also been encouraged by Umbanda politicians, who in the interest of gaining maximum numbers of supporters have welcomed support from diverse sectors of Umbanda. Some Umbanda federations even name themselves as representatives of both Umbanda and Afro-Brazilian religions in their official titles.

The nationalist emphasis in Umbanda has also continued to have wide appeal and is disseminated by both Umbanda politicians and the mass media.

Contemporary Umbanda literature also contains explicit restatements of the notion, developed at the First Umbanda Congress in 1941, that Umbanda's mission is to combat the evils of Quimbanda. One such statement, published just after the 1964 military coup (and probably written shortly before it), expounds upon Umbanda's mission to combat black magic, ignorance and superstition. It carries strong overtones of both the middle sector's wish to rescue the masses and its fear of them.

> Umbanda has come as a universal message from the heart of Brazil, a country still backward due to egoism, ambition, evil and false faith, as an antidote to these nefarious practices [black magic, Quimbanda] directed by men of the lowest social orders. The evil which they wreak in the Brazilian lower classes is profound. These huge, disenfranchised and defenseless masses, ignorant, spiritually blind and illiterate, with no religious defense except that of fanticism which is an identical evil, put themselves in the hands of these religious criminals [practitioners of black magic] with their tricks, illusions, their vain promises, and waste their meager finances for nothing. Their only defense is Umbanda, the other pole of mysticism, which provides an antidote. (Freitas 1965:11)

This quotation also suggests a powerful political metaphor. The shading between the stated fear that the masses will succumb to religious fanaticism and the implicit fear that these "huge, disenfranchised, and defenseless masses" will be roused to *political* fanaticism is a very fine one. The quote suggests a fear of the potential political threat posed by the urban lower sectors, as well as a sense of their exploitation and a measure of humanitarian concern for their welfare. Umbanda, then, may be offered as a political as well as a religious antidote.

The continuing degree of innovation within Umbanda and the low level of concern with dogma among both Umbanda leaders and its rank and file membership is reflected in two popular contemporary definitions of the meaning of the term Umbanda, both of which stress its unifying tendencies and move away from any concern with linking it to a particular, narrowly defined tradition. One, from an Afro-Brazilian Umbanda publication, states that while "in the African language [*sic*] Umbanda means a reunion of different tribes for religious purposes," similarly in Brazil it does not signify a particular ritual, religion or cult, but rather "the unification of all the rituals of Afro-Brazilian cults, which in its liturgy respects all the different tribal customs of the different nations of Bantu peoples" (Mironga Vol. I, 1969:25). An even more all-embracing definition now gaining popularity—one that emphasizes Umbanda's Brazilian identity—is that which was given to me several times during interviews with Umbandistas. They suggested that the word "Umbanda" was a contraction of *"uma" "banda,"* which in Portuguese means "a group" or "one group." Umbandistas interpreted this to mean that Umbandistas are all one group together.

4

Caboclos and Pretos Velhos in the Umbanda Cosmos

My focus now shifts away from the historical background of Umbanda and the period of its founding to contemporary aspects of belief and practice. This also represents a shift from the concern with influences upon Umbanda, its progenitors and the ideological concerns of its founders, to an ethnographic description and analysis of this religion. However, the links between the previous chapters and those to follow remain crucial ones. Continuity of personnel within the networks of middle sector Umbanda leadership links the perspectives of the early leaders to contemporary ones. Similarly, the type of Umbanda (Umbanda Pura, now customarily referred to simply as Umbanda) that these leaders continue to practice and promote still reflects many of the early leaders' concerns: with whitening and de-Africanizing Umbanda, with rationalizing and bureaucratizing it, and above all, with civilizing and domesticating it and delivering it from its primitive and barbaric past. It reflects as well their interest in nationalism and charity and in embracing the lower sectors of Brazilian society.

These concerns are now encoded within Umbanda belief and practice and are reflected in the structuring of the Umbanda cosmos, the position and significance of the figures within it, and the selective emphasis given to certain practices while others are marginalized or even absent. The rarity in contemporary Umbanda literature of ideological statements concerning the underlying principles according to which Umbanda's origins, cosmology, and ritual should be formulated reflects the process of encodement. Such statements are now superfluous because they have through time become translated directly into cosmology and ritual. Ideology is now expressed directly in other symbolic languages, those of belief and practice. Statements concerning Umbanda ideology can now be made, and different positions expressed, by defending particular forms of cosmology and belief.

The process of encodement has not been a neat one. First, as I have already indicated, the leaders who have espoused Umbanda Pura, while they have been privileged by the resources and connections of their class position, have neither gained control over Umbanda nor achieved consensus within it. Their particular Umbanda code may be ignored or opposed by those with differing ideological positions, which are, in turn, encoded in contrastive forms of belief and ritual. In addition, even within this form of Umbanda, its high level of eclecticism has produced internal contradictions within the cosmological system. Often highly significant in themselves, these contradictions also offer flexibility to Umbanda practitioners, who may thus identify with or stress particular interpretations of Umbanda and ignore others.

This chapter will explore the Umbanda cosmos and the figures in its pantheon. I will first discuss what I describe as two levels of its cosmological system: a more esoteric and intellectualized interpretation of the cosmos as a formal system, which follows Umbanda dogma and is mainly the province of Umbanda specialists, and a more widely shared, less complex, and somewhat contrastive lay interpretation based on ritual practice. I will suggest ways in which these interpretations encode different aspects of contemporary Umbanda ideology. The latter part of the chapter will elaborate on the figures in the Umbanda pantheon, focusing particularly on the Caboclos and Pretos Velhos. I will analyze the ideological significance of their centrality within the Umbanda cosmos, in contrast to other more marginal figures, and will argue that this positioning in itself provides a particularly clear expression of the civilizing, whitening, nationalizing process within Umbanda.

Cosmology

Leaders of Umbanda centros and authors of doctrinal tracts, more Kardecist-oriented Umbanda practitioners, and those who are interested in the complexities of Umbanda dogma maintain what I refer to as the specialists' view of the Umbanda cosmos. According to this view, the Umbanda cosmos is a complex formal system that contains three levels: the astral spaces, the earth, and the underworld. Powerful personages with dual identities, African and Catholic, inhabit the astral spaces, together with the Caboclos, the Pretos Velhos, and a host of other, less evolved spirits. The earth forms an intermediate plane that offers a temporary residence for spirits passing through their various human incarnations at lower stages of spiritual evolution. It is also visited by various categories of spirits, such as the more evolved Caboclos and Pretos Velhos, who return during ceremonies at Umbanda centros to visit and to further their own evolution through performing *caridade* (charity). Evil and ignorant spirits from the underworld also visit the earth and are chief causes of the harm that Caboclos and Pretos Velhos must work to undo. The underworld is the realm of these harmful spirits, the Exús, and the forces of Quimbanda.

God, a distant and otiose creator, presides over the astral spirit world.[1] Below him, the other inhabitants are organized into a complex hierarchical system based on the number seven. There is a vertical division into *as Sête Linhas de Umbanda* (the Seven Lines of Umbanda) whose leaders are powerful personages, most of whom have dual identities as *Orixás* (African deities) and Catholic holy figures (see figure 1). *Oxalá* and his counterpart Jesus Christ head the first line, *Xangô*/St. Jerome the second; *Ogum*/St. George the third; *Oxôssi*/St. Sebastian the fourth, etc. (see figure 2).[2] The seventh, and lowest line, known as the *Linha das Almas* (the Line of Dead Souls), headed by St. Michael, has no African counterpart. While Umbandistas generally accept the division into Seven Lines of Umbanda, the specific identities of these lines is somewhat flexible; for example, certain of the Afro-Catholic lines may be merged to make room for a Kardecist-influenced "Oriental Line" or a "Children's Line" (see figure 2).[3]

The vertical sevenfold division into lines is crosscut by another sevenfold horizontal ranking system that subdivides each line internally into seven "sub-lines" and further into seven legions. Legions are divided into sub-legions; sub-legions into *falanges* (phalanxes); phalanxes into sub-phalanxes, each with a spiritual leader. Umbandistas today often liken this structure to that of an army, with each unit or subunit under the command of a particular spiritual personage, in just the same manner as codifers at the first Umbanda Congress, who described the pantheon as a "whole spiritual army under the command of Jesus Christ, or *Oxalá*, his African counterpart" (Anon. 1942:190–92). This continuing usage of military imagery in referring to the structure of the Umbanda cosmos, which undoubtedly reflects the military background prominent among both Umbanda's founders and many of its current leaders, stresses the impersonal, rational, bureaucratic nature of this formal system.

Caboclos and Pretos Velhos are located among the lower echelons of the Seven Lines of Umbanda, at the ranks of legion leaders and below. Caboclos have been incorporated into the lines of the Orixá / Saints and form their lower ranks,[4] while the Pretos Velhos are the sole occupants of the seventh and lowest ranked line, the "Line of Dead Souls," also known as the *Linha Africana* (African Line). "African" in this case refers not to the African deities but to African slaves.[5]

Caboclos and Pretos Velhos are said to be associated in these lower ranks because, unlike the Orixás, who are commonly interpreted as deities, the Caboclos and Pretos Velhos are disincarnate spirits of individuals who lived during the Brazilian colonial and slave periods. Their associations with one another are often explained in terms of their common historical experience as enslaved peoples (see for example McGregor 1967:196; Bandeira 1961:114–15), although Pretos Velhos are sometimes said to be somewhat less evolved than Caboclos by virtue of having been more recently deceased.

Still lower ranking, below the Caboclos and Pretos Velhos, are vast

Figure 1. The Central Supernatural Figures of Umbanda and, Their Catholic, "Bantu" and Indian Counterparts

Diety	Candomblé (Yoruba Dieties) Association	Umbanda		Catholic Counterpart	"Bantu" Counterpart*	Indian Counterpart*
		Supernatural	Association			
Olorum	Supreme Diety	Olorum Zambi	Supreme power	Deus	Zambi Zambipongo Ganga Zumba	Tupan Tupi-Guarani
Obatalá Orixalá	Sky God	Oxalá		Jesus Cristo		
Xangô	Thunder, lightning. rain, rocks	Xangô	Thunder, lightning, rocks	St. Jerónimo		Tupan (God of thunder)
Ogum	Smiths and war	Ogum	War	St. George		
Oxôssi	Hunting, agriculture		Hunting			
Yemanjá	Salt water	Yemanjá	Sea, salt water	N.S. da Conceição N.S. da Gloria	Calunga	Janaina
Oxum	Fresh water, sensual love	Oxum	Fresh water, sensual love	Sta. Barbara		
Yansã	Storms	Yansã	Storms	N.S. da Gloria N.S. da Conceição		

Exú	Messenger for dieties	Exú Pomba Gira	Messenger, evil spirit	Satan Lucifer Jezebel	Bonbongira
Shapanan, Omulú, Obaluaie	Medicine, smallpox	has no counterpart, but is associated with Exú, or with the Linha das Almas			
Erês	Child spirits	Cosme e Damião	Child spirits	Sts. Cosmos and Damion	

* Bastide, 1971, 85: 108-9.

Figure 2. Examples of "The Seven Lines of Umbanda"

Sources*	Oxalá	Yemanjá	Ogum	Oxóssi	Xangô	Oxum	Linha das Almas	Linha do Oriente	Yansã	Cosme e Damião
1.	Line 1	Line 2	Line 3	Line 4	Line 5	Line 6	Line 7			
2.	Line 1	Line 2	Line 3	Line 4	Line 5	Line 6	Line 7			
3.	Line 1	Line 2	Line 6	Line 4	Line 5		Line 7	Line 3		
4.	Line 1	Line 2	Line 5	Line 3	Line 6	Line 6	Line 7		Line 4	
5.	Line 1	Line 5	Line 2	Line 3	Line 4		Line 7			
6.	Line 1	Line 2	Line 6	Line 4	Line 5		Line 7	Line 3		
7.	Line 1	Line 2	Line 4	Line 5	Line 3		Line 7			Line 6

* Sources:
1. McGregor 1967:185ff.
2. Freitas and Cardozo n.d.
3. Braga 1961.
4. Anon. 1942:245
5. Freitas 1939:21-22
6. Fontanelle 1961:136-41
7. Matta e Silva 1969:59-86

numbers of unidentified *guias* (spirit guides) and *espíritos protetores* (spirit protectors). An example of this hierarchy is given in figure 3. The underworld—the realm of Quimbanda, a mirror image of the Umbanda cosmos, the domain of negative and evil forces ruled by the Exús—is, like the Umbanda cosmos above it, composed of seven internally ranked lines, all of which are headed and staffed by Exús (see, for example, Braga 1961).

This elaborate sevenfold grid establishes a formal system for organizing and ranking the figures in the Umbanda pantheon, which resembles a complex, impersonal bureaucracy. However, its full range of complexity is known principally to religious specialists. Only the division into the Seven Lines of Umbanda is widely known to all practitioners. Mediums, who form a sort of intermediate category of semi-specialists, together with some lay Umbandistas interested in these matters, are also likely to be familiar with some details of the subranking system. Mediums are generally familiar, for example, with the ranking of the spirits that they and others in their centros receive.

In contrast to this formal hierarchy, participation in Umbanda public rituals produces another, somewhat different and far less formal interpretation of the Umbanda cosmos, which I refer to as the lay Umbandista interpretation. This is far more generally known and less complex than that of the specialists. However, specialists themselves, as they participate in Umbanda rituals, also participate in and validate this lay interpretation of Umbanda. The lay interpretation transforms the formal cosmos in two important ways: first, it shifts the focus of attention from the most powerful spiritual personages to the more accessible ones, and second, it ignores the formal ranking system and recognizes only major status differences. Within the formal hierarchical system just described, Orixá/Saints are, next to God, the most powerful and highest ranking figures in the Umbanda cosmos, who together combine the forces of nature under the control of the major African deities with the miraculous powers of the Catholic saints. However, these powerful dual figures are, like God, distant from human activity. Evolved beyond the point of returning to earth, they have become permanent inhabitants of the astral spaces and therefore no longer descend to visit Umbanda centros. Instead, they send their lower ranking emissaries, the Caboclos and Pretos Velhos.

The Caboclos and Pretos Velhos are most important and most active in Umbanda rituals in identifying the causes of human misfortune and prescribing countermeasures and cures. Though lower ranking than the Orixá/Saints, they take center stage during these rituals, displacing in importance the more powerful Orixá/Saints and the powerful Exús as well. Messengers of the Orixá/Saints, the Caboclos and Pretos Velhos serve as intermediaries between humans and these more powerful spiritual entities.

Figure 3. The Formal Hierarchical Structure of the Umbanda Cosmos*

	Line 1	Line 2	Line 3	Line 4	Line 5	Line 6	Line 7
Head of Line (Chefe da Linha)	Oxalá (Orixala)	Yemanjá	Xangô	Ogum	Oxóssi	Cosme e Damião	As Almas (Pretos Velhos)
First Astral Plane:							
Heads of Legions	Caboclos (male)	Caboclas (female)	Xangô	Ogum	Caboclo	Tupanzinho	Pai Guiné
Sub-Legions Phalanxes Sub-Phalanxes	Ubiratão Ubirajara Ubiritan	Iara Indaya Nana Burucú	Cao 7 Montanhas 7 Pedreiras	da Lei Yara Mêgê	Arranca-Toco Jurema Arariboia	Ori Yarira Doum	Pai Tomé Pai Arruda Pai Congo de Aruanda
	Aymoré Guaraci	Estrela do Mar Oxum	da Pedra Preta da Pedra Branca Agodô	Rompe Mato do Malê	Guiné Arruda	Cosme Damião	Maria Conga Pai Benedito
	Guarani Tupí	Inhassa Sereia do Mar		Beira-Mar Matinata	Pena Branca Cobra Coral		Pai Joaquim
Second Astral Plane:							
Guias	Caboclos	Caboclas	Caboclos	Caboclas	Caboclos	Crispin	Pai João d'Angola
	Grajauna	Estrela Dalva	Cachoeira	7 Espados	Pena Azul	Crispiniano	Pai João da Aruanda
	Grauna Agua Branca Tupan	Jupira Jupiara Jandira	Pena Verde Gira Mundo Sumaré Alofim	7 Lanças 7 Escudas Timbiri	Pena Dourada Tupinambá Guaraná	Mariazinha Zequinha Chiquinho	Vovó Ana Vovó Conga Tia Chica d'Angola

Rompe Nuvem	da Praia	Rompe Ferro	Tira Teima	Tabajaras	Joãozinho	Pai Miguel das Almas
Yarima	Jucana	Rompe Aço	Humaitá	7 Flexas		Vovó Catarina
Tamoio			Rompe Mato	Tupiara		Pai Congo do Mar
						Vovó Cambinda
Guaraná			Araguari	Tupaibo		
Iamacutara			Icaraí	Turiaçu		
Gira Sol				Mata Virgem		
				Tei da Mata		
				Rei do Oriente		
				Rompe Folha		

Third Astral
Plane:

Espíritos Protetores
(Protective spirits)
(These have no names)

* Matta e Silva. 1969: 59-86.

Umbanda practice shifts the complex, impersonal, bureaucratic, formal ranking system to another mode of relationship based on personalistic patronage exchanges and focused ritually on charitable curing and advising activities. It reveals another dimension to the operation of the Umbanda cosmos, one which, like the photographic enlargement of a detail in a larger canvas, highlights a particular segment of the Umbanda cosmos, the lower ranks of the formal ranking system, and throws its upper ranks into shadow. It does not contradict the basic status categories of the formal system, nor does it invert the subrankings among the Caboclos or the Pretos Velhos (i.e., legions, sublegions, phalanxes, etc.). It simply merges them within the more important collective identities of the Caboclos and Pretos Velhos. It refocuses relationships which in the formal system are based on impersonal rights and duties associated with rank to personalized patronage relationships within a larger astral patronage network. This refocusing, since it occurs during Umbanda rituals, involves all participants in Umbanda, specialists and mediums as well as the lay Umbandistas who attend the centros as members of the congregation and as clients.

These two views of the cosmological system present contrastive world views, deriving from different religious sources, encoding different aspects of Umbanda ideology, and expressing different aspects of contemporary Brazilian social structure.

The formal structure, the specialists' interpretation of the Umbanda cosmos, is very close to that of Kardecism. It obeys the same laws of evolution and reincarnation, with the resulting panorama of spirits evolving slowly but inevitably upward from a state of spiritual ignorance to enlightenment through a succession of early incarnations and in the process moving gradually away from the earth's orbit. As in Kardecism, Christian charity, in combination with reincarnation, provides the motor for spiritual evolution. The complex sevenfold grid, according to codifiers at the first Umbanda Congress in 1941, derives from theosophy and Rosicrucianism rather than from Kardecism (Anon. 1942:101). These codifiers may well have been the ones to incorporate this scheme into Umbanda, since it is not found in Kardecism and the first mention I found of it in Umbanda was in the proceedings of this Congress. Moreover, the inclusion of elements from European mystical traditions was directly in line with the interests of these early leaders in connecting Umbanda more closely with the esoteric religious traditions of the civilized world.

This formal structuring of the Umbanda cosmos encodes the founders' view of a structured, bureaucratized, highly ordered and regimented world, for which their usage of military metaphor seems both apt and politically suggestive. The inclusion of Kardecist and theosophical borrowings suggests as well the highly desired association with the educated, civilized, great traditions and distance from those of the lower sectors and from Africa. At the same time, this cosmos presents a middle sector utopian dream of a rationally ordered bureaucratic society. Moreover, it is based on enlightenment views of inevitable progress and slow but inexorable spiritual upward mobility according to rational and scientific laws, from ignorance to knowledge, from spiritual darkness to light. It presents an image of spiritual betterment, assured upward mobility through a rational process of education and the performance of charitable duties.

The informal Umbanda cosmological system, in contrast, emphasizes personalized relations between petitioners and providers of charity, which takes the form of patronage, with ritual homage exchanged in return for cures and advice. This interpretation of the Umbanda cosmos strongly resembles the relationship between petitioners and patron saints in Popular Catholicism, in which mortals seek favors and help from particular patron saints, promising acts of homage and devotion in return for aid granted. The Catholic saints themselves are present in the Umbanda pantheon in a strategic position as higher patrons and thus as direct models for the activities of the Caboclos and Pretos Velhos, who serve as their intermediaries. Moreover, aid received from the Caboclos and Pretos Velhos has a strong aura of the miraculous cures associated, for example, with Catholic pilgrimage centers, an emphasis that is strengthened by the presence of the saints' alter egos, the African Orixás, who also serve as sources of supernatural forms of aid. Although the Orixás' powers, significantly, are somewhat disparaged and marginalized as "magical," in contrast to the "miraculous" powers of the saints, the Orixás also provide models for the provision of supernatural aid.

Popular Catholic belief, then, shapes and reinforces a frankly religious and mystical emphasis within Umbanda, in opposition to the rational interpretation of spiritual aid provided in the Kardecist-influenced formal cosmological system. However, in the matter of providing both spiritual and material forms of *caridade* (charity) which is Umbanda's central project, it is probable that Catholicism, with its longstanding traditional emphasis on the practice of charitable activities and good deeds, has provided an underlying basis for both Umbanda and Kardecism.

This informal view of the cosmological system, with its emphasis on personalized patronage exchanges, also encodes a contrastive mode of organization and exchange, whose satisfaction is unpredictable—miraculous or magical—rather than the predictable rewards for duties performed within the formal bureaucratic system. This patronage view of the universe is a static one, reminiscent of models of a static patriarchal system, where statuses and their occupants are fixed and immutable: humans, disencarnate spirits, deities all exchange services, but all remain permanently in their places.

The view encoded in this lay interpretation of the Umbanda cosmos might be called a more realistic and less utopian image of the workings of the Brazilian bureaucracy, perhaps of the realities that for Brazilians underlie the idealism of a Weberian order: the unpredictable nature of rewards, the importance of personal ties over formal statuses, the illusion of social mobility.

It is clear that the utopian vision encoded within the formal system has not gained ascendancy within Umbanda but has remained the somewhat arcane province of specialists and more Kardecist-oriented Umbandistas, mainly from the middle sectors. Not only is this view not accepted by all Umbandistas; even among the followers of Umbanda Pura, it is both less known and secondary to the more common lay interpretation of a world that operates on the basis of patronage. For the majority of Umbandistas, this utopian vision of the world is counteracted by the experience of gritty daily realities. The more pragmatic lay interpretation is a clearer expression of praxis within the contemporary Brazilian political economic system. At the same time, the two interpretations together articulate the basic contradiction of Brazilian social reality, between the conscious effort to modernize and bureaucratize the political economy, and the reality that it operates on the basis of patronage.

Caboclos and Pretos Velhos

I now want to elaborate further upon the Caboclos and Pretos Velhos, the central figures in Umbanda. After characterizing them and discussing their symbolic significance for various sectors of Umbandistas, I will analyze the significance of their central position in Umbanda in relation to the marginalization of the Orixá/Saints and the Exús. I will suggest that the selective emphasis on the Caboclos and Pretos Velhos, and the complementary marginalization of these other figures, represents a central means through which Umbanda's ideological emphasis on purifying, civilizing, whitening, and de-Africanizing has been encoded within its cosmology. The Caboclos and Pretos Velhos, I will suggest, represent the selection of a Brazilian rather than a foreign identity, of the civilizing process over the forces of savagery and barbarism, and of the controlled over the uncontrollable.

Caboclos and Pretos Velhos are known to Umbandistas through oral tradition, through written literature, and particularly through the texts of *pontos* (sacred songs) sung at the ceremonies, and which are now available in inexpensive paperback volumes. In addition to the collective identities of these spirit categories, more individualized identities—spirits with particular names and histories—may also emerge within them. These may be heightened as well in the ritual performances of the mediums who receive them and who may add highly individualized interpretations of their particular spirits to the standardized gestures and stances appropriate to the spirits' collective identities.

Caboclos are collectively identified as unacculturated Indians, inhabitants of the Amazonian forests.[6] They are men and women at the height of their powers and vitality, hunters and warriors who are arrogant, brave, and often somewhat vain. In describing the personality traits of Caboclos, leaders and mediums at Umbanda centros repeatedly used the terms "proud," full of *força* (power), arrogant, aggressive, authoritarian, *mandão* (domineering).[7] They are considered to be highly intelligent and talented specialists in curing and advising on a variety of problems.

Caboclos draw their power from the forces of nature: waterfalls, rivers, the virgin forest, the sun, the moon, and from forest creatures, particularly snakes, who are often their companions. Some of their names derive from such associations, as for example, *Caboclo Mata Virgem* (Virgin Forest), *Caboclo da Lua* (Moon), *do Vento* (Wind), *Cobra Coral* (Coral Snake). Many Caboclos' names are drawn from particular objects sacred to them, and these are often represented in their costumes when they possess mediums: for example, *Caboclo Pena Branca* (White Feather), *Sete Flechas* (Seven Arrows), *Pedra Azul* (Blue Stone). Another source of Caboclo names is provided by actual tribal groups of Brazilian Indians, such as *Tupinambá, Tapirapé, Guaraní*. Still other "tribal" names are derived from Brazilian romantic literature on the Indians. Names such as *Aimoré, Perí, Iracema, Ubirajara* derive from the writings of José de Alencar, Brazil's foremost nineteenth-century Indianist writer, as do many of the habitats and associations with animal spirits (Carneiro 1964:146–49). Whole lines of the poetry of Gonçalves Dias, another nineteenth-century Indianist writer, are repeated in the pontos sung to Caboclos (Ibid.:148). Caboclo are often arranged in lineages and connected with specific heroic exploits. The individual details and lore of their identities are learned and transmitted in the beautiful pontos sung to them in Umbanda ceremonies, accompanied by handclapping or drums. The flavor of these individual Caboclo histories may be provided by a small sampling of these pontos. One Caboclo family, from the Guaraní tribe, includes Caboclo Aimoré, to whom the following ponto may be sung:

Valente em sua tribo	Valiant in his own tribe
E caçador audaz	He is a daring hunter
Em nome de Tupã	In the name of Tupã (God)
Foi cacique e foi Pagé	He was a chief and a shaman
Da tribo dos guaranís	Of the Guaraní tribe
O seu nome é Aimoré	His name is Aimoré
Aimoré, moré, moré...	Aimoré, moré, moré...
(bis)	(repeat)
	(Decelso 1967:52)

The lineage continues with his son, Caboclo Tupiaba:

Nos somos dois guerreiros	We are two warriors
Dois irmãos unidos	Two brothers united
Meu nome é Tupiaba	My name is Tupiaba
Sou filho de Aimoré	I am the son of Aimoré
La na tribo Guaraní	Of the Guaraní tribe
Meu irmão chama Perí	My brother's name is Perí
	(Anon. 1969:43)

While the above lineage is Guaraní, Caboclo Aracatí comes from the Goitacáz tribe:

Sou filho das montanhas	I am a son of the mountains
Da tribo Goitacáz	From the Goitacáz tribe
Meu pai era Cacique	My father was a chief
Minha irmã era Arací	My sister was Arací
Eu me chamo Aracatí	My name is Aracatí
	(Figueiredo 1967:89)

Another ponto, variously attributed to several Caboclos, among them *Jurema,* the most important of the female Caboclos, begins with an adaptation of the Biblical story of Moses:

Com sete mêses de nascido	At the age of seven months
A minha mãe me abandonou	My mother abandoned me
Salve o nome de Oxossi	Praise the name of Oxossi
Foi Tupí quem me criou...	It was Tupí who brought me up...
	(Ibid.:86; Anon. 1969:91)

The affinity between Caboclos and snakes may stem from Afro-Brazilian sects in Northeast Brazil. It is seen in the following ponto, sung to Caboclo Beira-Mar (Edge of the Sea):

Era na beiro do rio	It was at the edge of a river
Quando eu ouvi uma cobra piar	That I heard a snake hiss
(bis)	(repeat)
Era uma linda jiboia	It was a beautiful boa constrictor,
meu Deus	good heavens!
No bodoque do Seu Beira-Mar	In the quiver of Sr. Beira Mar

Caboclos are identified as inhabiting the Brazilian jungle *(mato),* but they are also frequently thought to have a spiritual home whose name and location may differ, depending on which aspect of Umbanda's syncretic tradition is emphasized. Sometimes Caboclos are said to live in the *Cidade da Jurema* (city of Jurema), a mythical, paradisiacal, distant land in the mato (see also Carneiro 1964:149).[8] Caboclos, when they are summoned to Umbanda centros, are often said to be arriving from Jurema, as for example in the following ponto, which begins: *"Ele vem de longe da Cidade da Jurema ... "* (He comes from far away, from the city of Jurema). They are also sometimes said to come from *Aruanda,* a version of *Luanda,* one of the largest slaving ports of Angola. While this would seem to represent a shift toward assimilating Caboclos into an African origin (Ibid.: 145), it need not be taken as such. Aruanda, for many Umbandistas, has lost its geographical significance and is located in the astral spaces, the home of both Caboclos and Pretos Velhos (Fontanelle 1961:86), or simply referred to as "the spiritual dwelling of the Indian and Negro spirit guides" (McGregor 1967:179).

The Caboclos are characterized as proud, free leaders and warriors with natural nobility, whose power comes from the forces of nature and who have never been subjected to the yoke of servitude. Descriptions given me by mediums and leaders and the many ritual dramatizations of these spirits I witnessed consistently stress their arrogance and vitality. Yet early Umbanda codifiers had perceived a contradiction in the Caboclos' status. Although proud, arrogant, and independent, they were at the same time helpers who must fulfill their duties to visit Umbanda centros to practice charity. One early ideologue presented the contradiction and its resolutions in the following way:

> The caboclo, because he comes from the *mato* [the forest] is full of intolerant enthusiasm, like a New Christian, is intransigent and points out our defects. Upon hearing the complaints of those who suffer he replies angrily that Spiritism is not meant to help anyone with the problems of their earthly lives, and he attributes our own sufferings to our own errors and faults for which we must pay. But after two or three years of contact with the bitter miseries of life he softens and ends up giving material aid. (informant, quoted in Freitas 1939:43)

This is a clear statement of the civilizing process, the process of conversion, in Catholic terms: conversion through the knowledge of suffering. Proud, free, yet bound to bureaucratic duties. Neither in talking to Umbandistas with whom I discussed the Caboclos, nor in any contemporary Umbanda literature, did I encounter any reference to this contradiction. This may be because in the dominant interpretation of Umbanda cosmology, the lay view which emphasizes patronage, there is no necessary contradiction between independence and duty. The patron is free to be as arrogant as he wishes; he is not bound by the duties of his position; he is seeking homage.

The Pretos Velhos present a striking contrast to the Caboclos. These "Old Blacks" are the spirits of Africans enslaved in Brazil, generally slaves from Bahia. All are elderly, and they are named and addressed familiarly and affectionately in kin terms: *Vovó* (Grandmother) or *Vovô* (Grandfather), *Tia*

(Aunt), and *Tio* (Uncle), *Mãe* (Mother), and less often, *Pai* (Father).[9] They are characterized as humble, patient, long-suffering, and good. Umbanda leaders repeatedly stressed to me their *humildade* (humility), *bondade* (friendship), and *caridade* (charity) and tended to characterize them as subservient. In contrast to the Caboclos, they are considered to be naturally endowed with humility and extremely anxious to help humans in any way they can. It is said that they love to exercise their many talents in curing and resolving family problems. As described by an early Umbandista,

> Preto Velho...cannot see tears without crying and almost always helps the needy without being asked. [He] is filled with pity, thinking of the difficulties which bad sentiments bring to him who cultivates them. (Freitas 1939:43)

Many of the names of Pretos Velhos reflect the tradition common in slave times of a Catholic first name followed by a tribal or nation affiliation, such as Maria *Congo* or Maria *Mina da Bahia, Mãe Maria d'Aruanda, Vovó Catarina.* Others are known simply as *Vovó Conga, Pai Guiné, Pai Angola-Zulu, Vovó Cambinda.* They are sometimes addressed collectively as the *Povo da Bahia* (People from Bahia) or by nation, as in *Povo de Moçambique* (People from Mozambique), or *Povo do Congo* (People from the Congo).

The pontos sung to them make frequent references to African and Afro-Brazilian culture, to *feitiçaria* (sorcery), and to the miseries of slavery and poverty. They include many words of African derivation and often contain ungrammatical constructions, said to reflect the Pretos Velhos' lack of familiarity with the Portuguese language and their lower class origins. The following sacred songs will suggest the character of the Pretos Velhos:

Eu é preto feitiçeiro	I am (lit. I are) a black sorcerer
Eu chego pra trabaiá	I have arrived to work (practice charity)
Eu é filho de Angola	I am (are) a son of Angola
O meu pai é da Guiné	My father is from Guiné
Minha Mãe é de Carangola	My mother is from Carangola
Eu me chamo Pai José	My name is Pai José
	Anon. 1969:103)
Andei sête noite, andei sête dia	I walked 7 nights, I walked 7 days
Chegou Maria Mina	Maria of Mina arrived
Com o seu povo da Bahia	With the other "People of Bahia"
	(Pretos Velhos)
Pimenta lá da Costa	Pepper from the (African) coast
Azeite de Dendê	Palm oil
Chegou Maria Mina	Maria of Mina came
Para as filhos vir benzê	So all her children (Umbandistas) could be blessed
Chegou Maria Mina	Maria of Mina came
Dona do Gongá	Owner of the altar
	(Priestess of feitiçaria)
Chegou Maria Mina	Maria of Mina came
Que veio trabalhá	She came to "work"
	(Ibid.: 102)

O galo cantou lá na Aruanda	The cock crowed in Aruanda
O dia já amanhecia	The day was already breaking
As Almas me avisavam	The spirits of the dead told me
Que na banda	That in their group
Tia Maria chegaria	Aunt Mary (A Preto Velho) would arrive
Tia Maria	Aunt Mary
A boa velha não despreza	That good woman never scorns
Quem lhe estima	Anyone who cares for her
Tia Maria	Aunt Mary
A boa velha	That good woman
Sempre trouxe alegria	Always has brought joy
	(Ibid.: 102)

Dá licença Pai Antônio	Forgive me, Father Anthony
Que eu não venho lhe visitar	That I haven't come to visit you sooner
Eu estou muito doente	I am very sick
Vim prá sucé me curá	I have come to be cured
Se a doença fôr feitiço	If the illness should be sorcery
Emburará em seu gongá	It will be stubborn at your altar
Se a doença fôr de Deus	If the illness comes from God
Ah! Pai Antônio vai curar	Ah! Father Anthony will cure it
Preto Veio curandô	Preto Velho the curer
Foi pará na detenção	He was jailed
Ah! por não ter um defensor	Ah! because he didn't have a defender
Pai Antônio é de Quimbanda	Father Anthony is from
é curandó	Quimbanda [black magic],
	he is a curer
É Pai de mesa, é curandô	He is an initiate, he is a curer
	(Ibid.:93)

The Pretos Velhos are polar opposites of the Caboclos: elderly, humble, patient, subservient, where the Caboclos are young and vital, arrogant and vain. Pretos Velhos' pontos, too, are quite different in tone, further from a formal literary convention and closer to the vernacular form of expression found in the song fragment quoted earlier from the Candomblé das Cambindas. The significance of these Caboclo and Preto Velho spirits can be analyzed from quite different perspectives, which derive from and articulate with the different sectoral interests and ideological concerns outlined in the previous chapter.

The Caboclos may be seen as stereotypic representations of the Noble Savage, and the Pretos Velhos of the Faithful Slave, or more precisely, Uncle Tom. Portrayals of the Brazilian Indian as a heroic figure developed in Brazilian Romantic literature during the mid-nineteenth century, under the influences of Brazilian independence, European traditions, and the American writings of Longfellow. They found their most popular expression in the writings of José de Alencar and Gonçalves Dias, whose inclusion within the Caboclo pontos of Umbanda has already been noted. During the Romantic period, the Indian became a symbolic national hero and a symbol of independence, an image far removed from the reality of his socio-economic and political status. Although "the Indian as an individual was scorned, as a symbol he was cherished. He came to represent the original Brazil before the coming of the detested Portuguese ... " (Burns 1968:144). Researchers concur that the Caboclos as portrayed in Umbanda are not derived from any long process of actual contact with Indian populations but are of recent formation and are manifestations of popular *Indianismo* (Teixeira Monteiro 1954:472; Carneiro 1964:143–45).

It is tempting to cite the same literary models as sources for the Pretos Velhos, who bear an equally strong resemblance to literary portrayals, in this case of the faithful slave, a popular stereotype in nineteenth-century literature, especially in the writings of Castro Alves, Machado de Assis, and Artur Azevedo (Sayers 1956:110–57; Degler 1971:9–13). Machado's typical slave is described by Sayers as "patient, understanding... filled with love and kindness and innocence; his soul unstained by the world" (Sayers 1956:121–22). These portrayals were influenced by *Uncle Tom's Cabin,* which appeared in Brazil soon after its American publication, was quickly translated into Portuguese, and enjoyed wide popular success (Ibid.:166). This stereotype of Uncle Tom has been preserved in twentieth-century Brazilian novels of plantation life, such as Lins do Rego's *Menino do Engenho (Plantation Boy).*

Early Umbanda leaders had even explicitly characterized Preto Velho spirits in this way. For example, one is quoted as saying: "I love the humility of the Pretos Velhos, poor things, with their black skins and their white souls, sufferers and friends of all men" (Freitas 1939:44). But while they interpreted Preto Velho spirits in this way and celebrated this image, it is not clear whether they themselves helped to shape the Pretos Velhos in this fashion, or whether they simply emphasized a pre-existing interpretation which ideally suited their own goals of whitening Umbanda. Differences in the racial stereotypes of Indians and Africans would, according to this interpretation, reflect upper sector stereotypes of Indian and African-descended populations. Sayers has observed that the nationalist emphasis in the nineteenth century was focused mainly on the Indian (Ibid.:165), who had the exotic role, while Africans and their descendents appeared in the distinctly more humble and inferior stereotyped role of the faithful retainer or the melancholy slave (Ibid.:75).

The strong resemblance of these Umbanda spirits to nineteenth and early twentieth century literary portrayals suggests that such romantic, nationalistic stereotypes probably influenced characterizations of these spirits within certain sectors of Umbanda. Nevertheless, it would certainly be an error to take this as the only possible derivation and symbolic meaning of these figures in Umbanda, since both of them appear to have originated within lower sector, Afro-Brazilian religious traditions and not within the dominant sectors. The meaning of these figures within the Afro-Brazilian milieu is obscured by the lack of data on their origins and by a lack of attention in more recent studies of race in Brazil to Afro-Brazilians' own representations of their cultural history.

I did discover one source, an account of the origin of the Pretos Velhos, which suggests that Umbandistas of African descent may have perceived Preto Velho spirits in a manner distinctly different from middle sector, white Umbandistas. It should be remembered that since slavery had ended only in 1888, at the time of my research many Brazilians of African ancestry had grandparents, and some even parents, who had been slaves. The author of this account, himself the descendent of slaves, is the same champion of Umbanda's African origins quoted in the previous chapter. I was unable to document his story, yet it has great historical plausibility, and, like the account of Umbanda's founding, may serve as an origin myth for the Pretos Velhos. It suggests the wide difference in interpretation that the figure of an African slave might summon up for lower sector blacks than for upper sector whites.

This account of the origin of the Pretos Velhos begins with the 1886 law freeing all slaves 60 and over (the *Lei dos Sexagenários*) and the well-recognized plight of elderly slaves abandoned to their freedom without any means of livelihood. Some of these individuals possessed or acquired considerable skills and reputations as curers and sorcerers. They turned to these pursuits for sustenance, a situation which, as already indicated, appears to have been common in Rio at the turn of the century. A number of such elderly curers, so the story goes, settled together on a piece of vacant land in the State of Rio and began to offer curing and other services in return for payment of cash or kind. Their settlement became known as the *Arraial dos Pretos Velhos* (The Settlement of the Old Blacks), and after they died, their spirits, identifying themselves by their slave names, began to appear in diverse Afro-Brazilian religious centers in Rio to continue their good works. They became known as Pretos Velhos and thus became a part of the Afro-Brazilian religious tradition (*O Dia* 12/1–2/68:20).

The terms in which these figures are described stress qualities opposite to those found in the image of the faithful slave or Uncle Tom: their intelligence, their skill as curers, and the courage and ingenuity with which they managed to survive in so hostile an environment. Whatever its meaning for white, middle sector Umbandistas, whose attitude toward Pretos Velhos is respectful but often somewhat patronizing, the image of Preto Velho clearly lends itself as well to a radically different interpretation. These figures here demonstrate the heroic ability not only to survive but to transcend their experience of slavery, retain their humanity intact, and still be able to care and to give to others despite the horrors of their oppression. This image of Preto Velho bears little resemblance to the decidedly passive and accommodating figure that most middle and upper sector Brazilians and Americans associate with Uncle Tom.

Still another common interpretation of the meaning of Pretos Velhos frequently given me by Umbandistas stressed their ability to transcend illness and suffering. This interpretation ignores both class and racial associations and appeals directly to the many sufferers who seek Umbanda explicitly for the alleviation of an illness or problem. For these men and women, Pretos Velhos symbolize the courage to endure the difficulty and the hope of emerging from it.

If Pretos Velhos symbolize the transcendence of various forms of suffering—slavery, oppression, and illness—Caboclos may represent the other face of non-European Brazil: the independence of those who never experienced slavery, age, illness, oppression, or the yoke of foreign colonization. These two figures thus present complementary images: a utopian image of youth, vigor, health, independence, pride; and the reality of oppression, suffering, age, and infirmity. Multiplex symbols, they lend themselves to interpretation as emblems of literary romanticism, nationalism, independence, heroic forefathers, and the transcendence of suffering.

Caboclos and Pretos Velhos in the Umbanda Pantheon

I want now to explore the context and significance of the Caboclos' and Pretos Velhos' central role in the lay interpretation of Umbanda shaped by its ritual practices. I will suggest that their position of centrality, as well as the complementary marginalization of both Orixá/Saints and Exús, in itself makes a strong ideological statement, or encodement, of Umbanda Pura. It concentrates attention on all that these figures stand for: a Brazilian identity, a domesticated, whitened image of Africa, and charitable and benevolent intentions. It marginalizes an unacculturated "barbaric" African identity, evil, and immortality.

I will first characterize the Orixá/Saints and the Exús and the values they encode, contrasting them with the Caboclos and Pretos Velhos. Then, based on my analysis of the Umbanda cosmos and its spirits, I will challenge the interpretation of that cosmos as representing a symbolic inversion of Brazilian social structure.

My discussion of the Orixá/Saints will focus primarily on the significance of their African, rather than their Catholic, identities. The Orixás in Umbanda resemble and may be modeled on the deities of the same name in Bahian Candomblé. The term "Orixá" (the Yoruba term for deity), these deities' individual names, and their characteristic attributes and identities (associations with particular forces of nature, colors, days of the week, foods and drink, and symbolic items) are similar to those in Candomblé.[10] However, the pontos, which celebrate their powers and their mythical exploits and resemble those sung to other figures in Umbanda, are sung in Portuguese, unlike the musical offerings to the Orixás in Candomblé. Likewise in Umbanda, while the Orixás are unequivocably associated with Africa, theirs is often a generalized rather than a specific "African" identity, and though in particular centros they may be regarded specifically as Yoruba, in others they have Bantu or even Angolan names.

The main difference, however, lies in their relative importance in ritual. In Candomblé, the Orixás are the sole objects of worship, both at public rituals where they descend to possess initiates and in the extensive and time consuming private rituals. In Umbanda Pura, these deities are reduced to little more than symbolic presences. They are represented in the statuary on Umbanda altars, in either their African or their Catholic persona, according to the preference of the particular centro for emphasizing the Catholic or the African presence. They are also celebrated in Umbanda pontos during the opening phases of the Umbanda public rituals when homage is sung to each of the leaders of the seven lines of Umbanda. Orixás are also objects of more elaborate forms of ritual homage (called *obrigações,* or "obligations") that take place outside of the public rituals, on the special day of the Catholic saint with which the Orixá is associated. These are conducted at special sites that reproduce as closely as possible the natural forces with which the Orixá is associated: large rock piles (for Xangó), fresh water (for Oxum), salt water (for Yemanjá), the forest (for Oxossi and Ogum). These offerings include the items of the Orixá's special preference and may involve considerable expense. But they are infrequent, involve only the ritual personnel of the centro, and occur separately from the public ritual ceremonies that so dominate Umbanda. The Orixás do not appear at the public rituals in Umbanda Pura, though they do appear at more African-oriented Umbanda terreiros. Orixás in Umbanda Pura are honored, but at the same time they are marginalized.

I will now suggest an interpretation of the marginalization of these figures in Umbanda Pura, in relation to the central importance of the Caboclos and Pretos Velhos. The Caboclos, too, share some similarities with the Orixás. Their powers are both drawn from the forces of nature; both are proud and arrogant and celebrate a natural, unacculturated morality untouched by the forces of modern life. Viewing them as parallel figures suggests that the Brazilian Caboclos' displacement of the African Orixás in Umbanda Pura represents the displacement of foreign (African) figures by indigenous Brazilian ones. The Catholic saints have also been displaced, and although the Catholic identity is an integral part of the national Brazilian identity, it, too, is foreign in origin and represents the intrusion of a colonial regime. The marginalization of the Orixás and the saints, in contrast to the prominence of the Caboclos, thus may be seen to encode the nationalist interests of Umbanda founders. At the same time, it contributes to Umbanda's de-Africanization.

The Pretos Velhos' displacement of the Orixás encodes other aspects of the transformation of the African identity. The Orixás represent proud, free deities, the Africans before their arrival in Brazil, while the Pretos Velhos represent the Brazilian transformation of the African into a slave and his acculturation, domestication, and whitening within the Brazilian environment into an African with black skin but a "white" soul. The elevation of the Pretos Velhos in Umbanda thus may be seen to represent the selection of servitude over freedom, of humility over pride, in short, the domestication of the African identity and its transformation into an Afro-Brazilian identity. This also represents the incorporation of the African into a national, Brazilian identity. Moreover, it directly encodes the process of whitening the African and acculturating him to a humble demeanor and status in Brazilian society.

The marginalization of the Exús represents the marginalization of evil and immorality, or perhaps, better, amorality. Exú also derives from the Yoruba pantheon, where he has the status of a lesser deity, messenger to the major Orixás. He has undergone an extensive transformation in the Brazilian context of Umbanda. A sort of trickster deity in the African pantheon, believed capricious and fickle, capable of both good and harm, and swayed by promises of rich rewards, Exú under strong Catholic influence in the Brazilian context has become merged in and largely transformed into the devil. He has spawned innumerable underlings and acquired a female counterpart, known by the collective term *Pomba Gira*.[11] Umbanda statuary customarily portrays male Exús as devil figures, painted red, with horns and grasping tridents. Females, also portrayed in red, are scantily and provocatively dressed to resemble temptresses. Exús are often referred to directly by Biblical names as the Devil, Satan, Lucifer; Pomba Giras as Jezebel.

In Umbanda rituals, Exús, after being placated before the beginning of the public ceremonies, are exorted to remain absent from them. They do, however, make unscheduled appearances among the clients at these rituals, and then, cajoled into revealing their identities as the spirits who are tormenting and persecuting clients, they are exorcised. They are also, like the Orixás in Umbanda, the objects of ritual homage, which is always made to them at crossroads. The familiar form of these offerings, known as *despachos,* is assemblages of candles, *cachaça* (rum), cigarettes, and sometimes sacrificed black chickens. These may be seen in profusion in the streets, even in affluent neighborhoods and in the business districts of the city, to the dismay and disgust of some of its citizens. If the Exús appear in any other ritual context in Umbanda—and especially if they become central figures, defying the code of Umbanda Pura—the rituals will tend to be identified with Quimbanda.

So strongly are the Exús now identified with the devil that they often seem to have lost their African identity and to have become personifications of evil, immorality, danger, exploitation. Their banishment from Umbanda represents the banishment of all of these negative and evil forces which, as has been seen, has threatened Umbanda's image in the minds of its codifiers. Their banishment encodes Umbanda as moral and pure and as rejecting evil, exploitation, and black magic.

Exús have another form of identity, however, through which they often exercise their black arts. Exú may be "crossed" with a Preto Velho. He may thus regain an African identity, which goes far in suggesting the degree to which, as a simple Exú, he has lost it. An Exú crossed with a Preto Velho, one of the most potent figures in Quimbanda, represents a figure familiar in Brazilian history and literature: the evil or amoral slave, the *feitiçeiro* (African sorcerer). As historical figures, sorcerers were active in opposing individual masters and in fomenting slave revolts. They were greatly feared by slaveowners and represented symbols of resistance to the slave regime. They were still feared even after abolition, as is evident in João do Rio's account of sorcery in Rio. The feitiçeiro has become another powerful stereotype in romantic Africanist literature. Unlike the humble slave, which I suggested as a model for the Preto Velho, the feitiçeiro is his polar opposite: the dangerous, uncontrollable, subversive African slave who does not accept his or her lot, who plots against his or her master and foments revolution (Sayers 1956:173–79). This figure of Exú as the feitiçeiro was clearly for the founders and codifiers of Exú a potent symbol of evil and danger, directly associated with the African. Thus, the selection of the humble slave over the sorcerer Exú represents the selection of the docile slave over the dangerous subversive. This selection encodes the image of the good and subservient African and expunges the subversive, evil one. This interpretation may not hold true for all practitioners of Umbanda, but it certainly seems to be a central message of Umbanda Pura.

The triumph of Preto Velho over Exú, then, represents the celebration of the African as an acculturated Brazilian slave, while both he and his culture are rejected in their "barbaric," unacculturated state. Umbanda, in making this selection, presents a metaphor of acculturation, in which, implicitly, people of African descent are accepted in the degree to which they, in turn, accept the loss of their African culture. They are "whitened" in the image of the Preto Velho, who is elevated symbolically only in his capacity as a slave, thus as a person of inferior status.

This interpretation of the significance of the Caboclos and Pretos Velhos in the Umbanda pantheon must now be compared to that of Willems (1966), who has suggested that these spirits in Umbanda signify a symbolic inversion of the social order, in which "Indians and Africans occupy the higher levels of

spiritual perfection, and the . . . 'masters' [are] relegated to the lower levels"
(1966:230). The inversion of the statuses of African and Indian spirits and
humans, who are spiritually their inferiors, is taken by Willems to represent
lower class practitioners' rejection of their role of social subordination and to
express in symbolic terms their embrace of new, egalitarian relations. It is a
major point in Willems' interpretation of Umbanda as an expression of the
new, egalitarian direction of social change within the lower classes.

While it is true that Caboclos and Pretos Velhos are higher in rank than
humans, the overall cosmology within which these relations are embedded is
extremely complex. For example, the Pretos Velhos, while spiritually
superior to man, still have the status of humble slaves and thus present a
contradiction in status: the paradox of the slave who may outrank his former
master but remains a slave. His appears to be a moral rather than a social or
political victory. The Caboclos and Pretos Velhos do have lower ranks than
the Orixás/Saints. Are these latter figures to be seen as symbolically
reproducing Catholic or African domination over indigenous and slave
populations? This would be a logical corollary to Willems' argument, yet I
have just argued to the contrary, that though of higher rank, these dual figures
are marginalized within the central context of Umbanda ritual, and that ritual
meaning takes precedence over the formal and bureaucratic ranking within
the spirit pantheon. I am also convinced that the inversion represented by the
master who is dominated by his slave is both an incomplete inversion and one
that is fraught with ambiguities. Ultimately, however, and most importantly
for Willems' argument, neither this inversion nor the wider picture of the
cosmos, in either its formal, bureaucratic forms or its informal patronage
network, suggests egalitarian relations. Whatever multiple ambiguities of
status relations are encoded within this complex cosmos, it cannot be
construed as egalitarian. Thus it cannot signify the kind of social
transformation imputed to it by Willems.

The ambiguities and complexities of Umbanda's cosmology, which form
part of the ongoing dialectical process of its development, give it enormous
flexibility of interpretation and permit different sectors with different interests
to identify with it in different ways. But they also make any simplistic
generalizations concerning status reversals hard to sustain in the area of
cosmology, and I will argue that this is true as well of inversions of social and
ritual status relations. In view of the extent of middle sector influence in
Umbanda and the wide spectrum of sectors who participate in it, it seems
unlikely that Umbanda could serve unambiguously to express a symbolic
reversal of their social situation by oppressed sectors of society.

Since I have bypassed many of these ambiguities in my characterizations
of the Umbanda deities and spirits in order to make them emerge more clearly,
let me illustrate their extraordinary flexibility and the manner in which they

may be brought into line with different cosmological interpretations. Through word play and punning, their identities may be shifted and even transformed entirely.

The Caboclos, for example, are as a category unacculturated Brazilian Indians. This identity is so strong that it has even led their African counterpart and superior, the Yoruban deity Oxôssi, to be identified as a Caboclo. However, I have indicated that this definition of the term *Caboclo* is not the usual secular one, in which the term refers, somewhat disparagingly, to a rough-hewn rural dweller, a "hick" (see this chapter, note 6). Some Caboclo spirits are drawn according to this secular meaning of the term Caboclo; one of the best known of these is *Caboclo Boiadeiro* (Cowboy), a bawdy and independent rural frontiersman spirit. I encountered still another form of word play on the term Caboclo, in a centro of the "Oriental Line," where I met a spirit named *João Indio*. He explained to me, playing on the word *Indio*, that he was a Caboclo and an Indian but not a Brazilian Indian, an *Indio da India* (an East Indian), one of the highly evolved spirits of the Oriental Line.

The Exús present an even more complex situation. Exú is an African Orixá, a trickster and a messenger of the major Orixás, whose main identification in Brazil, under the influence of the Catholic Church, is with the devil, although an alternative, more African interpretation still portrays him as an amoral trickster, capricious and changeable, capable of giving help as well as harm. However, there is another, Kardecist interpretation of Exú, which defines him not as a deity but a disincarnate spirit, not evil by nature or by intent but through ignorance.[12] He is said to be *atrasado* (spiritually backward), but under Kardecist law, ignorance is susceptible to reason, indoctrination, and enlightenment. Exú's capability to undergo a transformation is expressed by turning once again to a Catholic model. In his or her ignorant state, Exú becomes known as an *Exú pagão* (Pagan Exú) while in an enlightened and moral state, he or she becomes an *Exú batisado* (Baptized Exú). Once again, the model of acculturation appears here in the form of baptism. The primitive, pagan African deity acquires the basis of Brazilian culture.

These varied shadings, which suggest the almost limitless possibilities for reinterpreting Umbanda deities and spirits, also reveal a continuing pattern of opposition between Catholic models and Kardecist ones: Catholic interpretations with their fixed and immutable identities in which Orixás are deities, Exú is evil, and the cosmos is divided into Heaven and Hell, recall the lay interpretation of Umbanda. The Kardecist view of continual transformation and mobility, in which all are spirits capable of improvement, recalls the formal bureaucratic interpretation.[13] It is interesting that within this opposition, the African Orixás, static and fixed as well, appear far closer to the Catholic interpretation than to the Kardecist model. However, these two opposing interpretations, Catholic and Kardecist, meet and are mediated in the metaphor of acculturation, conversion through baptism or through spiritual evolution, both of which act together to civilize and transform the primitive, pagan, ignorant spirits, to educate them, and to make them into responsible moral beings.

5

Umbanda Ritual

Umbanda ideology and belief and the various figures of the Umbanda cosmos find their principal form of expression in the public religious ceremonies known as *sessões* (sessions). These take place at Umbanda centros, which may also be called *tendas* (tents) or by the Afro-Brazilian term *terreiros* (open spaces or terraces). At the time of my research, there were reported to be some 20,000 such centros practicing various forms of Umbanda throughout the city of Rio and its outskirts.

At these sessions, the spirits descend to earth, take possession of the bodies of mediums, and then, in most forms of Umbanda, give spiritual consultations to members of the congregation. The public ritual is the main form of participation for all who practice Umbanda, for *chefes* (centro leaders) and mediums, and for the members of the congregation, many of whom become clients during the consultation period. This public ritual provides the basis for the dominant, lay interpretation of Umbanda.

This chapter will focus on these public ceremonies and on the ritual form of Umbanda Pura.[1] I will describe a typical ritual in detail and interpret it in relation to Umbanda ideology and cosmology.[2] I will also briefly describe other, more African-oriented ritual variants of Umbanda, and Quimbanda, and will suggest ways in which changes in ritual emphasis in these variant forms convey shifts in meaning and interpretation.

A Public Ceremony

Public rituals in Umbanda Pura usually take place in the evenings two or more times each week in special buildings constructed for the purpose, in rented rooms, and in private homes. The physical setting I describe here will identify this centro as a relatively affluent one. However, the ritual itself is found at all social levels.

The centro is a one-story building especially designed and built for the purpose and located in a suburban district of the city. From the outside it resembles the neighboring houses, and only an insignia, the *ponto riscado* (sacred sign) of the centro, placed inconspicuously on an outside front wall, identifies its function. This building houses the centro proper, dressing rooms at the rear for the mediums and, in the front anteroom, a window for the registration and payment of membership fees and a bar where coffee, soft drinks, and cakes are sold before and during the ceremony. Ceremonies are held here three times a week, on Monday, Wednesday and Friday, beginning at 8:30 p.m. and lasting until around midnight.

The room where ceremonies take place is rectangular, about 30 by 50 feet square, painted white, its walls decorated with paintings of Caboclo and Preto Velho spirits. The room is bisected by a low fence with a gate in the center, which separates the ritual area from that of the congregation. The ritual area, at the front, contains a hardwood dancing floor and the altar, a niche set in the center of the end wall facing the congregation. On the altar stand statues of the principal Umbanda spirits: Caboclos, represented as Indian warriors; Pretos Velhos, as elderly Blacks, humbly dressed and seated on low benches or leaning on canes; and the Orixás, represented by statues of their Catholic counterparts, the saints. The altar also holds glasses of water, which are said to attract beneficial forces (a Kardecist influence), and flowers.

About 8:00, the members of the ritual corps begin to arrive, carrying small satchels in which they keep their ritual garments.[3] They greet the caretaker of the building, herself an initiate of the centro, who cleans and cares for the building in return for free lodging, then they retire to the dressing rooms to don their ritual dress in preparation for the ceremony. They reappear shortly, dressed in freshly laundered white outfits: women in nurses uniforms, shortsleeved dresses buttoned down the front and ending at mid-calf; men in one-piece coveralls known in Brazil as *macacão* (monkey suits). Both sexes wear white socks and tennis sneakers, and all have the insignia of the centro (the same one that appears on the outside front wall) embroidered on their left breast pocket. They move around the centro, greeting friends as they arrive or performing the many small chores that precede the service.

Members of the congregation begin to arrive, and after genuflecting to the altar as they enter, they take seats on the hard wooden chairs set in rows facing the ritual area and the altar, the women to the right of the central aisle, men to the left. Many, before taking their seats, stop with an attendant to obtain a *ficha,* or token, which will permit them to consult during the ceremony with the spirit of their choice. They sit in the brightly lit room, sometimes talking quietly with friends, waiting for the cermony to begin.

Shortly after 8:30, an initiate enters the ritual area carrying a smoking and fragrant incense burner, which signifies the beginning of the *defumacão* (ritual purification with smoke), which banishes harmful spirits lurking in the centro or hovering around the individuals present. The incense is swung over the altar, in front of each of the ritual performers, and then over the congregation, and the service begins. The initiates, joined by members of the congregation, sing a *ponto de defumacão* (special sacred song), and, when this is finished, another ponto opens the service: *"Abrimos a nossa gira, com Deus e a Nossa Senhora"* ("We open our service with the blessing of God and Our Lady"). Initiates kneel facing the altar on the white ritual *toalhas* (towels) they each carry. (These towels will be used later to wipe the streaming faces of the mediums possessed by the various spirits.) The singing continues with greetings to the pantheon of Umbanda deities and spirits. A Catholic prayer is said, and a short passage from Allan Kardec is read by the chefe, the leader of the centro.

Now the members of the ritual corps rise, and the tempo of the service changes. Joined by members of the congregation, they begin to sing the pontos celebrating the Caboclo spirits and inviting them to "come down and work" (*vem trabalhar*), to practice their charity upon those present in the centro. Each week, this particular night is devoted to the Caboclo spirits, and most of the visiting spirits tonight will be Caboclos.[4] These pontos are accompanied by handclapping, and the members of the ritual corps move around the ritual area in a slow circle, executing a modified version of a samba step. As they dance, the spirits begin to appear, each spirit possessing the particular medium who is accustomed to receive him.[5] Mediums, as they become possessed, stop dancing, begin to perspire and often look slightly ill, sway, and then, bending over and giving a series of rapid jerks, receive their spirits. Upon straightening up, they have taken on the facial expressions, demeanor, and body motions characteristic of the particular spirit they have received. Caboclos wear stern, even fierce expressions and utter loud, piercing cries. They move vigorously around the dance floor in a kind of two-step, often dropping to one knee to draw an imaginary bow, and they smoke large cigars, whose smoke will be blown over their clients as a form of ritual cleansing and curing.[6]

As the Caboclo spirits arrive, they first kneel at the altar to pay respects to the Orixás/Saints represented there. Then, rising, they call upon ritual servants to bring their accoutrements: ritual beads and other items such as Indian feather headdresses and equipment, which some Caboclos require as part of their ritual identities.

The spirits now begin a series of elaborate ritual greetings, first heartily embracing their fellow spirits and then leaving the ritual area to greet important members of the congregation. If I was known in the centro, as a foreign visitor and a student of Umbanda, I was likely to receive an entire set of such embraces. These spirits then return to the ritual area, where they dance or stand about, swaying gently on their feet, puffing on their cigars, and uttering periodically the piercing cries that mark Caboclo spirits.

In contrast to the initiates who receive Caboclo spirits, the chefe of the centro receives Pai João (Father John), a Preto Velho. Even when, as tonight, the service is dedicated to Caboclos, this chefe always receives Pai João, the highest ranking and most respected spirit visitor to the centro. Like all Pretos Velhos, he is old and walks with difficulty, bent over with age and stiffness and leaning on a carved wooden staff. In contrast to the Caboclo spirits, who smoke cigars, Pretos Velhos smoke pipes. Because of his high rank, Pai João receives deferential ritual greetings from all the other spirits.

Some members of the ritual corps do not receive spirits.[7] They continue to sing and clap until all the spirits have arrived, received their ritual accoutrements, and performed their greetings. At this point, the singing and clapping stop. The ritual area appears to be the scene of restless, disorganized activity, and to the inexperienced observer it may even appear that the service is ending. On the contrary, it is about to enter its most important phase, the period of *consultas* (consultations), when the members of the congregation are able to consult with the spirits about their problems. Spirit consultants, who possess high-ranking, fully initiated mediums, station themselves at intervals around the ritual area and prepare to give consultas. Caboclos remain standing, while Pai João, as is the custom with Pretos Velhos, is seated upon a low bench. In contrast to the Caboclos, whose demeanor during consultas remains arrogant and aggressive, Pai João, sucking on his pipe, listens to all of his clients' problems with the patient and sympathetic ear common to Pretos Velhos. His advice is much sought, and he will attend to the most important clients and the most serious problems at the centro. His first client is a woman who has not obtained a *ficha* (token) for a consulta but who is obviously very ill. She is led directly to Pai João, who greets her with a kindly air and listens attentively to her problem.

Other clients must follow the protocol prescribed for consultas. An attendant in charge of fichas steps to the gate in the center of the low fence separating the ritual sector from the congregation and calls *Caboclo Tupinambá, Numero Um* (Number One), and a member of the congregation comes to the gate, where he surrenders his ficha, removes his shoes, and is led over to stand in front of the waiting spirit. Caboclo Tupinambá, a much respected Indian warrior who works through a tiny white-haired woman of perhaps 60, commands in a loud voice for the servant attending him to fetch another of his favorite cigars. Puffing steadily and pausing to utter a long, piercing cry, he turns to his first client and begins the consulta by giving him a big ritual hug. Next he gives him a ritual cleansing involving *passes,* in which he touches him lightly with his fingers, drawing off the evil fluids into his own hands, and shaking them off with a snapping sound. Then he anoints him with large puffs of smoke. "Now, my child, what is your problem?" he asks. And the consultation begins.

The attendant continues to summon clients to consultas with the various spirits, and the ritual area becomes crowded with such pairs. The air, already heavy with incense, is overlaid with the strong smell of cigars. Ritual servants (low-ranking initiates who do not have possession roles during the consulta period) move back and forth, supplying the Caboclos with fresh cigars and copying down long recipes for herbal baths or other ritual preparations recommended to clients to solve their problems. Servants help to interpret the advice of the spirit consultants, which is often delivered in a ritual code language difficult to understand, though it is intelligible to those familiar with it. In addition, servants help to protect clients who may themselves become possessed during a consulta. Possession states often occur spontaneously among clients during consultas, or they may be induced by the spirit consultant as part of the cure or evidence of spirit persecution. In contrast to the extremely controlled possession states achieved by experienced mediums, possession, when it occurs among those inexperienced in controlling it, is often violent, and clients must be protected from injury to themselves or to others.

If a client's problem is diagnosed as persecution by an ignorant, backwards, or suffering spirit or an Exú, still other mediums of intermediate rank may be required to draw out or *tirar* (pull out) the spirit. It is a dramatic moment indeed to see as many as four or five initiates surround a client, place their hands on his or her shoulders, and, one by one, become suddenly possessed, erupting into the wild laughter, obscenities, or poses of sexual invitation characteristic of Exú spirits or falling senseless and rigid to the ground. Such mediums are said to have absorbed these dangerous forces into their own bodies, which, because of their ritual training, are protected against their harmful effects. After such an experience, clients often appear dazed or horrified at this physical evidence of the forces troubling them.

The consultas continue until all those with fichas have been attended to (a total of 61 people on this particular evening). By midnight the benches of the congregation are almost empty, since most members of the congregation have come for a consulta and leave immediately after. Only the most sought after spirit consultants are still in attendance; other spirits have finished their duties and departed, leaving the mediums whom they had possessed looking exhausted. Finally, only Pai João remains attending his last client, and as the consulta ends, Pai João, too, departs. The chefe emerges from his state of possession and leads a prayer and a brief series of pontos, which end the service. Members of the ritual corps then retire to change into street clothes and depart quickly for their homes. It is a week night, and many have an hour or more of traveling time back to their homes and must be up early the next day to go to work. Most will return to participate in at least one more session during the week. The chefe, a man in his early 60s, an engineer with an important managerial position in a large company, presides over each of the three weekly ceremonies, as he has for over 20 years. In contrast to some of the other participants, he appears fresh and wide awake, commenting that his religious duties are never a burden but always leave him feeling rested and relaxed, as he appears to be.

After the session just described, I rode home with several of the initiates in a carpool transporting them the ten or so miles to the other side of the city. The talk passed to the chefe, the inspiration he provided to members of the ritual corps and the wonderful cures that his spirit, Pai João, had performed both for the initiates who consulted with him and for members of the congregation. They spoke also of other marvelous cures and aid that spirits in the centro had provided. "It is the help that people get from consultas which is the real key to understanding Umbanda's popularity," said one initiate, and all agreed. The conversation then turned, as it so often does among Umbandistas, to a recital of the various problems that they and their families had had solved through consultas at the centro.

Interpretation

The public session just described expresses in ritual form many of the interests and aspirations of Umbanda's original codifiers. It dramatizes the lay Umbandista interpretation of Umbanda cosmological relations and reveals the syncretic blending of the religious traditions from which Umbanda derives and which, in turn, permits Umbandistas with different religious backgrounds and ritual preferences to identify with it.

Elements of Catholic, Kardecist, and Afro-Brazilian traditions are easily identifiable within this ritual. The altar with its statues of the Catholic saints, the incense, the genuflection, the recitations of a Catholic prayer all provide strong reminders of the Catholic influence in Umbanda. Kardecism is represented in the doctrinal passage from Allan Kardec, the glasses of water on the altar, and the form of spiritual cleansing given to clients, known as *passes*. Afro-Brazilian traditions provide the basic structure of the ceremony, which takes the form of collective dancing and singing and of group spirit possession, and are represented as well in various spirits and deities that appear.

This public ritual is also an expression of many of the central concerns among Umbanda's founders. The principle of charity is enshrined in Umbanda's principal drama: the consultas, private consultations enacted in public between spirit consultants and their human clients. Directly identified as *caridade* (charity), these highlight Umbanda's benevolent and moral purpose, as well as constituting a public denial of the constellation of "immoral," exploitative, and "barbaric" practices associated with such consultations in other forms of Umbanda and in Quimbanda. In other Afro-

Brazilian religions, in Quimbanda, and even in the more "African" oriented Umbanda, consultations are held outside of the public ceremonies, in the centro or in the home of its leader. In contrast to those just described, they are private, unsupervised, secret, and thus suspect, sometimes rightly so, of dealings with Exús, of serving immoral purposes or goals, of employing various substances and rituals proscribed in Umbanda and associated with Quimbanda, such as the sacrifice of animals and other elements and substances of believed witchery, and of charging exorbitant, exploitative fees.

In Umbanda Pura, the public context of the consultas precludes such ritual secrecy (although the content of individual consultations remains private) and any connections with disapproved spirits or substances. Even the manner in which the consultations are arranged, and the tokens (free or available at nominal cost) state that this form of caridade is indeed charity and not a form of exploitation.

The de-Africanization of Umbanda is clear in this public ritual. The Orixás are present only in their Catholic representations on the altar and as celebrated in the opening sacred songs of homage. Although the underlying structure of the ceremony may resemble other Afro-Brazilian religions, these points of indentification are muted, the Orixás replaced by Catholic images, drums replaced by handclapping. The only strong African presence is that of the Pretos Velhos, elderly African slaves. The whitening, which is an important counterpart of de-Africanization, can be measured in the absence of overt references to Africa, and, as if to give further emphasis, it is restated in the simple, even severe white ritual garments and the bare white walls of the centro.

The rational bureaucratic process of the formal cosmological system permeates the organization of the consultations, by numbers, with tokens, according to an orderly process. And this is reflected as well in the tone of this public ritual, which is generally sedate, decorous, restrained, and controlled. Certainly it is not as sedate or static as Kardecist rituals, with their long doctrinal lessons, given by mediums seated at a table. Nor are these rituals as static or as rigid in their division between congregation and ritual specialists as Catholic rituals. This form of Umbanda includes dancing and singing, the colorful ritual accoutrements of the Caboclos spirits, the individual dramas of spirit possession, the consultations, and the occasional wilder dramas provided by the Exús. Nevertheless, these rituals are considerably more sedate than those toward the more African end of the Umbanda spectrum and those of Quimbanda, which I will touch on in a moment.

It might be suggested that the sedateness and decorum of this particular ceremony is related to the affluent setting in which it occurs, and that the tone is thus a function of its class locus rather than of its ritual type. There is some truth to this, yet not only are many of the mediums at this centro poor; many centros in irrefutably impoverished settings have the same tone. I visited many centros located in favelas and followed narrow paths, which also served as open sewers, to wooden shacks with dirt floors—small, precariously lit, and crowded with people. The membership here was extremely poor and predominantly black. In fact, this was the stereotypic setting for what was popularly called "Macumba," and it was this that had originally led me to select a favela as the setting for my research. Even in such settings, however, the ritual was often in all essential respects similar to the one I have just described, including the organization and the restrained, controlled ritual tone. While this tone doubtlessly expresses the preferences of the middle sector who developed this ritual, it is now widely popular and has influenced all sectors of practitioners.

The ritual emphasis on consultas reveals the way in which the public ritual shifts the bureaucratic interpretation of the Umbanda cosmos to the lay interpretation, marginalizing the high-ranking Orixás and elevating the roles of the Caboclos and Pretos Velhos. All attention is drawn to the Caboclos and Pretos Velhos who are the consultants and to the members of the congregation who are their clients. While the rank of the Preto Velho received by the chefe is generally known to be higher than that of any other spirit received at the centro, the ritual dramas of the consultas obscure this and instead highlight personalized exchanges in which the powers of the individual curers, rather than their official rank, determine their importance. Their form, that of dyadic, personalized exchanges, forms the basis for the lay interpretation of the Umbanda cosmos as a mode of relationship based on patronage.

Umbanda public ceremonies also reveal the contradictory postition of the Exús: although marginalized, they can still, on occasion, claim center stage when they are revealed as the perpetrators of illness and suffering. This is an important reminder of their powers. Although banished from participation in benevolent curing activites, they remain an evil presence, unbidden among the clients, thus restating Umbanda's mission and its raison d'etre—to combat evil and ignorance. As Umbandistas often say, "if it weren't for Quimbanda, Umbanda would have no reason to exist." In an important sense, the powers of Umbanda's benevolent spirit heroes are set off by glimpses of the powerful enemies whom they must defeat. Exús thus must be continually ritually banished.

The allotment of ritual time within this public ceremony and the uses of ritual spaces suggest the interplay among contrastive modes of rationalized, bureaucratic, and informal patronage relationships found in Umbanda cosmology. Consultas, and the patronage mode, comprise well over half of the ceremony, in this particular case almost three hours, compared to just over one hour devoted to the bureaucratically oriented opening and closing ceremonies. The rational, orderly ritual opening, with homages and greetings that closely observe the formal ranks of the participants—the chefe, the mediums, the spirits who lead the seven lines of Umbanda—restates the formal hierarchy of the Umbanda cosmos and of the centro. Then comes a liminal period of apparent disorder before the ritual is reorganized along the lines of the personal, dyadic, patronage relations of the consultas. This disorder highlights a moment of the ritual system in which individuals are disconnected from their bureaucratic relationships and as yet unconnected to dyadic relations. It is the disorder of those who, in a patronage system, are without connections until, through the consultas, they are reintegrated, reconnected in a new manner. The ceremony ends with a perfunctory restatement of the formal hierarchy.

Similarly, in terms of ritual spaces, the secular, bureaucratic space is contrasted to sacred, patronage-oriented space. Secular space, on the other side of the fence from the ritual space, is that of the bureaucratic world par excellence, with its neat rows of chairs and the central aisle marking off the sexually segregated seating. It is the area of bureaucratric activites: the payment of dues, the distribution of fichas, the sale of food. Sacred space is the "ritual area" occupied by the chefe and mediums during the opening ceremonies. However, at a crucial point at the beginning of the consultas, members of the congregation, removing their shoes, which anchor them to their secular lives, pass through the gate into sacred space, breaking down the barrier as well of sexual segregation. Now, within this sacred space, the two groups, secular (human) and sacred (spirit), of unequal rank, confront each other in pairs to enact the ritual drama of patronage.

Since, as I suggested in the previous chapter, the two modes represent two inextricable twined aspects of Brazilian reality, a bureaucracy in which exchanges are enacted on the basis of patronage, Umbanda public rituals represent the ebb and flow, the alternating faces of what is in reality a single cosmological and ritual system.

Other Ritual Variants

A short foray into some of the ritual variations within Umbanda, the forms that shade off into more African-oriented practices and into Quimbanda will help to locate the ceremony I have just described within the spectrum of Umbanda's ritual heterodoxy. Practitioners and Umbanda's major leaders now identify a wide range of ritual practices as forms of Umbanda, and no general consensus exists as to when particular practices should or should no longer be identified as Umbanda. Variants of Umbanda are often distinguished, like Umbanda Pura, by the use of qualifiers. Thus, there are *Umbanda Kardecista* and *Umbanda Oriental* and a wide variety of qualifiers used to identify more African forms of Umbanda, including *Umbanda Africana, Umbanda traçada* or *misturada* (crossed or mixed), and *Umbanda Culto de Nação* (cult of an [African] nation).[8] Other forms are considered to lie outside the pale of Umbanda, though it is impossible to establish empirically, on the basis of ritual practice, when such a boundary has been crossed, and this remains a matter of individual opinion. These include Candomblé, some of the *Cultos de Nação,* and Quimbanda.

Three principal features seem consistently to characterize Umbanda rituals of the general type I have just described: 1) the presence of caridade within the religious service in the form of consultas; these are 2) given by Caboclos and Pretos Velhos; and they are 3) provided free of charge or at nominal cost. These features, however, are not found in all Umbanda centros, especially as they shade off either toward more African practices or toward Quimbanda. Differences between Umbanda Pura and other variants of Umbanda—the more African practices and Quimbanda—coincide with the differences in cosmological emphasis described in the previous chapter.

Umbanda Kardecista shows, as the name suggests, a greater influence of Kardecism. The rituals in such a centro may even include Kardecist as well as Umbanda sessions (usually held on different days). Or they may include the use of a Kardecist *mesa* (table), with mediums seated, Kardecist fashion, around it. In these centros, singing and handclapping during the service may be replaced by soft background music, Gounod's "Ave Maria" or similar semi-classical works with religious overtones played on a phonograph. Greater weight is generally given in such centros to the teachings of Kardecist doctrine and to various forms of spiritual instruction.[9] Spirits from the Kardecist pantheon, the Arab, Chinese, Hindu or Aztec spirits identified in Umbanda as belonging to the "Oriental Line," may also be present.

Umbanda da Linha Oriental (of the Oriental Line) is similar in ritual orientation to Umbanda Kardecista and works with similar spirits, but rather than the teachings of Kardec, it emphasizes occult literature: Hinduism, Rosecrucianism, the theosophy of Mme. Blavatsky and Annie Besant, and the writings on the Kabbala. I discovered one centro devoted only to the study and interpretation of the Kabbala and composed entirely of Jewish Umbandistas. Here, spirits from the Old Testament were received along with Caboclos and Pretos Velhos. Such dual religious affiliation is discussed further in chapter 8.

These two forms, as suggested in their descriptions, emphasize an intellectualized form of Umbanda. They are closer to the formal bureaucratic cosmological interpretation of Umbanda specialists and stress learning, order, rationality. They are almost completely de-Africanized and place little emphasis on either the Caboclos and Pretos Velhos or on the nationalism that these spirits represent. The strong emphasis on charity is more of the

Kardecist type: disinterested, nonreciprocal, impersonal. These two forms of Umbanda are found principally among more affluent sectors.

The more African-oriented centros, usually called terreiros, show increased emphasis on ritual elements associated with African practices. Ceremonies tend to be held on Saturday nights, beginning around 10:00 p.m. and lasting into the dawn. This schedule, which locates the ceremonies directly within the prime weekly hours of leisure activity, emphasizes their entertainment orientation, in contrast to the more instrumental orientation of ceremonies of Umbanda Pura, which can be integrated into working hours. These ceremonies do show a far greater emphasis on drama and entertainment, on dancing, drumming, and singing. Ritual participants customarily wear brightly colored ritual costumes, often made of satin and trimmed with rich layers of lace. Spirit possession is principally by African Orixás, who may require additional and more elaborate ritual costuming and engage in long and elaborate dances. Although the Caboclos and Pretos Velhos may appear in such ceremonies, they are often marginal and may even be absent. Mediums may also be possessed by Exús after the clock strikes midnight, the Orixás depart, and the altar with their images is covered. These rituals may include the drinking of alcoholic beverages by the spirits and members of the congregation and other ritual practices formerly identified with "Macumba" and now identified by many Umbandistas with Quimbanda. They may also include such activities as eating flaming candles or exorcising evil spirits through the explosion of gunpowder. Consultas are much reduced in scope, in number, and in visibility—they too are peripheral to the entertainment or may be absent, held instead during scheduled consulting hours, usually afternoons during the week and Saturdays before the service begins. They take the form described of private consultations and may be identified with black magic or Quimbanda. In such terreiros, one finds no mention of Kardecist doctrine; it may be unknown or scorned as completely extraneous to Umbanda. While practitioners may consider themselves Umbandistas, the ritual and doctrinal orientation is far from the doctrine and ritual of Umbanda Pura. It was only during the 1950s, some 25 years after Umbanda's founding, that the middle sector leaders of Umbanda Pura began to accept these more African-oriented, self-defined "Umbandistas" as part of Umbanda.

Certainly these traditions, with their many elements of African origin, have continued to appeal to those of Afro-Brazilian descent and are probably more popular in general among the lower sectors than among the middle and upper ones. But as with Umbanda Pura, the appeal of these more African forms of Umbanda is not restricted to a particular sector or class. For example, these more exotic rituals seem to appeal to people in the entertainment world and the arts, to members of the upper sectors who seek alternative life styles, and to the gay world.

Quimbanda

Like the Afro-Brazilian terreiros, many Umbanda centros include ceremonies that focus on Exú and are therefore associated with Quimbanda. These may be held after midnight, or in special weekly or monthly sessions, usually on Friday nights, which are dedicated to the Exús. Such ceremonies are sometimes justified by explaining that these Exús are enlightened and baptized and now work for moral ends. This explanation, however, does not dissociate them from Quimbanda and accusations of the practice of black magic and exploitation, which are a chief form of malicious gossip among centro leaders.

There are some centros, however, that overtly practice Quimbanda and whose leaders openly refer to themselves as "Quimbandeiros." I know one such centro personally and attended ceremonies there many times. This centro overtly fulfilled all of the stereotypic associations attached to Quimbanda by Umbandistas, so much so that it almost seemed designed expressly to challenge not only the middle class morality of Umbanda Pura but all of the revered institutions of Brazilian society as well: the family, the Church, the state. The centro was located in a shack with a dirt floor, lit by gas lantern, high on a steep hill in Rio's fashionable south zone overlooking the mansions of the rich. Its chefe, who worked in a janitorial capacity, identified two of the prominent mansions visible from his doorstep as belonging to well-known state politicians; he was fond of pointing them out to his visitors as examples of the fruits of political graft.

In this shack, he received an Exú crossed with a Preto Velho. Dressed in a red and black outfit (the colors of Exú) and a cap with horns sewn on, he gave consultas and held ceremonies. The clients' problems were made public to all who attended, and this Exú/Preto Velho would gleefully and candidly point out the immorality of some of the requests he set himself to grant, such as breaking up a marriage to satisfy a lover's desire. These discussions were conducted with gusto and bawdy humor and were punctuated with lewd remarks. One especially memorable all-night ceremony, which I attended with several Latin American journalists (see also Galeano 1970), was held on Good Friday. It began with the sacrifice of several black goats and fowl. To the accompaniment of pontos sung to Exú, the dead animals were carved up, and their private parts arranged into offerings to Exú, together with other items of food, drink, and cigarettes. Everyone present alternately drank the blood of the victims and quantities of sweet wine out of a common bowl, passed from hand to hand. Then all of the clients and visitors were invited to make lists with the names of their enemies. These, including a highly approved list containing the names of various Latin American dictators, were read out and then stuffed into the animal victims' mouths, preparatory to burial, which would slowly destroy those named in the lists. The victims' mouths were too small to take the long lists, so a large toad was produced to accommodate the rest, along with a small cloth-covered red and black coffin for the toad.

In perhaps the strangest daybreak I ever experienced, the rising sun illuminated us on the beaten earth in front of the shack, surrounded by lush tropical growth: I was holding the toad, whose mouth was now bulging with the last lists of enemies, while the red and black horned figure of the Quimbandeiro, possessed by the feitiçeiro, carefully sewed up the toad's mouth with red and black thread. The following day I attended the burial of the little coffin, deep in the forest. As the toad slowly expired underground, so would those named in the lists be slowly destroyed.

In this ceremony, anger at personal enemies—lovers, spouses, and false friends—merged with defiance and mockery of a major Catholic holiday and easily embraced as well visiting intellectuals' more explicit opposition to dictatorships, thus dramatizing a symbolic union of the economically and politically oppressed and expressing anger and opposition to enemies, local and national. Here was the quintessence of all the activites most feared and despised by Umbandistas: the open flaunting of morality as well as the barbaric and "primitive" rituals—animal sacrifices, the drinking of blood, the uses of toads. In the setting of extreme poverty, which contrasted with the rich mansions below, this constituted an unequivocal symbolic statement of defiance and resentment against the upper classes, the political system, and the Church as causes of oppression. It was a reenactment of the drama of the African sorcerer plotting to destroy his oppressor.

Ceremonies of this type, which are clearly rituals of rebellion against the dominant institutions of Brazilian society, would seem a more logical choice than Umbanda, especially Umbanda Pura, to serve as examples of religions of the oppressed. It is tempting to generalize from this type of ceremony and to see Quimbanda as primarily a lower sector of political expression of anger and hatred against oppressors (see also Galeano 1970; Luz and Lapassade 1972). However, it is important to recognize that Quimbanda is far more varied and complex than this single example would suggest. The Exús are associated with attaining power, money, and sex, not only in their illicit form but of any kind. I have known affluent businessmen who routinely consult Exús before all of their major business dealings. And their assistance to help in winning soccer games is widely sought by players and fans alike. In their broader sense, Exús seem to assert the power and autonomy of the individual to have and to pursue his/her own self-interests, as against the interests and moral codes established by the state, civil society, and the family.

Conclusions

The variations I have described in Umbanda ritual and cosmology, the influences upon them, and the gradations among them represent distinct ritual and cosmological features and encode particular social, political, and moral stances. Umbanda Pura encodes the morality, the propriety, and the values of the Brazilian middle sectors and their racial ideology of a whitened Brazil. It upholds the legitimate power of major Brazilian institutions: the state, the Church, and the family. The Afro-Brazilian terreiros have been associated with both an African ethnic identity and the articulation of class antagonisms, and they retain their potential opposition to the class and racial values of the middle sectors of Brazilian society as represented and encoded within Umbanda Pura.

Quimbanda and the Exús pose a more fundamental opposition to Umbanda Pura, that between the individual and society, individual interests and goals in collision with the social contract. This position encompasses political opposition to Umbanda Pura, which accepts, approves, and legitimizes socially constituted institutions and authority. Quimbanda challenges and denies that legitimacy. However, while it offers the potential for political opposition to unjustly constituted or inegalitarian forms of authority, its broader meaning is an assertion of selfhood and individual personal demands against the impersonal institutions that deny them.

6

Through the Gate of Suffering: The Social Meaning of Caridade

The next several chapters move from the interpretation of cosmology and ritual to an analysis of social participation in Umbanda. They examine the way in which practitioners articulate with Umbanda beliefs and practices and organize their religious activities, presenting data on their socio-economic and religious background and the details of their participation.

This chapter explores *caridade* (charity) in Umbanda, and the relationship between the religious context of its meaning and practice and its place in the lives of Umbanda practitioners. I will suggest that this central component of ritual and belief also forms the core of social praxis, the interface between religious meaning and social practice. A principal element in attracting participants and in generating faith and conversion, caridade, in the form of the consultations already described in Umbanda rituals, so dominates Umbanda that it has come to define and shape the character of this religion as a whole, giving it a pragmatic, instrumental orientation toward the solution of personal problems rather than the communal emphasis often associated with religious practice. This has led to its characterization in the comparative literature as a "thaumaturgical sect" (Wilson 1959:1973).

I have shown caridade to be the mechanism of spiritual evolution, the means through which the Caboclos and the Pretos Velhos gain their dominant ritual position and demonstrate their powers. The ritual form of caridade, the consulta, which consists in the personalized, dyadic exchange between spirit consultant and human client, is at once the central form of ritual expression and the dramatic highlight of the public ceremonies.

Consultas have the same central importance in the social lives of all categories of Umbanda participants. They are the principal links between Umbanda and the lay population who constitute Umbanda's potential clientele and membership. Almost invariably, for lay persons, a consulta forms the initial source of contact with Umbanda. I found that almost all the individuals who formed the congregations at Umbanda ceremonies had themselves come to consult, or were accompanying a relative or friend who had come to do so. Occasionally when I attended a session, I would remain seated during the consulta period to watch the activities. Invariably, someone seated near me would ask, "Don't you want to consult with one of the spirits? Then why did you come?" People become clients at Umbanda centros because they want help with their problems, and they view centros primarily as places that will provide such aid. If the consulta is considered successful in resolving the illness or difficulty, such a positive resolution, which takes on the aura of a miracle, generates or reinforces belief in the efficacy of this form of spiritual aid and may provide a stimulus to continued participation. Successful consultas create believers and converts and through time may make the centro the natural place to bring a wide range of troubles. Faith, for the great majority of believers, develops as a result of the spiritual cures and assistance found within the centros. This is expressed in a common saying among converts that *"Umbandista entra pela porta do sofrimento"* ("People come to Umbanda through the gate of suffering").

In order to give an idea of the popularity of consultas, I have estimated their volume per year in Rio during the period of my research. At the ceremony I described in the previous chapter, which was in an average-sized centro, on a less well attended weeknight, 61 clients each had individual consultas. On this basis, I would make a conservative estimate that some 30 million consultas are held per year in Rio alone.[1] Since the consultas are in part a response to the demands of the clients, this figure suggests the level of interest in obtaining this form of aid. In other words, consultas are not just the symbolic focus of Umbanda rituals but are a powerful source of its attraction for the Rio population.

In addition to providing the basis for continued participation in Umbanda, consultas also provide the main source of recruitment of clients to more active roles in Umbanda centros, as members and mediums. Responses by mediums to a questionnaire, the results and methodology of which are elaborated in chapter 8, indicate that of the 403 individuals interviewed, 249, or 62 percent, had originally sought out their present centro for aid in resolving some kind of problem (see table 1). However, many of those who obtain aid through consultas remain only casual participants and utilize Umbanda centros only in emergencies.

Once they enter the ritual corps and begin to learn mediumship, mediums continue to consult about their own problems. In addition, they enter the ranks of those who help to provide the spiritual aid, that is, who take ritual roles as vehicles for the spirit consultants. For members of the ritual corps, and particularly for the leaders and mediums who have roles as spirit consultants, the consultas now acquire an additional and quite different social

Table 1.   Why Respondents Joined Their Current Centro

	No.	%	No.	%
Had problems			249	61.7
Health	154	38.2		
Financial or other material				
problems	18	4.5		
Drinking	3	.7		
"Spiritual problems"	9	2.2		
"Needed to visit a centro"	65	16.1		
Someone brought them			79	19.6
Curiosity			45	11.2
To help *(para ajudar)*			8	2.0
Founded the centro			14	3.5
No informtion			8	2.0
TOTAL			403	100.0

significance. They provide the chief sources of ritual prestige and status within the centro. The greatest asset a medium can have is talent in serving as a vehicle for the spirit consultants. Mediums whose spirit consultants are successful and sought after for their consulting abilities will gain great prestige and advance rapidly through the ritual hierarchy of the centro; they may even come to challenge the prestige and status of the leader. Consultas are thus a source of prestige, of status mobility, and of competition among mediums within the centro. Outside of it, in the wider community of members and prospective clients, the collective abilities of the spirit consultants in any centro are crucial in establishing its reputation and will determine its continuing ability to attract clients. A large congregation of eagerly awaiting clients at a public ceremony is the sure sign of a successful centro, while a dwindling clintele just as clearly marks a centro's declining reputation. Consultas thus stand at the center of a circular process in which mediums' talents in receiving the spirit specialists who provide the aid at consultas in turn determine the numbers of clients who will seek aid at that particular centro. Consultas not only dominate the religious aspects of Umbanda, but subjectively, from the point of view of the participants, they constitute the principal motive for attendance among all categories of participants, ritual specialists as well as lay participants.

I now want to treat briefly another aspect of the interface between social participation and ritual and belief which emerges within the context of the consulta: the nature of the exchange between specialist and client. The consulta is the moment when the client expresses his illness or difficulty in lay terms, and the specialist translates and treats it within the framework of Umbanda belief and ritual. The spirit consultant, acting through the body of a trained medium, becomes the professional who listens to the client's complaint and diagnoses its cause. The specialist also performs ritual treatments on the spot, recommends additional treatments, and gives practical advice, based on an Umbanda interpretation of the spiritual causation of the illness and difficulties.

The common opinion among Umbandistas that most of the problems brought by clients for these specialists to solve concern health is confirmed by other researchers (Camargo 1961:64; McGregor 1967:214) and by my own interviews with mediums. Health problems constituted 62 percent of the problems listed in the interviews as the reason for joining the respondent's current centro and totaled 64 percent of the problems that respondents and members of their immediate families said they had brought to their centros in the period since their initial contact (see table 1). I do not have detailed information on the nature of these illnesses. The complexity of working with definitions and symptomologies of folk illnesses, together with the circumstances of the interviews (see chapter 8), unfortunately put such data far beyond my reach. Furthermore, the complex interrelationship described between clients' illnesses and their other, nonhealth problems, distress about which often in itself produced illnesses, often made distinctions between illnesses and other problems difficult to make.

The use of nurses' uniforms as the prescribed ritual outfit highlights the ritual emphasis on the treatment of health problems in ceremonies such as the one I described. This does not appear to be the result of conscious or deliberate intent; these garments are generally explained as an inexpensive and easy means of standardizing the required white ritual dress. Nevertheless, the outfits give the ceremonies, particularly during the consulta period, the appearance of large public medical clinics and reinforce their image as proper places for the treatment of illness.[2]

Individuals also seek the solution to many other sorts of personal problems in Umbanda centro: problems of love, family relations, unemployment, finances, drinking, moral anguish, loneliness, and despair (see table 2).

However, even among clients with great faith in the spirits' power to cure and advise, consultas do not take precedence over secular, material efforts to resolve difficulties. For most types of problems, Umbanda remains a last resort, to be sought after more obvious secular specialists and channels for resolving the particular problem have failed to yield results. I found this to be particularly true of illnesses. Among clients complaining of serious, chronic illness, doctors had commonly been consulted, often many times, though this

Table 2.   Problems Brought for Consultas by Respondents and Members
of Their Families

Category of Problem	No.	%	No.	%
Health problems			297	64.0
Common illnesses	131	32.5		
Serious illnesses	48	11.9		
Mental health problems	18	4.5		
Miscellaneous (drinking, car accidents, etc.)	13	3.2		
Unspecified spiritual or material health problems	87	21.6		
Family problems			55	12.0
Sentimental problems			10	2.0
Employment			43	9.2
Financial problems			34	7.3
Unidentified spiritual problems			26	5.5
TOTAL			465	100.0

was not true of minor complaints, such as colds, for which medical aid would
not normally be sought. Commonly, the clients with chronic illnesses were
ones for whom medical specialists had provided no help. For this reason,
Umbanda's facilities attract not only the poor, who cannot afford or lack
institutional access to various health and other medical services.[3] Spirit
consultants are not simply poor people's doctors and social workers,
functional equivalents of secular specialists for those who cannot afford them.
Umbanda attracts individuals of any social class who have failed to resolve
their problems elsewhere and therefore bring them to Umbanda spirit
consultants.

After the client has described the problem, usually very briefly, the spirit
consultant gives the diagnosis. Clients' problems are commonly, though not
always, attributed to spiritual causes. For example, a client may be said to be
perseguido or *perturbado* (persecuted or perturbed) by ignorant, backward,
suffering, or evil spirits whose influences must be removed through ritual
cleansings. Still other ills may be attributed to an individual's own lack of faith
or bad actions (sometimes those of past lives, which according to the law of
Karma are said to require expiation) or to the evil intentions of their human
enemies (see table 3).

Undeveloped potentialities as a medium are said to be another common
cause of illness and other difficulties. Mediumship is believed to be inherent

Table 3.   Beliefs Among Respondents Concerning Spirits,
Their Roles, and Reasons for Causing
Illness and Suffering

	No.	%	No.	%
Believe that spirits do not cause illness and suffering			79	20
Believe that they do cause illness and suffering			281	70
Because the person needs to become a medium	66	16		
Because the spirits are ignorant or backward	97	24		
Because the spirits are evil	72	18		
Because the person lacks faith	7	2		
Because the person is doing evil	31	8		
Because the person's human enemies wish him ill	8	2		
Doesn't know			15	3
No information			28	7
TOTAL			403	100

rather than acquired, and those who have this capacity bear the moral
responsibility to develop their mediumistic talents *(desenvolver a
mediunidade)*. Natural mediums who through ignorance or recalcitrance
abnegate such a responsibility are believed to be a common source of harm
both to themselves and to others, especially to members of their immediate
families. In such cases the problems can be resolved only by undergoing
initiation in an Umbanda centro. Consequently such a diagnosis forms an
important source of recruitment of new members to the ritual corps and may
even exercise a coercive influence in recruitment. A few mediums admitted to
me that they wished to leave their duties in their Umbanda centro but dared
not do so for fear of immediate spiritual retribution. This situation, however,
is an uncommon one, and the vast majority of mediums seem to enjoy
participating in Umbanda and look forward to the ceremonies (see table 4).

The various curing techniques used in treating clients' problems include
the ritual cleansings and exorcisms mentioned in the description of the
Umbanda ceremony in the previous chapter. The spirit consultant may also
prescribe other rituals, to be performed outside of the centro, such as the
lighting of candles in the home to ward off evil spirits and attract benevolent
ones, the setting up of an Umbanda altar in the home, or paying homage to
one of the Orixá/Saints believed able to resolve the particular problem. They

Table 4. Greatest Satisfactions Listed by Respondents
Concerning Their Activities in Their Umbanda Centro

Satisfactions	No.	%
Practicing charity and seeing the sick cured, and their problems solved	168	41.7
Developing their *mediunidade* (mediumistic talents)	45	11.2
The sense of peace, order, or tranquility	31	7.7
Learning the doctrine, gaining better understanding	24	6.0
Singing the pontos	22	5.5
Having responsibility, feeling useful	6	1.5
Everything (Tudo)	51	12.6
Doesn't know	36	8.8
No information	20	5.0
TOTAL	403	100.0

may prescribe herbal or homeopathic remedies and innumerable special Umbanda soaps, incenses, and potions designed to bring about or restore the desired condition. Such items line the shelves in the many Umbanda stores around the city, together with ritual beads, candles, and statuary of all sizes and variations representing the Umbanda deities and spirits.

Spirit consultants also provide practical advice as to how to resolve conflicts and impasses ranging from family problems to complex bureaucratic tangles. They may assign material rather than spiritual causes to their clients' problems and recommend secular or material solutions: consultations with a doctor, lawyer, or some other secular specialist. I did not find a unified body of beliefs concerning the causative factors of human suffering among the group of mediums whom I interviewed. Instead, the varied responses given by this group of mediums to an open question concerning the causes of illness and difficulty revealed that while many respondents believed in the primacy of spiritual causation or the working of Karmic law, others stressed material causes. Still other respondents introduced additional elements such as secular, folk theories of the causes of illness. Typical of these latter was the response given me by an elderly woman, who stated flatly that "Illness comes from the night air, the wind, from storms, but difficulties are financial, and come from a lack of money." When questioned directly as to whether spirits could cause illness and other difficulties, 70 percent of the sample believed they could, but 20 percent answered they could not (see table 3). No clear boundary is drawn between spiritual and material causes of suffering, nor, as will shortly be seen, is a clear distinction made between spiritual and material forms of its alleviation.

In keeping with the tradition established in Kardecism, many Umbanda centros extend the concept of caridade beyond the spiritual aid provided in the consultas to include material forms of aid, such as access to doctors (both homeopathic and allopathic) or dentists, free or cut-rate medicines, burial funds, and food and clothing. These are often made available free or at a minimal cost to members and, occasionally, to the local community as well. The various types of social welfare services offered by the centros in which the questionnaire was administered are listed in table 5. In addition to such regularly available forms of aid, in certain cases employment, loans, and other forms of help may be arranged on a personal basis within the centros (see table 6). In this fashion, many Umbanda centros are coming to resemble the voluntary organizations that serve as mutual aid societies so common in other urban areas of the world (see for example Kerri 1976). The social services provided by Umbanda centros are not yet available on so grand a scale as those provided by the Kardecists, but they are rapidly increasing.

Table 5. Social Welfare Services Available in Umbanda Centros
Where Interviews Were Conducted

Centro No.	1	2	3	4	5	6	7	8	9	10	11	12	13	14	Total
Doctor	x			x	x						x	o	o		6
Dentist	x								x			o	o		4
Psychiatrist				x											1
Legal Aid	x					x						o	o		4
Medicines	x	x		x		x		x				o	o		7
Food distributions				x		x									2
Clothing		x		x	x										3
Day care											x				1
Burial funds	x														1
Classes for preschoolers								x			x				2
Hospital				x											1
Orphanage	x														1

Key: x aid available
        x in construction
        o available through membership in an Umbanda federation

Table 6.   Social Welfare Services Obtained by Respondents
in Their Centros

Type of Service	No.	%
Medical care	66	16.4
Dental care	22	5.5
Free medicines	47	11.7
A financial loan	11	2.7
Employment	3	0.7
Had received no services	285	70.7
No information	20	5.0

   The provision of secular social services as well as spiritual aid extends the notion of caridade beyond the realm of the spirit world into the material one and often results in the interpenetration of spiritual and material forms of assistance. Since the consultas customarily form the beginning point of any help-seeking activities in Umbanda, any help received, material as well as spiritual, will tend to be interpreted as provided by the spirit consultant.

   Umbanda's strongly pragmatic and instrumental orientation is accompanied by a corresponding lack of emphasis on social activities. The coffee hours, group activities, clubs, picnics, and dances frequently found in Catholic or Protestant churches, which encourage members to become better acquainted with each other, are notably rare and downplayed in Umbanda centros. Most socializing occurs in the limited time before the ceremonies begin. While friendships and sometimes even marriages may develop among members of a centro, most individuals seem to both join and attend Umbanda centros for practical, personal ends rather than for social ones. The responses of mediums interviewed to an open-ended question concerning their greatest satisfaction in participating in Umbanda are revealing in this context (see table 4). No one listed social contacts or activities as their greatest satisfaction. They emphasized instead their participation in the consultas (referred to as "practicing charity") or some other aspect of the ritual. Similarly, responses to questions on both socializing and forming new friendships within Umbanda centros indicated that these are infrequent. Although respondents had introduced many members of their own pre-existing networks into their centros, they did not add to them through their centros (see chapter 8, tables 26–29).

   Umbanda centros are not places where one goes to be seen and to enhance one's social prestige in the local community, as often occurs in local Catholic and Protestant churches. In Rio, Umbanda centros most frequently draw their membership from diverse areas within the city, and a predominantly local membership is rare. Even those who attend centros in their own neighborhoods may do so discreetly, since there are always neighbors who disapprove. Discretion, even secrecy, is facilitated by the fact that the ceremonies occur at night. Members of the middle sectors, who are more likely to suffer disapproval from their peers for attending centros, may even prefer to join a centro located a considerable distance from their homes, where their activities need be known only to their fellow centro members. In some cases, Umbandistas even attempt to conceal their participation from members of their own families. Thus, the fear of social disapprobation, which undoubtedly inhibits public communal rituals in Umbanda, particularly those of a local community type, also hinders the development of strong communalism within Umbanda. This, in turn, reinforces its pragmatic and instrumental orientation.

The practice of caridade in Umbanda, in both its ritual and material forms, presents a strong contrast with what I have already outlined for Kardecism. Both Kardecist ritual and its secular forms of charity discourage the participation of the lower sectors. Charity, specifically, involves an impersonal, nonreciprocal donation by the rich to the poor and provides for no form of return. The poor are only objects of charity and are spurned as coreligionists. Ritual and charity together, and in parallel fashion, act to restrict active participation to the middle sectors and to prohibit the entry of the lower sectors. Caridade in Umbanda acts exactly to the contrary. It provides for a redefinition of charity as a ritual form of spiritual aid that occurs in a reciprocal, personalized form of exchange and binds clients ritually into reciprocating through obligatory acts of ritual homage, suggestively called *obrigacões* (obligations), in return for aid. Similarly, in social practice, caridade, in the form of consultas, is a translation of the concept of charity which is designed to draw clients, without selection as to social sector, education, or "culture," into regular attendance and more active ritual and social involvement in its activities. Moreover, clients may themselves become ritual specialists—mediums or leaders. The result of this is that clients of the lower sectors flock to Umbanda centros, join them, and are drawn into active participation in Umbanda's many forms of reciprocal obligation.

The central theme of caridade in Umbanda ritual is restated as a form of social practice. Just as the elevation of the Caboclos and Pretos Velhos to central positions in Umbanda may be interpreted as a central symbolic encoding of the middle sectors' ideology of embracing the lower sectors, so Umbanda's form of caridade, too, embraces the lower sectors and draws them into active practice in Umbanda centros. It does so in a form of personal patronage relationship which is embodied in the consultas and reiterates a principal form of reciprocal, vertical relationship found within Brazilian society.

7

Structure and Organization of Umbanda Centros

This chapter examines various aspects of social structure in Umbanda centros, beginning with the organization of the ritual and administrative hierarchies and the relationship between them. I will then present a model of the way in which centros are founded and will discuss the factors that influence their growth and demise and their class composition. Special attention will be given to centros with a socio-economically heterogeneous membership, which is characteristic of Umbanda Pura. Finally, I will return to the issue of symbolic inversion in Umbanda ritual, and discuss the relationship between ritual and secular statuses in Umbanda centros. Like my treatment of caridade, this chapter continues to explore the interface between ritual and social practice, between ritual structures and the social and class structures of the centros that provide their context. The themes of bureaucracy and patronage and their ritual transformations will also reappear in discussions of social organization.

Ritual and Administrative Hierarchies

Umbanda centros have two spheres of organization and potentially two hierarchies of power: the ritual hierarchy, which provides the social structure for religious practice, and the secular or administrative hierarchy, which attends to the bureaucratic details of centro activities. The ritual hierarchy includes all individuals who participate in the religious ceremonies already described. Participants fall into three minimal status categories: the leader; the *corpo mediúnico* (ritual corps), who together with the leader wear the ritual white uniform; and the congregation, whose members participate in the consultas. These three categories are basic to all Umbanda centros, although they may undergo further internal differentiation.

The leader, known as the *chefe* (chief) or *mãe* or *pai de santo* (mother or father of the saints),[1] and who is also nearly always the founder of the centro, is ultimately responsible for all of its activities and has authority over all who are connected with it. Some chefes, however, delegate administrative authority to others, and concern themselves principally with activities in the religious sector. Chefes direct the religious ceremonies and instruct the mediums in both ritual and doctrine. They are responsible for the quality of performance in all religious rituals, and their capabilities in these matters, their leadership qualities, and their ability to inspire loyalty among their followers are all crucial in determining the success of the centro.

Almost without exception, chefes are mediums, who receive the highest ranking spirits in the centro, those expected to be the most gifted in curing and counseling.[2] As in the ceremony I previously described, the most serious and difficult problems and the most socially distinguished of the centro's clientele will be brought directly to them for consultas. Chefes also lead the prayers and may even deliver sermons during the ceremonies, taking a role similar to that of a Protestant pastor.

The *corpo mediúnico* (ritual corps) forms the second category in the ritual hierarchy. It is composed principally of mediums in various stages of initiation and consists minimally of two ranked statuses: *médiuns de consulta* (consulting mediums), full initiates who serve as *aparelhos* (vehicles) or *cavalos* (horses) for the spirit guides who give consultas; and *médiuns em desenvolvimento* (mediums in training) in lesser stages of ritual preparation. A further differentiation may be made between mediums in training and *cambonos,* novices at the beginning stages of initiation. Mediums may also be known as *filhas* and *filhos de santo* (daughters and sons of the saints).[3] The ritual corps may also include a few individuals who are not mediums but assist in the ritual and have various titles.

In smaller centros, where the ritual corps is likely to average somewhere between 10 and 60 individuals, these status categories may not be further distinguished. But as the size of the centro increases, so does the likelihood of further internal subdivisions in the categories of both chefe and corpos mediúnico. In large centros, the ritual corps may number as many as several hundred individuals, and chefes may be assisted by *sub-chefes,* who help with or substitute for the chefe in directing religious ceremonies (especially when these are held several times a week). The ritual corps may likewise be differentiated into substatuses on the basis of degree of ritual preparation. In one of Rio's largest centros of Umbanda Pura, the ritual corps numbers some 450 individuals who occupy seven ranked statuses ranging from chefe (rank 7) to cambono (rank 1). All participants have their rank number sewn on the left sleeve of their ritual uniforms. Drawing on the military imagery so often employed in describing the organization of the Umbanda cosmos, the chefe likens the organization of his centro to that of an army, and his religious ceremonies have the precision and order of military drills.

Status differences within the ritual hierarchy are reflected most clearly in the possession roles taken in the ceremonies during the consulta period. At this time, full initiates, the médiuns de consulta, receive their spirit consultants and give consultas, while lower ranking initiates become their assistants and ritual servants. Mediums of intermediate rank, sometimes called *médiuns de passagem* (mediums of passage), assist in the rituals for the exorcism of ignorant and evil spirits, laying their hands on the client and drawing these negative spirits into their own bodies, in the manner already described. Cambonos, the lowest ranking members of the ritual corps, do not have public spirit possession roles but are servants to the spirits, bringing them their cigars and pipes and performing other errands.

The different statuses and the roles connected with them depend principally on a medium's level of skill in trance performance. *Desenvolvimento mediúnico* (development as a medium) is commonly acknowledged to be the main route to advancement through the ritual hierarchy. Novices without prior experience in Umbanda must master the rudiments of Umbanda cosmology, and classes are sometimes offered in this and in Kardecist doctrine. They must also learn the pontos sung to the various spirits and a variety of personal ritual obligations *(obrigações)* to them. However, their principal task is to learn the highly controlled possession behavior required in Umbanda ritual. The wild frenzies often popularly attributed to Umbanda possession states by its detractors are found only among the most inexperienced of beginners or those possessed by extremely ignorant or evil spirits. In fact, it is easy to discern a medium's level of experience and relative rank within the centro by the ease with which he or she enters and leaves possession states and by the degree to which this behavior is controlled.

Possession roles are learned and practiced during special training sessions, *sessões de desenvolvimento*, held in the centro as often as once a week. These resemble the regular religious ceremonies and are usually open to the public, but in these ceremonies less advanced mediums, who in the regular sessions are not permitted to have possession roles, are encouraged and taught to receive their spirits. The chefe and the more advanced mediums devote considerable time to inducing possession and instructing beginners in gaining physical control over their actions while possessed.[4]

The learning of possession roles in Umbanda proceeds in two stages, in a manner similar to that described by the Leacocks for the Batuque, in Belem (1972:173–82). The first stage of this process is the learning of what the Leacocks term a "generalized trance role," that is, the minimal skills and control expected of anyone who is possessed (Ibid.:174). First encounters with possession are often uncontrolled, violent, and even potentially dangerous to novices, who may reel about as if drunk, oblivious to their surroundings, and frequently bump into objects and other individuals. They may even pitch straight over forward or backward onto the floor or become totally rigid. At the very least, beginning possession states generally involve extremely awkward physical behavior, and novices must learn to enter, maintain, and leave possession states without violence and in response to ritual cues. While possessed, they must learn to control their movements and to relax into a more or less graceful shuffle or to execute an abbreviated samba step.

The successful novice, having mastered this generalized trance role, begins to learn specific "subroles," the more patterned behavior appropriate to the particular spirits he or she receives (Ibid.:174). This involves learning particular motor patterns, gestures, and, eventually, as the medium moves toward the role of spirit consultant, acquiring verbal skills and proficiency necessary for such a role. I have already suggested that spirit consultants often acquire high levels of individual expression and quite distinctive personalities, which enhance their individual reputations and prestige and the belief in their powers to cure and counsel.[5] Their skill in learning spirit possession roles lies behind their spirits' success in helping clients and directly affects both their own prestige as mediums and the reputation of the centro.

The selection and process of learning these subroles are expressed in Umbanda as the "revelation" by the spirits of their identities. Novices often explain that they "receive spirits, but they haven't yet revealed their identities." Revelation may come during spirit possession, when the spirit suddenly speaks his name, or it may be ascertained through a consulta with the more evolved spirit consultant of the chefe. Gradually, through time, the medium will receive other spirits as well, each with a separate identity. The length of time required for this learning process varies greatly according to the aptitude of the individual medium and probably according to his or her degree of familiarity with the requirements of possession performances.[6] Individuals do not progress equally, nor do they automatically attain a high rank in the centro. Some never succeed in spirit possession and may take nonpossession roles in the rituals. Others who never gain control over their possession behavior, i.e., whose spirits never reveal their identities, remain in the lower ranks of the ritual hierarchy or, dissatisfied with their lack of progress or promotion, may leave to go elsewhere. Mediums are generally able to transfer their former ranks to a new centro, provided that they can demonstrate the capabilities demanded by the new chefe.

The level of skills demanded varies considerably among centros. For example, in the large centro whose military ranks and precision I just mentioned, possession begins with about 200 mediums in two lines, the men facing the women. A bell is rung, signaling the approach of the spirits, and within less than a minute the entire group has received their spirits.[7] At the other extreme lie centros such as one that I visited out of curiosity because of its local reputation for being poorly run and on the verge of closing due to the ineptness of its chefe and the lack of order in its public rituals. Mediums in possession staggered about, bumping into each other and into the few members of the congregation, who appeared to become more and more restless and bored as the services progressed and exchanged uncomplimentary remarks on the confusion and disorder. One individual left shortly before the consulta period, and when I inquired about this, he replied, "I don't want to consult with any of the spirits *here*."

The third status category in the Umbanda ritual hierarchy is composed of the *assistência* (congregation), who watches the proceedings, participates in the singing, and furnishes the clientele at the consultas. These are noninitiates, and the greatest potential source of recruitment to the ritual corps. They may or may not be members of the centro, since it is customary to offer free consultas to visitors on a sort of get-acquainted basis. However, if an individual wishes to consult regularly at the centro, he or she will probably be required to become a member.

I have already suggested that the consultas create a realignment of cosmological and ritual roles. In a parallel fashion, they also create a realignment among some members of the ritual hierarchy. The status of spirit consultant ignores the formal distinction between chefes and their high-ranking mediums, since they serve together in these roles. Theoretically, the chefe's superior formal rank will be reflected in the higher status and greater importance of the spirit consultant he or she receives. In practice, however, chefes and their most accomplished mediums now enter into direct competition for clients. Their relative success may be directly observed in both the numbers and the social prestige of their clienteles. It is not uncommon for the spirit consultant received by a particularly gifted but lesser ranking medium to challenge the reputation and the prestige of that received by the chefe. Given the importance and prestige of this activity, such a situation represents a direct challenge to the chefe's entire ritual position and status. The usual result of such a situation is that the chefe's spirit consultant will call the medium involved for a special consulta, at which the medium will receive notice of a new and special spiritual mission—to leave his or her current centro and found a new one. It is by this route that chefes retain their ascendancy within the centro and that experienced mediums make the status change from médiun de consulta to chefe of their own centro. Just as the role of spirit consultant can threaten to unbalance the formal system, it can also be utilized by the chefe to restore balance, regain control, and encourage the departure of the too successful medium from the centro. If this is not done, the medium is likely, over time, to take over the chefe's prestige, clients, and eventually, the centro as well.

Parallel to the ritual hierarchy is an administrative hierarchy that consists formally of a board of directors: a president, vice-presidents, secretaries, treasurers, and various other officials, who uphold the by-laws stating the purposes, comportment, and rules to be observed by members. Legal registration, which is now sought by virtually all Umbanda centros,[8] requires such a formal structure. However, in practice, the relative importance of these administrative structures varies greatly according to the size, financial status, and range of activities of the particular centro. It assumes greatest importance principally in the larger and wealthier centros, which tend to be more highly organized and more bureaucratically oriented, as well as offering a wider range of social services to their memberships. In such centros, the administration may be vital to the smooth running of the centro, and formal administrative positions are likely to be fully elaborated and to involve a variety of tasks, including the registration of new members, the collection of monthly membership dues, fundraising, the administration of charitable activities and of any social activities that may take place, and even the publication of a monthly journal. In addition, administrators may supervise the distribution of *fichas* (tokens) to potential clients before the ceremony begins, and in some of the larger centros, oversee the prompt arrival and regular attendance of members of the ritual corps. While ultimately responsible within the centro to the chefe, administrators are in fact legally responsible for the centro, and they bear a direct responsibility as well for the efficiency and success with which the centro operates. The individuals who occupy these positions tend either to be members of the chefe's immediate family or close personal friends, and they may also include spouses of members of the ritual corps.

While the administration may also be significant in smaller centros such as the one whose ceremonies I described in chapter 5, it tends to decrease in importance as centros become smaller and poorer, to the point where administrative posts may exist as a mere formality. In such cases, ritual statuses will determine administrative ones, with the chefe serving as president and high-ranking mediums as vice-presidents and secretaries.

Of the two spheres of organization just described, ritual and administrative, the ritual sphere is the primary one. Concerned with the performance of the religious ceremonies that lie at the heart of Umbanda practice, the ritual hierarchy is a constant feature of social structure in all centros, while the administration, though a de facto legal necessity, is variable, and its degree of elaboration and its very social existence depend upon the size and wealth of the centro. Whatever the importance of the administrative sector, the chefe, who is the head of the centro and director of rituals, emerges as the centro's dominant figure. It is not surprising that chefes try to fill key positions, both ritual and bureaucratic, with relatives and personal friends who form the core of the loyal following that is necessary for a centro's successful operation.

A Model of the Growth and Demise of Umbanda Centros

This loyal following is crucial to all aspects of a centro's success, from its inception through the possibility of its continuity beyond its original founder. Since there are no effective ecclesiastical controls over religious leaders, anyone may open a centro. Usually, however, the founder is an experienced initiate and médiun de consulta who has served an apprenticeship in another Umbanda centro and who may well have left in the manner just described, by threatening the position of the chefe. Beginning leaders gather a small core of supporters: family, friends, and individuals who have been clients of their spirit consultants at their previous centro. Operations begin on a small scale. Basic needs are simple and require small investment: a place in which to hold religious services, which may be arranged in a room of the leader's home or on his premises; the ritual garments, and the candles, flowers, and other ritual items necessary to the ceremonies, which are customarily the responsibility of the mediums.

From this original nucleus the centro is formed, organized, and officially registered and becomes an independent group supported by a dues-paying membership, which will provide the financial support for maintaining the centro. The membership includes the individuals in the ritual corps, the administration, and others who join in order to use the centro's facilities on a regular basis—for consultas and any other material welfare services the centro may provide. It may also include a few individuals, such as local politicians, who provide financial support without necessarily utilizing the centro. While a specially constructed centro may be a costly affair, involving considerable expense for overhead and upkeep and possible only with a more affluent membership, a smaller centro, with ceremonies continuing to be held in the chefe's home, entails far less expense.

Members pay an initial registration fee and monthly dues, which vary according to the expenses of the centro and the socio-economic composition of its membership.[9] Of course, not all members pay their dues on a regular basis. The most faithful are members of the ritual corps and administration, while those who join only in order to obtain consultas and other services tend to let their dues lapse until times of need. Consultas, if they are not offered free of charge to members, may furnish an additional source of income.[10] Other sources of financial support to the centro include the individual gifts sometimes made by grateful clients in return for successful cures or resolution of problems; funds raised by activities such as lotteries, raffles, bakery sales, and, more rarely, the financial or other contributions made by politicians.

Centros expand mainly through the social networks of their original membership. Members bring their families, friends, acquaintances, business colleagues, and even their employers or servants to consult with the spirits about their problems. Some join, and the numbers of members and attendance at the religious service grow. Demands on space lead to cooperative efforts by members to raise the funds to acquire a larger centro. Most desirable is to purchase land and, using members' contributions of labor, building materials, and funds, build a proper Umbanda centro. However, this is beyond the means of most centros, which seek alternatives such as renting a building or an apartment which is then remodeled as a centro. This may even be shared by two or up to four other centros, all of which arrange the hours and days of their religious ceremonies so as not to overlap and are thus able to minimize the costs of rental. I visited two such places in downtown Rio.

Choice of a new location for the centro depends on the material resources of the membership, the availability of space, and certain ritual considerations. Centros that do not utilize drums in their rituals generally try to locate as close as possible to central commercial areas where transportation is most convenient. Rents in Rio's southern residential zone are generally too expensive for these purposes, and the majority of centros are located in the more industrial *Zona Norte* (North Zone) and in the city's suburbs. Centros and terreiros that use drums, particularly those holding all-night ceremonies, are much more restricted as to their location. In densely populated areas the *lei do silencio* (law of silence, a state ordinance outlawing the use of drums past the hour of 10:00 p.m.) is sure to be constantly invoked by irritated and complaining neighbors. Their telephone calls to the police may occasion the extremely disruptive arrival of official police delegations in the middle of Umbanda ceremonies. I even witnessed ritual participants, dressed in their ritual garments, being escorted to the local delegacia. Centros that use drums in their ceremonies may locate in favelas. Although rent may be cheaper and police fewer, these locations are preferred mainly by favela inhabitants; others are put off by their popular image as unsavory, violent, and dangerous places. Alternatively, such ceremonies may be held in the open air, in the *mato* (dense forested areas), which rises up steep slopes in the heart of the city. However, since these areas belong to the city and construction is not permitted, ceremonies held there are subject to weather conditions. The areas preferred by these centros, most of which are the more Afro-Brazilian centros, are Rio's far suburbs or even sites in the neighboring State of Rio,[11] where semi-rural conditions permit sufficient privacy for all-night drumming. These less central locations may make transportation difficult for some members, necessitating carpools to transport members to and from the ceremonies. The greater distance from the densely populated areas of the city, and pressures against the use of drums in the increasingly dense urban surroundings, tend to create ritual drift away from the more Afro-Brazilian style of rituals toward the style of Umbanda Pura. Drums are the indispensable core of more Afro-Brazilian forms of Umbanda.

Spatial and ritual considerations, together with the influence of social networks in the membership of centros, mean that members often live a considerable distance both from one another and from the centro. While difficulties of travel will eventually lead some participants to choose another centro closer to their homes, many others, particularly members of the ritual corps, maintain their loyalty to their centro over many years, commuting considerable distances (up to two hours each way) several times each week to participate. Once located, a centro will tend to attract some local membership. But the membership of an established centro is rarely of a purely local nature, and if its spiritual cures become widely known, it will continue to attract a nonlocal membership.

Most Umbanda centros stabilize with an active membership—including ritual participants, members of the administration, and steady clients—at somewhere between 50 and 150 people. The size may be held down and membership controlled by lack of space or the deliberate maintenance of the centro in a private home. At the other extreme, a small minority of centros have increased in size to several thousand members. These inhabit entire multistory buildings and offer daily religious ceremonies and many varied social welfare services. Such size and scope are possible only when the centro has considerable financial resources, and thus are found only among the wealthier centros.

Because Umbanda's growth has occurred principally since World War II, it is hard to get a clear idea of the potential longevity of Umbanda centros and their ability to survive the death or retirement of their founders. I found several cases among the largest and wealthiest of the older centros, in which leadership had already been successfully transferred. It had almost always remained within the nuclear family of the founders, passing to their sons, daughters, or spouses, as in the centro founded by Zélio de Moraes, which passed to his daughter. In only rare cases had it been transferred to nonrelatives who were high-ranking initiates in the centro. Outside of these few examples, it appears that the majority of centros, which are small, informally run, and lack a large resource base, are unlikely to survive the tenure of their founders. I heard of many centros that had simply closed down, their personnel dispersed to join other centros, some perhaps eventually to found their own. The ability to effect a successful transfer of leadership appears to be related to resources and financial stability and to the strength of family members' interest in maintaining the centro.

This model reveals the importance of the personal networks of the chefes and their members in recruiting the loyal supporters upon whom the centros' success and survival depend. While chefes may be considered to be charismatic leaders whose power lies in a personal appeal to their followers rather than upon their status in a particular organization, it is clear that their success depends on more than personal appeal alone; they must generate and maintain a small but crucial core of loyal followers in order to ensure their centros' success.

Socio-Economic Composition of Umbanda Centros

In view of the extremely wide socio-economic spectrum of Umbanda practitioners and the tendency for particular forms of ritual practice to be associated with particular sectors, different sectors might be expected to practice separately and individual centros to form relatively homogeneous socio-economic units. This has been a common pattern, for example, within Protestant churches in Brazil, in nineteenth-century England, and in the United States.

I did find many examples of such relatively homogeneous centros at all levels of the Umbanda population. I will refer to such centros as homogeneous in socio-economic composition. However, I also found another quite different and yet similarly widespread pattern of centros that were heterogeneous in their socio-economic composition. These centros conformed, almost without exception, to a standard pattern in which the chefes and top-ranking members of the administration occupied the highest among a wide range of different socio-economic statuses found within the centro, while lower ranking members ranged from socio-economic equals of the chefe to individuals of substantially lower socio-economic status. This pattern of heterogeneous socio-economic composition was particularly noticeable in centros practicing Umbanda Pura. I thus thought at first that it might be a unique form, related specifically to some particular feature of Umbanda Pura. Further investigation, however, convinced me that it was more widespread and was the logical result of broader and more general principles of centro affiliation operating throughout all forms of Umbanda. These appeared to reflect class factors involved in individual choices of centro membership and to be related to the pragmatic and instrumental focus of Umbanda and its individualistic rather than collective nature as a religion.

I have condensed the factors that influence membership in Umbanda centros into two broad principles: first, that the socio-economic status of the centro's chefe will be the key variable in determining the socio-economic level and range of individuals who will be attracted to the centro; and second, that potential members respond to social class clues in their choice of membership in a centro, choosing one whose socio-economic and status level at least equals their own.

The first principle derives from the chefes' crucial roles in decision-making and in forming and drawing together the centros' key personnel. These nuclei tend to be drawn from among chefes' primary networks of family and friends, thus tending to reproduce the socio-economic status of the chefes themselves. The pooled skills and resources of these groups will, in turn, determine the basic parameters of the centros' operation. Chefes may determine matters of ritual and belief, but the groups around them and their resources, interests, and values, affect many aspects of the centros: their location and decor, the organization of their administrations, their tone and general class image.

Following from this, the second principle states that these aspects of the centros' class images will, in turn, influence potential members in their choice of a centro. While clients respond to a centro's reputation for success in curing, and when in trouble may visit a wide range of centros in search of spiritual aid, they will tend to choose membership in a centro whose affluence, ritual, efficiency of organization, and membership manifest a social level at least equal to their own. They may choose to join a more affluent centro, but they will not choose a less affluent one. Thus, for example, individuals of any socio-economic level may be attracted to a centro run by their social peers, and individuals from the lower sectors may be attracted to affluent middle sector centros, but individuals from the middle sectors will not tend to join a centro run by members of the lower sectors.

The workings of these principles may be illustrated through examples provided by two discrete research populations: my survey of the Umbanda centros in the favela where I lived for several months (see also Brown 1966); and the data from my questionnaires, which included 14 centros of widely varying socio-economic composition. The favela survey suggests membership patterns among the lower sectors.[12] In 1966, the favela, which had a total population estimated at 50,000, contained fifteen small Umbanda centros, all of whose chefes and memberships came from the lower sectors, most living locally in the favela. I found, however, that a far greater number of the Umbandistas in the favela belonged to or attended centros *outside* the favela run by members of the affluent middle sectors. Informants who attended these centros told me that they preferred them because the *ambiente* (atmosphere or surroundings) was better, the people *mais elevado* (of higher social status), and more social services were available there. These data illustrate the lower sectors' varied preferences for centros whose members are their social equals, often their neighbors, and for the social and economic benefits derived from membership in more affluent centros. These varied preferences result in the formation of homogeneously lower sector centros and contribute as well to producing heterogeneous ones.

Data from my later and broader questionnaire survey confirm the above patterns and reveal at the same time the more restricted membership preferences found within the more affluent middle sectors. The 14 centros in which interviews were conducted showed the memberships of the ritual corps to be consistently of lower or of equal sectoral and socio-economic status, but not of higher socio-economic status, than their chefes. The only exceptions to this pattern proved to be a French immigrant couple whose occupational level, education and salary greatly exceeded those of anyone else in the centro in which they were undergoing initiation, including that of the chefe. Since they were recent immigrants, their ready crossing of class boundaries may be attributed in part to their unfamiliarity with the subtleties of Brazilian class behavior. It is important to note here that this pattern refers to active members only, not to those who remain occasional clients. If the French couple mentioned had only been clients, their presence would not have been surprising. I also found wealthy clients attending ceremonies in the favela; many of them could not conceal their embarrassment at my discovery of their presence there. But wealthy clients would not be likely to become regular members at such a centro. This survey also revealed two small but affluent middle sector centros operating out of their chefes' homes, where membership was deliberately restricted to the middle sectors. The majority of the centros, whether Umbanda Pura, more Kardecist, or more African-oriented, however, showed the pattern I have characterized of socio-economic heterogeneity, with their chefes at the top levels of both income and occupational status found within the centros.

This pattern of heterogeneous socio-economic composition reflects Umbanda centros' openly pragmatic and instrumental orientation, as for example in favela residents' preferences for more affluent, service-oriented centros outside the favela. It also establishes a particular socio-economic context for the exchanges that take place within these centros which influence as well the character of the relationships formed through these exchanges. This topic will be further developed in chapter 10.

A second important aspect of the socio-economic composition of centros is that it sets the framework within which ritual and administrative hierarchies are elaborated. Heterogeneous centros thus have an additional, class-stratified hierarchy, which must be considered when examining questions of whether ritual status categories provide for inversions of secular statuses. I have questioned Willems' interpretation of Umbanda cosmology as either egalitarian or representing inversions of secular social relations (see chapter 4) and have suggested that, at best, the issue of cosmological status relations in Umbanda is too complex and ambiguous to support such easy generalizations. The same appears to be true with respect to ritual inversions of secular class or racial statuses. The overall status structure in heterogeneous centros reproduces the secular class structure of Brazilian society, with chefes and their nuclei of supporters occupying the highest ritual and administrative statuses within the centros and their subordinates ranged as equals or below them. In such situations, these leaders' ritual and administrative positions reinforce their secular positions of dominance rather than reversing them.

It is true that there is a saying in Umbanda, sometimes quoted by mediums, that *"aqui todo o mundo é igual"* ("here, everyone is equal") and that in Umbanda "there are neither classes or castes" (Zespo, quoted in Willems 1966: 226). Even in centros of Umbanda Pura this statement has some limited truth. The ritual corps' use of simple white outfits and the absence of such class indicators as jewelry and accessories do away with many visible indicators of socio-economic status. And the importance of spirit possession skills as the basis of rank within the ritual hierarchy permits many situations of status reversal, in which poor mediums outrank more affluent ones, blacks outrank whites, and women outrank men. During the consulta period, as well, mediums may significantly outrank their clients. At this time, elegantly and expensively dressed white men and women from the professional sectors may be seen humbly asking advice of a Caboclo or Preto Velho spirit possessing a médiun de consulta who is poor and black (see also Bastide 1960:467–68).

However, the reverse situation also occurs: many médiuns de consulta are affluent whites attending to clients who are both poor and black. At the Umbanda Pura ceremony described in detail in chapter 5, the chefe who received Pai João, the humble Preto Velho, was a polished, commanding, and successful white man in his early 60s, a mechanical engineer. Watching this chefe, possessed by Pai João, giving a consulta to a poor black woman, I used to wonder with whom the client was really identifying. Clients always insisted that they disregarded the physical presence of the medium and saw only the possessing spirit, but I could not escape the feeling that such situations, at least subliminally, presented a great deal of status ambiguity. A telling comment was made by one of the poorer members of this centro when I asked him what was the secret of Pai João's success: *"Pai João é Pai João porque Seu Silva e Seu Silva"* (in effect, "Pai João is who he is because of Sr. Silva, the chefe who receives him"). He further explained to me that since Sr. Silva is a kind, successful, and experienced businessman, knowledgeable on many matters, it is natural that the spirit he receives should possess these same qualities. This kind of comment suggests the degree to which underlying factors associated with socio-economic and class status may contribute to legitimizing and justifying the superior ritual status of chefes.

Certain ritual moments and activities, then, seem to hold secular, socio-economic factors in suspension and to support the potential for everyone to be equal. However, these are statements not of truth but of ideology, and while they may momentarily seem tenable, they are ambiguous. They occur within the total social context of the centro, within a nest of hierarchical structures that often contradict equality and provide instead repeated restatements of hierarchy and inequality. It is thus dangerous to take these statements at face value and out of the total social context in which they occur. Even within the context of Umbanda centros, they may be only temporary reversals of the social order, serving to mask and camouflage other social inequalities found within the centros.

On the other hand, I have paid particular attention to socio-economically heterogeneous centros and have somewhat neglected homogeneous ones. I found the ritual emphasis on hierarchy and inequality to apply widely to centros of all types of socio-economic composition, homogeneous as well as heterogeneous. However, further research would clearly be necessary to establish the significance of ritual reversals and statements of egalitarianism in centros where socio-economic homogeneity among members might well change the meaning of such statements and the egalitarian emphasis might indeed be greater. But even if this should be true in specific types of Umbanda centros, it would still be misleading to attribute such instances of greater egalitarianism indiscriminately to Umbanda as a whole.

8

The Social Background of Umbanda Practitioners

The errors contained in scholars' previous interpretations of Umbanda's social and political significance have derived in important measure from false assumptions concerning the class backgrounds and rural origins of its practitioners and an absence of systematic investigation of these topics. As my own research came increasingly to challenge these previous interpretations, it became essential to me that I not commit a similar error. I resolved to conduct a survey of practitioners that would test my own interpretations by providing empirical data on their backgrounds and on other aspects of their religious beliefs and practice.

I therefore prepared a questionnaire, which I administered to 403 chefes and mediums in 14 Umbanda centros. This chapter presents my findings and discusses their implications. It provides a profile of those who seek out and practice Umbanda in Rio and suggests ways in which these data help to illuminate further the character of this religion as a whole. I begin with data on participants' socio-economic background: vital statistics, aspects of social class and race, and rural-urban migration history. I then present material on their religious background, their involvement with Umbanda, and their family and other social ties within Umbanda centros.

Methodology

My choice of methodology in conducting this survey was dictated by two concerns: first, I wanted to be able to understand the details of individuals' participation in Umbanda within the social context of their particular centros, rather than simply to interview random individual practitioners throughout the city. This method enabled me, for example, to observe the different patterns in the socio-economic composition of centros that I discussed in the previous chapter. In order to do this, it was necessary to select a small number of centros from an estimated 20,000 in Rio, for which there was at the time no even minimally adequate census available. Taking a random sample of Umbanda centros was clearly out of the question. I chose the centros for interviewing from among the over 200 centros of various types that I had visited in the course of a year's fieldwork. Rather than focus exclusively on centros of Umbanda Pura, I resolved to include a range of various forms of Umbanda practiced in Rio and to present an aggregate picture that would suggest the common characteristics of the sample and its range of variation. I selected centros that would represent major variations found in Umbanda centros: in social composition, type of ritual practice, location within the city, and size. The 14 centros included a number of heterogeneous centros and a few that seemed to be more uniformly middle or lower sector in composition. They represented Umbanda Pura, Umbanda Kardecista, Umbanda Oriental and Umbanda Africana; were located in the fashionable south zone, in the industrial north zone, in favelas, and in the semi-rural periphery; and ranged in size from a very small one with a total of 8 mediums to one extremely large centro with over 1500 mediums.

My second major concern was to concentrate on the most active sector of Umbanda participants: the chefes and other members of the ritual corps, mediums and helpers who dressed in their ritual clothes to participate regularly in the public ceremonies. I felt that this sector would have the greatest degree of commitment and the longest experience with Umbanda.

I then prepared an 11-page questionnaire consisting mainly of semistructured questions, and a few open-ended ones. With the help of a team of Brazilian university students, I administered it individually to respondents.

The interviews themselves presented extraordinary difficulties. We conducted them in the centros on the evenings of the public ceremonies, during the period preceding the ceremony. Most chefes agreed to ask that the mediums come early, and one chefe insisted on delaying the beginning of the ceremony for over an hour in order to allow us to complete the interviews. This setting made the interviews hectic, often rushed, and far from ideal. However, it was the only one that proved feasible. Since the centros do not serve a primarily local community, interviews in participants' homes would have necessitated excessive travel. Moreover, practitioners of Umbanda, particularly those of the middle sectors, were often extremely reluctant to discuss publicly, with strangers, their connection with this religion, since it suffers from considerable social disapproval and is often a target for criticism. Individuals' homes often proved to be the least satisfactory places for a free discussion of their participation in Umbanda, since, unless all family members were Umbandistas, at least some of them disapproved, and sometimes the subject could not even be broached. Interviewing in the centros, with individuals already dressed for participation in the religious ceremony, precluded any disavowal of faith and placed the interview within the only setting in which Umbanda could be discussed without fear of social censure, since nonbelievers were not present.

The resulting 403 interviews include 389 with mediums, and 14 with chefes (whom I interviewed separately and of whom I asked additional questions concerning the history and social organization of the centro). This number of mediums represents 75 percent or better of the total number of mediums present at each centro on the night of the interviews, with the exception of the extremely large centro where 150 (10 percent) of the 1500 mediums were interviewed. Characteristics of the centros, as well as the numbers and proportions of mediums interviewed, are given below in table 7. Because of the manner in which the sample was selected, the data provide a descriptive rather than a statistically valid characterization of the most active sector of participants in Rio. In addition, because the sample represents various types of Umbanda centros, but not necessarily the proportion in which they are found in Rio, it is likely that the sample includes a greater proportion of middle sector practitioners than is found in the total Umbanda population.[1] With these qualifications, the results provide much data concerning the participants in Umbanda and help to correct misconceptions about their social background. My findings are presented in table form and discussed below. The sample has been analyzed in aggregate form, and thus gives the broad characteristics and range of variation within the sample as a whole. Analysis of internal variations within the sample remains an important task for the future.

Vital Statistics

This section, which treats the age, sex, and marital status of the sample, compares data on the 14 chefes to the sample as a whole and discusses the findings in relation to data on other Afro-Brazilian religions and "possession cults."

The Umbandistas in the sample are predominantly adults of middle age. They have a mean age of 40, and over half of the sample (52 percent) falls between the ages of 30 and 49. Twenty-six percent are 50 or over, and the sample extends upwards to the age of 79 (see table 8). Twenty-two percent are under the age of 30, but only 6.5 percent are under 20. These figures reflect the fact that becoming a medium or joining the ritual corps in an Umbanda centro, because it is a time-consuming activity and requires much responsibility, appeals mainly to adults. Chefes and parents reinforce this pattern by discouraging mediumship before the age of about 18, although a few precocious young mediums, including one 14-year-old in the sample, provide exceptions to this rule. Mediums bring their children and other family members to their centros, but conversion to Umbanda, and especially mediumship, is very much an individual and primarily an adult affair.

Women predominate over men in the sample by a ratio of 2:1 (see table 8). This level of female representation might suggest that Umbanda conforms to

Table 7. Characteristics of the Centros in Which Interviews Were Conducted

Centro No.	1	2	3	4	5	6	7	8	9	10	11	12	13	14
No. of mediums in the centro	1500	20	11	35	8	35	60	58	32	80	25	23	55	22
No. of mediums per session	100-200	20	11	35	8	20	30	35	18	30	15	20	34	22
No. of mediums interviewed	150	16	8	29	5	15	27	29	15	27	15	16	32	18
Percentage of total No. of mediums interviewed	10%	80%	73%	82%	63%	43%	45%	50%	47%	34%	60%	70%	58%	82%
Type of ritual practiced	Umb.	Umb. Linha Oriental	Umb. Linha Oriental	Umb. Kardecista	Umb. Oriental	Umb. Pura	Umb. Pura	Umb. Pura	Umb. Africana	Umb. Pura	Umb. Pura	Umb. Africana	Umb. Africana	Umb. Pura
Location of centro	North suburb zone	North sub. zone	South zone	South zone	North suburb zone	South zone	Cen. Bus. zone	North suburb zone	North rural zone	North rural zone	North sub. zone	North rural zone	State of Rio rural	State of Rio sub.
Socio-economic composition of membership	mixed	mostly middle sector	all mid. sector	mixed	all mid. sector	mixed	mixed	mixed	mixed	mixed	all lower sector	mixed	mixed	mixed

Table 8. Age and Sex of Respondents

Age Group	Females		Males		Total		Age Brackets
	No.	% of total number of Females	No.	% of total number of Males	No.	%	
10-19	20	7	6	4.5	26	6.5	22%
20-29	43	16	20	15	63	16	
30-39	72	27	36	27	108	27	52%
40-49	71	26	30	23	101	25	
50-59	46	17	25	19	71	18	26%
60 and over	17	6	15	11.4	32	8	
No info.					2	.5	
TOTAL	269	100	132	100	403	100	100%
Percentage of total sample by sex	67		33				

the gender pattern described for other Afro-Brazilian religions and to the crosscultural patterns of "peripheral possession cults" described by Lewis (1971). A contexual analysis of my findings, however, indicates that Umbanda follows a quite different pattern.

The Leacocks, in their study of the Batuque, an Afro-Brazilian religion in Belém, estimate a 3:1 ratio of female to male participants (1972:103), a somewhat higher degree of female participation than I found in Umbanda. They claim that this is the result of cultural deterrents placed upon male participation, rather than of the Batuque's greater attraction for women. The participation of males, according to their findings, is limited by the stigma of homosexuality attached to male spirit possession, which is said to conflict with the concept of *machismo* (Ibid.:106-7). In Candomblé as well, males seem to be largely absent from spirit possession roles (Carneiro, 1940; Hamilton 1970; Herskovits 1943; Landes 1947), which seems also to be related in part to the perceived threat to their masculine image.

In Umbanda, however, spirit possession per se seems neither to be viewed as threatening to the masculine image, nor to carry the suspicion of homosexuality. An exception to this is the case of male mediums who, possessed by female Orixás, act in an exaggeratedly effeminate manner,[2] a situation that occurs chiefly in the more Afro-Brazilian centros. A few such centros have an openly gay orientation and a large gay clientele. Elsewhere, however, such a performance would run a high risk of open ridicule and even of expulsion from the centro. Umbanda, then, is unlike Afro-Brazilian religions such as the Batuque where this type of performance has come to dominate and stigmatize the public image of male spirit possession as a whole. In this respect, Umbanda, and particularly Umbanda Pura, seems rather to resemble Kardecism, where male spirit possession carries no stigma whatsoever. The influence of Kardecism on Umbanda may well have helped to legitimize spirit possession for male participants in Umbanda.

Another difference between patterns of male participation in Batuque and Umbanda is that while most of the mediums in the Batuque are young men, with male participation reportedly decreasing markedly among middleaged and older men (Leacock and Leacock 1972:106-7), in Umbanda the proportion of male participation increases slightly with age. Thus 53 percent of the male participants are 40 or over, a slightly higher proportion than that found for women (50 percent). This same pattern of increased male participation with age is also found in Kardecism (Renshaw 1969:119).

An even more significant aspect of male participation in Umbanda, that it also shares with Kardecism, is the disproportionate representation of males in leadership roles. My small sample of chefes, which includes 8 males and 6 females, accords with my wider observations in other centros that there are more male than female chefes, despite the smaller overall number of male participants. Moreover, the fact that the mean age of female chefes (55) is nearly ten years greater than that of male chefes (46) (see table 9) suggests that while women may hold leadership roles, they may require greater age to be accepted in these roles than do men. For example, one of the male chefes in the sample is 23, and he has been the chefe of a very successful centro since the age of 15. It is not uncommon for young men who give early evidence of superior spiritual talents to become accomplished religious leaders by their early 20s, as was the case also with Zélio de Moraes, Umbanda's founder. Yet, when I asked mediums in this young leader's centro whether a young woman of this same age might take a similar leadership role, they responded emphatically that she would be far too young to do so, and some men showed great amusement at my query.

Men, most of them from the middle sectors, are found almost exclusively in the top Umbanda administrative positions, as presidents and directors of Umbanda centros and leaders of Umbanda federations. This reflects both general patterns of male dominance in Brazilian society and the fact that Umbanda leadership positions attract aspiring politicians, most of whom are male. The selective factors that favor males in leadership positions, however, do not preclude the emergence of a number of female chefes, some of whom have become well known, and of a few successful women Umbanda politicians. Patterns of male dominance also do not apply among the lower ranks of the ritual hierarchy, where skills in trance performance take precedence over both sex and age, and where even very young women may hold prestigious positions as médiuns de consulta. In general, though, the smaller overall numbers of men than of women in Umbanda conceal their political dominance.

Another significant point is that the ratio of male participation in Umbanda appears to be *higher* than in Afro-Brazilian religions such as Batuque. It may also be higher than male participation in Brazilian Catholicism, which has traditionally been regarded as "woman's business" (Azevedo 1962:68; see also Brody 1973:449; Willems 1953:71; 1957:43). It has even been suggested that the general lack of male involvement in Catholicism may be related to a conflict between the image of male virility and the ideal of priestly celibacy (Azevedo 1962:68). Priests may be ridiculed and even accused of homosexuality (Brody 1973:355). Lower rates of male than female participation in Umbanda, then, may in reality reflect wider cultural patterns of gender participation in other Brazilian religions. Ironically, what may be emerging in Umbanda, and in Kardecism as well, is a *higher proportion* of male participation, with less stigma for male virility, than has been customary within areas of either Catholic or Afro-Catholic religious practice.[3]

This leaves the important question concerning the significance of the extensive female participation in Umbanda largely unexplored, and my data can only suggest directions to pursue. With respect to women in leadership

Table 9. Chefes in the Sample by Age and Sex

Age	29-29	30-39	40-49	50-59	60+	Total	Mean Age
Females	0	1	0	3	2	6	55
Males	1	2	1	2	2	8	46
TOTAL	1	3	1	5	4	14	

positions, it appears crucial to consider class distinctions. While relatively few female Umbanda leaders have emerged within the middle sectors, which remain dominated by men, I have the impression that female *chefes* are far more numerous and influential in the lower sectors. This would suggest a pattern long observed in Bahian Candomblé (see for example Landes 1947), whose lower sector environment has spawned many female religious leaders who have achieved considerable influence within the city.

Another possible interpretation of predominantly female possession religions has been proposed by Lewis (1971), who suggests that certain kinds of "peripheral possession cults" provide vehicles of self-expression for women and lower status men who are excluded from full participation in the society in which they live (Lewis 1971:88). However, the class and gender composition of Umbanda's membership, and particularly of its leadership, suggests that just as Umbanda cannot be categorized as a religion of the oppressed, it also does not fit this related model of a possession cult of the oppressed, although other Afro-Brazilian religions such as the Batuque in Belém may do so. Umbanda appears to fit far more closely the category at the other extreme of Lewis' polar model, the "central possession religion" in which "men of substance compete for positions of power and authority in society" (Ibid.:34). This suggests that an important distinction may exist between Umbanda and other Afro-Brazilian religions with respect to the significance of gender participation.

The significant degree of joint nuclear family participation in Umbanda centros also argues against an uncritical interpretation of this religion as a domain of women. Of the total sample, including both men and women, 59 percent are married (including common-law marriages), 27 percent single, 10 percent widowed, and 4 percent *desquitado* (separated—Brazil until 1979 had no legal divorce) (see table 10). Married women between the ages of 30 and 49 form the largest category (38 percent) of the entire sample, while married men make up another 21 percent. Single men and women fall mainly below the age of 39, and there is a sizeable group of widowed women (9 percent of the sample), most of whom are over 50, but very few widowed men. Of the married mediums in the sample, over one-third (36 percent) report their spouse also attends the centro regularly (see table 28), a pattern also noted in Umbanda in Belém (by Leacock and Leacock, 1972:106). Frequently, both husband and wife are mediums, or a medium's spouse may work in an administrative capacity in the centro. Mediums often bring their children to their centros as well. Over two-thirds (69 percent) of those with children report that they, too, attend the centro, and 6 percent report their children are mediums in their centro (see table 19). Thus, Umbanda attracts men and women of all types of family situation, those who are single or widowed, and many who participate together as families.

The complex picture of women's participation in Umbanda that emerges

Table 10. Marital Status of Respondents According to Age and Sex

	10-19	20-29	30-39	40-49	50-59	60 + over	Total by sex		Total	
							No.	%	No.	%
Married									238	59
Women	0	21	52	52	22	7	154	38		
Men	0	3	22	24	21	14	84	21		
Single									109	27
Women	20	22	15	8	5	0	70	17		
Men	6	16	11	3	3	0	39	10		
Widowed									39	9.7
Women	0	0	3	6	17	10	36	9		
Men	0	0	0	2	1	0	3	1		
Separated									15	3.8
Women	0	0	2	5	2	0	9	2.2		
Men	0	1	3	1	0	1	6	1.5		
No Information									2	.5
TOTAL	26	63	108	101	71	32			403	100.0

from these data indicates clearly that the numerical dominance of females in Umbanda, which might suggest that it is a woman's domain, must be qualified. It is clearer in Umbanda than in some other Afro-Brazilian religions that this predominance of women is due to its greater attraction for them and not to cultural barriers inhibiting active male participation. Yet the central questions of how Umbanda serves as an important domain for women's participation and leadership, and what it may express of women participants' own viewpoints, aspirations, and dissatisfactions, still remain to be investigated.

Social Class, Race, and Rural-Urban Origins

I have made extensive reference to Umbanda's middle and lower sectors and have indicated that because these groups cannot be treated as classes in the sense of groups having social or ideological cohesion, I have used the term middle and lower sectors in a very broad sense, referring to the social and occupational distinction between nonmanual and manual labor (see also chapter 1, note 1). This classification has been followed in Brazil and elsewhere in Latin America, for example, by Soares (1966; 1968) and by Adams (1967).

Individuals in the sample are classified as "middle sector" if they are engaged in white collar, nonmanual occupations, and "lower sector" if engaged in blue collar manual occupations. Full-time housewives are classified according to their husband's occupation, and unemployed, unmarried individuals below the age of 25 and living at home, according to the occupation of their parents. Based on this classification, 51 percent of the sample can be classified as middle sector and 38 percent as lower sector (see table 11). Eleven percent remains unclassified due to a lack of information. As I have indicated, the sample reveals the significant degree of middle sector participation in

Table 11.   Race and Class of Respondents

	White		Mulatto		Black		Totals	
	No.	% of Whites	No.	% of Mulattos	No.	% of Blacks	No.	%
Middle sectors (non-manual labor)	144	68.2	48	40.3	14	19.4	206	51.1
Lower sectors (manual labor)	48	22.7	54	45.4	50	69.4	152	37.7
Unclassified	9	4.2	2	1.6	6	8.3	17	4.2
No information	10	4.7	15	12.6	2	2.7	27	6.7
TOTAL	211	100.0	119	100.0	72	100.0	403	100.0

Umbanda in Rio but not necessarily the proportional representation of different social sectors.

In order to consider in more detail the occupations of those employed in paid labor, it is necessary to exclude 41.5 percent of the sample, who are *donas de casa* (housewives) engaged in unpaid household labor, and 3.5 percent who are full-time students. Thirty-three percent of the total sample are employed in sectors of the economy associated primarily with middle sector, nonmanual activities: 13 percent in commerce, 8 percent in the civil service, 7 percent in the professions (of which the highest proportion are school teachers), 4 percent in the military officer corps, and .5 percent as owners or managers of small industries. Twenty-six percent of the sample is engaged in occupations involving manual labor, both skilled (15 percent) and semi- or unskilled (10 percent) (see table 12).

Salaries range from 15 percent of the sample who, as unskilled laborers, *biscateiros* (odd jobbers), domestic servants, and washerwomen, make the minimum salary or below (in 1969–70 the minimum salary was NCr$156, or $39.00, per month), to 12 percent who make a clearly middle sector salary of over NCr$1,000 per month ($250.00) in managerial positions in large business or as professionals (see table 13). Figures on salaries were unobtainable for a large proportion (29 percent) of the respondents,[4] but even if this 29 percent were to fall into the two lowest census salary categories, there is still a higher

Table 12.   Economic Sectors in Which Respondents Were Employed

Category	No.	%
Housewife	155	38.5
Student	14	3.5
Employed: non-manual sectors		
Civil servant	32	7.9
Military (Officers)	17	4.2
Professions	24	6.0
Commerce	53	13.1
Employed: manual sectors		
Transport	4	1.0
Industry	9	2.2
Skilled labor	50	12.4
Semi- and unskilled labor	44	11.0
No information	1	.2
TOTAL	403	100.0

Table 13. Salaries of Respondents* Compared with Working Population of Guanabara

Salary per Month ($NCr 4 = $1.00)	Lower Sectors (manual labor)	Middle Sectors (non-manual labor)	Total		Salaries of the Working Population of Guanabara, 1969[+]
			No.	%	
Minimum Salary (NCr$156) or below	59	2	61	15.1	29%
NCr$156-400	57	57	114	28.3	47.6%
NCr$401-800	7	43	50	12.4	15.3%
NCr$800+	1	60	61	15.1	8.0%
No information on salary	28	44	72	18.0	
No information on class or salary			45	11.2	
TOTAL	152	206	403	100	100%

*Housewives are classified by their husband's salary and occupation and unemployed, unmarried individuals below the age of 25 and living at home according to the salary and occupation of their parents.

+ Anuário Estatístico, 1971:535.

proportion of individuals (27 percent of the sample) who make NCr$400 per month or more (roughly $100.00) than occurs in the working population of Guanabara in 1969.

The level of education of the respondents shows a similar range of variation: 12 percent have had no schooling, 44 percent have some primary school education, 36 percent have attended high school, and 8 percent have attended college (see table 14).

The racial composition of the sample of Umbandistas has been classified as 52 percent white, 29 percent mulatto, and 18 percent black.[5] The Umbanda sample shows a somewhat higher proportion of mulattos and blacks than is found in the general population when compared with census figures on race for 1960 (the last year in which the census included such figures), which classified the population of Guanabara as 70 percent white, 11 percent *pardo* (mulatto) and 11 percent black (I.B.G.E. 1960:8). When these racial categories are correlated with social class, it is evident that participants in Umbanda reflect the prevalent Brazilian distribution of race according to class, with the majority of the whites in the sample (68 percent) found in the middle sectors and the majority of the blacks (69 percent) in the lower sectors. However, several interesting points emerge: although the representation of whites in Umbanda (52 percent) is somewhat lower than that among the general population of Guanabara (70 percent), they form a significant portion of Umbanda's membership (see table 11) and demonstrate clearly that Umbanda cannot be

Table 14.   Educational Background of Respondents

Category	No.	%		Educational level of Guanabara Population 15 and over*
None	48	11.9		
Primary School			= 56.3	66%
incomplete	92	22.8		
complete	87	21.6		
Secondary School				
incomplete	59	14.6		
complete	30	7.4	= 35.4	28%
College preparatory	54	13.4		
College	33	8.2		8.3%
TOTAL	403	99.9		

*I.B.G.E., Censo Demográfico de 1960. Vol. I, Tomo XII(2):19.

considered primarily a "religion of a colored proletariat," as suggested by Bastide (1960:519–58) in terms of either class or race. Whites form an even more significant proportion of Umbanda leadership. The race/class membership of the chefes in my sample may somewhat overrepresent the proportion of middle sector whites: 12 of the 14 chefes had middle sector occupations, and of these 11 were whites and one mulatto, while the two lower sector chefes were mulatto and black. These figures cannot be taken to represent Umbanda chefes as a whole, but they do illustrate and support my wider observations concerning the frequency of white middle sector centro leadership.

The proportion of middle sector mulattos and blacks in the sample (40.3 percent of the total number of mulattos, and 19 percent of the blacks) also deserves comment. While it reflects the generally lower representation of these racial categories in the middle sector, their representation is at the same time significant enough to refute predictions made by earlier researchers working principally in northeastern Brazil that upwardly mobile mulattos and blacks would seek to dissociate themselves as much as possible from all aspects of the African cultural heritage (see Azevedo 1955:191; Hutchinson, in Wagley 1952:42; Pierson 1942:313). Clearly this has not occurred in Umbanda. These predictions appear to have derived from ideas, prevalent in modernization theories, that with access to education and upward mobility, "backward" or "traditional" practices such as Afro-Brazilian religions would be abandoned. What these theories failed to take into account was that just as individuals may, at least in theory, become upwardly mobile, so may cultural practices. Umbanda, as it has gained a measure of respectability and has ceased to be identified with either an exclusively Afro-Brazilian or a lower sector membership, has continued to attract upwardly mobile blacks and mulattos. What is not clear and remains a subject for future research is how middle sector Brazilian blacks and mulattos view Umbanda: whether they participate simply as members of the middle sectors, for whom Umbanda has now become a legitimate religion, or whether they do so because they retain an identification with their African roots.

According to another prevalent misconception, Umbanda participants are primarily rural migrants, and one of Umbanda's most important functions is the integration of these migrants into urban life (Camargo 1961:65–69; Levy 1968:28; 43ff.; Willems 1966:224–25). This hypothesis seems to be based on the convergence of Umbanda's emphasis on providing solutions to personal problems with the timing of the period of its expansion, which began after 1945 and coincided with extensive internal migrations from rural areas of Brazil to Rio and other major cities. Researchers assumed a functional relationship between these migrations and the growth of Umbanda.

My data on the respondents' place of birth and major residence suggest, to the contrary, that Umbanda is preeminently a religion of urbanites. The overwhelming majority of the respondents are urban-born: 43 percent are natives of Guanabara (the city of Rio), which is now regarded in the official census as totally urbanized, and of the remainder, 17 percent were born in state capitals, 18 percent in municipal capitals, and 10 percent in small towns. Only 10 percent were born on the *roça* (farm), and less than 2 percent list this distinctively rural setting as their major residence (see table 15). Since the great majority of Umbandistas are adult converts, it is likely that even for the 10 percent of the sample with rural origins, many had already become urban residents prior to joining Umbanda. In fact, I have the impression that in Rio, at least, for the great majority of Umbandistas, joining an Umbanda centro might better be taken as an *indicator* of socialization to urban life than as a means of acquiring it.

Table 15.   Rural-Urban Background of Respondents: Place of Major Residence

Residence	No.	%
Guanabara (urban)	295	73.2
Other states:		
State capital	65	16.1
County seat	23	5.7
Small town	8	2.0
The *Roça* (farm)	7	1.7
No information	5	1.2
TOTAL	403	99.9

My data, then, challenge the hypothesis that Umbanda's expansion in major southern cities is to an important degree a result of rural-urban migration. The Leacocks, studying the Batuque in the northern city of Belém, also concluded that rural migration had not been a major factor in that religion's growth (1972:113). I would not preclude the possibility that Umbanda, with its strongly instrumental, problem-solving orientation might, in other specific settings, help to integrate rural migrants. This might occur, for example, in the so-called "dormitory cities," such as Caxias and São João do Meriti in the surrounding State of Rio, which are principal receiving areas for rural migrants. I did not conduct research in these areas. Nevertheless, the data from my questionnaire suggest that rural-urban migration neither has provided the bulk of Umbanda's membership nor explains its growth. From its founders and early leaders to its present membership, it presents a consistently urban picture.

Religious Background and Participation in Umbanda

This section explores the religious background and current affiliation(s) of respondents to the questionnaire, as well as some of the dimensions of their participation in Umbanda.

Since Umbanda is of recent origin and many adherents join as adults, they have been raised in other religions. While this situation might seem to lead naturally into a discussion of conversion to Umbanda, the issue is more complex. Participation in Umbanda may overlap with continued participation in other religions, and the boundaries between them are often blurred. Many practitioners of Umbanda do not consider themselves exclusively Umbandistas (some Umbanda mediums do not consider themselves Umbandistas at all), and many practice and identify with other religions in addition to Umbanda.

This is partially a result of the structure of Umbanda, its lack of central institutional controls, and the resulting high levels of autonomy of individual chefes to encourage or discourage their members' participation in other religions. However, a tacit or sometimes quite explicit universalist stance seems to have developed within Umbanda, according to which it is said to tolerate and embrace all other religions. Its practitioners, therefore, need neither abandon their former religions nor consider them incompatible with Umbanda. Overlapping or multiple religious affiliations are also affected to an important degree by the attitudes and controls exercised by the other religions toward their members' participation in Umbanda, for example, a dramatic contrast can be seen between the Catholic Church and Pentecostal Protestant sects. Catholicism, at least nominally, is the official religion of over 90 percent of the Brazilian population. Yet despite the Church's continuing efforts to prevent Catholics from practicing Umbanda, its lack of effectiveness is revealed in the data from my questionnaire, while the same data suggest that the Pentecostal churches are far more effective in this regard.

Eighty-seven percent of the sample reported they were raised as Catholics, 9 percent as Spiritists (5 percent as Umbandistas and 4 percent as Kardecists), 0.7 percent as Protestants, and .5 percent as Jews (see table 16). Respondents were then asked whether they still considered themselves to be adherents of their former religion (see table 17). Of the group that had been raised as Catholics, a majority (56 percent) stated they no longer considered themselves Catholics. In this respect Umbanda appears to differ from Afro-Brazilian religions, in which the great majority of adherents continue to consider themselves Catholics (see for example Pierson 1942; Leacock and Leacock 1972:82). It closely resembles Kardecism, whose practitioners also tend to dissociate themselves from Catholicism (Renshaw 1969:128). This willingness to assume an identity as Umbandistas may be related to Umbanda's increasing legitimacy within Brazilian society. However, I am convinced that the data

Table 16.   Religion in Which Respondents Were Raised

Religion	No.	%
Catholic	351	87.1
Protestant	3	.7
Jewish	2	.5
Umbanda	22	5.5
Kardecism	15	3.7
None	8	2.0
No information	2	.4
TOTAL	403	99.9

Table 17.   Relation of Respondents to Their Former Religion

Natal religion	Still retain former religious affiliation		No longer retain former religious affiliation	
	No.	%	No.	%
Catholic	153	44	198	56
Protestant	0	0	3	100
Jewish	2	100	0	0
Kardecist	13	87	2	13

from my questionnaire also reflect respondents' far greater willingness to declare their faith when interviewed within their centros than to do so on official religious census forms. This group may properly be spoken of as "converts" to Umbanda.

Respondents who considered themselves both Umbandistas and Catholics (44 percent of those raised as Catholics) were then asked whether they believed Catholicism and Umbanda to be 1) "complementary religions which form part of a single religious system," (2) "separate religions," or 3) "religions in conflict with each other" (see table 18). Over half (60 percent) of this group selected the first response and several commented, "Catholicism and Umbanda? It's the same thing," which suggests that the distinction between the two religions is frequently blurred or may be entirely lost. In such cases, where the two religions are seen as parts of a single religious system, the notion of dual religious affiliation may not be an appropriate one to use for Catholic Umbandistas. Only the Catholic Umbandistas who felt either that there was no relation between Catholicism and Umbanda (28 percent) or that there was conflict between them (11 percent) may properly be considered to hold dual religious affiliation.

Table 18. Catholic Umbandistas' Attitudes Concerning the Relationship
between Umbanda and Catholicism*

Response of Catholic-Umbandistas	No.	%
Felt that Catholicism and Umbanda are "complementary religions which form parts of a single religious system"	92	60.1
Felt that there "is no relation between the two religions"	43	28.1
Felt that "there is a certain amount of conflict between them"	17	11.1
No Opinion	1	.7
TOTAL	153	100.0

*Respondents were asked to select from the above three choices.

The percentages of those in the sample who were raised as Protestants (0.7 percent) or Jews (0.5 percent) are far too small to be statistically significant, yet they provide interesting comparisons with the group raised as Catholics. The two individuals raised as Jews still consider themselves to be Jews as well as Umbandistas. Rather than the preservation of an ethnic Jewish identity subsequent to religious conversion, this appears to be dual religious affiliation. Umbanda's eclectic and universalist tendencies and the perceived continuity of mystical traditions stemming from the Kabbala are seen as providing a bridge between Umbanda and Judaism. One respondent declared that the origin of Umbanda lay in Judaism. The other had formerly belonged to the Umbanda centro mentioned in chapter 5 as composed entirely of Jewish-Umbandistas oriented to the study of the Kabbala.

The three individuals raised as Protestants, on the other hand, show no tendency to maintain their former religion. This supports my strong impression, from conversations with both former and practicing Protestants not included in the sample, that Brazilian Protestants, most of whom are Pentecostalists, regard their religion and Umbanda to be totally incompatible. This impression of mutual exclusivity between Protestantism and Umbanda is further supported by data on the religious affiliations of nuclear family members of the respondents, where a similarly low incidence of Protestantism is found among the parents (1.2 percent among fathers, 2.2 percent among mothers) and among spouses (1.0 percent) (see table 19). This exclusivity, which appears so marked in contrast to the relationship between Umbanda and Catholicism, seems to be more a result of aggressive campaigning and stringent pressures from Protestant pastors than of individual practitioners' own sense of incompatibility. The sense of an incompatibility, or even a conflict, between

Table 19.   Religious Affiliation of Respondents'
Immediate Families

| | Father | | Mother | | Spouse | |
	No.	%	No.	%	No.	%
Umbandista	65	16.1	83	20.6	124	30.8
Catholic	240	59.6	258	64.0	102	25.3
Kardecist	32	8.0	27	6.7	29	7.2
Protestant	5	1.2	9	2.2	4	1.0
Jewish	3	.7	2	.5	3	.7
No religion	25	6.2	11	2.7	25	6.2
Don't know	28	6.9	10	2.5	0	0.0
No information	5	1.2	3	.7	9	2.2
TOTAL	403	99.9	403	99.9	296	73.4

Catholicism and Umbanda among 39 percent of the Catholics in the sample, for example, does not prevent them from actively identifying with and practicing both religions. The Protestant ministers' smaller congregations and greater degree of personal contact with and control over their members than is found in the Catholic Churches may well be a crucial factor in their ability to prevent dual affiliation between Protestantism and Umbanda.

The majority of respondents (64 percent) have had no contacts with Spiritism prior to their entry into Umbanda. However, 26 percent report that they have previously attended or been mediums at Kardecist centros, and another 5 percent have participated in other occult forms of Spiritism. Thirteen percent report previous contact with Afro-Brazilian religions, which are identified variously as "Candomblé," "Macumba," or "Quimbanda" (see table 20). Both of Umbanda's progenitors, Kardecism and Afro-Brazilian religions, have provided sources of Umbanda's membership. The greater proportion of former Kardecists may be significant in confirming a migration from Kardecism to Umbanda, or it may simply reflect a disproportionate number of middle sector individuals among the respondents and a concomitantly stronger representation of Kardecist traditions.

The majority (62 percent) of the respondents originally visited their current centro seeking some kind of aid: 38 percent report an illness, 5 percent financial and other material problems such as unemployment, and 18 percent unspecified *problemas espirituais* (spiritual problems). Similar problems undoubtedly lie behind the responses of the 20 percent who report more vaguely that "someone brought them" (see table 1, chapter 6). Only 13 percent list non-problem-oriented reasons for their initial contact with their current

Table 20. Attendance at Other Forms of Spiritism Prior to Umbanda

	No.	%	No.	%
Have attended other forms of Spiritism			141	35.0
Kardecism	106	26.3		
Occult groups	20	5.0		
Candomblé	24	6.0		
Macumba	11	2.7		
Quimbanda	14	3.5		
Have not attended other forms of Spiritism			257	63.8
No information			5	1.2
TOTAL			403	100.0

centro: 11 percent came out of curiosity and 2 percent "to help." A high proportion of Umbandistas among the parents and spouses of respondents, however, suggests that although individuals may join Umbanda for personal motives, there may also be a considerable degree of family influence involved in such a choice. Sixteen percent of the sample have fathers who are Umbandistas, 21 percent have mothers who are, and 31 percent (roughly half of those married) have Umbandista spouses (see table 19). The pattern of family influence continues among Umbandistas' children. Of the 64 percent of the sample with children, over two-thirds report that their children attend their centro; of these, 39 percent attend only their Umbanda centro, while 30 percent attend a Catholic Church as well (see table 21).

Social Networks in Umbanda Centros

While I have described illnesses and problems as providing the principal motive for seeking Umbanda and successful solutions to various difficulties as an important reason for joining a centro, the data suggest that social networks also play an important role in the selection of a centro. For example, my model of the growth of Umbanda centros suggested that successful centros depend on a loyal and stable membership core, the nucleus of which is provided by the chefe's immediate family and friends. The chefes in my sample show an extremely high level of participation by members of their immediate families. Seven of the ten who are married have a spouse who also serves as a medium in the centro, while two other spouses are important figures in the administration of the centro. Three of these chefes have children who are mediums in the centro, one of whom is being groomed to succeed his father when he retires. Of

Table 21.   Attendance of Respondents' Children at Umbanda Centros

	No.	% of Sample	No.	% of Sample
Those with children			257	63.8
Children attend only centro	100	24.8		
Children attend centro and other church	76	18.9		
TOTAL	176	43.7		
Children do not participate in any religion	33	8.2		
Children are Catholics	37	9.2		
Children are Jewish	1	0.2		
Children ae Baptists	1	0.2		
Children are Quimbandistas	1	0.2		
Children are considered too young to attend	3	0.7		
TOTAL	76	18.9		
No information	5	1.2		
Have no children			142	35.2
No information			4	1.0
TOTAL			403	100.0

those not married, one has a mother and the other two have sisters who are important mediums in their centros.

Nonfamily members of the ritual corps may also give long and faithful service within Umbanda centros and are crucial in the recruitment of all categories of new clients and members. There appear to be two distinct patterns of membership: a stable core of mediums with many years of loyal participation in their centros, and what might be called a "fluctuating periphery" of mediums who remain only a short time and move frequently from one centro to another. Forty percent of the respondents have been mediums in their current centro for five years or more; 21 percent for ten years or more, and 5 percent for twenty years or more (see table 22). The long-time participants, particularly those remaining ten years or more, give stability to centros, and each of the older centros reveals a core of participants whose length of service equals the age of the centro. Of the 56 percent of those who have been mediums in their centros for less than five years, many must be eliminated from the category of short-time participants either because their centros themselves are less than three years old (12 percent) or because of their own relatively short span of participation in Umbanda.

Table 22. Length of Time in Present Centro

No. of Years	No.	%
0-4	224	55.6
5-9	75	18.6
10-14	36	8.9
15-19	28	6.9
20+	19	4.7
No information	21	5.2
TOTAL	403	99.9

For half of the sample (48 percent), their current centro is the only one they have ever attended (see table 23). The other half (48 percent) have attended other centros, as visitors (20 percent), as members (2 percent), or as mediums (25 percent). The fact that the majority of those who have been mediums elsewhere are among those who have attended their current centro for less than five years suggests that there may be another roughly 20 percent of mediums who belong to the fluctuating periphery.

Table 23. Previous Participation in Other Umbanda Centros

	No.	%	No.	%
None			194	48.1
Some			192	47.6
As a casual visitor	81	20.1		
As a member	9	2.2		
As a medium	98	24.3		
As a founder or chefe	4	1.0		
No information			17	4.2
TOTAL			403	99.9

Over half the sample (58 percent) report that they participate twice or more weekly in Umbanda ceremonies, and 17 percent three or more times weekly (see table 24). Since most of the ceremonies are held weeknights, and mediums must often go directly to the centro from their employment, regular participation three times a week is undertaken mainly by chefes (who may spend almost every evening at the centro) and by mediums who do not hold full-time jobs or have families. Those who participate only once a week (22 percent) or once every two weeks (12 percent) include many of the participants in more Afro-Brazilian style rituals, which are held less frequently, usually on Saturday nights.

Table 24.   Frequency of Participation at Current Centro

	No.	%
Every two weeks	49	12.2
Once a week	90	22.3
Twice a week	169	41.9
Three times a week	55	13.6
Four or more times a week	12	3.0
No information	28	7.0
TOTAL	403	100.0

Mediums rarely visit centros other than the one to which they currently belong, except on occasions when the chefe and the ritual corps together make a ceremonial visit to another centro to participate in a joint religious ritual. This occurs only when the chefes are friends and share a similar ritual orientation.[6] Otherwise, chefes tend to disapprove of and even forbid visits to other centros. Only 8 percent of the sample report they attend other centros, 5 percent for occasional visits and 3 percent on a regular basis (see table 25). This latter category includes exceptional cases such as one woman who reported to me in an interview that her spirits demanded she dedicate every evening to Umbanda. She had become a full medium in three different centros, where she participated in rituals on different nights of the week. Unlike the great majority of mediums, this woman appeared to be highly nervous and perhaps emotionally disturbed.

The number of the respondents' family members, friends, neighbors, and business acquaintances who also attend their centros suggests the importance of personal networks as a source of recruitment to Umbanda centros. Eighty-

Table 25.   Attendance at Other Centros

Attendance	No.	%	No.	%
No			354	87.8
Yes			34	8.4
Infrequently	19	4.7		
Regularly	6	1.5		
Member of another centro	9	2.2		
No information			15	3.7
TOTAL			403	99.9

two percent of the respondents had been introduced to their current centro through such connections: 31 percent by family members, 35 percent by friends, 11 percent by neighbors and more casual acquaintances, and 6 percent by contacts at their place of work (see table 26). This latter category refers primarily to workmates, but it also includes six individuals introduced into their centros by their employer. Of these, two worked in firms, and four worked in paid domestic labor and had been brought to their centro by their *patroa* (female boss). The reverse situation may also occur, although it is not represented in the sample: I met several affluent women who had been introduced into their centros by their own domestic servants. Only 11 percent of the sample reported making their initial contact with their current centro through such impersonal means as advertisements on the radio or in weekly Umbanda columns in the newspaper (2 percent), passing the centro on the bus (3 percent), or living nearby (6 percent).

Table 26.   How Respondents Made Contact with Their Present Centro

	No	%	No.	%
Personal Contacts			329	81.6
Through relatives	123	30.5		
Through friends	141	34.9		
Through colleagues at business or school	16	4.0		
Through their employer	6	1.5		
Through acquaintances	43	10.7		
Impersonal Contacts			45	11.2
Through the mass media	9	2.2		
Live nearby	23	5.7		
Passed it on the street	13	3.2		
Founded the centro			14	3.5
Don't know			4	1.0
No information			11	2.7
TOTAL			403	100.0

Primary networks of members are also important in the ongoing recruitment of new personnel to the centros. Fifty percent of the respondents report that they themselves have introduced other members of their social networks into their centros. Of these, over half (54 percent) have brought two or more relatives, friends, neighbors, *compadres* (ritual kinspersons), and 30 percent have brought three or more (see table 27). Some of these have, in turn, become mediums. Eighty percent of my sample reports that at least one

Table 27.   Respondents' Activities in Introducing New Individuals to
Their Centro

	No.	%	No.	%
Introduced no one			192	47.6
Introduced others from their social network			202	50.1
Relatives	50	12.4		
Compadres	2	.5		
Neighbors	9	2.2		
Colleagues	4	1.0		
Friends	28	6.9		
Two of the above categories	48	11.9		
Three or more of the above categories	61	15.1		
No information			9	2.2
TOTAL			403	99.9

member of their social network from outside of the centro presently attends it, and 51 percent reports that three or more do so (see table 28). Sixty percent report that some member of their *parentela* (kindred) attends their centro: 14 percent have parents, 21 percent have spouses, and 15 percent have children who attend. In addition, 21 percent have siblings, 18 percent cousins or nephews, aunts or uncles, and 11 percent in-laws there. One-third (33 percent) of the sample reports that at least one of those relatives is a medium at their centro.

Forty percent of the respondents have friends who attend the centro, 31 percent have neighbors, 17 percent school or business colleagues, and 11 percent have compadres. The importance of these primary networks in recruitment means that for the majority of members, going to the centro provides a regular basis for visits with members of their networks and thus helps to maintain the networks themselves.

A striking contrast emerges between the importance of these primary networks and the infrequency with which respondents report that their centros serve as sources of new friendships or contacts. Of the sample, 70 percent report they do not socialize outside the centro with anyone they have met there. Of the 28 percent who do, most pay only occasional visits to other centro members in their homes (see table 29).

This suggests that the majority of Umbandistas do not utilize Umbanda

Table 28. Members of Respondents' Social Networks
Who Currently Attend Their Centros

	No.	%	No.	%	No.	%
No one					77	19.1
Some					318	78.9
Relatives			239	59.3		
Parents	56	13.9				
Siblings	88	21.8				
Children	61	15.1				
Spouse	86	21.3				
Collateral relatives	74	18.4				
Affines	45	11.2				
Compadres			46	11.4		
Neighbors			126	31.3		
Friends			159	39.5		
Colleagues from office or school			67	16.6		
No information					8	2.0
TOTAL					403	100.0

Table 29. Degree of Socializing Outside the Centro with Friends Made
Within the Centro

Socializing with them	No.	%
Never	288	71.5
Sometimes, go to a movie or take a walk	10	2.5
Yes, visit them in their homes	86	21.3
No information	19	4.7
TOTAL	403	100.0

centros as a means of expanding their social networks (although, as will be seen, important contacts of a socio-economic or political nature may be established within the centros). It would thus appear that centros form around previously existing social networks of their members to a far greater degree than they are instrumental in creating new ones.

9

The History of Umbanda in Rio

I now want to examine various aspects of Umbanda's development within the broader context of socio-political change during the period 1930-1970, giving particular attention to the ways in which Umbanda has been shaped by and has participated in the wider development of Brazilian populism and clientele politics during this period. After relating the activities and ideology of Umbanda's early, formative phase to the political context of the Vargas dictatorship, I will then move to the period of its explosive expansion, beginning with the return to electoral politics in 1945. Shortly after this time, Umbanda began to take shape as a political interest group. I will consider the role of the Umbanda federations and the Catholic Church in this process and the effects upon Umbanda of the 1964 military coup. Finally, I will evaluate Umbanda's level of social legitimacy at the end of the 1960s, by which time it had achieved its current dimensions.

Umbanda under the Vargas Dictatorship 1930–45

The beginnings of Umbanda closely coincided with Getúlio Vargas' rise to power in 1930. Rio was at that time the national capital and, like other southern cities, was experiencing both rapid industrial growth and tremendous expansion within the middle and lower sectors of the urban population. Vargas' takeover represented the economic and political victory of new urban upper sector interests over those of older agrarian elites. His support of industrial development, his strongly nationalistic stance on both economic and cultural matters, his expansion of the state bureaucracy to provide employment for the middle sectors, and his extension of the franchise and provision of social security benefits to workers all formed part of his effort to gain the support of these new expanding urban populations and to bind diverse regional interests into a strongly centralized national state. These policies effectively masked for many of those affected by them what was in fact the creation of a highly authoritarian regime, consolidated in 1937 with the creation of the *Estado Nôvo* (New State), which was modeled on the Italian Fascist State.

Umbanda's founders and early leaders, like many members of the middle sectors during the period, were enthusiastic supporters of Vargas' policies. Zélio de Moraes, Umbanda's "founder," became a local Vargas politician in his home town. Among other early Umbandista leaders were young military officers sympathetic to the extreme nationalism of the *tenentes,* a group of young army officers who during the early years of Vargas' regime furnished him with some of his strongest support. Vargas' intense nationalism and his efforts to create a national culture as a basis for the unification of the Brazilian state were undoubtedly important stimuli to the development of the strongly nationalist themes in Umbanda.

Despite their support of Vargas' policies, Umbandistas suffered considerably under the repression that characterized the period of the Estado Nôvo (1937-1945). Although this was directed mainly against leftist political organizations and labor unions, it touched as well far less radical social and religious groups: the Masons, the Kardecists, and Umbanda and the Afro-Brazilian religions. A 1934 law placed all of these groups under the jurisdicition of the Rio Police Department's Vice Squad (*Departamento de Tóxicos e Mistificações,* or Department of Toxicants and Frauds), in the special division of *Costumes e Diversões* (Customs and Diversions) which also handled problems of alcohol, drugs, illegal gambling, and prostitution. These groups were required to obtain special registration from their local police departments in order to function, and the police set their own fees. This law thus categorized their practices in social terms as marginal, deviant activities and, by implication or association, as vices requiring punitive rather than simple regulatory social controls. This classification remained in force for Umbanda centros until the 1964 reorganization of the Rio Police Department.

The police, who were the main agents of repression during this period (Skidmore 1967:29-30), were apparently given a free rein in dealing with what were construed as potential enemies of the state. Kardecists, who had both a well-established and nonpolitical middle sector following, including a core of influential defenders from the professions, survived with little difficulty, despite the reported suppression of a few of their publications. Umbanda and the Afro-Brazilian religions, however, enjoyed no such protection. Afro-Brazilian terreiros had been subjected to sporadic police harassment since at least the 1920s, and probably considerably before. Feared and despised by the upper sectors, and used mainly by the lower sectors, they were vulnerable targets for various forms of persecution and extortion. Umbanda, still a small and unknown religion, was publically indentified with these Afro-Brazilian religions, and suffered the same fate.

The 1934 law placed practitioners of Umbanda and Afro-Brazilian religions in a double bind: in theory, registration allowed them to practice legally: in fact, however, it attracted the attention of the police and increased the likelihood of harassment and extortion. Registered or not, Umbandistas and their Afro-Brazilian coreligionists incurred severe police persecution in Rio, as did other Afro-Brazilian religions in the northeast (see for example Landes 1947; Ribeiro 1952). Police raided and closed down terreiros, confiscating ritual objects and often jailing the participants as well. In addition, they reportedly extorted large sums of money in return for promises of protection. I spoke with several old-time Umbandistas who vividly recalled the police raids of this period and the fear and secrecy in which ceremonies were conducted.

Though they were required to register, understandably few Umbandistas wished to attract the notice of the police. The majority, like the Afro-Brazilian terreiros, went underground and performed their rituals in secret, behind locked doors. Even in the late 1960s, long after the Vargas regime, when the registration policy had been changed to require only a civil registration—the filling in of forms, a payment of $25.00, and a wait of two or three weeks—the continuing legacy of fear and isolated cases of police harassment made many centros extremely reluctant to register.

The police evidently justified the persecutions of this period by claiming that "Macumba" was riddled with subversives. I interviewed one highly placed Rio police official who openly admitted his own role in the harassment and assured me that "Macumba" terreiros had been hotbeds of Communist activity. He claimed that Ogum, the Yoruba deity of war popularly represented by statues of his Catholic counterpart St. George, mounted on a white horse and wearing a large red cape, had been popularly known and worshipped during the 1930s and early 1940s as the *Cavaleiro Vermelho da Esperança* (the Red Horseman of Hope). Older Umbandistas who had been active participants in Umbanda and other Afro-Brazilian religions during this earlier period scornfully denied any acquaintance with such an interpretation of Ogum or St. George, and while I found scattered indications of leftist sympathies among a few terreiros during the period,[1] I found no evidence either of a leftist or of any other clearly defined political orientation among any of these religious groups.

Today, Umbandistas, like many other sectors of the Brazilian population, seem to have forgotten these repressive aspects of the Vargas regime and look back upon Vargas with favor.[2] Until 1964, when with the advent of the military dictatorship any form of public political expression became politically dangerous, many Umbanda centros displayed his photograph along with representations of the Umbanda spirits. Many Umbandistas are convinced that Vargas was himself an Umbandista. One elderly man I met claimed to remember the centro, now defunct, that Vargas had attended. Umbandistas and some sectors of the public now remember

Vargas as a friend to the cults, and blame the persecutions of this period on earlier governments. A 1967 article in the *Jornal do Brasil,* Rio's leading newspaper, for example, named a particular police chief in the government of Washington Luis (president of Brazil from 1926 to 1930) as the one responsible for the persecutions and claimed that Getúlio Vargas was their liberator. He "not only permitted the terreiros to function openly, but frequented them as well" (*Jornal do Brasil,* 11/30/67). Thus, the ideology of the Vargas dictatorship is reflected in Umbanda, and the harsh treatment of its practitioners has been erased from memory.

The police harassment of this period had another important effect upon Umbanda: it stimulated Umbandistas to organize for their own protection. It was in 1939, during the height of the Estado Nôvo, that Zélio de Moraes and other leaders of major Umbanda centros formed the first Umbanda federation, the *União Espírita de Umbanda do Brasil* (Spiritist Union of Umbanda in Brazil) for the express purpose of providing protection against police harassment to all Umbanda centros who affiliated with it. While this federation, which I will refer to hereafter as the UEUB, had only a limited effect in counteracting the persecutions of its member centros, it almost immediately became an important base for organizing other activities. It was this federation whose leaders in 1941 organized and sponsored the first Umbanda Congress, the major early effort to formally codify Umbanda doctrine and ritual, discussed at length in chapter 3. The intensity of these leaders' efforts to dissociate Umbanda from its Afro-Brazilian image may even have been due in part to their desire to escape the persecutions to which the Afro-Brazilian religious groups were subjected. This federation continued to be a major influence in Umbanda in the postwar period.

The Vargas regime's repression of Afro-Brazilian religions in northeastern Brazil also stimulated the formation of federations for their protection, in Recife in 1935, and in Salvador, Bahia in 1937. Unlike the Rio federations, whose organizers were themselves founders and practitioners of Umbanda, the founders of the northeastern federations tended to be outsiders. Some were scientists interested in studying the mental health and capacities of Brazilians of African descent, and others were intellectuals interested in preserving the Afro-Brazilian cultural heritage (see for example *Estudos Afro-Brasilieros* 1935; Freyre 1937). In the northeast, the sponsorship and protection of Afro-Brazilian religions took the form of a paternalistic noblesse oblige, combined with scientific and artistic interests on the part of the intelligentsia, while in Rio it may be viewed as representing an effort from within the expanding middle sectors at a new form of self-identification in religious terms. In both of these regions, however, these federations quickly assumed the role of upper or middle sector patrons to unprotected lower sector religious practices. In Rio, this was soon to become translated directly into political activity and the middle sector mobilization of lower sector voters.

This new interest from within the more affluent sectors in learning about, protecting, and thus preserving Afro-Brazilian religions reflected several convergent currents of interest in the Afro-Brazilian heritage. Artistic and intellectual circles felt the influence of the intensely nationalistic modernist movement, which had begun in 1922, and the Romantic interest in Indianist and African themes which had permeated Brazilian literature. I have already mentioned the growing interest of social scientists in these religions during this period. While in Rio Artur Ramos made disparaging comments about "Macumba," in the Northeast, sociologists and folklorists were discovering the value of many aspects of the Afro-Brazilian heritage and becoming interested in their preservation. The organizer of the first Congress of Afro-Brazilian religions, in Recife in 1934, was none other than Gilberto Freyre, the author of *The Masters and the Slaves,* who was himself from Recife. He was also instrumental in organizing the first protective federation for these religious groups in that city the following year (see *Estudos Afro-Brasileiros* 1935; Freyre 1937). The Vargas government, which had its own strong reasons for encouraging public interest in discovering the ingredients of the Brazilian identity, both built upon and played to these growing nationalist concerns. Umbanda, then, absorbed its form, its themes, and its ideology from the socio-economic and political environment of the period and was not the only Afro-Brazilian religion to be so affected.

Many details concerning the development of Umbanda during the 1930s and early 1940s remain obscure. The identity of its early leadership, their organizational activities, and their aspirations for their religion are reflected in the early literature, especially in documents such as the proceedings of the first Umbanda Congress (Anon. 1942), yet little is known of the extent of the activities of rank and file Umbandistas. Undoubtedly the political climate of persecution and its negative public image acted to limit both Umbanda's size and its appeal, although to what degree is impossible to judge. It clearly experienced some growth, since several of the leaders who were to emerge during the postwar period first became active during this time. Umbandistas have suggested that anxieties and tensions created by the combined effects of the Estado Nôvo and the Second World War stimulated many individuals to seek comfort and solace in Umbanda and other forms of Spiritism (see Pessoa, quoted in Anon. 1944:148-49; and *O Semanário* 8/1-7/59).

The years prior to 1945 comprise an initial phase during which Umbanda appears to have remained limited mainly to a small group in Rio. Judging by the first Umbanda Congress, its major early landmark, Umbanda during this period remained confined mainly within the circle of its original founders. Only local Umbandistas and their invited guests attended the Congress. These included Kardecists, with whom Umbandistas felt considerable affinity, and members of the press. Apparently, in keeping with the effort to de-Africanize Umbanda, practitioners of Afro-Brazilian religions were not invited. The radical change in attitude toward these groups that was to begin during the 1950s and to result in efforts to draw them into Umbanda, was not yet in evidence.

Umbanda and Electoral Politics 1945–70

The year 1945 marks the beginning of Umbanda's period of tremendous expansion and its rapid transformation from a small local sect into a national religion. This year brought not only the end of World War II but also the end of the 15-year Vargas dictatorship and the return to constitutional government. For Umbandistas, the period of systematic persecution ended. Umbanda could now be practiced openly, and this new freedom resulted in a tremendous burst of organizational activity. New centros opened, new federations formed, and Umbanda began to appear in the mass media, in radio programs, in weekly columns in major Rio newspapers, and in numerous publications of its own. As Umbanda gained thousands of new adherents in Rio, among both the middle and lower sectors of the population, and as its activities gained attention, many Afro-Brazilian terreiros began to identify themselves publicly with this new image of Umbanda. Sometimes this involved a move towards the rituals and cosmology of Umbanda's founders; often it did not. Umbanda also began to diffuse rapidly to other states and regions of Brazil, gaining, as in Rio, new adherents and influence over various regional Afro-Brazilian religions. Like the Brazilian state within which it had emerged, Umbanda now began to exercise a homogenizing influence over many regional religious traditions, muting their distinctiveness and shaping them in the direction of a national Afro-Brazilian religious culture.

In this postwar period, Umbanda continued to respond to political developments in Brazilian society. In fact, both its expansion and its increasing legitimation are enmeshed in national and local level political processes and cannot be understood apart from them. The return to constitutional government in 1945 brought with it the return to electoral politics for the first time in 15 years. Vargas' electoral reforms of the 1930s had greatly extended suffrage within the urban lower sectors, and from 1945 onward this sector of the population became significant electorally at all levels of politics. In Rio and other large cities, where the size of the lower sector electorate soon greatly exceeded that of the middle and upper sectors, politicians were quick to follow the example set by Vargas in wooing the support of the urban masses, utilizing, as had Vargas, techniques of populism and personal appeals to various clientele and interest groups.

Umbanda leaders' efforts to protect their practitioners from police persecution had already led them to organize the first Umbanda federation. Umbanda federations now began to proliferate, and their leaders sought further legitimacy and protection for Umbanda through the political process, forming alliances with elected politicians and themselves attempting political careers. Diverse politicians in search of access to political supporters, particularly within the lower sectors, also recognized in Umbanda and Afro-Brazilian religions important potential sources of such support. The ensuing political activities that resulted from the interest of these various politicians played an important part in creating publicity, new members, and social legitimacy for Umbanda.

In examining the interrelated processes of Umbanda's political involvement and its growth in greater detail, I will continue to view these from the perspective of middle sector Umbanda leaders from the same networks involved in the codification of Umbanda Pura. I will take as my principal vantage point the *Jornal de Umbanda,* a monthly publication begun in 1949 by founders of the first Umbanda Federation, the UEUB, who had also sponsored the First Congress of Umbanda, in 1941. The *Jornal de Umbanda* provides a good point from which to observe this group's developing interest in politics in the postwar period. Though today this newspaper is of only minor importance, it was Umbanda's major newspaper during the 1950s and early 1960s, and represented the most influential middle sector interests.

The Jornal de Umbanda covered both local and national Umbanda events. In addition, it contained articles and debates on points of doctrine and ritual; a column entitled *"O Que os Outros Dizem de Nós"* ("What Others Say About Us"), which quoted both friends and enemies and discussed Umbanda's public image; and reviews of the many books and periodicals on Umbanda that now began to appear. There was also a women's page entitled *"O Nosso Lar"* ("Our Home"), which dealt with fashions, food, comportment, and the many types of subservience to men considered fitting for female Umbandistas. This newspaper was financed by subscriptions and through advertising, a large part of which came from the makers and sellers of items used in various aspects of Umbanda ritual: statues, candles, beads, and other ritual decorations, herbal baths, soaps, magical powders, incense.

Its first issue indicated clearly that the *Jornal de Umbanda* did not intend to remain an internal house organ for members of the UEUB. It hoped to become a national forum for reportage and discussion and to provide extensive coverage and maintain contacts with Umbandistas in other states. By the early 1950s, Umbanda was already well established in Rio Grande do Sul,[3] and it was also beginning to appear in the capital cities of São Paulo and

Minas Gerais. The editors and writers of the *Jornal de Umbanda* initiated contacts with leaders of new centros and federations in these areas and encouraged all who traveled there to visit their organizations and report on their activities.

The *Jornal de Umbanda* also reported on a wide variety of events taking place in Umbanda in Rio, including the emergence of new political figures and the activities of new, rival Umbanda federations. Space was also provided to newcomers to Umbanda, such as Attila Nunes, a young journalist who in 1947 started the first Umbanda radio program, *Melodias de Terreiros* (Terreiro Melodies), which featured the pontos sung in Umbanda rituals performed by various guest centros over the air. This program also publicized social and religious events in various Umbanda centros and federations and their activities throughout the city. In seven years, the program grew from 15 minutes once a week to a twice-weekly two hour program, and just over ten years after its founding, Attila Nunes became the first Umbandista in Rio to be elected to public office.[4] He was elected *vereador* (city councilman) in 1958, and in 1960 he became Rio's first Umbandista state deputy. The *Jornal de Umbanda* and Attila's radio program exchanged free publicity for each other's news and events, and leaders of the UEUB cooperated with Attila in organizing various social and religious gatherings.

The Umbanda Federations

News items in the *Jornal de Umbanda* soon began to feature the activities of new Umbanda federations appearing in the wake of the publicity generated by the UEUB, and especially by Attila Nunes' radio program. These followed the general organizational model of the UEUB, with boards of directors, composed of chefes of centros and administrators, working to affiliate individual Umbanda centros by offering them protection and various kinds of services in return for a small monthly dues (in 1969 this ranged from $1.00 to $5.00) and their participation in the various religious and social activities that the federations organized and sponsored.

Although Umbanda centros were no longer targets for systematic harassment, they were still required to register (until 1964 with the police and after that, in the civil registry office). They continued to experience incidents of extortion by police officials and many complaints from their own neighbors, who objected to their activities, particularly to the noise level during ceremonies. Federations' offers of protection now centered on providing assistance in legal registration and supplying lawyers and bureaucratic advice in cases of harassment or infringements of freedom of religious practice. In addition, they sponsored collective religious ceremonies, organized religious processions on the principal Umbanda holidays, and sometimes offered classes in doctrine or ritual practice. While intended as a way of attracting new member centros, these latter events were also used as a means of influencing their members' ritual practices and doctrine. More affluent federations that championed the cause of Umbanda Pura were especially concerned with promoting this particular ritual form. Although they tended to accept for membership any centro that defined itself as practicing Umbanda, they subsequently attempted to impose their own standards for ritual practice upon them. Some even organized periodic unscheduled visits to member centros to check on the type of ceremonies being held, (I was occasionally mistaken for an inspector for one or another of the federations). Umbanda federations competed actively for affiliates and measured their respective strengths by the numbers of their member centros and the size of the turnouts at their various public activities. The high frequency of federation leaders' involvement in politics further suggests that political ambitions lay behind the fierce competition among them and that they viewed their affiliated centros as potential political clienteles.

The extent of the federations' influence over Umbanda is a complicated issue. Certainly they have never at any point in their history affiliated more than a small minority of the Umbanda centros in Rio; most have preferred to remain autonomous. Through their ties to the mass media and to politicians, however, the federations have been able to exercise a degree of influence on Umbanda that has been disproportionate to the actual numbers of their affiliates. For example, their ritual guidelines, while not always complied with by member centros, have, through the mass media, had a standardizing influence on Umbanda ritual practice. Moreover, links forged among centros have helped to create a sense of group identity among Umbandistas. Through overseeing the registration of individual centros, the federations have also had an important role in legalizing Umbanda practice. As intermediaries between their affiliates and local community leaders, politicians, and the mass media, they have helped to smooth relations with non-Umbandistas, improve Umbanda's public image, and thus contribute to its social legitimacy.

The numbers of Umbanda federations that continue to operate at the local, state, and national level testify to the ongoing political competitions and rivalry among them. Umbanda federations, like most Umbanda centros, have resisted any permanent moves toward centralization and unification. Umbanda, in this respect, contrasts strongly with Kardecism, the great majority of whose centros throughout Brazil have joined and accepted the standards of doctrine and practice set by the *Federação Espírita Brasileira* (Brazilian Spiritist Federation). The fact that Umbanda federations continue to represent different and competing interpretations of Umbanda ritual and different social sectors is unquestionably a source of the dynamism, flexibility, and innovative spirit that characterize this religion.

By the mid 1950s, six new Umbanda federations had been formed in Rio and the adjoining State of Rio, in addition to the UEUB. Three of these had been organized by middle sector Umbandistas and followed the general lines of ritual and doctrinal orientation of Umbanda Pura. One was formed by a former affiliate of the UEUB, the chefe of a large Umbanda centro who had run unsuccessfully for town councilman and then abandoned the UEUB to found his own rival federation, apparently in an effort to create a base for his own future political activity.

The other three federations championed an African-oriented form of Umbanda. Their leaders were mainly from the lower sectors, and many were blacks and mulattos. The first of these federations, which was formed in 1952 under the name "Spiritist Umbanda Federation," was led by Tancredo da Silva Pinto, the same Afro-Brazilian leader named as a defender of an Afro-Brazilian identity for Umbanda in chapter 3. Tancredo was also able to acquire a weekly column in the largest of Rio's daily tabloids, *O Dia,* through connections with its owner, Chagas Freitas, himself a politician. In this column, Tancredo solicited affiliates for his new federation, promised them protection, and recommended an African form of Umbanda ritual. These affiliates and supporters came almost entirely from the lower sector, African-style terreiros, many of them located in the city's favelas. Tancredo became their major spokesman and a legendary leader who gained the title *Tata de Umbanda* (Pope of Umbanda). At the time of my first research in 1966, I was struck by his reputation and fame in favelas throughout the city. In each one that I visited, someone was sure to mention his name, and many of the centros in these surroundings were long-time affiliates of his federation.

Tancredo also maintained alliances with leaders of other, similar federations in the State of Rio, and together with them he coauthored a number of books on African-style Umbanda, one of which was quoted in Chapter 3 as stating the "Africanist" opposition to Umbanda Pura. A network of Umbanda federations thus formed within the lower sectors paralleling that organized by middle sector Umbanda leaders but representing a quite different understanding of the word "Umbanda." I have already alluded to this Africanist voice in opposition to middle sector "White Umbanda" and to its insistence on Umbanda's identity as part of the African heritage.

It might seem that the emergence of parallel Umbanda networks, white and black, represented a move toward racial separatism. Racially separatist organizations had appeared in both Rio and São Paulo in the early 1940s, for example *The Teatro Experimental do Negro* (Experimental Negro Theater), founded in Rio in 1944 (cf. Costa Pinto 1955:270-90). Individuals from this experimental theater even visited Afro-Brazilian Umbanda centros during the early 1950s to suggest that they, too, should take a similar separatist stand. These visitors voiced their support of Umbanda, but proposed that black

Umbandistas should worship a black Christ (Freitas and Pinto 1956:84-85). Tancredo and other Afro-Brazilian religious leaders angrily rejected this suggestion, calling it part of an "ugly campaign"

> to provoke racial and religious separatism ... and to divide the population into whites and blacks. ... It might seem at first glance that the idea of a black Christ is designed to elevate the negroes ... but in fact it is an attempt at agitation and racial separatism, which our historical traditions have always rejected. (Ibid.:84-85)

At this point, in the mid 1950s, black Afro-Brazilian Umbanda leaders, while they clearly recognized the racial issue involved in the dispute over Umbanda's African identity, rejected the more radical position of racial separatism. They seem to have been preoccupied with the narrower concerns of defending Umbanda's African identity rather than with wider issues of racism in Brazilian society; they couched their criticisms and exchanged insults in the language of social class and religious differences rather than in terms of race. However, it seemed that two forms of Umbanda had developed: one within the middle sector, influenced by Kardecism and the desire to create a socially respectable, non-African image; and the other representing more Afro-Brazilian forms of practice. The two were mutually hostile, with conflicts on the level of ritual deepened by the class and racial differences that underlay them. There seemed little basis for or prospect of a political coalition between these two Umbandas.

Nevertheless, in 1956, the same year in which the book quoted above was published, the *Jornal de Umbanda* announced that the leaders and federations representing these two different forms of Umbanda had joined together to form a coalition. Named the *Colegiado Espírita do Cruzeiro do Sul* (Spiritist College of the Southern Cross), this new coalition brought together the five most active federations in Rio to work for the unity of Umbanda. With the UEUB as its main sponsor, it included Tancredo's Umbanda federation, and Tancredo himself was named as a copresident.

What could have occurred to stimulate such a rapprochement? From the middle sector perspective, the answer suggested by subsequent events is that as the political advantages of such an alliance became more evident to Umbandistas, similar political interests came to outweigh class, racial, and ritual differences. The political campaign to gain support and representation for Umbanda and to elect Umbanda leaders to public office had so far met with little success. In the period from 1950–54 at least three leaders of large and affluent Umbanda centros, with upwards of 500 members, all affiliates of the UEUB, had run for city councilman. Each had made a respectable showing, gaining upwards of 1500 votes, about one-half the number required for election, but none was elected. Middle sector Umbanda leaders recognized that neither an individual centro nor an individual Umbanda federation could provide a sufficient base for successful election and that a broader coalition was required in order to amass sufficient numbers of political supporters. The Afro-Brazilian terreiros offered a potential source of such supporters, and thus middle sector leaders resolved to enlist these terreiros, submerging their own doctrinal and ritual concerns in the interests of winning elections. Some of these middle sector Umbanda leaders wanted to extend this coalition to include Kardecists as well, but these efforts were generally not successful, since most Kardecists were not interested in either politics or Umbanda. However, perhaps in the interests of reaching potential individual Kardecist supporters, Umbandista politicians throughout this period often chose to use the inclusive (and more socially acceptable) term "Spiritist" rather than "Umbandista" in their political appeals in the mass media.

Why Afro-Brazilian Umbandistas should have joined in this coalition remains more problematic, since far less is known of the political activities of this sector of Umbanda. I would speculate that their leaders were attracted by promises of protection, social legitimacy, and potential political advantages to be had from an alliance with middle sector leaders. Some of these Afro-Brazilian leaders also had their own political goals in mind, as will be evident in the next chapter.

With the formation of the Colegiado, the pages of the *Jornal de Umbanda* immediately began to reflect greatly increased political activity among Umbanda leaders. By the time of the 1958 elections, this newspaper presented a large slate of Spiritist candidates, making no reference to the type of Spiritism that they practiced. This political effort extended beyond candidates from the city of Rio de Janeiro (then the State of Guanabara) to include candidates from the adjoining State of Rio and from São Paulo. "Let us go to the polls...and vote for Spiritist candidates," urged the *Jornal de Umbanda* (8/58). In Rio, their campaign resulted in the election of two Umbandista *vereadores* (city councilmen).

The Colegiado was not the only organ interested in mounting political efforts. The leader of one Umbanda centro called a meeting of leading Umbandistas in Rio to propose the formation of a Spiritist political party, an idea that found much popular support but was rejected by the Umbanda leadership. *O Semanário,* a nationalist political weekly which during the late 1950s devoted an average of two pages per issue to Spiritist news, launched a third effort to create a pan-Spiritist political alliance and to promote Umbanda as the national religion of Brazil.

These various competitive coalitions were successful in gaining considerably more political representation for Umbanda, although they did not result in permanent alliances or have any lasting effect in creating a higher level of unity within it. In 1960, Umbandistas succeeded in electing their own candidates in several states. In Rio, Attila Nunes, the young journalist who in

1947 had begun the first Umbanda radio program and in 1958 had been elected city councilman, became the first Umbandista to be elected state deputy in Rio primarily through reliance on Umbanda voters. Several more local Umbandista politicians would undoubtedly have been elected there as well, had it not been for the conversion earlier that year of the Federal District into the new State of Guanabara and the ensuing abolition of all elective offices below the rank of state deputy.[5]

In the state of Rio Grande do Sul, Umbandistas had also recently elected another state deputy, Moab Caldas. Like Attila Nunes, Moab had begun his career in Umbanda as a radio announcer, which attests to the importance of the mass media in Brazil as a basis for political campaigning. Rio Grande do Sul also elected three Umbandista mayors and some 20 city councilmen, which indicated Umbanda's political strength in that state.

The Second Congress of Umbanda, organized by the Colegiado and held in Rio in 1961, was a measure of the changes that had occurred in Umbanda during the 20 years since the First Congress in 1941. This Second Congress took place in a large Rio soccer stadium and several thousand Umbandistas attended, including representatives from ten states and various state and city officials. Discussions of doctrine and ritual shared the stage with politics, and Umbanda's newly elected politicians were euphoric about the movement's political potential both locally and nationally. "Umbandistas," declared one state deputy, "this is only the beginning. If you all unite, then we can elect federal deputies and even state governors" (quoted in McGregor 1967:181). "Umbanda is the national religion of Brazil," the other deputy declared: "[Its] electoral force has become a reality... not only in the small cities of the interior but in the large cities as well" (quoted in *Manchete,* 11/61).

If these political victories seem limited and the euphoria exaggerated, it is important to remember that only 15 years before, in 1945, Umbanda could not even protect itself against police harassment, let alone mobilize political representation. It had now emerged into public view. Members of the professional sectors and elected politicians openly declared their belief in it, and championed their religion in state legislatures, defending the issues of religious freedom, and making impassioned speeches against the legal constraints still placed upon many aspects of its practice.[6] Its new representation within the formal political process now put it in a position to achieve still greater levels of institutionalization and legitimacy.

These gains were in important measure the result of Umbanda's electoral expansion through alliances with lower sector Afro-Brazilian Umbanda terreiros, which provided access to the lower sector electorate. It is debatable whether they could have been achieved without this electoral support. Together with the creation of alliances with Afro-Brazilian terreiros, federation leaders now expanded Umbanda's ritual boundaries and moved from a narrow insistence on Umbanda Pura to a position of ritual heterodoxy. They now spoke of Umbanda as embracing several *seitas* (sects, or ritual styles), all of them equally valid expressions of Umbanda. Some federations even renamed themselves as federations of Umbanda and Afro-Brazilian sects.

Umbanda as a Political Interest Group

Before discussing the effects of this political representation in helping to create legal and social legitimacy for Umbanda, I want to touch briefly on the nature of Umbanda's involvement in politics. It had come to constitute a religious interest group and provides a very clear illustration of the workings of interest group politics in the postwar period. Umbanda voters represented considerable diversity in their social and political interests and opinions; many had little in common beyond their support of Umbanda. Umbandista politicians represented different political parties as well, but campaigners avoided as much as possible both references to the party affiliation of political candidates and any discussion of political ideology or specific political issues that might divide Umbandista voters. The *Jornal de Umbanda,* for example, rarely mentioned party affiliations and never the specific political persuasion of the candidates whom it publicized and supported in the political slates published in the months before election time. Likewise, it avoided mention of all political issues outside of Umbanda. In reading almost the complete run of over 20 years of this newspaper, I found only two overt references to secular political issues, both of which advocated democratic ideals and warned against extremism, a common middle sector position during this period. A 1953 article condemned extremism of both the left (Communism) and the right (Integralism)[7] as threatening to the current regime and the interests of democracy, and recommended the proper course of action towards Communists in Umbanda centros: "to give *passes* (a spiritual cleansing) to a Communist is permitted, but they must not be allowed to infiltrate our organization" (*Jornal de Umbanda* 1-2/53). In 1959, the *Jornal de Umbanda* came out in favor of agrarian reform: "If we do not pass this, the Communists will take over" (6/59).

The same strategy of avoidance may be seen in other efforts at political unification, such as that launched from the pages of *O Semanário,* which represented a considerably more leftist and socialist position. Although *O Semanário* made a strong appeal to Umbandistas' nationalist sentiments, promoting the election of candidates who represented leftist political positions, it too avoided any reference to the party affiliations and political platforms supported by these candidates.[8] Nor were these topics mentioned at the Second Umbanda Congress.

Umbanda thus managed to become involved in politics without assuming any clear and unambiguous political identification. Voters were urged to support candidates because they supported or were themselves Umbandistas. This emphasis on the narrow, unifying interests of a particular group, which is typical of interest group politics, is a major reason why interest groups and the patronage structures that support them often undermine both the effectiveness of party politics and any confrontation with wider political issues. Interest groups may also serve to mask underlying differences in the class interests of their leaders. Undoubtedly, many of the politicians who supported Umbanda and courted its voters used Umbanda as a means of gaining support for their own middle and upper sector political agendas, which had little, if anything, to do either with Umbanda or with the sectoral interests of its less affluent supporters.

Umbandistas and the politicians who courted the Umbanda vote rallied around two principal causes: nationalism and the defense of religious freedom. Articles in the *Jornal de Umbanda, O Semanário,* and in many other Umbanda columns and publications referred repeatedly to Umbanda as "Uma Religião Brasileira" (A Brazilian Religion), "Umbanda, Religião Nacional do Brasil" (the National Religion of Brazil), "Umbanda, ideal religiosa para o Brasil" (the religious ideal for Brazil). They frequently alluded to the Freyrian theme of Brazil as the unique product of miscegenation and Umbanda as the true and unique Brazilian religious expression of this intermixture. In the post-1945 period, nationalism remained a central theme in secular politics for politicians of all political persuasions, ranging from the far left to the far right. It was closely identified with the development of populism during this period and was employed as a political tool for winning the support of the urban masses. Nationalist themes in Umbanda resonated with those in secular politics; they were ideally suited to unify the diverse social and political interests represented within Umbanda and to mask the differences among them.

The Role of the Catholic Church

The Catholic Church provided Umbandistas with their major rationale for Umbanda's entry into the political arena. Since the late nineteenth century the Church's official communications had periodically warned against the Spiritist heresy, and soon after 1945, these began to make specific references to Umbanda. In 1952, perhaps influenced by the results of the 1950 religious census which revealed Catholicism to be losing ground to both Protestantism and Spiritism,[9] the Catholic Church launched a major attack on these religions. The newly created CNBB (Conselho Nacional dos Bispos Brasileiros), formed to facilitate communication within sectors of the

Brazilian Church hierarchy and to give the Church a base for wider and more active social participation in Brazilian life, declared the Spiritist menace its first order of business. At its first meeting, held in Belém in August 1953, it concluded that of all the threats to Catholic supremacy, among which it counted Protestantism, Communism, Masonry, and others, "Spiritism is at the moment the most dangerous doctrinal threat to the natural religiosity of the Brazilian people" (quoted in Kloppenburg 1961b:17). The CNBB then formed an anti-Spiritism committee "to draw up a plan for a national campaign against Spiritism" (Ibid.:9). This campaign, which was launched from the pulpit and through the mass media, both refuted the Spiritist heresy and denounced "hybrid types of Catholic-Spiritists" (Ibid.:120), threatening them with excommunication (Ibid.:77). This attack was directed primarily at Umbandistas, whose members tend far more than Kardecists to hold dual religious affiliations. The Church declared its duty "to strip the mask of Christianity from the face of Spiritism and to tell Catholics that it is impossible to be at the same time a Catholic and a Spiritist" (Ibid.:13).

The campaign soon came to focus on Umbanda. Public conferences and TV appearances denounced Umbanda as a "fraud" and attacked it in books, pamphlets, and articles. The leader and major spokesman in this campaign, Franciscan friar Boaventura Kloppenburg, summed up the attack on Umbanda in a book entitled *Umbanda no Brasil: Orientação para Católicos,* (*Umbanda in Brazil: Orientation for Catholics*), whose publication date was timed to coincide with the opening day of the Second Umbanda Congress in 1961. Published by the official Catholic press and designed for both clerics and laymen, it is a well-researched polemic that attacks Umbanda on religious, moral, racial, and political grounds and declares it a menace to mental health. In addition to labeling it a heresy, this book identifies Umbanda as pagan, fetichistic, and based on superstition and fraudulent magical practices (Kloppenburg 1961a:207). It is accused of encouraging generally loose and permissive moral attitudes towards sexual practices and favoring abortion and the use of birth control (Ibid.:91-92).[10] Umbanda is then belittled with racial slurs as the "result of the black blood which runs in the veins of 33 percent of [the Brazilian] population" (Ibid.:207) and of the African racial heritage which "turns religion into mere superstition." The book further attacks Umbanda in particular, and Spiritism in general, as favoring the spread of Communism: "The pantheism and latent materialism of Spiritism provide the best basis for the atheism and materialism of the Communists" (Kloppenburg 1964:371-72). Finally, with regard to mental health, Spiritism of all kinds (here, read "spirit possession") is said to be based on and to encourge pathological and deviant behavior, madness, hysteria, and epilepsy. Not only are all mediums said to be of an "abnormal type, insane, neurotic, disequilibrated, degenerate, hysteric," but Spiritism is said to cause these pathological reactions in spectators as well (Kloppenburg 1961b:167-68).

This violent attack seems to have had very little effect in curbing Umbanda's growth, though it certainly must have contributed to its negative public image among nonbelievers and encouraged many practitioners to keep their religious beliefs to themselves. However, it provided Umbanda leaders with a most effective political rallying point and a justification for unification and political mobilization: the need to defend freedom of religious practice against attack. Umbandistas were able to follow closely the Church's denunciations of their religion which were quoted in the *Jornal de Umbanda*, the columns of *O Semanário*, and other new media. These provided kindling for their anticlerical sentiments, and more importantly, they provided a rationale for Umbanda's entry into politics. Umbanda's founders had expressly prohibited their religion from becoming involved in politics, and injunctions against participating in political activities were routinely written into the statutes of virtually every Umbanda centro and federation. However, in the face of both the Church's declaration of war against Spiritism and its own participation in electoral campaigning through the *Liga Católico Eleitoral* (The Catholic Electoral League), Umbandista leaders declared themselves compelled to organize politically in defense of their own religion. "It is impossible for us to organize a 'Liga Umbandista,'" declared the *Jornal de Umbanda*, "but Umbanda, in order to defend itself [against the Catholic Church's accusations] needs political organization" (8/54). It advised: "Vote carefully. Do not vote for LEC [Catholic] candidates; vote for Umbandista candidates in order to protect Umbanda" (8/55). A 1958 article discussing the dictatorial manner by which the Church sought to maintain its monopoly over Brazilian religious life declared: "Although we must not involve our religion with politics, it is clear that [Umbandistas] must not abdicate their civil rights ... to maintain freedom of religious practice" (8/58).

Those who proposed in 1958 to found a Spiritist political party similarly based their appeal on the grounds that Umbanda was threatened by the clergy and that the only way it could protect itself was through the formation of a political party which would unify all Umbandistas (reported in the *Jornal de Umbanda* 4/58). This suggestion received considerable popular support but was rejected by the Umbanda leadership—probably a wise political decision since Umbanda certainly did not have enough support to become effective as a political party. However, politicians were able to use these pleas for defense against the Catholic attackers to urge Umbanda voters to form a religious interest group, and they succeeded in mobilizing electoral support along religious lines.

The Church, then, not only failed dramatically to stem Umbanda's growth; but by its frontal attack, which stimulated Umbandistas to unify and mobilize politically, it probably contributed to it. Umbanda's unity and level of political mobilization achieved their height during the period of the Church's major attacks; the end of the Church's crusade against Umbanda robbed Umbanda politicians of an effective rationale for mobilization.

After 1962, following the directives of the Second Vatican Council, the Catholic Church in Brazil revised its posture toward Umbanda and other forms of Spiritism, adopting a stance of "liturgical pluralism." Abandoning its attack on Umbandistas, it now began a new campaign to appease them and to declare them valid religions in their own right. It even made some attempts to capitalize on exactly the syncretic aspects of Afro-Catholicism that it had formerly worked to abolish (see Kloppenburg 1969:7-8). In Rio, for example, the Church commissioned an Afro-Brazilian popular mass entitled the *Missa do Morro* (Shantytown Mass). Afro-Brazilian masses also began to be celebrated in Bahia (see Hamilton 1970:359) and promoted by the CNBB, the group that had spearheaded the anti-Spiritist campaign in 1953 (*O Globo* 10/69:12). It is ironic that at the same time that middle sector leaders of Umbanda Pura were working to influence Afro-Brazilian groups in the direction of a "whitened" and de-Africanized Umbanda, the Catholic Church was attempting to move in exactly the opposite direction, toward a greater tolerance of African influences in popular rituals.

On the level of individual pratice, Umbandistas seem to have been no more affected by the Church's new efforts at reconciliation than they had been by its earlier attacks. No one with whom I spoke felt that either the Church's attack or its later appeasement had affected their participation in Umbanda, although some appeared to be glad that the Church's open hostilities had ended. One said to me, "We never had anything against the Church, and we're glad they don't have anything against us any more, either."

The Effects of the 1964 Military Coup

The 1964 military coup, which abruptly reversed the liberal and radicalizing tendencies of the previous 15 years and once again imposed a harsh dictatorship, had significantly few negative effects on Umbanda. After the coup, a very few of the more openly leftist Umbanda politicians in Rio Grande do Sul and São Paulo were *cassado* (stripped of political rights). This did not happen in Rio, but a few of the more leftist federation leaders did abandon the Umbanda political scene. This had a minor effect in reducing the spectrum of political views among Umbanda's leaders, and created a somewhat greater degree of homogeneity and conservatism among those who remained.

Military officers quickly became far more visible and numerous as leaders of Umbanda centros and federations. Umbanda, like Kardecism, has always drawn many members from among the military officer corps. "This is the military's hour," one Umbandista remarked to me. "After all, when they are in command of the country, you are likely to find them in command of Umbanda as well." He was not implying simply that the military had taken over Umbanda, but rather that they now became the preferred candidates from among the Umbandistas contesting leadership positions. Umbandistas clearly recognized that this increased visibility of the military presence in Umbanda would improve their image with the government and their security in a period of harsh repression. Strengthened links to the military government also increased opportunities for closer cooperation between it and Umbanda leaders. On the one hand, it raised the possibility that Umbanda might be utilized as an instrument of political control. I know of at least one effort by an Umbanda leader who was a high-ranking military officer to obtain government funds to set up an information service for monitoring the presence and activities of Communists in Umbanda centros. The government refused his offer, but the initiative in itself reveals Umbanda's vulnerability to serve the government's ends. Undoubtedly these military linkages also strengthened the dictatorship's ideological influence within Umbanda. On the other hand, these same factors increased the opportunities for protection, support, and favors to be channeled downward from the government to the Umbanda federations, then to the individual centros and their memberships.

Umbanda fared well at the hands of the military dictatorship instituted in 1964. Unlike the previous dictatorship under Vargas, this new military government did not deny Umbandistas their political rights as Umbandistas or freedom of religious practice. Instead, it supported the social and political gains of the previous 15 years and helped to institutionalize them. It was under the military dictatorship that the registration of Umbanda centros moved from police to civil jurisdiction, that it gained recognition as a religion in the official census,[11] and that many of its religious holidays were incorporated into official national and local public calendars. While these gains were largely the work of local politicians and public officials, they were unopposed by the federal government. This benign attitude toward Umbanda's increasing social legitimacy was itself significant. In a period of 30 years, Umbanda had moved from repression under the Estado Nôvo, to the enjoyment of governmental protection. Its leaders could even offer themselves as instruments of repression.

The dictatorship's tacit support of Umbanda was probably also in part aimed against the Catholic Church. During the 1950s and early 1960s, many Brazilian Church leaders had moved to the left and into positions of clearly defined opposition to the military regime. Thus, the government's open toleration and support of Umbanda, the Church's traditional archenemy, was a way of expressing its opposition to the Church. Instead of allying itself with the Catholic Church against Umbanda, as had occured under Vargas, the state saw Umbanda as an ally against the radical Catholics. Once again, the Church's activities appear to have created unintended benefits for Umbanda.

The regime's support for Umbanda highlights both Umbanda's success in creating a public position of political nonalignment and the essential political conservatism underlying this position. That Umbanda should have been able to command equal support from radical politicians during the early 1960s and from post-1964 military leaders testifies to the political flexibility that a politically nonaligned religious interest group can attain. The dictatorship's creation of a climate in which political issues and positions could not be openly discussed simply brought the world of secular politics closer to the position that Umbandista politicians had maintained from the beginning of their political activities—that political issues and positions *should* not be discussed.

Umbanda and Social Legitimacy

Assessing Umbanda in 1970, and in contemporary Brazil, one can see the tremendous gains in its social legitimacy during a 40-year period, as well as the social stigma that continues to be attached to it. In a way analogous to changes in status associated with minority groups in general, Umbanda leaders have won many battles against legal discrimination, but they have not yet succeeded in erasing social prejudice against it. This can be seen in the limited nature of its changes in status, their incompleteness, and the contradictions that still surround Umbanda's public image. For example, while Umbanda's shift in status from police to civil jurisdiction represented a clear gain, it still was not recognized legally as a religious entity or given the special automatic tax exempt status accorded to world religions. Umbanda centros have to apply individually for such nonprofit status as charitable organizations, and only a few of the most affluent and established ones have attained it. Likewise, while the appearance of Umbanda as a separate category in the official Brazilian religious census was a major achievement, the social stigma that still surrounds its practice prevents the majority of practitioners from avowing their faith.

Another area that demonstrates the social contradictions still surrounding Umbanda concerns its public image; its treatment in the media, in religious celebrations, and in Rio public life. While it has gained a far greater degree of public attention, there is still a conflict between its image as a religion and its emergence as an aspect of Rio regional folklore.

Its gains are particularly visible in the media, where, in addition to its own media coverage—radio programs, newspapers, and columns in the daily press—a vast Umbanda literature is on sale at public newsstands throughout the city, including doctrinal tracts, manuals on ritual practice, books of prayers, and sacred songs. Moreover, Umbanda and other forms of Spiritism hold a fascination for the secular media, especially for the illustrated weekly magazines, and hardly a week passes without a feature article on some public ritual or story of miraculous cures.

Umbanda religious holidays have taken their place in national as well as local public calendars. December 31, the *Dia de Yemanjá* (Day of Yemanjá), Rio's major Umbanda holiday, has now become a tourist attraction second only to *Carnaval*. Yemanjá is the female Orixá who guards the domain of the sea and of fertility.[12] On this day each year thousands of Umbandistas, onlookers, and tourists gather on Rio's beaches to pay homage to Yemanjá. Believers offer her gifts of cosmetics, flowers, and even jewelry, which they throw into the sea or launch in small boats that are left to float out to sea with the tide. Meanwhile, hundreds of Umbanda centros hold religious ceremonies in her honor in the sand along the water's edge. The Rio Department of Tourism, patron of this event, helps to publicize it in the press and weekly newsmagazines, and provides permits and police protection to Umbanda federations that hold religious processions in honor of Yemanjá in various parts of the city, including the fashionable Copacabana section. In 1967, through the efforts of a Rio deputy, this date, December 31, was officially declared a Rio holiday, the *Dia dos Umbandistas* (Umbandistas' Day).

Umbandistas have also succeeded in weaving Umbanda themes into public celebrations of another major Brazilian holiday, Abolition Day, on May 13. This has become the special day dedicated to the Pretos Velhos, spirits of African slaves. This tradition began in the early 1960s, with the unveiling of a statue honoring a local octogenarian who was a former slave, in a park in Campo Grande, one of the more distant barrios of the city. This statue has become a focus of the public Umbanda celebration of Abolition Day; deputies, local officials, and even governors have lent political and financial support and appeared to make speeches there. Umbandistas have also increased their participation in Catholic religious holidays when they give joint homage to the saints and the African Orixás. Public processions through the streets in celebration of these dual figures are now commonplace. They might easily be mistaken for the Catholic processions common since the colonial period, except for the white or gaily colored ritual garments of the marchers, the Umbanda sacred songs that they sing, and the details of the statues carried at the head of the processions. Local politicians help to arrange permits for these processions and often march at their head, thus gaining a bit of free publicity.

Umbanda has become increasingly institutionalized in Brazilian social life and culture as well as politics. Yet it still constantly risks being patronized by both politicians and the general public as a quaint aspect of folklore rather than a religion. Even politicians who publicly defend it as a religion may at the same time be openly patronizing and play to its exotic and spectacular aspects. Because of this, most of the participants in public Umbanda celebrations of the sort just mentioned tend to be more African-oriented centros. Middle sector Umbanda leaders deeply resent both the folklorist emphasis and patronizing attitudes by officials. Many refuse to participate, and counsel their followers as well to "practice religion in the church and not in the street."

The huge celebration at the fourth centennial of the founding of the city of Rio de Janeiro, in 1965, provides a good example of this patronizing, folkloric treatment of Umbanda in secular Brazilian public life. The secretary of tourism successfully lobbied to have an entire evening of the four-day celebration devoted to the Afro-Brazilian religious heritage. Many of those charged with organizing this segment of the program, however, were Rio folklorists, and although the participants invited were members of local Umbanda centros, the evening was entitled, *Você Sabe o que é a Macumba?* (Do you know what Macumba is?). Moreover, it featured the more African-style terreiros performing dances in elaborate, highly colored garments reminiscent of Candomblé. It stressed these groups' exoticism and downplayed their religious meaning. The outdated and deprecating use of the term "Macumba" and the folkloric orientation of the program as a whole incensed leaders who advocated Umbanda Pura, and they refused the invitation to participate.

These contradictions in Umbanda's contemporary public image are the result of the tensions between its legal gains as a religious interest group and the racism persisting in social attitudes toward aspects of its cultural content. Activities of some of the different politicians who have courted Umbanda voters have helped to perpetuate this contradiction. Politicians who have emerged from within Umbanda, particularly the elected Umbandista state deputies, have pressed for religious legitimization and defended religious freedom. They have represented mainly Umbanda Pura and have helped in the diffusion of this form. However, non-Umbandista politicians, who have courted mainly the lower sector Umbanda voters, have tended to adopt the more stereotypic non-Umbandista interpretation of Umbanda (or "Macumba") as an exotic and folkloric form. Like the sponsors of the fourth centennial, they have tended to downplay its religious significance. Umbanda's involvement in contemporary Brazilian political life, then, is a source not only of its increasing legitimacy but also of the tension and dynamism that mark its continuing heterodoxy.

10

Patronage Relations in Umbanda

Patronage relations have emerged at many points in my discussion of Umbanda, in cosmology, rituals, and the developing involvement with secular Brazilian politics. I want now to focus directly on patronage in Umbanda, to juxtapose its expressions within these various contexts, and to explore the significance of its presence for understanding Umbanda's political and social meaning within Brazilian society. I will suggest that patronage is a dominant mode of relationship in Umbanda, and that this autochthonous urban religion has adopted the form of relationship that also dominates its secular environment.

The chapter begins with a brief discussion of forms of patronage and their relevance for contemporary urban Brazil. I then examine the organizational forms of patronage in Umbanda centros and federations and their use by individual Umbanda politicians. I relate these to transcendental forms of patronage in Umbanda rituals and cosmology, closing with a brief comparison of urban forms of patronage found in Umbanda with their rural counterparts found in Popular Catholicism.

It is useful to begin by distinguishing two rather different kinds of patronage relations found in secular Brazilian society and represented in Umbanda. The first is the anthropological model of patron-client ties, informal, asymmetrical, personalistic relations between individuals in which the patron provides employment, protection, and other favors to the client, who reciprocates with loyalty, respect, and political support (see Wolf 1968; Foster 1963; Weingrod 1968; Scott 1972; Powell 1970). The second form of patronage is that defined by political scientists for complex political systems of the clientelistic type (Weingrod 1968), in which individual forms of asymmetrical exchange are amplified into state systems involving the widescale distribution of jobs or special favors by politicians or by state bureaucracies, in return for political, particularly electoral, support.

While patron-client relations and patronage systems have often been assumed to be associated predominantly with agrarian societies, where "authority is dispersed, and state activity limited in scope," (Weingrod

1968:381), studies of developing countries have revealed that as state power and centralization increase, patron-client structures may persist, developing into state organized political patronage systems. Power may continue to be exercised principally through patronage and clientele relations (Weingrod 1968:381).Such political systems are often identified as clientelist states (see Powell 1970:415).[1] They continue to be based on personalistic authority and on material incentives and rewards (Powell 1970:415). However, political parties may now also emerge as important arenas for these new forms of patronage and as mediators between different levels of the social order and the state (Weingrod 1968:381).

Even the transition to urban-based, mass societies need not imply the breakdown of systems based on patronage. Powell notes that

> where the political culture is a carrier of patron-client patterns of behavior, the disintegration of peasant clientelist politics does not mark the demise of the generic pattern. To the contrary, urban based clientelist politics may proliferate. They may become more subtle and complex, but function in essentially the same manner.(1970:423)

In such clientelist states political patronage continues to operate through informal networks of asymmetrical personal relationships. Patron-client relations are still found within these political patronage systems, but they are fewer and less comprehensive in form (Scott 1970:106-9).[2] Under these conditions political middlemen or brokers (see Wolf 1965; Mayer 1968:114) assume a key role, mediating between patrons, the state, or politicians working within the framework of political parties, on the one hand, and their clienteles or political followings, on the other. Patrons and their clienteles may no longer be in direct contact, each maintaining personal relations only with common middlemen who form the links between them. In contrast to the relative stability described for patron-client relationships, political patronage relations involving middlemen tend to be far more evanescent and to occur with greatest intensity during election campaigns (Weingrod 1968:380).

Brazil is often characterized as a clientelist state. As urban areas began to expand rapidly at the end of the nineteenth century, federal patronage was instituted as a means of winning the political support of the emerging urban middle sectors, mainly through offers of employment in the government bureaucracy (Jaguaribe 1968:41). During the 1930s, as Vargas shaped and consolidated a highly centralized, integrated urban-based Brazilian state, he vastly extended federal patronage powers. He continued to enlist the support of the middle sectors by increasing the numbers of patronage positions in the bureaucracy and the military (Ibid.:144), and he extended patronage to the expanding lower sectors, mainly through newly created, federally controlled labor unions and extensive social welfare systems (Erickson 1970:334; Skidmore 1967:39-40). Through the period of the Estado Nôvo "the federal executive gained enormous patronage power, in the sense of favoritism or discrimination inherent in the exercising of the growing administrative powers," and this was especially true for urbanizing areas of Brazil (Skidmore 1967:35). Jaguaribe describes the Brazilian political system at this time as a *Estado Cartorial* (Clientelist State), where "the state exercised a policy of patronage, securing political support in return for government employment" (1968:144).

The downfall of the Estado Nôvo in 1945 and the return to electoral democracy did little to modify this system: with continuing scarce employment for the growing urban populations and their lack of access to urban services, "the clientelistic demand for government employment continued unabated.... The bargain on which the Estado Nôvo had been founded—patronage in return for the promise of [political] support—served as a buttress to the political parties of the Second Republic (1945-64), votes being exchanged for political posts" (Ibid.:144; see also Ianni 1963:29). Patronage activity now burgeoned in the arena of electoral politics, taking the form of populism. This form of clientelist politics has been associated with a general absence of developed political ideologies and platforms, as well as a heavy reliance on interest groups and local clienteles that support them (Powell 1970:422). The strength of interest groups in Brazil has been credited by political analysts with hampering the development of coherent ideologies and platforms, discouraging individual politicians from focusing on political issues (Brandão Lopes 1967), and "blurring the meaning of political parties," which, rather than developing national scope, tend to respresent the the local interests of political clienteles (Jaguaribe 1968:169). State forms of patronage have also remained a crucial avenue for gaining access to employment and a wide variety of urban goods and services. The civil service (Graham 1968:125-39), labor unions, social welfare services, and social security (Erickson 1970:62) are all heavily infused with patronage. Patronage ties are also a major source of career mobility for individuals of both the lower and the middle sectors of the population (Leeds 1965; Leeds and Leeds 1970).

Patronage politics continued under the military dictatorship that came to power in 1964, despite the military's vows to end it. Patronage has remained integral to Brazilian political life and has continued to structure social relationships at all levels of the Brazilian population. Given its omnipresence within Brazilian society, it should not be surprising to find it a prominent aspect of an endogeneous Brazilian religion as well.

Forms of Patronage within Umbanda Centros

The analysis of patronage structures in Umbanda begins with Umbanda centros, which form its basic structural units and lend themselves easily to the formation of various kinds of patronage relationships. Centros are small, autonomous units, hierarchical in structure and dominated by the figure of their chefes, whose authority over all religious matters in the centros, and ultimately over all secular matters as well, takes a personalistic form. Because centros rarely exceed 50 to 100 active members, who come together frequently over long periods of time, chefes know their members personally and are familiar with their histories, their families, and their problems. Chefes' authority thus takes the form of personalistic, familistic relationships. Chefes refer to members, particularly to mediums, as *meus filhos do centros* (my children of the centro), becoming their ritual godparents in the Umbanda ceremonies of baptism and marriage which have recently begun to become popular.[3] Members always address chefes in the centro as Pai or Mãe (derived from "Father" or "Mother" of the saints), often regard them as parental figures, and may comment that "the chefe is like a father (mother) to me." These familistic relationships are to a great extent independent of the age and sex of the chefe and of kinship or friendship relations between members and chefes that may obtain outside of the centro.[4]

Centros, with their strongly instrumental focus, are also focal points of requests for personal aid. Clients request assistance in gaining access to health care facilities, solving legal and bureaucratic problems, finding employment, housing, and financial aid, and resolving interpersonal conflicts and emotional crises. They bring these problems to Umbanda when they have not been able to solve them through formal, institutional channels, in other words, when their solution requires the intervention of an intermediary or recourse to a noninstitutional source of help. Centros, on the other hand, are equally pressured to provide help because their ability to resolve clients' problems, spiritual and/or material, is an important component of their reputations and their continued successful operation.

Chefes are at the center both of requests for aid and of the resources for providing it. Their mediums seek them out to resolve their own various personal problems. Clients at the centros, although they begin by consulting with a spirit, are likely, if the problem has material dimensions, to discuss it informally with the chefe as well. Alternatively, one of the ritual servants who attended the consulta may transmit word of the problem to the chefe. In this way, the chefes, as well as the spirits, become aware of their clients' problems and needs. They are then responsible for mobilizing resources to deal with these problems. Although a few centros do provide their members with social welfare services, such as medical or dental care or a legal advisor, such forms of aid are only beginning to be available. Chefes must use their own personal authority to pressure, enjoin, and persuade other members of the centro to contribute their resources or expertise, or they must seek it from outside sources.

These ingredients lend themselves ideally to the formation of various kinds of patronage relationships. Chefes' personalistic authority over members, and their positions as chief targets for those seeking aid, places them in patron-like positions and defines their members as potentially dependent, needy clients. In fact, a patron-client-like atmosphere seemed to pervade relationships in all of the many Umbanda centros I observed. While there is a clear difference between an atmosphere of patron-clientism and the actual formation of patronage relations, the shift between them is frequent and often almost imperceptible. All that it appears to require is the presence of the proper categories of social and/or political actors and the willingness of the parties involved. The formation of patron-client relations will not tend to result simply from the imbalance between chefes and their clients created by the chefe's positon of leadership and control of redistribution. However, if socio-economic imbalances are superimposed upon it, patron-client relations may result. Likewise, while all centros resemble in embryo the political clienteles composed of eager followers who depend on their leaders to provide favors, they will be transformed into political clienteles and appended to larger political patronage systems only if a politician is interested in acquiring such a clientele and the chefe is willing to provide it.

Since true patron-client relationships depend on economic inequalities between patron and client, these are clearly limited to socio-economically heterogeneous centros. They appear, that is, only when the essential asymmetry in the chefe-member relationship is overlaid by marked economic inequalities. The greater the disparity between the affluence of the chefe and the poverty of the individual members, the greater the likelihood that such relationships will develop. Instances of these relationships appear to be very limited in any one centro, but it seems quite common for heterogeneous centros to contain one or even several such relationships. They depend upon and are constrained only by the limits on the patron's ability and willingness to provide general protection and security for the welfare of clients; the supply of hopeful clients is endless.

An example of an incipient patron-client relationship will illustrate the situations of both patrons and clients and the kind of exchanges that may occur between them. The chefe in whose centro this relationship was developing was a high school teacher. The client, a woman in her 50s, had originally come there as a friend of one of the mediums. This medium had brought her to the centro for a consulta because her eyesight was failing, and she had been told by doctors that unless she had an immediate operation she would soon be blind. However, she was very poor and had no hope of raising the necessary funds. She was first taken for a consulta. After the ceremony, her friend arranged for her to be introduced to the chefe, and she explained her problem to him. He in turn discussed the problem with other members of the centro and later, at the chefe's urging, another member agreed to pay the costs of her operation, which eventually amounted to several hundred dollars.

Grateful for this help, the woman then joined the centro and became a loyal member. The spirits helped her to discover that she was a medium, and she was in the beginning stages of her ritual training when I met her.

This client, although she later learned of the manner in which her operation had been arranged, of the chefe's role, and of the actual donor of the funds, remained firm in her belief that her good fortune emanated from the spirit with whom she had the consulta. She was enormously grateful, particularly to the chefe, whom she viewed as the spirit's human agent and as a possible future source of economic aid and protection. The human intervention that made the operation possible, however, only strengthened her belief in the powers of the spirits.

This client's story highlights several dimensions of patron-clientism in Umbanda centros. A poor woman with an incapacitating and, for her, insoluble health problem receives the financial aid for her operation; she reciprocates with what promises to be long and loyal service as a medium. A relationship is begun in which the chefe acts as a patron, and the client reciprocates with service in a form that encourages the relationship to continue through time. In this case, the chefe himself did not donate the funds but used his position of influence to requisition the resources of one of his members. Yet it was the chefe, and not the donor of the funds, whom the grateful client envisaged as her future human provider. The stage was then set for a further elaboration of a lasting patron-client relationship. The client's interpretation of her good fortune as spiritually derived did not interfere with her recognition of a potential human patron. This case illustrates very clearly the blurring of lines between material and spiritual aid and the way in which material aid may contribute to, rather than undermine spiritual faith.

For the very poor, misfortunes such as this one, involving sudden and unpredictable events—death, job loss, sickness, or accident—can produce life-threatening situations. In such circumstances, individuals turn to support-in-crisis groups—family, neighbors, or patron-client ties, which provide a kind of informal insurance mechanism (Leeds and Leeds 1970:243). Members clearly view their centros, and their chefes, as sources of such informal support. If a chefe has the resources to provide such aid and is willing to continue responding to a series of such appeals, a patron-client relationship may be formed. I found ample evidence that even nonpractitioners of Umbanda regard affluent Umbanda centros as potential sources of patron-client relationships. One woman in the favela where I lived commented to me: "I like Umbanda myself, though I've never gone to centros very much. But I have a friend who joined an Umbanda centro *lá fora* (outside the favela), a big and luxurious one, and the chefe became her patron. I'm tempted to try my own luck there myself if anything should go wrong, though Praise the Lord nothing bad has happened to me or my family recently."

While the potential for the formation of patron-client relations in any centro is limited, the fact that a few such relationships do occur enhances their attraction. Even if actual patron-client relationships are few, the centro, or its chefe, remains a potential source of help in any specific crisis, and this charitable aspect of Umbanda centros greatly adds to their attraction, particularly for members of the lower sectors.

A few examples of fully elaborated, long-term patron-client relations will indicate how initial contacts of the type just described may work out over time. One centro, whose chefe was a married woman with a professional career, contained three patron-client relationships. One client was an elderly woman who was an expert and high-ranking médiun de consulta. She had attended this centro for over 20 years and informed me proudly that in all this time, she had missed a religious ceremony only on one occasion several years before when she had suffered a serious illness. She had no family in Rio, lived in a rented room, and had been employed as a domestic servant in the chefe's home for some 18 years.

Another of her clients was a single man in his mid-40s, also a high-ranking médiun de consulta in the centro, which was located at some distance from the chefe's home. He lived at the centro, in a small room upstairs, and served as caretaker for the property, keeping it clean and purchasing ritual items for the centro as they were needed for the religious ceremonies. This seems to be a common pattern: I found four cases in which clients, in addition to their duties as mediums, served as caretakers for the centro and acquired free housing in the process.

A third client was a middle-aged woman whose husband was seriously ill and unable to work. She was second-in-command in the centro and directed the ceremonies when the chefe was unable to attend. She lived near the chefe, who helped her to find temporary employment in domestic service and as a seamstress in the neighborhood.

The chefe in this centro had assumed ultimate responsibility for all three of these clients, providing employment or housing and protection against any crisis that might befall them. In return, they contributed to the success of her centro with their ritual competence and their long and regular attendance. Moreover, their vocal praise of her kindness and generosity contributed to her prestige. One commented to me: "If it weren't for her I don't know what my husband and I would have done. . . . We would be dead. Over the years she has helped me out every time something happened."

Another chefe, a man, also with a professional career, had two patron-client relationships in his centro, both of many years' standing. One client was a médiun de consulta who served as caretaker at this centro. The other was third-in-command in his rather large centro, serving directly below the chefe's son. This client explained to me that the chefe had helped her and her family out of numerous difficulties, finding employment for her with other members of the centro, for whom she washed clothes, and personally financing the cost of a serious operation for her mother.

This chefe commented to me,

> A lot of people come to me looking for a patron (*buscando patrão*). It's very hard. A lot of these people are terribly poor, and their problems are endless. We do all we can to help, but it's never enough. There are two mediums here [referring to his clients] who are completely dependent on the centro—on me—for support. They're good mediums, dependable, and they've been here for many years. And there are a lot more people here who would like to be in that position. But we can't provide for them. Some continue to hope and eventually the others go somewhere else.

As well as providing aid to clients, these patron-client relations have important advantages for chefes. A chefe, in becoming a patron and assuming continuing responsibilty for the general welfare of clients and their immediate families, receives in return a loyal and dependable supporter, who as a medium or caretaker of the centro will contribute greatly to the quality of its religious ceremonies and to its success. Clients join the chefe's family and close friends in forming a core of loyal and dependable personnel in key positions in the centro. The requirements for the operation of a successful centro share some similarities with those of any successful business enterprise, and yet, unlike businesses, Umbanda centros are voluntary organizations, whose personnel are not paid in wages nor bound by formal contracts. While religious zeal and belief help to forge such loyalties, as do personal satisfactions and the hope of receiving favors, still these must be balanced against the rigors of service: the long and often exhausting hours, the length and difficulty of travel, and the obligation to participate regularly. Chefes meet this burden of responsibility through recruiting members of their immediate families, where family pressure helps to ensure commitment, and through patron-client ties, which bind the client to loyal service. Thus clients are often interspersed with the chefe's kinsmen in key ritual positions.

This brings about the ironic situation that patron-client relations, which are inherently asymmetrical, nonegalitarian, and dependent upon socio-economic inequalities, may contribute to an image and ideology of egalitarianism in Umbanda centros. The ideology that "in Umbanda everyone is equal, and there is neither class nor caste" rests principally on the idea that in terms of ritual status, everyone has equal opportunities for advancement. The proofs most often cited in support of this maxim are the many examples of poor, often black, mediums who have high ritual status; these mediums are offered as evidence that the Umbanda status system constitutes a denial of the secular one. However, my discussion of patron-client relations suggests that the presence of these poor mediums in such high ritual positions is often due to the presence of patron-client relations, which serve to select such individuals for high ritual positions. Thus institutions that are in themselves inherently inegalitarian give credence to avowals of egalitariansim. This example of the disjunction between ideology and social reality reveals additional difficulties with the interpretation of Umbanda as egalitarian, or as an inversion of the secular status system. Moreover, it points up the importance of evaluating and interpreting ideological statements within the full social context in which they occur. Only through careful analysis of the social relationships within which these ritual statuses are embedded is it possible to see that the rituals through which these statuses are expressed may act to mystify socio-economic inequalities rather than to subvert them.

Although patron-client relations highlight one important aspect of exchanges in Umbanda centros involving the redistribution of economic resources downward from wealthier members to poorer ones, the variety of problems is such that many exchanges do not require financial solutions. Wealthier members, for example, may seek qualified and dependable employees, whom the chefe can provide from within his centro's membership (which also may provide employment to another of his clients). I met an affluent man who had conquered his alcoholism "with the help of the spirits and of a fellow centro member," a man far poorer than himself who, unknown to all other centro members except the chefe, had himself recently conquered a similar drinking problem. It was the chefe who had arranged for this assistance. In this way, chefes act, often unobtrusively, to assist individuals of widely differing socio-economic circumstances in obtaining solutions to their problems. The nature of the problems and the sources of aid, which are ultimately attributed to the spirits, act to downplay economic inequalities and class differences among the members of the centros. All, within the ritual and social context of the centro, appear to be equally dependent on the chefe.

For both clients and chefes, patronage, like such relations the world over, acts to maintain rather than to eliminate economic inequalities. For clients at Umbanda centros, these redistributive systems are not sources of upward mobility or career building but serve principally to retain the status quo. Individuals seek Umbanda when things have gone wrong, and solutions, if available, are provided on the basis of need. Aid is utilized to resolve difficulties, to regain personal or household stability, and, in more serious crises, to prevent downward mobility.

For Umbanda chefes, the problem is a more complex one. For affluent middle sector chefes who practice Umbanda Pura, successful leadership depends upon their continuing generosity to their clienteles, and their prestige may even be heightened by a degree of personal economic privation. This does not imply that chefes live in penury but rather that they tend to live modestly within the style dictated by their occupation and income. Some chefes even live considerably below that standard: for example, I knew two chefes of large and prosperous centros, both of them widowed in their 60s, who lived in small, austere cubicles on the upper floors of their own centros and were almost continuously available to the many individuals who visited them to pay compliments and solicit help. The entire income from their centros, and much of their personal incomes as well, went toward the maintenance of their centros and their members. This may also occur among chefes who are married with families. One wife of a prosperous chefe, an electrical engineer, confided to me somewhat wistfully when I visited their modestly furnished home, "As you can see, we live very simply—most of our income goes to Umbanda."

Most of the chefes I met, female as well as male, and of all socio-economic levels, carried out their Umbanda duties in addition to full-time employment, and did not regard their centros as additional sources of income. On the contrary, many chefes periodically used their own personal resources to meet the overhead on their centros. While monthly income (from dues, nominal fees for consultas, if charged, and any cash contributions presented by grateful clients) is intended to cover these centro expenses, it often does not suffice, and chefes dip into their own resources in order to make up the difference. Some even do so on a regular basis.

This picture of the abstemious Umbanda chefe certainly runs counter to their detractors' negative stereotype of chefes as grasping, exploitative figures who systematically bilk their clients. Yet even the minority of chefes I met whose positions as chefes constituted their only source of income tended to live rather modestly. I found such full-time chefes at all socio-economic levels, but chiefly among the more African-oriented forms of Umbanda, which tend to charge higher fees for consultas than occurs in Umbanda Pura. I obtained reliable accounts of only a few chefes who, fulfilling the popular image, had exploited their positions for their own economic benefit, drawing heavily upon centro funds and fees from private paid consultas in their homes for personal expenditures and investments in financial ventures or real estate. Such cases, when they come to public attention, receive enormous publicity in the daily tabloids and are cited by Umbanda's detractors as evidence of the essentially corrupt and exploitative nature of this religion. However, among chefes influenced by the humanitarian ideology of Umbanda Pura, I encountered none reputed to have seriously violated the ideal of charity. The centros' clientele structures, since they make chefes' prestige and the loyalty of their followings dependent upon their continuing generosity, reinforce humanitarian ideals on the part of chefes.

For the great majority of chefes, then, leadership in an Umbanda centro is not a source of upward mobilty. Unlike patrons in the secular world, who may put their gains toward further capital accumulation, in Umbanda there are religious ideals and structures that both encourage the redistribution of resources and militate against individual economic aggrandisement. These structures, however, do not cause Umbanda chefes to forfeit either power or class position, even though they often convert wealth into prestige. While Umbanda reinforces redistribution both structurally and ideologically, it should not be seen either as advocating egalitarianism or as negating class differences.

This profile of Umbanda chefes, in focusing on Umbanda Pura, neglects other forms of Umbanda, particularly Quimbanda, which accept and even advocate the exploitation by chefes of their clients. Power in these cases may be assumed to be basically amoral, and high fees an accepted norm. Under these circumstances, a chefe's ability to exploit clients may even be regarded as a dimension and symbol of his or her spiritual power. This reveals another dimension of the contrast between Umbanda Pura and Quimbanda.

Umbanda Centros as Political Clienteles

In order to examine the ways in which centros become incorporated into broader patronage networks of secular Brazilian political life, it is necessary to return to the point that while full patron-client relations are limited to heterogeneous centros, all centros, irrespective of their socio-economic composition, have a patronage-like structure. This allows them to be easily converted into political clienteles. Patron-clientage may be enhanced by economic inequalities, but in its political form it is clearly not dependent upon them. In all of the centros I visited, regardless of their socio-economic composition, the relationships I observed between chefes and their members were invariably strongly asymmetrical ones. Chefes were strikingly alike in their positions as dominating figures, while the treatment they evoked from their members, at least within the centros, exuded deference and dependence.

Chefes' dominating positions derive first and foremost from their religious authority and their control over the supernatural world. They have superior spiritual powers to control and command the spirits, to summon and dismiss them, and to compel their obedience. Moreover, the high-ranking spirits whom the chefes receive are believed to exercise the same superior powers over the other spirits received at the centros.

In addition to their religious authority, chefes control personal information concerning members and their resources, which, as I have already indicated, enables them to become redistributors of resources within the centros and to pressure and persuade their members. Successful redistribution does not necessarily depend on economic inequalities. Even between economic equals, a particular individual may, at a particular moment, be in a position to provide a crucial resource that another, at that moment, urgently needs. Chefes' superior knowledge of their member's resources allows them, even in centros with minimal socio-economic differences among the members, to gain ascendancy and influence as redistributors of the members' resources.

This influence may in turn be converted into a political relationship, in which chefes use their position to influence the political behavior of their followers, offering their memberships as political clienteles to higher level politicians. In such cases, chefes become political middlemen, and their memberships become political clienteles. Such political alliances may even enhance chefes' positions in their centros, giving them access to additional resources with which to supply their members' demands.

The nature of the involvement of Umbanda centros in the formal political process reveals both their potential as sources of political clienteles and their limitations as bases for their leaders' election to political office. For chefes willing to use their clienteles for political purposes, the common starting point is to make contact with elected or aspiring politicians and to serve them as political middlemen, offering to deliver the votes of their members in exchange for the politicians' favors and promises to promote the interests of Umbanda. In this way, a chefe may become a *cabo eleitoral* (local ward heeler), an informal participant in the formal political process. The cabos play key roles, since it is often they, rather than the elected politicians, who maintain personal contact with the voters. The cabo has even been identified as "the most important figure in Brazilian elections" (Medina, quoted in Morse 1965:57). This position is usually held by local level leaders "who control a few dozen or a few hundred votes, too few for themselves to be elected" (Singer 1965:74). Cabos eleitorais use the favors provided by politicians to augment the resources with which they satisfy the demands of their own clienteles. In return, they promise the politicians their clienteles' electoral support (Ibid.:75).

Umbanda centros are even listed among the voluntary associations that are potential sources of such local political clienteles (Ibid.:74).[5] Chefes are in ideal positions to serve as cabos eleitorals, since their members provide a continual demand for services, while the chefes' personal influence and authority may be utilized to influence members in their voting behavior. Of course, chefes have no guarantee of success, since their members are exposed to diverse political influences through family, friends, and the mass media and may hold to their own personal political persuasions. However, the ability of chefes of large Umbanda centros, cited in the previous chapter, to mobilize 1500 votes apiece in their own bids for local political offices in Rio during the 1950s demonstrates their considerable electoral influence over their memberships and members' families as well. Each of these chefes mobilized a sizeable number of votes, but well below the number needed for election. It is likely that chefes would be able to generate a greater degree of political loyalty for their own candidacies than for those of outside politicians, particularly if the latter are not Umbandistas. Moreover, these unusually large centros offer the prospect of many more votes than the more typical, smaller centros. Still, the prospect of even a small number of votes is reported sufficient to interest politicians in forming alliances with local leaders (Ibid.).

Umbanda centros' magnetic attraction for politicians supports this observation. Particularly in the months before election time, dozens of candidates for state and federal deputy, and representatives of the candidates for governor as well, can be seen ploughing through the pouring rain and rivers of mud at all hours of the night to visit even the small Umbanda centros located high in favelas or in the labyrinthine recesses of distant Rio suburbs. They make their visits in the hopes that the chefe will introduce them to the members and permit them to say a few words in defense of Umbanda. One politician, a state deputy and not himself an Umbandista, commented to me,

Well, we can't make official visits to the labor unions because they are government controlled and don't allow politicians in there, and the factories will only let us in at lunch hour, when no worker wants to listen to political speeches. What are we going to do? We visit the samba schools, the *futebol* (soccer) clubs, and we go to religious groups such as Umbanda centros. You never can tell how many votes you will gain by these visits—maybe 50, maybe five, maybe none. But you have to try everything. A friend of mine lost in the last election by 27 votes.[6] You can't take the risk. If we can, we set up a close relationship with chefes at the centros and get them to plug for us. But we also make the rounds of lots of other centros, hoping the chefe will at least let us say a word or two.

Such comments offer insight into the importance of Umbanda and other voluntary associations in the Brazilian political process, and they indicate, by the type of groups listed, that the politicians' primary targets are the lower sector voters. Voluntary associations such as Umbanda centros assume crucial political importance in reaching this segment of the electorate in the absence of formal institutional channels of access to it. I have already indicated the increasing importance of this segment of the electorate in the period after 1945. In Rio (the State of Guanabara), the lower sector was estimated in 1960, for example, to constitute some 70 percent of the total electorate, more than double the size of the middle (28.5 percent) and upper (1.5 percent) sector constituencies combined (Coutto 1966:25). Candidates for political offices must thus make tremendous efforts to attract lower sector voters. In order to do this they turn to interest groups with significant lower sector memberships, such as Umbanda.[7]

While chefes serve as cabos eleitorais at all socio-economic levels of Umbanda, I have the impression that chefes from the lower sectors do so far more often than do those from the middle sectors. This may in part reflect the politicians' pursuit of lower sector votes, but it also appears to reflect the interests of the chefes themselves. Poorer chefes who have less access to power or resources, either for themselves or their memberships, find the hope of favors through a political alliance far more attractive than do more affluent chefes. Thus lower sector chefes and their memberships tend to provide the bulk of the clienteles in the wider patronage networks in which Umbanda centros become involved.

The politicians, who are usually the ones to initiate contacts with Umbanda chefes, direct their main efforts at centros with lower sector memberships. Customarily, they will first request permission through an emissary to attend a religious ceremony, to be introduced, and to state publicly their support of Umbanda. They thus gain an initial contact with the chefe and his clientele, and both chefe and politician have a chance to assess the potential for a further relationship. If both are interested, they may agree to exchange favors and the chefe may become a cabo eleitoral.

One of the three chefes unsuccessful in his bid for election as city councilman in the 1950s subsequently served as a cabo eleitoral at different times to various state deputies. One provided him with construction materials with which to finish building his new centro and another helped him to gain *utilidade pública* (nonprofit status), giving his centro tax exemption and making it eligible to receive *verbas* (financial donations) from state deputies.[8] Two other deputies have since given him such donations, which he has used to extend the social welfare services in his centro. When members have had special problems requiring solutions beyond the capabilities of his centro, his political patrons have sometimes helped to provide them. In return, he has permitted these politicians to introduce themselves at his centro's religious ceremonies, has himself urged his clientele and their families to vote for them, and has closed his doors to competitors. I found several similar cases and heard of many others in far smaller centros with only a few dozen members.

Certainly politicians' initial visits to Umbanda centros produce varying results; the chefe does not necessarily become a cabo eleitoral. Politicians may make only one hasty visit to a centro without seeking to establish a closer relationship with its chefe. Others attempt, often successfully, to exploit chefes with promises of favors in return for the chefes' services as cabos, promises that they have neither the intention nor the ability to fulfill.[9] I met several chefes who were waiting with diminishing hopes for the political favors promised them in return for their electoral campaigning and some whose experiences had left them openly cynical about any future dealings with politicians. Chefes may also play this political game, offering the votes of their clienteles simultaneously to several politicians. Some chefes consider it a community service to permit any politicians who desire to do so a chance to introduce themselves at the religious ceremonies, but they still refuse to attempt to influence their members' voting behavior. The frequency with which chefes serve as cabos eleitorals is hard to estimate, but this certainly occurs in only a small proportion of the centros in Rio. The great majority of chefes refuse to engage in these political activities, and seem content to derive personal satisfaction from their religious and humanitarian activites, as well as their prestige within the centro and their local communities.[10]

Chefes may also invoke their centros' statutes, which expressly prohibit any political activities within their confines, and cite the general maxim that one must not mix religion with politics. This norm, whether or not it is followed, is widely invoked against chefes in all sectors of Umbanda. Those who do not engage in politics use it to censure those who do, and those who are politicaly active censure their political rivals. Accusations and denials of political ambitions and involvements, together with accusations of exploitation and the practice of sorcery, are major topics of malicious gossip among Umbanda chefes, especially among leaders of Umbanda federations, where the level of political involvement is considerably higher than it is among chefes. This gossip provides a telling popular view of the Brazilian political system, in which political ambitions are considered synonymous with an interest in exploitation for individual gain and thus run directly counter to the ideal behavior of Umbanda chefes, which rests on generosity and humanitarian concerns. Umbandistas' doubts about politicians' sincerity are embodied in their calumnies against politically ambitious leaders, yet at the same time, they both permit and engage in these activities.

Politically ambitious chefes counter these accusations by basing their justifications for entering the political arena on Umbanda's need for public defenders who will work for its greater legitimacy. All of the politicians who court the Umbanda vote resort to such populist political appeals, defending and promoting Umbanda as an accompaniment to their links with cabos eleitorals. This helps to establish their credibility and their effectiveness in individual clientele relationships with Umbanda chefes. In their public speeches in the state legislature, in their sponsorship of the participation of Umbanda groups in state celebrations and public religious events, these politicians treat and recognize Umbanda politically as an interest group, rather than simply as an aggregate of discrete political clienteles. As I have indicated in the previous chapter, these activities in turn contribute to Umbanda's legitimacy and public image.

Umbanda Politicians

Umbanda politicians seeking elected offices use centros, federations, and the mass media to create patronage networks sufficient for them to attain statewide political offices. I will look first at these activities within the Umbanda federations and will then examine the careers of three Umbanda politicians.

For Umbandistas who aspire to elective offices, leadership of an Umbanda centro provides only limited possibilities for political career building; it is not sufficient *trampolim* (springboard; see Leeds 1965:387) from which to launch a political career or win an election. Even in the largest Umbanda centros in Rio, chefes have made good cabos eleitorals precisely because they control too few votes to be elected themselves and thus are not a source of competition to politicians. Politically ambitious Umbandistas must turn to wider sources of patronage, to positions of leadership in Umbanda federations, and to the mass media.

Leadership in an Umbanda federation offers far more extensive possibilities for the building of extended clientele networks than does an individual centro. Federations may affiliate as many as several hundred centros. Federations, resources, and their leaders become additional sources of personal favors for affiliated chefes and their memberships, while the centros' chefes and members form a part of the federation's following, or extended clientele, the size of which will help to determine the federation's relative influence within Umbanda and in the wider political process. The fact that Umbanda federations are structured and used as clientele networks underlies the fierce competition among them, both for members and for influence and power within Umbanda. The often hostile attitudes of federation leaders toward each other, which are frequently lamented as chief causes of a general lack of unification in Umbanda, reflect competitive efforts at career building.

Federations have served successfully as bases for their leaders' election to local level political offices in several states. Rio Grande do Sul in 1960 elected three Umbandista mayors in smaller cities of the interior and several city councilmen in the capital, all of whom gained election through their leadership of Umbanda federations. Another city councilman founded an Umbanda federation soon after his election as a means of maintaining his clientele. In the State of São Paulo, in the capital, and in Santos, Umbanda federations have formed the basis for election of city councilmen.

In Rio, in the period prior to 1960, when local elective offices still existed, several leaders of Umbanda federations laid foundations for their candidacies. One of these, after trying unsuccessfully to use his centro as a springboard for election to city councilman during the early 1950s, founded his own Umbanda federation soon after his electoral defeat. His subsequent intensive efforts to affiliate centros for his new federation and to form alliances with politicians convinced his Umbandista colleagues that his federation was intended to further his own political ambitions. His colleagues attributed his subsequent failure to reemerge as a political candidate to both the 1960 abolition of elective offices and his own inability to generate a sufficiently large clientele. Abandoning his elective aspirations, he later used his federation successfully to gain influence within Umbanda. He began to sponsor huge ceremonies, which generated widespread visibility and won him frequent publicity in the popular press for his participation in Umbanda events in Rio. He was often cited as a successful promoter of rituals of the type of Umbanda Pura. Other Umbanda leaders agree that he is one of Umbanda's major leaders in Rio, and he has been included in all major coalitions among various federations and in all major decision-making activities. Thus he successfully refocused his political ambitions upon gaining influence within Umbanda.

Federation leaders in Rio ceased to become political candidates after 1960, when the office of state deputy—a post which required upwards of 7,000 to 8,000 votes—became the lowest remaining elective office. This may well represent their political assessment that an Umbanda federation was not likely to generate enough votes. However, Umbanda federations could be used in other ways as political clienteles. The following case provides a dramatic example of both the potential and the dangers involved in clientele entanglements. It concerns a lower sector federation leader, who in trying to increase his resources through political patronage relationships, lost control of his federation to his patron. In addition to revealing the process of backstage clientele politics, it provides another example of class-based patronage. This case suggests the vulnerability of lower sector leaders to cooptation by their middle sector competitors.

The individual involved, whom I will refer to as Roberto, was the founder and president of one of the African-oriented Umbanda federations that dated back to the early 1950s. He had been active and influential in Umbanda during that time and had been a member of the major Umbanda coalition formed in 1956. However, by the early 1960s his influence had declined considerably. His downfall occurred in 1965, as a result of his entry into political negotiations surrounding the election of the new governor of Rio (the State of Guanabara). The outgoing governor, Carlos Lacerda, had made extensive campaign funds available to his political friends to help in electing his chosen successor. Lacerda had always represented the interests of the middle and upper sectors and had had great difficulty in reaching the lower sector electorate (Coutto 1966:81). Learning of these campaign funds shortly before the election, Roberto approached one of Lacerda's political supporters to offer the votes of the member centros of his federation in return for a portion of the campaign funds. His offer was quickly accepted.[11]

Lacerda's chosen successor subsequently lost the election. However, the distributor of the campaign funds to Roberto's Umbanda federation, a high ranking military officer, was himself interested in Spiritism and undertook a closer investigation of the clientele whose support he had enlisted. He concluded that the federation was badly organized, out of contact with its affiliated centros, and greatly in need of more efficient administration. But he evidently considered it to be potentially valuable as a clientele, so he and Roberto agreed that he would become its patron. He donated an office for its headquarters, funds, and his own administrative talents. Within a year he had become the effective leader of the federation. Roberto, although he remained its ritual president, was increasingly ignored in decision-making and was described to me by the federation's new leadership in 1966 as "a mere figurehead." He eventually withdrew entirely from the activities of his own federation.

Its new leader now reorganized and expanded this federation, using his own resources and contacts to increase its number of local affiliates and to form alliances with Umbanda federations in other states. By 1966, he headed one of the largest Umbanda federations in Brazil. His own personal resources, contacts, and bureaucratic expertise permitted him to expand the range of its activities far beyond the capacities of its former leader. He also made changes in the ritual orientation advocated by this federation. Although it continued to affiliate the Afro-Brazilian terreiros recruited by its former leader, the federation now began to advocate the ritual orientation of Umbanda Pura, urging its member centros to give up drums, animal sacrifices, and elaborate ritual costumes and to follow "White Umbanda." This example is not unique. I heard of similar middle sector takeovers of lower sector Umbanda federations in São Paulo and in Piauí. Within these competitive situations, the socio-economic resources and connections available to leaders themselves may become more significant than they are on the level of the individual centros. The competitors are fewer, the potential stakes higher, and the competition fiercer. The greater resources controlled by more affluent federation leaders give them a distinct advantage over poorer leaders. While the competition among the various Umbanda federations has not produced unity within Umbanda, it has favored the increasing ascendancy of the middle sectors. This situation within the federations parallels politicians' efforts to gain control over the lower sector Umbanda electorate, both of which favor the reproduction of class based patronage patterns found in secular Brazilian society.

Three Umbanda Political Careers

The career patterns of three leading Umbanda politicians, two elected state deputies and one an aspirant to this position, reveal the coordinated use of a full range of Umbanda patronage bases, including those in the mass media. Umbanda radio programs and regular space in leading daily newspapers have exponentially increased politicians' access to Umbanda voters and have formed an important foundation for their success.

The increased importance of the mass media in Brazilian politics since World War II is well recognized. In Rio (the State of Guanabara), with its high index of urbanization and the highest literacy rate of any state in Brazil,[12] politicians routinely utilize newspapers as well as radio and television for reaching all levels of the population (Brasileiro 1967/68:154). For Umbanda politicians as well, radio programs, newspapers, and weekly columns in major daily papers are highly sought after political plums and appear to be prerequisites to the successful election of Umbandista candidates to state offices.

Attila Nunes, the Umbandista deputy elected from Guanabara mentioned in the previous chapter, came from a middle sector Rio family and began his career as a journalist with a law degree, an interest in Spiritism, and political ambitions.[13] During World War II he converted from Kardecism to Umbanda, and in 1947, in his early 30s, he founded the first Umbanda radio program. As already indicated in the previous chapter, he formed an alliance with leaders of the UEUB *(União Espírita de Umbanda do Brasil)*, the only federation in existence at that time, publicizing the federation in his radio program and inviting its member centros to sing their favorite Umbanda pontos and discuss their activites. In return, the UEUB's publication, the *Jornal de Umbanda*, publicized and praised Attila's activities in support of Umbanda. Since radio reached a far wider audience than did the *Jornal de Umbanda*, Attila's publicity was advantageous for the federation, which gained new affiliates through this means. It was advantageous for him as well, since through his connections with the federation he was able to establish personal relationships not only with its leaders but with the chefes and members of its affiliated centros. In clientele fashion, he created an extensive personal following.

Attila soon became a well-known figure in Umbanda circles. The publicity generated by his radio program was instrumental in bringing Umbanda Pura to the attention of practitioners of Afro-Brazilian Umbanda, leading some of them to shift their own ritual orientations. As various other Umbanda federations formed during the early 1950s, Attila Nunes established similar relationships with many of them as well. His program, meanwhile, was expanding. In 1952 it was extended to a half-hour weekly, and gradually through the late 1950s and early 1960s it grew to an hour, two hours, and finally to the two weekly four-hour programs that he maintained at the time of my research. By this time leading Rio newspapers also carried his weekly columns on Umbanda, which provided the same type of news and publicity offered on his radio program.

In 1958, Attila Nunes, through his activities in Umbanda and the vast network of personal relationships he had established, waged a successful electoral campaign for city councilman, becoming the first Umbandista in Rio to be elected to a political office. In 1960 he was elected state deputy, a position that allowed him to make many more chefes his cabos eleitorals. His failure at reelection in 1962 appears to have been due more to the political unrest preceding the 1964 coup than to any personal failure with his clientele. He was reelected in 1966, under the military government, and served as vice-president and secretary of the state legislature. He spoke there many times in defense of religious liberty and Umbanda, launching public protests against its persecutors, mainly Rio police officials, and (prior to 1964) against the laws that still required Umbanda centros to obtain police registration, which he was instrumental in changing.

He was still in office at the time of his death in 1968. His obituary in one of Rio's leading newspapers, the Catholic-oriented *O Globo,* emphasized his career as a defender of Umbanda. It recalled his devotion to his religion and described the Umbanda funeral services performed for him in the Legislative Assembly and held at his burial (*O Globo* 10/28/68). The strength of the political clientele that he had established through his activities in Umbanda was such that after his death in 1972, his son, Attila Nunes, Jr., then only 20, was elected in the place of his father. Attila, Jr., became the youngest deputy ever to serve in the Guanabara state legislature.

Despite Attila Nunes' popularity, few Umbandistas could recall his political party affiliations. One commented to me, "It doesn't matter what party he belonged to; he was an Umbandista." His political career thus provides a good example of a successful interest group politician. The several parties under which he had campaigned turned out, when I had looked them up in the archives of the state legislature, to be populist-oriented parties to the left of center, which derived their greatest support from the lower sectors.[14] This same political identification also characterizes the other Umbandista politicians discussed here.

The other state deputy, Moab Caldas, who was elected in Rio Grande do Sul, had a similar career pattern in Umbanda. He was born in the 1920s in the capital city of Alagoas to a family of modest means. As a young man he enlisted in the army, where he first encountered and converted to Kardecism. After serving in various parts of Brazil, he was transferred toward the end of World War II to Porto Alegre, the capital of Rio Grande do Sul. Umbanda was already popular in military circles in that city, and Moab, now a sergeant, served under an officer who was an Umbandista. He formed a close friendship with this officer and he, too, converted to Umbanda. After the war, when the officer decided to make a political career in Umbanda, Moab became his partner and protégé.

In 1952 they founded an Umbanda federation in Porto Alegre and quickly built up a clientele that the officer was able to utilize as a successful base for his own election as city councilman. In 1954, he helped Moab to acquire the first Umbanda radio program in Rio Grande do Sul, and together they and another man, the author of several books on Spiritism and Umbanda, formed a *panelinha* (little saucepan—an informal group of associates who exchange their different resources and thus contribute to each other's careers; see Leeds 1965). As had happened in Rio, the radio program generated much publicity and attracted many new adherents to Umbanda, including some practitioners of Afro-Brazilian religions known locally as Batuque or *Casa de Bara*. After encountering strong opposition to Umbanda from the Catholic leaders in Porto Alegre, the panelinha decided that in order to defend Umbanda they should enter state politics and elect an Umbandista state deputy. Moab was young, personable, and, through his radio program, the best known of the panelinha, so they selected him as the best candidate among the three although he had held no prior political office. In 1958, with extensive campaigning by the members of the panelinha, each of whom utilized his respective clientele in vote-getting activities, Moab ran for state deputy. He was elected easily, receiving the third largest vote of all the candidates. His campaign provides a good example of what Leeds describes as a common form of panelinha cooperation to elevate one of the members to political office in order to gain greater access to political power for everyone in the group (Leeds 1965).

Once elected, Moab was able to perform numerous patronage services for his friends and his clienteles. He defended and publicized Umbanda in the state legislature, acquired a land grant for the construction of an Umbanda hospital from the then mayor of Porto Alegre, Leonel Brizola, a political ally. He obtained free bus service to transport Umbandistas to Umbanda social events in various cities of Rio Grande do Sul and funds for the celebration of Umbanda holidays. In addition, he was able to perform numerous personal favors. He became an enormously successful clientele politician.

Moab was reelected in 1962, but his career was seriously affected by the 1964 military coup. The political party he represented (the PTB) lost support, and he was defeated by a narrow margin in the 1966 elections. In 1970, shortly before election time, he was *cassado* (stripped of office and political rights for a period of ten years). Moab's political career in Umbanda had been far more overtly political in tone than that of Attila Nunes in Rio, and further to the left. Consequently, he was more drastically affected by national political events.[15] At the time I left Brazil in 1970, he still retained his presidency of the Umbanda federation, though he had lost his radio program and his position in Umbanda was much weakened by his fall from political favor. A rival federation with more conservative political views had already begun seriously to challenge his leadership and influence.

The third Umbanda political career is that of a young man whom I will refer to as João, who at the time of my research aspired to the position of state deputy in Rio. He was a long-time practitioner of the African-oriented style of Umbanda and worked as a journalist for one of the larger Rio tabloids. João's political career building in Umbanda began during the mid-1960s when he formed an alliance with another journalist on the same newspaper, a Kardecist and long-time federal deputy who became his patron and helped him obtain a weekly column on Umbanda. Since federal and state deputies do not compete for votes, patron and client were not political competitors. João used his Umbanda column to generate publicity for himself, for his patron, whom he publicized as a defender of all forms of Spiritism, and for his Umbandista friends who were leaders of Umbanda centros in the African tradition.

His column became popular, and in 1968, again with aid from his patron who had influence with the editor of the newspaper, João was able to expand the column into an eight-page Sunday supplement on Umbanda. This vastly increased the opportunities for publicity and created employment for some of his Umbandista supporters, who were hired as reporters to visit and describe activities in various Umbanda centros and at larger public gatherings around the city. João's and his patron's activities always received extensive coverage. The federal deputy was able to widen his popular support by appealing to the Umbanda vote, while João gained publicity and prestige from having an elected politician as a supporter. His clientele expanded, and he began to be recognized and discussed by other Umbanda leaders in Rio as a competitor on the political scene.

Soon after its appearance, the Sunday supplement announced the founding of a new "Federation of Spiritist Religions," with João as president and his patron as financial director. The use of the more inclusive term "Spiritist" rather than "Umbanda" in the federation's title permitted João and his patron to participate and solicit support, although like the Sunday supplement, the federation itself, despite its name, remained oriented toward the more African-style Umbanda centros. The pages of the supplement began to solicit affiliates to the federation, offering as an inducement to membership extensive free medical services, in addition to the more standard forms of protection and legal registration. The federation also became active in sponsoring large public religious processions through the major streets of various districts of the city on the name days of the various Orixás/Saints. João and his patron always marched together at the front of these processions, and at the large social gatherings that followed them, participants had a chance to meet these new federation leaders.

Up to the time I left the field (1970), the subject of João's political candidacy was never raised publicly, although he admitted it privately and other Umbanda leaders gossiped about his political intentions. He had decided to run as a candidate of the MDB (the Opposition Party),[16] to which his patron also belonged. He explained to me that "in order to capture the Umbanda vote you would have to support the Opposition Party" (which in Rio had absorbed the former PTB, the Labor Party originally organized by Getúlio Vargas). Thus João's choice of party affiliation followed that of the other politicians described here—a political position to the left of center, associated with the more populist-oriented sector of politics, and oriented principally to the lower sector voters.

The separate careers of these three politicians reflect a remarkably similar use of Umbanda clienteles. Most striking is their use of the mass media, particularly radio programs, which were clearly a major asset in the election of the two state deputies. At the same time, these politicians also actively utilized the clientele networks provided by Umbanda federations and, in addition, formed clientele relations with individual Umbanda centros. Once elected, these politicians were able to use the perquisites of office as sources of patronage exchanges. Since both of the deputies gained office almost exclusively on the basis of Umbanda voters, their careers reveal the electoral potential of Umbanda as a political interest group. The form and content of their political ties with Umbanda illustrate the workings of populist politics described for Umbanda politicians in the previous chapter: the appeal to a particular interest group and the downplaying of secular ideological positions and party identities.

Transcendental Forms of Patronage

The examination of social structures in relation to the symbolic systems through which they acquire their meaning often reveals many inconsistencies, but Umbanda presents few such problems. Its symbolic structures are as suffused with images and metaphors of patronage as are the social structural aspects I have just described. I will briefly recall and amplify aspects of patronage that occur in Umbanda cosmology and ritual and will then compare transcendental forms of patronage in Umbanda with those reported for rural Popular Catholicism. The contrast that emerges between these two religions in their different contexts highlights the way in which Umbanda rituals and cosmology have taken on the contours of urban patronge.

The more popular, lay interpretation of the Umbanda cosmos, which overlays the formal bureaucratic one, takes the form of a vast heavenly patronage network linking spiritual patrons and middlemen to the human clients who form its base. Spiritual powers to heal and advise move downward in exchange for loyal and faithful homage and service, which move upwards. Patronage relationships between human clients and spirit patrons prevail throughout Umbanda belief and practice; specific groups of Umbandistas may even have their own patron spirits. For example, each centro has its

Padroeiro (patron spirit), usually the principal spirit received by the centro's founder. Since the founder is almost invariably its chefe, a parallel is thus established between the patron-like position of the chefe in relation to members and the patron-like role of the chefe's principal spirit in relation to clients. Ritual protocol often requires that a statue of the centro's patron spirit occupy the central position on the centro's altar and that mediums wear the patron spirit's *ponto riscado* (emblem) sewn or embroidered on their ritual uniforms. In centros that practice Umbanda Pura, many Umbanda prayers refer to the Caboclo of the Seven Crossroads, the spirit who "revealed" Umbanda to Zélio de Moraes, as *O Padroeiro de Umbanda* (the patron saint of Umbanda).

Most important of the spiritual patronage relations are those that individual practitioners of Umbanda have with their spirit benefactors, which take the form of patron-client relations. Mediums regard the principal among the spirits they receive as their chief spiritual patron, and form especially intimate and enduring patron-client relationships with these patron spirits. Umbandistas who are clients seek patrons from among the spirit consultants available at their centro during consultas. While clients may engage in a series of short-term exchanges with various spirits, promising specific acts of homage to each in return for the solution to particular problems, they often form stable, long-term patron-client relations with one particular spirit whom they believe to be most able to provide for their spiritual needs.[17] These transcendental patron-client relationships, like the earthly ones between chefes and their clients, involve reciprocal exchanges of protection and favors in return for esteem, obedience, and loyalty on the part of the clients.

Another parallel between social structures and symbolic systems is established by the Caboclos' and Pretos Velhos' roles as spiritual middlemen. Just as chefes in Umbanda centros may serve as middlemen in patronge networks linking members of their centros, as clienteles, to higher political patrons, Caboclos and Pretos Velhos are middlemen in the Umbanda spiritual patronage hierarchy, intermediaries between human clients and higher spiritual patrons, the Orixás/Saints. Likewise, Umbandistas' relationships to the distant though powerful Orixás/Saints are very much like their relationships to elected politicians. They have little direct contact with them and are uncertain of their concern. Politicians, like the Orixás/Saints, remain remote and inaccessible. Both patron-client and clientele relations are thus found in individual relations between humans and their spirit helpers, and the multiple and vertically connected levels of the spirit hierarchy resemble secular political patronage networks.

Patronage Relations in Umbanda and Rural Popular Catholicism

A comparison of patronage in Umbanda with that described for rural forms of Latin American Catholicism suggests ways in which Umbanda differs from the rural model and highlights its resemblance to distinctly urban forms of patronage described for Brazilian socio-political life. The interpretation of the relationship between rural Catholic populations and Catholic saints as supernatural forms of patron-client relations was first proposed by Foster for rural Mexico (1963:1280-94), and has subsequently been applied as well to rural Brazil by De Kadt (1967:196) and Gross (1971: 145-46). Since Umbanda has been influenced by Popular Catholicism, and the saints, together with their African alter egos, are present in the Umbanda pantheon, patron-client relations in Umbanda might easily be misconstrued as simply a result of the Catholic influence upon it, a holdover from a rural tradition. However, the pervasive presence of patronage in all sectors of contemporary urban Brazil, as well as the high degree to which it is articulated in Umbanda, argues against such an interpretation. A still more persuasive argument may be found in the comparison of the structures of supernatural patronage in rural Popular Catholicism and in Umbanda. The differences that emerge from this comparison are qualitative and indicate that patronage in Umbanda cosmology cannot be viewed simply as a rural holdover.

Descriptions of rural Catholicism stress both distance and uncertainty in the relationships between rural populations and patron saints, whose numbers are limited and whose degree of distance from their petitioners is believed to be considerable enough that their responsiveness to their clients' demands is not assured (Foster 1963:1286). Saints may not hear their petitions or may not acknowledge their demands. The same may be said of relations between humans and the Orixás/Saints in the Umbanda cosmos as well. However, in Umbanda, the limited number of the Orixás/Saints has been augmented by a potentially infinite number of Caboclos and Pretos Velhos, who may be recruited as patrons at a mediating level between the saints and humans and whose interest and availability for serving their clients are guaranteed.

Unlike the Catholic saints and the African Orixás, both of whose spiritual status is fully realized and fixed, the Caboclos and Pretos Velhos are lesser spirits, still evolving by means of their excellence in providing spiritual aid. That such aid both constitutes a moral imperative for the spirits and forms the source of their upward mobility reinforces the image of these spirits' direct interest in helping humans. The Caboclos and Pretos Velhos are portrayed as just willing and available to help as the Orixás/Saints are uncertain and undependable.

These cosmological differences between the two religions may easily be related to differences in the social contexts from which they derive. The rural patron-client relationships of Popular Catholicism which resemble traditional rural forms of patronage, involve large numbers of peasants or rural populations and limited numbers of patrons; their disproportionate numbers favor the patrons and disadvantage their clients. The greater complexity of the Umbanda cosmos, specifically the emergence of an intermediate level of supernaturals serving as patrons to man and middlemen between humans and their more powerful patrons, likewise resembles the contemporary urban political patronage systems I have described. The proliferation of these intermediate level patrons, the Caboclos and Pretos Velhos, which allows clients to choose from among them, and the greater degree of elaboration, complexity, and density of the patronage network, all reflect specific characteristics of urban patronage systems.

There are also striking differences in the availability of public ritual contexts within which these two systems of supernatural patronage, rural and urban, are realized. In rural Catholicism, these ritual contexts are limited to the *romarias* (pilgrimages) enacted at limited numbers of pilgrimage sites, where *romeiros* (pilgrims) come to pay a visit to the saint to whom the shrine is dedicated, or to render homage and fulfill *promessas* (ritual promises) made in return for aid received. Gross (1971:142) notes the importance of these shrines both for enhancing petitioners' feelings of personal contact with the saint and for increasing chances for receiving supernatural aid. However, opportunities for such rituals of intensification are few and far between, and pilgrims may attend only once or a few times in a lifetime. Thus, limited numbers of patrons, and the uncertain access to them that has characterized rural social relations, is reproduced on a ritual level by the scarcity of ritual contexts in which to enact and represent these relationships.

In Umbanda, by contrast, encounters with potential spirit patrons are legion and are readily accessible to clients. In any one of thousands of different centros, on any day in the year, clients may have a consulta. They may, and do, shop around in different centros for the most sympathetic and efficacious spiritual patron, with whom they may then consult regularly, should the need arise. In addition, the consultas, the focal points of Umbanda ceremonies, provide ritual enactments of patron-client transactions, visual evidence for believers of both the spirits' existence and their willingness and availability to enter into patron-client relationships with human clients. At Umbanda centros the members of the congregations who await their own consultas witness the repeated process of patron-client formations and the transactions of those who precede them in the waiting lines.

While rural Popular Catholicism, just as Umbanda, shows a tendency to credit any solutions to aid requested from a spiritual patron as the result of spiritual intervention (see for example Gross 1971:144), Umbanda has dramatically extended the possibilities for providing material aid in the resolution of problems. In rural Catholicism, the agreement between human client and supernatural patron, the promessa, is a personal affair made silently and privately. Only the testimonial rooms at pilgrimage centers dramatize the eventual successes of these petitions, in the intimate details of the miraculous cures pinned to the walls for strangers to read. No ritual or social context exists through which the help sought might be materially implemented. Umbanda, on the other hand, provides not only the ritual context of the consulta, in which the request is made, but the social context through which it may be answered and the centros' resources mobilized toward material solutions. This would seem both to increase the potentiality for resolving the problems and to strengthen the basis for faith in the spirits' powers and willingness to help. Umbanda has not only expanded the numbers of spiritual patrons, but it may strengthen faith in their efficacy as well, thus intensifying the reliance on patronage.

There are some broad similarities between these two cosmological systems. Umbanda, like Popular Catholicism, emphasizes the roles of spirits as patrons and of all humans as their clients. Umbandistas are offered an image of man as dependent for protection and aid upon individualized, personalized relations with superiors. Umbanda presents supernatural patron-client relationships as the ideal means through which humans may ensure their protection, solve their problems, and obtain aid, and at the same time it sanctifies this standard of behavior for both patrons and clients.

The emergence of Umbanda thus provides structural, behavioral, and ideological support for a predominant type of socio-political relationship found in Brazil. Umbanda did not innovate such relations; it has reproduced them, serving both to mirror and to socialize individuals to the dominant socio-political system. Problems, of whatever sort, are defined as individual rather than collective. Similarly, they require individual rather than collective action for their resolution. Umbanda ignores, and thus denies, the efficacy of collective action by human groups as a means to achieve solutions to the problems of human social life. It cannot possibly be construed, on any level, social or cosmological, as representing a "revolutionary break with the past," which "negates the traditional class structure by rejecting traditional forms of class relations based on paternalism and patronage of the lower classes by the upper classes" (Willems 1967:213).

However, in challenging Willems' interpretation of Umbanda (and I believe he is also in error in making these same claims for Kardecism), I do not intend either to discount the possibility that more egalitarian forms of religious innovation may be occurring in contemporary urban Brazil or to deny the validity of his interpretation for Pentecostal forms of Protestantism. Willems' interpretation of Pentecostalism, which forms the principal focus of his research, as representing new, more egalitarian forms of social relations among the lower classes may well be valid. If so, however, it would appear to make Pentecostalism substantially *different from* Umbanda rather than, as Willems has suggested, similar to it. One of the few studies that offers any comparative perspective on these two religions, a study of patients in a Rio mental hospital by Brody (1973), identified substantial differences between Umbandistas and Pentecostals with respect to another dimension of class-related attitudes: Umbandistas consistently showed far less concern than Pentecostals with occupational upward mobility and achievement (Ibid.:450–55). It is not clear what relation Umbandistas' apparently lower level of occupational ambition or achievement orientation might have to a political sense of dependency and fatalism engendered by Umbanda's combined emphasis on patronage and notions of spiritual causation, and its resulting greater image of human powerlessness. Nor is it clear what significance the apparently contrastive picture of a Protestant ethic among Pentecostals might have for comparing the nature of social relationships fostered within these two religions.

11

Conclusions

In these conclusions, I have resisted the temptation to reformulate my work in response to the current state of knowledge on Brazil and current theoretical issues and debates. I will leave this for the epilogue, in which I will also comment upon recent research on Umbanda. This chapter will remain faithful to my original conclusions and to the theoretical parameters within which the research was conducted. I will first summarize my findings, and then discuss some of their implications at the time of my research.

Umbanda is a mystical religion centered on the belief in spirits and on spirit possession as a means of achieving direct contact with the spirit world. Its principal supernatural figures are benevolent spirits believed able and willing to intervene directly in the affairs of men, and Umbanda rituals focus upon contacts and petitions of aid made to these spirits. The emphasis on spiritual aid and its implementation by forms of social welfare gives Umbanda a practical and instrumental orientation and makes its centros places that are sought out primarily for solutions to personal problems.

Kardecism, popular with the middle sectors, provides a rationalistic, scientistic framework for a belief in spirit possession and a humanistic emphasis on charity and social welfare. From "Macumba," a generic term for Afro-Brazilian religions in Rio popular mainly within the lower sectors, Umbanda draws its principal supernatural figures and many elements of ritual practice. Umbanda, as I have interpreted it here, began as a schismatic movement among middle sector Kardecists, who transformed Afro-Brazilian traditions according to their own class values and interests. However, it has also appealed to many members of the lower sectors, who have redefined themselves as Umbandistas. Practitioners of Umbanda in Rio now include most former followers of "Macumba." This same process has occurred as Umbanda has diffused throughout Brazil. As it has invaded territories formerly dominated by other regional traditions, it has become an important component of the ongoing changes to which leaders and practitioners of these religions must respond. While it has been modified in these regional settings, it has at the same time modified regional Afro-Brazilian religions toward greater homogeneity and created a new national religion.

Participants in this multiclass and multiracial religion range from upper class professionals to impoverished members of the lower classes. Middle sector participation is congruent with Kardecists' belief in spirits and spirit possession and with the growth, within the upper sectors of society, of nationalistic sentiments that highlight the contributions of Brazilian Indians and African slaves to the Brazilian cultural identity. The middle sectors' participation in Umbanda has been legitimized by the interest and involvement of politicians, who have contributed to its increasing institutionalization and acceptance within Brazilian society. For members of the lower sectors, participation in Umbanda and/or self-definition as Umbandistas has conferred legitimacy and prestige upon beliefs and practices formerly disparaged and persecuted, and it has provided a source of numerous benefits and services, both spiritual and material, available through Umbanda centros.

While my study has explored the spectrum of participation and ritual variation in Umbanda, my principal focus throughout has been on the middle sectors, particularly on the form of Umbanda Pura, "Pure Umbanda," which they developed and which remains identified with middle sector values and interests. I believe that their influence over ritual and belief and their attitudes toward legitimizing its practice have been crucial in setting Umbanda apart from the ongoing Afro-Brazilian religions out of which emerged, and in establishing its contemporary forms, dimensions, and status in Brazilian society.

Umbanda is composed of small groups of adherents organized around the personalistic and charismatic authority of their leaders. These vary considerably in ritual and ideological orientation and in class composition. Many remain autonomous; however, increasing numbers are affiliating with Umbanda federations, which provide an organizational superstructure and a degree of centralization for Umbanda on a local, state, and national level. Umbanda federations, although they affiliate only a minority of centros, are able through contacts with politicians and with the mass media to exert a disproportionate influence over Umbanda's public image. This centralizing tendency represents an effort by the middle sectors to organize and coopt formerly lower class religious centers. Middle sector domination is also apparent in individual centros of multisector composition, whose leaders are almost invariably from the middle sectors.

Relationships between individuals and groups in Umbanda commonly take the form of vertical, clientelistic, patronage relations, which are frequently translated into forms of class domination. Individuals of the middle sectors serve as patrons and the lower sectors become their clients and clienteles. This idiom of patronage extends beyond socio-economic and political relationships to become a generalized and pervasive model of relations between spirits and humans.

Middle sector dominance of Umbanda has also involved the projection of a middle class ideology and value system, which has become encoded in the ritual form of Umbanda Pura. This emphasizes rationalism and order, charity and social welfare, and restraint and decorum in matters of ritual. It rejects, under the heading of Quimbanda or "black magic," behavior and practices associated with violence, lack of control, immorality, and many practices specifically derived from Africa. Thus while acting to perpetuate and legitimize selected elements of Afro-Brazilian religious traditions, it also discredits and eliminates many others and "whitens" Umbanda. The central position of the Preto Velho exemplifies this reinterpretation of the Afro-Brazilian heritage, emphasizing subordinate, subservient, docile, acculturated Africans over the free, independent, and powerful figures of the Orixás.

These political, socio-economic, and ideological aspects of middle sector dominance are masked by ambiguities and status reversals in Umbanda cosmology and ritual practice. In the cosmology, the dual identities of the Orixás/Saints and the Pretos Velhos, spirit patrons who are slaves, create ambiguities in regard to their religious identity, on the one hand, and their social status, on the other. Ritual ranking provides for disjunctions between members' ritual ranks and their socio-economic statuses. Spirit possession leads to further ambiguities by creating disjunctions between the social status, race, and sex of spirits and that of the mediums who receive them.

These ambiguities create status reversals for members of the lower sectors and permit differing interpretations of Umbanda ideology and ritual historically associated with different social sectors to coexist within a single religion. At the same time, by obscuring the realities of power, they serve to reinforce and to perpetuate Brazilian structures of hierarchy, inequality, and patronage.

This process of mystification, however, should not be seen to have successfully eliminated overt and conscious class and racial conflict within Umbanda. Resistance to white middle sector hegemony was and continues to be visible in conflicts over leadership, over definitions of ritual and belief, and over Umbanda's African identity.

Umbanda draws together individuals from different socio-economic sectors, providing arenas for communication and interaction between them on a personal basis and for the formation of patronage relations that include the exchange of goods and services. More affluent participants may assume roles as patrons and derive personal and humanitarian satisfactions from their charitable services to the community. At the same time they may manipulate their roles to gain clients and followings that are a source of specific services, social influence and prestige, and political supporters. These same roles are open as well to the less affluent on a more limited basis, but lower sector participants derive principally the reciprocal benefits of protection, and of goods and services that contribute to their subsistence and are unavailable on a regular basis through institutional channels.

By reproducing and reinforcing social inequalities and forms of class domination found within secular society, Umbanda emerges as an essentially conservative religion which acts to preserve the status quo by redressing social inequalities individually through the classic mechanism of charity. Politicians, in exploiting Umbanda voters, also perpetuate Brazilian structures of hierarchy, inequality, and patronage. This conservatism is also expressed in Umbanda ideology and ritual, which stresses spiritual rather than social causations and solutions to life's problems, and individual rather than collective responsibility and action.

Umbanda is clearly a product and a part of the changes that have occurred in southern Brazilian cities during a period of rapid urbanization and industrialization, which has been marked by the shift of economic and political centers of power from rural to urban areas. During the early phase of this transformation, at the time of the emergence of Umbanda, the urban middle sectors made significant economic and political gains but failed to develop class solidarity, remaining fragmented both in their interests and in their social and ideological cohesion. They gained their ends through patronage ties with the federal government and through participation in elite political and economic interest groups. The urban lower sectors, which expanded at a far more rapid rate through both internal growth and rural-urban migrations, suffered from high rates of unemployment and underemployment and the lack of essential urban services. Their discontent presented an increasing political threat to the upper sectors of the population, who responded with the cooptation of political leaders, and federal patronage (particularly within the labor unions). For these and other reasons, working class solidarity developed to only a limited degree. Within this urban context, Umbanda served to facilitate the creation of vertical contacts and linkages between two sectors of the urban population, both of which lacked social or ideological cohesion and traditionally relied on patronage to gain their ends.

I have distinguished two phases of Umbanda's development: its formative period during the Vargas regime and its post-World War II political phase. Its initial phase may be seen as a response from within the middle sectors to the political and economic existence of the expanding lower classes, within the context of intense nationalist sentiment. Umbanda became almost a religious metaphor for nationalism and for the new socio-economic and political realignments of the Vargas regime.

Nationalist symbolism and political opportunism combined in Umbanda with a paternalistic and humanitarian concern with the urban lower sectors. In São Paulo during the early 1920s, similar attitudes were reported among the same occupational sectors of the middle sectors that predominated among Umbanda's founders and early leaders—professionals, civil servants and small merchants (Dean 1970:158). This same combination of nationalism, paternalistic humanitarianism, and political exploitation of the lower sectors was shortly to come together in the government of Getúlio Vargas. Umbanda's early years thus provided it with an ideological structure that both reflected its social context and laid the foundation for articulating the political interests of the middle sectors with those of the lower sectors.

Umbanda's second phase began with the postwar return to electorate democracy and the immediate impact of an expanded lower sector electorate. Umbanda leaders began to encourage lower sector adherents, and Umbanda emerged as a multiclass religious interest group. This becomes especially significant when seen in the political context of an increasing polarization of the middle and lower sectors of Brazil's large urban populations. As the lower sectors continued to expand, their demands for economic benefits and social services, supported by populist politicians, presented an increasing threat to the economic and political stability of the middle sectors, who responded with increasing political opposition to lower class interests and demands. This increasing polarization was a central factor in the 1964 military coup in which the middle sectors joined the elite to stand behind the army against the threat to its interests of urban lower class political participation (Love 1970:23).

Umbanda's political role during this period was as an interest group, organized around religion and nationalism. It furthered the ends of populism and mediated increasing polarization of the sectors involved in it by creating crossclass linkages and fostering the exchange of goods and services.

Without intending to do so, my study of Umbanda challenged several well established myths about Brazilian society: that patronage structures were essentially rural and not urban forms of organization; that urban Brazil lacked any significant independent coherent middle sectors; and that the middle sectors that could be identified in Brazilian urban areas acted differently from the middle sectors in developed countries.

My findings demonstrate how thoroughly the idiom and structure of patronage permeate urban Brazilian life. They provide an almost classic study of urban patronage relations and networks, showing how political interest groups may form around a popular religion and how local associations formed in this way provide clienteles that in turn articulate with the formal political process. They thus illustrate and reveal the workings of the infrastructure that supported the rise and success of Brazilian populism in the 1950s and 1960s, as well as providing empirical support for Singer's (1965) suggestion that Umbanda might be among the urban voluntary associations serving as sources of political clienteles.

My research also shows that the middle sectors as well as the upper sectors described by Leeds (1964) can use patronage to build, maintain, and further their own careers. The process is parallel to the one he describes for affluent upper sector businessmen, except that in Umbanda the patronage ties link the poor to middle sector patrons.

Many studies of Brazil, and Latin America in general, have observed that the middle sectors have tended to identify with and derive their culture, political attitudes and values from the elite, demonstrating little evidence of class consciousness, solidarity, or action in their own interests (Wagley 1963; Adams 1967). The formation and growth of Umbanda, however, reflects an initiative from within the middle sectors to create a new religious identity, independent from that of the elite. Umbanda contrasts with the mode of religious dissent traditionally adopted by the upper sectors, which, in seeking religious and philosophical alternatives to the dominant Catholicism have, since the mid-nineteenth century, turned to various European traditions: Positivism, Protestantism, and Kardecism, all of which reflected their identification with European culture and elites. The middle sector creators of Umbanda also drew upon these European traditions, but their simultaneous incorporation of Afro-Brazilian traditions represented a new and dramatic turn to non-European, Brazilian popular religious elements. The creation of Umbanda Pura, then, signaled a turning to non-European cultural sources as well as to lower class religious traditions, and reflected the emergence of middle sector claims to cultural and political autonomy.

Viewing Umbanda, other Afro-Brazilian religions, and Spiritism as voluntary associations also makes it clear that statements claiming the absence of such associations in Brazil, and in Latin America in general (see Wagley 1964; Goode 1970), are in error. Since so many of these religious associations, carrying out activities similar to those identified with associations within developed nations, are also clearly products of the middle sectors, the history of Umbanda is to some degree also the history of the increasing desire and ability of middle sector members to develop vehicles for the expression and realization of their own interests and identity.

As the first investigation of any Afro-Brazilian religion in the industrial south, my study helps to shift the focus of these religions from the north and northeast to the south, from the study of their cultural and psychological aspects to an examination of their political and economic dimensions, and from what has amounted to almost an obsession with their continuity to the legitimate study of their change.

My study portrays a religion that is highly eclectic and innovative; it is an important component as well as a reflection of urban religious, social, and political life. The evidence I have presented of its integration into Brazilian urban society refutes the impression that lingers in the literature, particularly that available in English, that these religions are exotic cultural forms that have, in some miraculous fashion, remained largely isolated from the social processes that have so dramatically affected other aspects of urban industrial life. Stripped of its exoticism, Umbanda is revealed as an exemplary urban voluntary association, with social, economic, and political roles characteristic of these associations in the industrial world.

However, even within its industrial context, Umbanda remains inescapably and essentially exotic. The extraordinary richness and variety of its ritual and cosmological eclecticism provide a symbolic universe with great potential for interpreting the transformations of contemporary Brazilian society. While it is true that Umbanda is far more eclectic and less African than, for example, Candomblé, levels of African retention must not be confused with issues of cultural or aesthetic worth. Obscurantist notions that more eclectic Afro-Brazilian religions such as Umbanda are, simply by virtue of their eclecticism, culturally inferior or aesthetically impoverished must be laid to rest.

If, instead of viewing Umbanda only with reference to Africa, as presenting an impoverishment of African traditions, it is placed in a wider international cultural context which includes Europe, then its eclecticism can be seen as an extension of its symbolic universe to embrace major European strands of Brazil's complex cultural and intellectual history, and as providing an arena where the Brazilianization of continental ideas meets the Brazilianization of the African heritage.

The discovery of the crucial role of the middle sectors in Umbanda's formation and subsequent development within Brazilian society raises new questions for other Afro-Brazilian religions. All of these, like Umbanda, have been assumed to be essentially independent and spontaneous creations of the lower sectors, translations into a religious idiom of their experiences and world views. While researchers have occasionally noted participation of more affluent sectors in these religions, their presence has been regarded as peripheral and insignificant. The case of Umbanda, however, raises questions as to whether this participation has been merely peripheral. For example, I have suggested the possibility of an extensive dominant sector influence in Bahian Candomblé. It is necessary to investigate the class composition of these religions empirically rather than accepting them uncritically as autonomous expressions of lower sector social and political attitudes. It is also important not to assume homogeneity of the lower sectors with respect to their identifications with and participation in Afro-Brazilian religions. For example, while Umbanda Pura has undoubtedly proved attractive to many members of the lower sectors, it has competed there with contrasting definitions of Umbanda, which have championed more African forms of ritual and a strong identity with Africa and have expressed hostility to the class as well as the ethnic implications of the whitened form of Umbanda. This same diversity of identifications and participation may also exist in other Afro-Brazilian religions.

With respect to previous treatments of Umbanda, this first full-length study interprets it quite differently from the impressionistic findings of my predecessors Bastide and Willems. I view it as inegalitarian rather than egalitarian, as presenting a continuation rather than a break with patronage relations, and as perpetuating class dependency within the lower sectors rather than fostering emergent working class autonomy and solidarity. These findings also challenge characterizations of Umbanda as either a religion of the oppressed or a simple example of a peripheral spirit possession religion.

My data also challenge major premises of modernization theory. Modernization models portray industrializing societies as dual societies composed, on the one hand, of a "modern" sector—urban, educated, and industrialized, structured in terms of horizontal class ties and forms of association, rational, bureaucratic, and open to change—and on the other hand, a "traditional" sector—rural, agrarian, structured through vertical ties of patronage, largely uneducated, associated with "irrational" folk practices, and deeply opposed to change. The second and related premise assumes that as the benefits of modern industrial development gradually trickle downward to the urban masses and outward to the traditional rural sectors, they will be accepted in these sectors and will come to replace traditional culture and forms of social structure.

Umbanda, with its practice of spirit possession, its association with preliterate, "primitive" Africa, its historical links to Brazil's colonial, agrarian, slaveholding past, even its dominant structuring of relations into forms of patronage should, according to the modernization model, be found within the traditional sector. It should be either absent or on the wane in the urban industrial sector, lingering on principally among traditionally oriented lower sectors, especially among recent rural migrants.

Many analysts of Afro-Brazilian religions appear to have accepted these premises. Their influence can be inferred, for example, both in the assumptions by Willems and Camargo that Umbanda's practitioners are from the lower sectors and primarily rural migrants, and also in the predictions that Afro-Brazilian religions in the northeast would gradually lose their vitality and disappear as the modernizing forces of education and upward mobility become available to all class sectors.

Umbanda has shown a contrary pattern of demographic growth, however, manifesting overall expansion and increased vitality rather than decline, with the most dramatic expansion occurring in the heart of the most modern industrial areas of Brazil, among its educated and affluent sectors. This same vitality is found as well in other Afro-Brazilian religions, and some of these appear, like Umbanda, to have been influenced by the participation of the affluent, educated urban sectors.

Umbanda, then, suggests the dangers of assuming either a dichotomy between rural and urban socio-cultural forms or the incompatability or irrelevance of "traditional" forms in the "modern" sector. The very associations with tradition that are assumed by modernization theories to relegate forms such as Umbanda to extinction can in fact serve as an important basis for evoking tradition within a contemporary urban context. It would seem to be precisely Umbanda's ability to evoke so many dimensions of Brazilian experience, past and present, that made it of such service to nationalist interests. It makes powerful symbolic references to a national identity that reaches far beyond the confines of urban industrial Brazil to embrace the slaveholding past of the northeastern Pretos Velhos and the vast Amazonian rainforests of the Caboclos. These figures, at the same time, symbolize the incorporation of ethnic minorities and, more broadly, of the lower classes into national life. Moreover, they provide a potential locus for expressions of cultural and political resistance by the urban poor to the dominant sectors of Brazilian society. Traditional elements are deliberately manipulated in Umbanda to serve diverse contemporary political ends.

The centrality of patronage relationships in the ideology and practice of this consummately urban religion also challenges modernization's dichotomous model of society, which associates patronage relations with rural social structures. My evidence concerning urban patronage in Umbanda converges with that of many recent analyses of urban Brazil which similarly indicate that despite its rapid industrialization and growth, patronage retains its importance in urban political, economic, and social life and should be viewed as an essential structural characteristic of Brazilian development.

In only one sense—and paradoxically, it is one which is generally ignored by modernization theorists—does Umbanda *conform* to the model of modernization: the activities of the middle sectors in creating Umbanda Pura, in codifying, organizing, bureaucratizing, and rationalizing it, reflect an effort within a traditional religious arena to modernize and to bring the principles and ideology of Brazilian development to the masses.

12

Epilogue

In the period since I completed this study, the expansion of anthropology within Brazil, together with growing theoretical interest in the study of forms of popular culture, has led to greatly increased research interest in Umbanda, especially among young Brazilian social scientists. What started in the 1970s as a trickle has become a flood of research and publications on diverse aspects of Umbanda, other Afro-Brazilian religions, and Spiritism. This final chapter will review some of this new work, focusing mainly on contributions to topics central to my own concerns and analyses (the bibliography also includes recent work not discussed here). I will also incorporate into the discussion recent studies concerning ongoing changes in Brazilian society and politics, mentioning some of the pertinent new theoretical perspectives within the social sciences. I will offer some critical reflections on my own study and identify what I regard as promising areas for further research.

Reflecting on the contributions that my own research has made to an understanding of Brazilian society, I think its main importance for the field of Afro-Brazilian religions lies in its identification of the influence of the middle sectors, their shaping of Umbanda ritual and ideology in conformity with their own attitudes and values, utilizing of Umbanda as a source of political clienteles and electoral support, and strengthening of Umbanda's structural emphasis on vertical, hierarchical patronage relations. These interpretations have now gained widespread acceptance, and they have helped to reorient studies of other Afro-Brazilian religions toward greater sensitivity and concern with class and political issues.

My findings have also proven to have more relevance and application outside the realm of Afro-Brazilian religions than was apparent at the time of my research, identifying wider processes of change and linking Umbanda to transformations in other areas of Brazilian culture and politics. I will mention briefly three examples of such linkages: one concerns the role of the dominant sectors and the state in the transformation of popular culture; a second, the articulation of self-conscious social and political goals by the middle sectors; and the third, continuities in local level populist politics.

The role of the middle sectors in transforming Umbanda ideology and practice now appears to me to represent only one example of a far-reaching process involving efforts, particularly during the 1930s, by the dominant sectors of Brazilian society and the Brazilian state to influence and coopt a wide variety of popular cultural forms. Unaware of the work of Antonio Gramsci, I was nevertheless discovering the role of the middle sectors in what more recent researchers have explicitly identified as the hegemonic process at work. My suggestion that this process might also be occurring in other Afro-Brazilian religions during the same period is confirmed in recent work in the northeast (Dantas 1982). All of these examples involve efforts to transform the religious heritage of lower class racial minorities into regional or national Brazilian culture (see also Dantas 1982; Fry 1982b).

This effort appears to have extended as well to other, secular forms of Afro-Brazilian popular cultural expression. It was during this same period, from the late 1920s through the Vargas dictatorship (1930–1945), for example, that the samba, the *escolas de samba* (samba schools) and *Carnaval* were similarly transformed from lower class practices, whose public manifestations were disapproved and often banned, to recognized, officially sanctioned, and central components of Brazilian national culture (Goldenwasser 1975; Fry 1982). *Capoeira,* a martial art of African derivation practiced first by slaves and later in the streets of lower class Afro-Brazilian neighborhoods as a form of self-defense (Rego 1968), was also elevated in status during this period, moving off the streets and into the salons of the middle classes as a form of recreation and incorporated into the repertory of national Brazilian folklore as a dance form (Myers 1983). Today, in urban centers of southern Brazil, capoeira is studied by the affluent sectors in conjunction with dance and other martial arts and has itself become Brazil's own national martial art.

While it is not clear to what degree these transformations were directly encouraged by the Brazilian state, they unquestionably coincided directly with the Vargas government's intense interest in promoting cultural nationalism and incorporating the traditions of Brazil's ethnic and racial minorities within a national culture. The state's nationalist interest extended as well beyond the realm of Afro-Brazilian culture. The Vargas government gave enthusiastic encouragement to activities of noted composers such as Villa Lobos to incorporate popular regional Brazilian folk themes into national upper class musical forms (see Squeff and Wisnik 1982). And Vargas also carried a nationalist influence into the realm of Popular Catholicism and supported the effort to have *Nossa Senhora de Aparecida* (Our Lady of Aparecida), already the object of a local shrine, elevated to the status of national patron saint.

Taken together, these concurrent transformations suggest that the intense nationalist sentiment that built during the 1920s and that Vargas consolidated as a central basis of his policy to modernize and centralize the Brazilian state may well have had wide-ranging effects in transforming and nationalizing various aspects of Brazilian popular culture, including Afro-Brazilian culture. Umbanda, in this case, would represent an instance of this process in which the middle sectors acted as brokers between the interests of the state and the rich cultural heritage of the popular sectors.

My analysis of the middle sector's role in the transformation of Umbanda also highlighted a broader process of class transformation in Brazil during the 1930s. This transformation involved increasing self-consciousness within the middle sectors, combined with their growing awareness of the potential political threat represented by the lower sectors. A recent analysis by Chauí (1978) of *integralismo* (Integralism), a political movement also centered in the middle sectors and contemporaneous with Umbanda, observes this same process to be at work. Integralism emerged during the 1930s, as a major right wing political party modeled on European Fascism, and despite the obvious differences between this explicitly political movement and Umbanda, the two offer some interesting parallels. (see also Concone 1981). Like middle sector Umbanda leaders, Integralists allied themselves closely with the nationalist interests of the Brazilian state. Integralism, with its passionate appeal to national unity and its denial of class and regional differences, was a call to action urging the middle classes to unify and assert their own standards of control and order, in order to avert the perceived threat of a Communist-inspired revolt from within the lower classes.

In fact, one of Integralism's major themes, which concerns the need to rescue the Brazilian workers (and of course, Integralism's own middle class constituents as well) from exploitation by Communist agents of false faith (Ibid.: 101), is remarkably close to the discourse of Umbandistas of the time, except that Umbandistas' expressed enemy was Quimbanda. I quoted their formulation of Umbanda's mission to save the miserable and ignorant masses from exploitation by the sorcerers of Quimbanda in my study, and I analyzed this as a metaphoric expression by the middle sectors of their fear of the political threat posed by the masses and their desire to order and control them, thus protecting themselves. The parallel with Integralist discourse suggests that Quimbanda may have served even more directly as a political metaphor for Communism. It may also be significant that several important early Umbanda leaders were reportedly supporters of Integralism, and at least one nationally known Integralist leader later served as the head of an important Rio Umbanda federation. The parallels and linkages between the two movements might be explored as examples of different arenas through which the middle sectors expressed their political ideologies during the period of the 1930s.

My analysis of Umbanda's involvement with populist politics has also gained new significance. At the time of my research, shortly after the 1964 military coup, many Brazilians believed populism to be in rapid and permanent decline. Statements to this effect, which dominated the discourse of the military government in the daily papers, appear to have been accepted as well by many Brazilian intellectuals, who apparently expected the military to succeed in their aim of replacing clientelism and populism with a more rationalized, bureaucratized political apparatus. These beliefs greatly limited the degree of interest in my political analysis of Umbanda, since I was thought to be observing the final moments of a dying political form. The activities of the Umbanda politicians whom I studied were even taken as evidence of their ignorance and political naivete and their hopeless distance from the current political realities.

With the reopening of the political arena in the 1970s, however, populism immediately reemerged, above all in Rio, and in the frenzy of new political activity, Umbanda clienteles became highly visible. Recent studies of populism have even highlighted Umbanda as a prime example of clientele and interest group politics (see for example Diniz 1982). The role of Umbanda and other religious clienteles in local electoral politics has become a popular topic of study (see Pechman 1982a and 1982b; 1983; Silverstein, Birman and Seiblitz 1982). I was astonished, reading a recent report on the involvement of Umbanda federations in the 1982 elections in Rio (Silverstein, Birman and Seiblitz 1982), to see that not only the process that I analyzed in my study, but many of the same groups and even the individual politicians upon whose activities I based my analysis, were still practicing the same politics and in much the same fashion as when I had observed them more than ten years ago. My own study thus provides a historical dimension to the current activities of Umbanda politicians and reveals the continuity and stability which such an interest group may maintain through time, in this case a period of almost 40 years. It appears to me, in retrospect, that Umbanda politicians' estimates concerning the long-range advantages of maintaining their clientele networks during a period of military dictatorship were based on sound political judgment rather than political naivete.

To shift now from discussing the strengths of my analysis to its shortcomings, I feel that my emphasis on middle sector influence, while it constituted a major strength in my work, also resulted in certain distortions. In stressing the middle sectors within Umbanda, which represented in part an attempt to compensate for the oversights of previous researchers who had ignored this sector, my own study in turn underemphasized the significance of lower sector participation. Even as I repeatedly stressed the dialectical interplays between different sectors within Umbanda (see also Brown 1977), the evidence I mobilized to document middle sector practices and influences greatly outweighed and nearly buried my treatment of similar activities among the lower sectors. I wish, for example, that I had explored forms of lower class black Afro-Brazilian Umbanda as extensively as I explored the world of middle sector Umbanda Pura. I also wish I had more systematically compared centros dominated by middle sector membership with those that were more uniformly lower class in composition, in order to test whether the emphasis on hierarchy and patronage was as strong throughout these as in the multisector centros which figured so prominently in my study. I have come to feel, in other words, that there may have been more divergence from the middle sector model on which I focused than I allowed for at the time.

The correlation between changes in the Brazilian political climate and interpretations of Umbanda's political significance made by successive generations of researchers leads me to suspect that we have all been at least as strongly influenced by the Brazilian political climate within which we have worked as by our respective theoretical baggage. It seems to me suggestive, for example, that the interpretations of Umbanda by Bastide and Willems, who regarded Umbanda as a harbinger of emergent class solidarities, the position from which my own research departed, were produced during a period of democratic optimism in Brazil (1955–1964) when liberal to increasingly leftist regimes created many expectations concerning both the autonomy and the degree of solidarity of the Brazilian lower classes. My own work, by contrast, began in 1966, two years after Brazil's political pendulum had swung sharply rightward after the 1964 military coup, which installed what soon became an extremely repressive authoritarian regime. My own focus on the middle sectors was certainly triggered by my early discovery of a retired general (who had served briefly on the national security council of the 1964 military government) at the helm of an important Umbanda federation and by the high visibility of military officers within Umbanda generally. The political climate of harsh repression within which I made this discovery led me, in turn, to look with special care and suspicion at the efforts of the middle sectors to control Umbanda and, through it, other aspects of religious and political life among the lower sectors. I felt compelled to expose these newly discovered elements of both cultural and political domination which, at the time, seemed more significant and more urgently in need of attention than the efforts of other sectors of Umbanda to maintain their independence.

More recently, the political shift toward redemocratization, known as the *Abertura* (opening) that began in the mid-1970s, has provided a new stimulus to researchers to explore popular traditions such as Umbanda as expressions of cultural autonomy and resistance to forms of state domination. The impact of these new interests is already visible in several recent studies of Umbanda and other popular religions which I will discuss presently. These new perspectives are beginning to apply a corrective lens to characterizations of Umbanda as an unequivocal agent of domination.

Turning now to chart some of the directions in recent research on Umbanda and other Afro-Brazilian religions, it seems to me that a striking feature of this new work, second only to its large quantity, is the almost total absence of any dialogue among the various researchers. With notably few exceptions, they appear to have conducted their research and published their results in mutual ignorance. The resulting body of literature is fragmented and has so far failed to identify developing areas of consensus and dispute or to adopt a self-critical stance. It remains an aggregated rather than integrated field of study. While a few notable studies, such as those by Dantas (1982), Fry (1975; 1977; 1978; 1982), and Velho (1975), explore new issues and approaches, many others remain largely descriptive and traditional in their focus, with interesting new observations emerging mainly in peripheral remarks. These problems greatly increase the reviewer's task and have led me to limit the topics reviewed here to those directly linked to my own interests.

The problems I have just outlined emerge with particular clarity in relation to the first topic I will take up: what may be called the social geography of Umbanda's expansion, its growth in relation to demographic shifts and regional differences in economic expansion and politics. Much new material is now available on the growth of Umbanda in diverse Brazilian settings, with interest focused on the major urban centers of the south, on Rio (Birman 1980; Pechman 1982a and 1982b; 1983; Perelberg 1980; Seiblitz 1979; Silverstein, Birman and Seiblitz 1982; Velho 1975); on São Paulo (Fry 1978; 1982; Fry and Howe 1975; Montero and Ortiz 1976; Negrão 1979; Ortiz 1978; Pressel 1973; 1974; 1977; 1980); on Belo Horizonte (Montero 1983); and on Porto Alegre (Lerch 1980). Smaller towns and cities of the interior of São Paulo have also received limited attention (Brandão 1980; Mott 1976), and Umbanda has been investigated in two northern Brazilian cities: Belém (Fry 1977; Vergolino e Silva 1976), and Manaus (Gabriel 1980), and in a small town in the northeast (Toop 1972).

No one has yet attempted to fashion out of this material a more comprehensive comparative picture of the processes of Umbanda's development under regional economic and political conditions, and these regional studies presently remain diverse in their focus. However, they do suggest the broad dimensions of Umbanda's diffusion from major southern cities in response to demographic shifts associated with economic development, commerce, and tourism; evidence of both regional and local variations in these patterns offers possibilities for comparative regional studies.

An exceptionally clear picture of the process of Umbanda's development in the Amazonian city of Manaus is provided in the introduction to the study by Gabriel (1980) although his main focus is on the political dimensions of spirit possession. He links Umbanda's arrival in that city, in the years following World War II, to migrations into the Amazon from the coastal areas during an economic boom, the same process that had earlier brought Afro-Brazilian religions to this area. The period of Umbanda's expansion and the beginning of its institutionalization and bureaucratization in the 1970s is linked to more recent economic changes involving the establishment of Manaus as a Free Port. This stimulus to economic development, principally through tourism, greatly increased the incidence of travel to Manaus from other areas of Brazil and produced a rapid penetration of the mass media. Moreover, among the many new migrants to Manaus were several Umbandista religious specialists and federation leaders who had undergone their religious training and orientation in Rio and São Paulo and who began to organize federations in Manaus. Thus, the form of Umbanda Pura reached Manaus and began to gain popularity. Gabriel stresses, however, that Umbanda's local evolution also involved a reflexive influence upon it of local Afro-Brazilian religious traditions.

In the coastal Amazonian city of Belém, Umbanda's penetration, as well as the important role of its federations in disseminating Umbanda ritual practice, appears linked principally to political rather than economic developments. In the wake of the 1964 military coup, the Brazilian government, in an effort to tighten state security in the Amazon area, mandated the State of Pará, of which Belém is the capital city, to create state level Umbanda and Afro-Brazilian protective federations as a means of organizing, legalizing, and controlling religious groups and their practitioners (Vergolino e Silva 1976); all Afro-Brazilian religious groups were required to join. The social conflicts between federation leaders and religious leaders, which are the focus of this study, take place in the shadow of state intervention, yet its influence is little treated. It would be fascinating to know how this state presence affected Afro-Brazilian religious life and practice, and to compare the effects of the two different forms of economic and political state expansion and intervention on the development of Umbanda in Manaus and Belém.

The only regional comparison yet to appear (Dantas 1982) reveals the rich possibilities of this approach. Dantas focuses on an Afro-Brazilian religion known as Xangô, rather than on Umbanda, and is concerned with the historical role of the local elite in a small town in the State of Sergipe in establishing and upholding the canons of African orthodoxy in Afro-Brazilian religious practice. While Xangô is found to claim fidelity to the same Yoruba traditions as orthodox Yoruba Candomblé houses in Salvador, Bahia, a comparison of the two sets of practices reveals that although each purports to be a faithful reproduction of Yoruba tradition, they differ substantially, at some points offering opposing definitions of that orthodoxy. Instead of writing off these ritual and ideological differences in a manner common to earlier studies—that is, by ascribing them to differences stemming directly from Africa, perhaps to a derivation from different towns—Dantas views them, correctly I believe, as having been largely created within their local Brazilian contexts. Turning to the theoretical literature on ethnicity, she suggests that each of these different definitions of Yoruba orthodoxy has been strongly influenced by the different perceptions and priorities of the dominant classes in their respective local Brazilian contexts. Then, extending her comparison to Rio, she suggests further that the contrastive regional attitudes toward the Afro-Brazilian heritage manifested in their religious traditions— the northeastern religions, which celebrate African orthodoxy, and southern Umbanda, which seeks to dilute it—reflect deeper regional differences in attitude toward that heritage itself. These differences she relates to differences in the demographic and racial composition of their populations.

Research on Umbanda in southern cities and towns, despite its proliferation, has so far given little further attention to local historical processes or to regional comparisons. This situation should be partially corrected by a major study now in progress of the history of Umbanda in São Paulo by Negrão (see also Negrão 1979), which will complement my study of Rio and permit what promises to be an interesting comparison of Umbanda in these two major industrial settings. Other studies of Umbanda in the south have tended either to be unconcerned with its historical dimensions or to produce global level comparisons.

One example of these latter types of global level analysis is provided by Ortiz (1978), a student of Roger Bastide. While Ortiz' analysis begins from a concern, similar to my own, with the emergence of this multiclass and multiracial religion in a modern industrial setting, he interprets the process in a quite different way. He sees Umbanda as the product of a process involving the simultaneous "whitening" of lower class Macumba and the "blackening" of middle class Kardecism, which he views as expressing the reciprocal acceptance by blacks of the world of white values and acknowledgment by the white middle class of the social existence of black Brazilians. He attributes this in turn to socio-economic and industrial changes acting upon the racial and class components of the urban populations in southern Brazil to produce a complementary exchange of cultural materials.

While this model fits the contemporary class and racial distribution of Umbanda, it seems to me to offer a somewhat mechanistic and overgeneral view of Umbanda's historical development, one which neglects politics, ignores historical specificity in regard to local events, and denies its participants the significance of their own actions or strategies. I find it hard to accept a model that portrays simultaneous processes of whitening and blackening in what Ortiz clearly recognizes as different socio-economic and racial sectors of the population as simply a mechanical result of unfolding universal processes. Moreover, he fails to consider the politics of class and race and the dynamic relations of power, aspects that seem to me integral to an understanding of Umbanda's growth, internal variations, and fluidity.

My difficulties with Ortiz' interpretation, as well as our differences, can be easily illustrated by comparing our different points of view on the origins of Umbanda. Apparently because he regards Umbanda as a product of universal processes of change, Ortiz interprets Umbanda's presence in different cities of southern Brazil as evidence of multiple origins, of its independent and spontaneous emergence in three different locations: Rio, Niteroi (former capital of the State of Rio), and the southern state of Rio Grande do Sul. On the other hand, I have suggested a particular moment, place, and set of individuals as "founders" of Umbanda, who embarked upon the transformation of the Afro-Brazilian heritage in a particular way according to their own class interests and values. I have been criticized for being overspecific on this point, and I agree that more detailed historical research would be necessary firmly to establish Umbanda's origin point. However, I find Ortiz' argument in favor of simultaneous independent origins for Umbanda unconvincing on several counts. First, Niteroi, the home of the man whom I identified as Umbanda's "founder," Zélio de Moraes, was only a ten-minute ferry ride across the bay from Rio, and while Zélio himself began his own practice in Niteroi, most of his early associates lived in Rio and began their own centros there. He himself moved his centro to Rio during the 1930s. It thus seems difficult to treat Rio and Niteroi as cases of independent development. As to Umbanda's independent emergence in Rio Grande do Sul, I think it far more likely that it spread there in the manner often recounted to me in various interviews in both Porto Alegre, the state capital, and in Rio; namely, through networks of young military officers, who were active participants in Umbanda from its earliest years and who traveled extensively between Rio and Porto Alegre, both of which were major army headquarters as well as important seaports. I remain convinced, in other words, that future local historical studies will provide evidence for the same kind of diffusion of Umbanda throughout southern Brazil as appears to have occurred in the north, involving networks of influence and communication, cycles of migration, and other social and economic processes associated with capitalist expansion. Moreover, whether or not Umbanda's specific point of origin lay in Rio, it is clear that the activities of the middle sectors that proved decisive in the development of Umbanda Pura (which Ortiz refers to as *Umbanda Branca,* "White Umbanda") did take place there. Rather than reducing Umbanda's development to a series of broad generalizations, I find it more interesting to examine the different socio-economic, cultural, and political factors that have shaped this highly fluid and racially and politically sensitive religion in the different contexts in which it is found. It should be possible, for example, to develop an interesting comparison between Rio and São Paulo. Rio has since the mid-nineteenth century had a rich and complex Afro-Brazilian and Spiritist tradition. The federal capital until 1960, and a bureaucratic and service city par excellence, it has been known for its deeply entrenched and pervasive patronage systems, which operate especially among the middle sectors, many of whose members have been employed in the bureaucracy. Moreover, Rio has also remained a major center of Brazilian populism.

São Paulo, by contrast, developed as a major city only at the end of the nineteenth century, with large infusions of European immigrant populations, and the density of its Afro-Brazilian population, and consequently of its indigenous Afro-Brazilian cultural traditions, has been far more limited in scale and influence than in Rio. Its industrial level surpassed that of Rio by the 1920s and differed significantly in character. Whereas Rio's industrial development favored state-owned enterprises, São Paulo for the most part was the center of private industrial entrepreneurship, which fostered the growth of a strong local industrial bourgeoisie and the corollary rise of a larger and more militant working class than that of Rio. As a consequence, forms of class patronage and populist politics compete in São Paulo with stronger class-based solidarities and political movements than have emerged in Rio. These differences, all of which have important implications for Umbanda practice, its class structure, and its political significance, are exactly the issues which Ortiz' analysis seems largely to ignore.

Two other broad treatments of Umbanda, by Fry and Howe (1975) and Fry (1978), contrast it with forms of Protestantism. Fry and Howe (1975) interpret Umbanda and Pentecostal Protestantism in Brazil as representative of two contradictory structural principles of relationship in Brazilian life: one magical, manipulative, and oriented toward vertical exchanges, represented in Umbanda; the other rational, bureaucratic, and oriented toward horizontal exchanges, associated with industrialization and represented in Pentecostalism. Fry (1978) extends this argument by comparing the religious development of Umbanda in São Paulo with the emergence of Methodism in nineteenth century Manchester. He suggests that the differences in the two religions relate to differences in the nature of each country's industrial revolution, as well as to the position and legitimacy of magic within the two societies. In Manchester, primary industrial growth, in a setting already largely purged of magical beliefs and practices by the Englightenment, produced a thoroughgoing bureaucratic, rational revolution in both social relations and ideology, of which Methodism came to express the quintessential values. In São Paulo, by contrast, a later and quite different, dependent form of capitalist development, in combination with a strongly persistent substratum of magical belief, fostered two contradictory modes of social relations and, in turn, two opposing forms of religious thought and development. Pentecostal Protestantism came to represent the rational, bureaucratic aspects of Brazilian development, while Umbanda expressed its other face, its magical, patronage orientation.

Fry's comparison of São Paulo and Manchester is intriguing. It highlights aspects of Brazilian history crucial to an understanding of the wide popularity that Umbanda and other mystical religious and philosophical groups enjoy among all sectors of Brazilian society. The weakness of Enlightenment influence upon the forms of Catholic belief and practice that were transported to and nurtured in Brazil, and the resulting persistence of mysticism and magic—to which I also alluded in my discussion of the mysticalization of Kardecism in Brazil as a precondition of Umbanda's development and acceptance—merit more serious investigation. It is also possible, though hard to demonstrate, that industrial growth within the context of dependent development in Brazil, by failing to significantly counteract existing levels of mysticism with rationalism, also contributed indirectly to its perpetuation. However, I think it equally possible to interpret the emergence and growth of Umbanda from the heartland of Brazil's industrial development as a challenge to assumptions that industrial development is incompatible with mystical interpretations of the world and thus will tend to replace them with rational ones.

The comparison of Umbanda and Pentecostalism in Brazil seems to me somewhat more problematic. The opposing structural principles of Brazilian society that the two are said to represent seem rather to be fused, on the level of praxis, in bureaucracies that operate on the basis of patronage and, at the national level, in a clientelist or corporatist state. Even within these two religions, Fry and Howe and my own research find a bureaucratic emphasis as well within Umbanda, while other interpreters have noted a complementary clientelistic and patronage influence within particular Pentecostal groups (see especially Raphael 1975).

Even if we accept the broad characterizations of the two religions and the opposition between them, there still remains a crucial question as to what aspects of Brazilian social and political life they relate to and represent. Fry and Howe suggest that the choice between them may be made by different individuals on the basis of familiarity or preference for one or the other mode of social relations, but they do not suggest what kinds of experiences might create such preferences. Various hypotheses have been put forth: I have suggested that this might be linked to participation in different occupational sectors (see Brown 1979), with occupations traditionally associated with patronage, such as the state bureaucracy or domestic service, associated with a preference for Umbanda, and other, less patronage related occupations, such as factory work, with a preference for Pentecostalism. Others have suggested that Pentecostalism may represent nascent class based solidarities and the rejection of vertical dependency on the dominant sectors (Willems 1967; Novaes 1980) while Umbanda might be seen as representing continuing class dependency. These questions are important ones, and they remain unanswered.

Returning to Umbanda, and as a prelude to the discussion of recent interpretations of its political significance within Brazilian society, I will comment briefly on its class composition in different settings to which it has been diffused. Recent research indicates that wherever Umbanda has spread, it has continued to attract middle as well as lower sector participation. Yet its class composition clearly varies with the size and level of anonymity within local environments and with the strength and local character of institutions such as the Catholic Church. Rio, the origin point and focus of Umbanda's struggle for legitimacy, still appears to have the highest proportion of affluent participants. São Paulo, probably for some of the reasons cited in my comparison of these two cities, seems to have a considerably lower proportion of middle sector participants, many of whom are European and Near Eastern immigrants, and a greater concentration of working class and lower sector adherents. In smaller cities, the participation of these affluent sectors appears to me to be significantly lower, which I would attribute in important part to the greatly limited degree of anonymity in comparison to that of large cities. The continuing stigma attached to participation in Umbanda, which increases proportionally with social status, leads more affluent participants to seek Umbanda further afield. I noted, for example, in my research during the 1970s in Campinas, a city near São Paulo with a population of just over 700,000, that while members of the local upper sector—doctors, lawyers, judges, and their families—participated in Umbanda, they almost never did so in Campinas itself, preferring instead the anonymity offered by attending centros in neighboring or even distant cities such as Santos or São Paulo. One woman expressed to me her horror at the idea of participating in Umbanda locally, explaining that it would never do to be seen by her peers at an Umbanda centro. In these smaller cities, middle and upper sector participation may also be limited by strong opposition from local Catholic Church leaders, who cannot exercise a corresponding degree of influence in the more anonymous environment of large cities.

In small towns, there is some indication that participation in Umbanda may be restricted to a still narrower stratum of the population. A recent study of popular religions in a small community in the interior of São Paulo (population 10,000) located the practitioners of Umbanda principally within the commercial middle sector, lodged between the Catholics and Spiritists in the local professional class and the varieties of Popular Catholic, Protestant, and diverse Afro-Brazilian practices found among the lower sectors (Brandão 1980). In the small town in Pernambuco studied by Toop (1972), on the other hand, Umbanda was found to be highly stigmatized, the object of "bitter attacks" by Protestant, lay, and Catholic leaders. Socially marginalized, it was reportedly attended almost exclusively by "the lower strata." Further exploration is needed of the contextual factors that affect the class composition and levels of legitimacy of Umbanda in different local settings, particularly since, as will soon become clear, class composition appears to be an important aspect of political orientation.

Recent research on political aspects of Umbanda falls into two distinct categories: one focuses rather narrowly on micro-political issues internal to Umbanda organizations; while the other is concerned mainly with Umbanda's broader political significance within Brazilian society.

The new literature emerging in the first of these categories, on micro-political issues in Umbanda, is concerned with the social and political dynamics of the interactions among and between leaders of centros and federations, aspects of Umbanda to which I gave relatively little attention. Much of it draws upon models of social conflict that have developed within the British anthropological tradition, and it includes case studies of small group dynamics that provide a close-up perspective of individual and group activities and actors that was absent in my own study. While these studies focus on different aspects of Umbanda's internal politics, they converge in identifying common themes and conflicts.

The best known of these, *Guerra de Orixá* by Velho (1975), is a fine and detailed ethnography of a centro in Rio. It examines the struggle for control between chefes, holders of ritual power, and administrators, holders of bureaucratic power. This same conflict is taken up by Vergolino e Silva (1976) in an examination of relations between the (secular) president of an Umbanda federation and the ritual leaders of its member centros in Belém, and again by Mott (1976) in an examination of competition and conflict among Umbanda centros in the city of Marília, in the interior of São Paulo. Gabriel (1980) provides further insights into the exercise of ritual power in his study of the role of spirit possession in the constitution of sacred authority in a convincing analysis of the ways in which the leader employs the different personae of the various spirits by which he is possessed to respond to and resolve conflicting demands among his constituency and thus maintain power over individuals who in secular terms are his social equals.

These studies help to illuminate the contradictory bases of sacred charismatic power and secular bureaucratic power within Umbanda, and they reveal the exercise of these different kinds of power to be considerably more complex and conflictual than I portrayed them in my own study, which treated them as complementary forms in which sacred authority dominated its secular counterpart. At the same time they consistently fail to relate the internal conflicts and struggles examined to changing economic and political bases of power within the wider society. For example, Vergolino's study of ritual and bureaucratic conflicts in Belém fails to explore the implications of recent state influence in the organization of Umbanda federations as an aspect of authoritarian intervention in a popular religion.

Even Velho's intensive study of the inception and unexpected demise of the Umbanda centro under study overlooks the class aspects of the conflict, which appear to me to be of central importance. The data provided, however, suggest a reinterpretation that does take class issues into account; they suggest that the clash between leaders involves far more than different bases of power. The president of the centro is a middle class, educated university student, while the principal chefe involved in the dispute is a poorly educated, lower class migrant from the northeast. The conflict, of which the sacred and secular strategies exercised by the combatants are given in fascinating detail, ultimately appears to me to involve a clash in which the educational level, financial resources, and prestige of the secular president act throughout to undermine and eventually to overthrow the basis of the ritual power of the unlettered ritual specialist. This case provides what is in my experience an unusual, even rare example of a ritual leader who is quite literally "outclassed" by his chief administrator. It also suggests an important factor in the pattern of class ranking that I identified in my own research, with the apex of the centro's class hierarchy occupied by the chefe, surrounded by close personal friends and family as occupants of top positions in the administrative hierarchy. This configuration, in which ritual authority is supported rather than contradicted by socio-economic status, minimizes both the vulnerability of the leader's power and the potential leadership conflicts of the sort revealed so clearly in Velho's study. This conflict reinforces my own conclusions as to the important degree to which secular statuses and inequalities impinge upon the exercise of ritual power within Umbanda. While ritual leadership clearly constitutes an important basis of power, only in rare cases of extremely successful charismatic leaders have I observed this power to transcend that of socio-economic status.

If these forms of leadership within Umbanda are viewed more broadly, with the bureaucratic form seen as the principal link to and representative of bureaucratic and political institutions of the wider society and the ritual form as representing an alternative (sacred) and autonomous source of power, the opposition between them emerges in its political dimensions as one in which ritual leadership presents a constant potential challenge to the larger social order. Personal networks of chefes' families and friends have important roles as mediators of this opposition and neutralizers of potential conflict.

Political analyses of Umbanda that fall within the second category and treat its wider political significance may be further subdivided into those interpretations that view it as an agent of domination and purveyor of hegemonic values and those that stress its opposite capacity to express an independent, anti-hegemonic potential. Differences in the research perspectives represented in these studies leave unclear whether these two positions represent contradictory orientations within Umbanda or between Umbanda and certain other Afro-Brazilian religions.

The first group of studies, which analyzes Umbanda as an agent of domination, includes two studies of individual centros in Rio (Birman 1980; Seiblitz 1979) that apply an explicitly Gramscian perspective to the analysis of Umbanda ideology and its expression in social action. They interpret it as an agent of hegemonic control which reproduces and transmits the value system of the dominant sectors and the state to the lower classes. Birman's study of a centro located in a large Rio favela indicates how deeply the structures of hierarchy, domination, and patronage may penetrate into lower class Umbanda settings. In an extremely revealing description of the centro's distribution of candy to the neighborhood during a local celebration of major Umbanda spirits, Birman finds ritual leaders who are economically as poor as their local followers using their positions to treat their neighbors with all the superiority, condescension, and rudeness associated by the poor with agents of the dominant classes. In this case, values and behavior associated with the dominant sectors are exercised by members of the lower sectors *toward each other.*

Examples such as this one, which suggests that Umbanda may serve as a vehicle through which economically oppressed sectors take on the mask of the oppressors to oppress their own social equals, reaffirm my own conclusions as to the contradictory and ambiguous nature of expressions of domination and oppression in Umbanda, as well as the dangerous error of regarding it unambiguously as a religion of the oppressed. For this reason, I find a recent revival of this earlier interpretation of Umbanda (Da Matta 1982) unconvincing. Da Matta's blanket characterization of Umbanda as a kind of safety valve, said to "compensate a daily life full of social and political frustrations with blind faith in the powers of the mystical entities" (Ibid.:258) and to provide status reversals in which "the poor and destitute . . . can act powerfully and advise or cure the rich" (Ibid.:260), ignores the now extensive evidence linking Umbanda to middle class influence and to expressions of domination. In addition, the notion of a compensatory religion as an *alternative* to political action avoids the important issue of Umbanda's own political efficacy, the ways in which it is a *form* of political action.

Umbanda again emerges as an expression of the values of the dominant classes in Brandão's study of religion in a São Paulo community (1980). This conclusion is particularly ironic, since his study, which is strongly influenced by the work of Bourdieu, explores the opposite issue, namely, the development of popular religions as vehicles for the expression of cultural and political independence from the values of the dominant Brazilian society. Yet his inquiry, which focuses on the activities of popular religious specialists in demarcating and establishing autonomous forms of religious expression for themselves and their followers, leads him to deny Umbanda leaders this role. Umbanda, and the members of the commercial middle sectors who are identified as its chief practitioners, are seen rather as posing a class-based opposition to more autonomous forms of popular Catholicism and Afro-Brazilian practices which Brandão identifies among the community's poorer sectors.

The second political interpretation of Umbanda emphasizes its potential for autonomy or resistance rather than accommodation to the dominant ideology (although it is important to note that it does not deny that Umbanda may also serve as an agent of domination). The strongest advocate of this interpretation is Negrão (1979), who acknowledges significant middle class influence upon Umbanda during an earlier historical period but asserts that, at least in São Paulo, this influence has begun to diminish, and Umbanda is reemerging as an authentic expression of lower class popular culture (1979:172). Negrão bases his interpretation on the preponderance of lower class genre figures in the Umbanda pantheon, the autonomy and ritual freedom of its religious leaders, and its overall current shift toward more African-oriented forms of practice and identity, which might be called the "re-Africanization" of Umbanda. The large list of spirits within the Umbanda pantheon: Pretos Velhos, Caboclos, and cowboys, sailors, hustlers, prostitutes, and, most recently, *cangaceiros* (northeastern outlaws) are interpreted as authentic representations by the lower classes of "the condition of the dominated." Leacock (1964) made a similar point concerning the pantheon of the Batuque in Belém. However, the fact that at the time of Leacock's study this religion had an almost exclusively lower class membership gives his interpretation credibility. Extensive middle class influence in Umbanda, together with evidence that several major Umbanda spirits have been at least in part defined by middle sector Umbandistas to represent *their* racial and politial ideologies, suggests more complex origins for Umbanda's pantheon of spirits. Negrão's argument offers an important topic for further research, but appears at the moment to be largely speculative and to rest on establishing how different Umbandistas identify and interpret these various figures.

The issue of Umbanda as a continuing reference and identification point with the African heritage is certainly a crucial one. Negrão's observation concerning the current re-Africanizing of Umbanda in São Paulo and federation leaders' increased acceptance for a variety of more African forms of

Umbanda accords with an observation made to me recently in Rio by an extremely astute participant and interpreter of the Afro-Brazilian religious scene in that city (Bandeira, personal communication). I believe that Negrão is quite right in linking this increased African presence in Umbanda to the current movement emphasizing African pride and racial identity. Umbanda's history indicates its enormous fluidity and sensitivity to changes in racial as well as political identifications and ideologies. I would hope that current reexaminations of race and racial inequality in Brazil, which tend to focus rather narrowly on quantitative issues (see Fontaine 1980; Hasenbalg 1979; 1983; Silva 1978; 1979), will carry as well into cultural expressions of race and racial identity and take advantage of the insights that the study of Afro-Brazilian religions can contribute.

To return to my review of political interpretations of Umbanda, the most convincing analyses to date concerning the presence of authentic, independent grass roots political expression from within Afro-Brazilian religions are presented in studies of religions other than Umbanda. Brandão, for example, identified several of the less systematized Afro-Brazilian and popular Catholic groups he studied as demarcating positions of autonomy, and two studies of Afro-Brazilian religions in northeastern Brazil, by Henfry (1981) and Ireland (1983) likewise find these to be articulating grass roots values and interests in lower class settings. Ireland's study is particularly interesting because it combines careful empirical analysis of particular groups with a delineation of the qualities by which such autonomy might be measured. Utilizing the concept of "intermediate groups" in which values, aspirations, and modes of relationship are rehearsed and articulated independently of state agencies and the hegemony of the ruling elites, Ireland finds several Afro-Brazilian groups in the small town expressing grass roots values and interests and an "anti-hegemonic sensibility," which he contrasts with the individualized, vertical, clientelistic relations reported for Umbanda (Ireland 1983:28).

The explicit contrast that both Brandão and Ireland make between the groups that they examine and Umbanda implies, contrary to the position taken by Negrão, that sources of grass roots autonomy in the area of Afro-Brazilian religions lie only outside its boundaries. I remain unconvinced on this point and feel that further exploration both of the socio-political aspects emphasized by these authors and of the cultural representations suggested by Negrão are likely to reveal that, at least in certain settings, autonomous grass roots forms of expression do exist within Umbanda as well. It seems to me that an understanding of this issue with respect to all of these religions depends on their class composition and class relations on the local level. The presence of significant numbers of middle or upper class participants and influence, especially when this is associated with the formation of strong patronage ties with the lower classes, will act against the emergence of autonomous, grass roots political expression in all of these religions. While their absence will not guarantee that the groups will develop anti-hegemonic sensibilities, it offers the potential for them to do so.

Discussions of this sort immediately invite the comparison of Afro-Brazilian religions with the Catholic grass roots ecclesial communities known in Brazil as *Comunidades Eclesias de Base,* or CEBs. These are an outgrowth of efforts by radical clergy, under the influence of Liberation Theology, to stimulate the development of autonomous lay Catholic discussion groups within the lower classes. There are now an estimated 80,000 of these groups in Brazil, and while they have been found to vary considerably in their levels of autonomy and social action, many are now well established (see Betto 1981; Boff 1979; Bruneau 1982; Krischke 1983; Mainwaring 1983; in press).

In a preliminary comparison of the CEBs and Afro-Brazilian religious groups in the town in which he worked, Ireland concluded that, like some Afro-Brazilian groups, some of the CEBs also possess the potential to act autonomously as intermediate groups. Another study of CEBs in the industrial, mainly working class southern city of Nova Iguaçú (Mainwaring 1983; in press) notes that despite their strongly ecclesial rather than political orientation, the CEBs have mobilized successfully to gain social services on the local level. Similar patterns of political mobilization have been described for Pentecostal groups in a rural Pernambuco town (Novaes 1980). I know of no studies that have investigated the possible role of Umbanda centros in such local level political organizing efforts. Certainly this would seem to be of major importance in evaluating its political role and offers another area for further research.

The continuities between the highly visible local level political activity of these religious groups and political parties and electoral politics are at this point unclear. Novaes found in her Pernambuco study that despite their collective mobilization in support of local issues, Pentecostal voters were not identified with either specific parties or platforms (Novaes 1980). In Rio, however, preliminary results of a study of the 1982 local elections show that Protestant candidates, most of them Pentecostals, mobilized higher levels of voter support and had more electoral success than did Umbandista candidates (Various authors, 1982/83).

On a structural level, the CEBs and Umbanda both represent attempts of the dominant sectors of the Brazilian population to mobilize the lower classes, although with different political intentions. Umbanda exemplifies the case of a once autonomous grass roots religion that became the target of middle sector cooptive efforts to implant hierarchical control and to mobilize practitioners in the service of electoral politics in support of nonegalitarian, often authoritarian political goals. The CEBs represent another effort, also from within an institution of the dominant sectors, to establish autonomous, grass roots religious groups, here in the service of more radical, egalitarian political goals. It seems paradoxical that the Catholic Church, the same institution that opposed and even sought to eradicate grassroots Afro-Brazilian religions on religious grounds, is now, on political grounds, seeking to create a similar structure and orientation.

Before leaving the topic of Afro-Brazilian religions and Catholicism, I want to comment on their interaction in practice and belief. It is necessary here to stress internal distinctions between more orthodox Catholicism and more "relaxed," mystical, "popular" forms. It is these latter forms that have permitted so many of Umbanda's practitioners to remain Catholics while practicing Umbanda and to identify Umbanda and Catholicism as complementary parts of a single religious system. This identification is epitomized in the fusion of Catholic saints and African deities described by Herskovits (see especially Herskovits 1937). The continuing vitality of this identification is highlighted by a recent event in the world of Bahian Candomblé. It is particularly revealing because Candomblé is considered to be the most orthodox and least syncretic of these religions. In 1983, the "Second World Conference of the Tradition of the Orixás" took place in the city of Salvador, attended by dignitaries of Yoruba worship, the majority from West Africa. Toward the end of the Congress, these leaders supported the idea that Bahian Candomblé houses, in the interests of Yoruba orthodoxy, abandon Catholic elements in their rituals, especially the presence of the Catholic saints, counterparts of the African Orixás. All but a small minority of cult leaders, however, reacted with horror, protesting the loss of what they identified as an integral part of their religion. Even many orthodox Afro-Brazilian practitioners view this identification as an essential element of practice.

However, in Candomblé, as in Umbanda, I strongly suspect that an increase in African pride may increase the willingness to suppress Catholic elements. Syncretisms are not fixed but are responsive to political and social conditions. This contextual definition of religious identity is dramatically revealed in another study of the "Brazilian" community in Lagos, Nigeria, composed of Yoruba ex-slaves and their descendents who returned to Nigeria during the nineteenth century. In their African context, these cousins of Candomblé opted to define their uniqueness by espousing a *Catholic*, rather than an African, religious identity (Carneiro de Cunha 1977).

Afro-Brazilian religions may also serve as shelters for the conservation of threatened aspects of Catholic belief and practice. In Rio in 1969, two of the most popular Catholic saints, St. Barbara and St. George, were removed from the Catholic ritual calendar. These saints are deeply venerated by both Umbandistas and Catholics; in Umbanda centros St. George is the counterpart of the powerful Orixá Ogum, and St. Barbara of Iansan. Their demotions and the subsequent removal of their icons from many Catholic churches created a great rush of Umbanda chefes to these churches to purchase these large and beautiful icons for their centros. In the ensuing months, I heard many visitors and members of Umbanda centros comment that now that they could no longer pay homage to these favorite saints in the Catholic Church, they had to attend Umbanda in order to do so.

Another example comes from the Batuque in Manaus (Gabriel 1980). During the late 1970s, more orthodox local Church leaders in Manaus, in an effort to increase the orthodoxy of Church practice, prohibited certain Popular Catholic rituals from being held in the churches. Leaders of these Popular Catholic rituals were then granted permission by leaders of the Afro-Brazilian Batuque to perform them in the local terreiros, and in this way, forms of Populist Catholic practice were kept alive. While in the earlier example those who sought St. George in Umbanda were arguably already frequenters of Umbanda, in this latter case they were not, and used Batuque centers as locations in which to continue a Catholic practice. This situation reverses that described for the early colonial period, when the Catholic religious brotherhoods are believed to have been crucial in sheltering and preserving Afro-Brazilian religious practice. Ironically, centuries later, the Afro-Brazilian religions are returning the service.

I will end with brief comments on three additional areas of research on Umbanda which have been neglected in the discussion of political and class issues: gender and health, which have become topics of major concern in anthropology since the time of my study, and symbolic analysis.

The recognition of religion as an important and neglected area for gender studies has so far had little effect on the study of Afro-Brazilian religions. Little has been done on female religious leaders since the early work of Ruth Landes (1947). One exception, Silverstein's work on female leadership in a variant of Candomblé (1976; 1979) focuses on the contradictions of leadership for lower class women, whose influence is dependent on kinship ties with their members but whose financial needs force them to seek the patronage of affluent white men. This economic dependence of even successful lower class women religious leaders contradicts the public image of the powerful *mãe de santo* (female religious leader), and raises a crucial issue concerning the relationship between public ideologies of gender and its daily realities in Afro-Brazilian religions.

My own attempt to bring together the data on the prevalence of women in leadership roles in Umbanda centros (Brown 1976) points up an additional socio-economic constraint on women religious leaders. I found that lower class women frequently become chefes and can achieve positions of considerable local influence (a situation that must be seen in relation to the relatively greater powerlessness of lower class men); however, in the middle sectors, this role for women appears to be rarer, since men tend to predominate in centro leadership and to exercise virtually exclusive domain over activities in the centros, the federations, the mass media, and in politics, a situation that is greatly influenced by their secular occupational statuses as professionals, military officers, and politicians. These observations provide only a beginning for an understanding of women as leaders. How do they gain access to and exercise influence, in comparison with male leaders? Do women's political negotiations and their construction of clienteles differ from those of male leaders? How does this role affect their other activities?

Umbanda as a domain for the creation and transmission of gender identities, world views, and meanings forms another underexplored area. Suggestions that Umbanda provides a context within which women can relieve stress resulting from stereotyped sex roles of virility and virginity (Pressel 1980) and can transcend their ordinary situation of powerlessness by exercising both supernatural and secular authority (Lerch 1980) represent promising beginnings to be explored, but they raise more questions than they answer. What is the structure and significance of gender relations within the Umbanda cosmos and ritual hierarchy, and what perceptions of themselves and of gender roles do women gain through participating?

Feminist anthropology raises many additional questions related to the study of gender that have not been investigated with respect to Afro-Brazilian religions: for example, how do these religions deal with gender-related issues, including homosexuality, birth control, child care, rape, and battered women? Are these issues dealt with differently by male and female mediums? The drama of spirit possession has created so strong a focus on the medium-spirit relationship that attention has been drawn away from the crucial relationship between medium and client, which is, in reality, the central interaction within Umbanda. Does the gender of the consulting medium play a significant role in such interactions, in relation to the parameters of experience, attitudes, and modes of expression which are often largely gender defined?

Studies of male participation in these religions also continue to focus on the issue of the role and significance of male homosexuality. Fry (1977) develops a contrast also noted in my own study, between the high levels and visibility of homosexual participation in Afro-Brazilian religions in Belém and their correspondingly less visible participation in Umbanda in São Paulo. Belém, smaller and less industrialized, offers little anonymity for the expression of either religious or sexual preferences, and consequently, Fry suggests, Afro-Brazilian religions and homosexuality, both marginalized, find affinity in their mutual social unacceptability. Industrialized São Paulo offers far greater anonymity for both religious and sexual preferences and results in less mutual affinity. Fry rejects social class as a factor in this contrast. However, evidence that Umbanda, even in northern cities, tends to be both more middle class and more legitimate and less associated with homosexuality than the Batuque suggests that differences between Umbanda and the Batuque may also be ones of religion and social class, rather than simply differences in degrees of social anonymity. Umbanda's greater social legitimacy, conferred by its middle class participants and image, may be significant in separating this religion from association with more marginal and stigmatized practices.

Wide agreement concerning the importance of illness in Umbanda ritual and belief and in motivating participation and conversion make the long neglect of this topic particularly surprising. (Important exceptions are the intriguing observations on Umbanda by Brody (1973) in his study of a Rio mental hospital and Warren's work on Spiritist curing (1968b).) It may be that Umbanda's initial visibility and success as a competitor of Catholicism fixed it so firmly within the framework of religious studies that researchers were blinded to the centrality of its curing activities. The recent growth of medical anthropology and interest in popular culture has begun to take cognizance of the enormous range in forms of treatment and the contexts within which they occur. Centros represent only one locus for curing, which is also performed in Umbanda and Spiritist hospitals and clinics and by individual healers, where long lines of patients awaiting treatment resemble those at Catholic pilgrimage centers. These various types of healing centers are popular throughout Brazil and have even diffused with Umbanda outside of Brazil. For example, I found spiritual healing to be the central attraction of the Umbanda centros in Newark, New Jersey (see Brown 1980).

Treatments range from those described in my discussion of consultas, involving the use of ritual objects, music, gesture, and the laying on of hands *(passes),* to more medicalized forms known as spiritual operations, which may be performed on the exterior of the body or may involve actual surgical incisions (see for example Fuller 1974; Greenfield 1984). Moreover, forms of Spiritist and Umbanda treatment are often found in conjunction with biomedical treatments. This is often the case in Spiritist and Umbanda hospitals and in private consulting rooms. In the course of research in Rio in 1976, I studied the practice of an Umbandista M.D., which was structured in the following way: patients were first diagnosed by an Umbanda medium in trance, through the use of a Spiritist technique known as *musicoterapia* (musical therapy), and then they were examined by the M.D., who utilized this diagnosis, together with standard medical diagnostic techniques, to prescribe treatment. This same doctor was part of a large referral network, which included a number of Umbanda and Spiritist centers, and forms of therapy including dance therapy and Spiritist psycho-drama.

This rich variety of practices and accompanying theories concerning the etiology and treatment of illness are now receiving their share of attention. Current studies are beginning to address the role of spirit possession in treating illness, stressing the therapeutic aspects of possession (Pressel 1974; 1977; 1980; Lerch 1980), and the role of such groups in integrating their patients within the local community (Serra 1976). Other studies are exploring theories concerning illness etiology and treatment in relation to concepts of the body (Ferreira 1983; Guedes 1974; Montero 1977; 1983). Comparative work is also beginning on the approaches of these forms of parallel medicine and orthodox biomedical practices, as well as on the roles they play on the lives of those who purvey and consume them. One study of patients in a Rio psychiatric unit compares beliefs held by the psychiatric personnel at the clinic and by Umbandista members of the patients' families concerning the causes of particular patients' mental illnesses (Perelberg 1980). I have also studied the process of diagnosis and treatment of clients at a Brazilian Umbanda centro in Newark, New Jersey (Brown 1980). A broader comparison of religious and scientific values among Spiritists, members of the medical profession, and the Catholic clergy and their activities with respect to health care is also in progress (Hess 1983).

Finally, considering the richness of Afro-Brazilian religions' symbolic systems, it seems incredible that so little symbolic analysis has been done. Umbanda, because of its pronounced eclecticism, internal variation, and dizzying rate of ongoing change, seems to pose a great challenge to a form of analysis that has traditionally examined more stable phenomena. The studies I have already mentioned, which examine figures in the pantheon and the symbolism of illness and the body, offer only a tantalizing sample of the vast and complex symbolic universe of Umbanda. Even in the far better known Candomblé, I know of only two full-length symbolic analyses, by Elbein (1976) and Trindade-Serra (1978). Elbein's study focuses upon concepts of death among the most "orthodox" Yoruba Candomblé houses in Bahia. This is a fascinating study, but it is flawed because rather than investigating these issues and their meanings for Brazilian practitioners, Elbein describes the beliefs and practices and analyzes their meaning almost exclusively with reference to Africa. She thus gives the impression that Bahian Candomblé represents not only a faithful but a nearly exact reproduction of Yoruba practice in Africa. This interpretation must be taken more as an expression of ideological commitment to African orthodoxy than as a portrait of the realities of Bahian Candomblé, even the most orthodox versions of which have been modified by their Brazilian environment.

This problem does not arise in the study by Trindade-Serra (1978) which, influenced by Turner and Levi-Strauss, examines symbolism in its social context in a Candomblé of the Angola type. This wide-ranging study explores the symbolic aspects of *axé* (sacred power) and its ritual expression and transmission, touching upon spirit possession, food, illness, and various aspects of divinity embodied in the Orixás. Most intriguing is his discussion of the *erês,* representations of the Orixás as children, which leads him into a discussion of the symbolic meanings of childhood in Candomblé. These *erês* emerge as contradictory, ambiguous, liminal figures, mediators who embody the transition between nature and culture, license and restraint, order and disorder. The richness of this interpretation suggests the possibilities awaiting researchers of Umbanda.

An intriguing but nonmainstream symbolic analysis of Xangô in Recife has been made by Motta (1983), whose work seeks to merge the dialectical approach of Robert Murphy with the materialism of Marvin Harris. Motta's central concern is the symbolic significance of food, which he relates to the analysis of the symbolism of family and ritual kinship. This allows him to construct a theology of Xangô, which he derives from ritual, dance, music, and food.

None of the above analyses, however, make a serious effort to relate the symbolic realm to the realities of class, power, and politics. A promising model for such an approach has been developed by Taussig (1979; 1980a; 1980b) in his work on popular religions and healing systems in another area of Latin America. His version of symbolic Marxist analysis, which treats these popular forms in their dialectic relations with the Catholic Church and other dominant institutions, and as expressions of a critical political consciousness within a context of class struggle, promises to provide rich insights as well into Afro-Brazilian religions.

Umbanda's vitality rests on the continuing importance of the Afro-Brazilian heritage to diverse social sectors: on the creativity of a dominated black and mulatto minority whose contributions to Brazilian culture continue to be vigorous 100 years after abolition, and on the interests of the more affluent sectors of society who have also found it symbolically significant and have drawn upon it to express their own attitudes and ideology. The mutual interests of these different sectors in the Afro-Brazilian heritage, and the often strained but nevertheless crucial alliance between them within Umbanda, provide a key to the dynamic growth that this religion has sustained. Umbanda's continuing popularity extends beyond its link to Brazil's African heritage. It stems as well from its involvement in and expression of so many aspects of Brazilian social, political, and religious life. It continues to exercise its fascination upon me, after 20 years of research and writing about it.

Notes

Chapter 1

1. I will use the term "sectors" rather than "classes" throughout this study. The middle sector refers to a wide range of white collar workers, from the affluent liberal professions and upper echelons of the military to various levels of bureaucrats and civil servants, to clerical and other relatively low-income occupations. The upper sector refers to the agrarian elite and the commercial and industrial bourgeoisie, and the lower sector refers to another wide spectrum of occupations ranging from industrial workers to the semi- and unemployed. I have been led to this cruder terminology by the well-known problems of applying either Marxist or Warnerian models of social class. The term "sector" does not assume class solidarity or an established class identity but refers to what are essentially broad occupational distinctions, which to some degree blur economic overlaps among sectors. These distinctions conform to an essentially bimodal model of Brazilian society based on the fundamental distinction between nonmanual and manual labor (see Fernandes 1973; Ianni 1963; Jaguaribe 1968; Saes 1974; Leeds 1967). In these terms, the middle sectors, however precariously, belong to the upper stratum. In terms of the historical process of Brazilian class formation, the middle sectors began to expand, to acquire visibility, and to articulate interests distinct from those of the upper sector toward the end of the nineteenth century, under the impulses of urbanization, industrialization, and the expansion of the state bureaucracy. This process has continued, and although this stratum still does not form a cohesive, self-conscious class, groups within it have shown much evidence of common interests, ideologies, and lifestyles. I refer to these as the middle sector's recognition of class interests and values. Umbanda, as I will argue, is a part and an example of this process.

2. I use quotations with this term, as I explain further in chapter 2, because of the extreme lack of clarity as to the various ways in which the term has been employed and as to the practices to which it refers.

3. See Bastide 1960; Carneiro 1961; Costa Pinto 1952; Ramos 1934.

4. Nina Rodrigues' other major publication in the field of Afro-Brazilian religions was the influential *Os Africanos no Brasil* (1906). His investigations focused mainly on the northeast, while Artur Ramos, his disciple, centered his own studies in Rio. Ramos, after occupying a major medical post in Rio, moved increasingly into the fields of psychiatry and the social sciences, eventually becoming a professor of anthropology and ethnology. In addition to his own major publications on Afro-Brazilians and their religions (1934;1935), Ramos was influential as editor of a major series of government sponsored publications on the Negro in Brazil, for the *Biblioteca de Divulgação Científica*. Between 1934 and 1940, 20

volumes on various aspects of African populations in Brazil appeared in this series. As director of social sciences for UNESCO, he designed in 1949 the important and pioneering UNESCO-sponsored study of race relations in Brazil, which was carried out during the 1950s (see Bastide 1974; Correa 1983; Wagley 1952). The effects of Ramos' biases on the study of Umbanda will be discussed at various points in this book.

5. See Carneiro 1940; Costa Eduardo 1948; Herskovits 1937; 1943; 1954; Peirson 1942; Landes 1947.

6. I use quotations with this term because it refers to an ideal of fidelity to traditional African practices. I do not mean in any sense to demean this ideal, but rather to recognize that it should be taken as having a relative rather than a literal meaning. Researchers have generally acknowledged that any exact replication of any particular African religious tradition was impossible, given the radical shift in environment and, particularly, the radical limitations placed upon its practitioners by their positions of servitude. For a discussion of this issue in the Caribbean, see Mintz and Price (1974).

7. While "cult" is a literal translation of the term *culto*, which is used in the language of the official census to refer to Catholic and Protestant as well as Kardecist and Umbanda groups, popular usages of the term, which oppose *cultos Afro-Brasileiros* to *a religião Católica* (the Catholic religion), clearly imply that the status of these Afro-Brazilian practices is inferior to that of a religion.

8. This problem is discussed, and the literature cited, in chapter 2.

9. See for example Fernandes 1964; Cardoso 1962; Ianni 1962; Bastide and Fernandes 1955; Cardoso and Ianni 1960.

10. The citations in this book are from the original 1960 edition in French.

11. Bastide's interpretation, published in 1960, was based on earlier observations. Willems' article appeared in 1966 but was undoubtedly written prior to the 1964 coup.

12. The discussions of both Afro-Brazilian religions and Kardecism are greatly reduced from the form in which they appeared in my dissertation. For a fuller discussion, see Brown 1974, chapters 1 and 2.

Chapter 2

1. This is a reduced version of the material presented in my Ph.D. dissertation. For more detail see Brown 1974, chapter 2.

2. These include *Livro dos Espíritos* (1857); *Livro dos Médiuns* (1961); *Evangelho Segundo o Espiritismo* (1864); *O Céu e o Inferno* (1865); and *A Gênese* (1868).

3. Renshaw's analysis of the distribution of the Spiritist population of the State of São Paulo leads him to link Kardecism specifically to industrialization rather than to urbanization (1969:116). This hypothesis would seem to require further testing.

4. Official census figures for 1967 listed just under 640,000 adepts nationally (*Annuário Estatístico* 1969:591). This discrepancy is partially a result of methods of census taking. The yearly religious census is compiled by sending a written questionnaire to those churches and religious centers that appear on the official census list. The many groups not on this list, newly formed groups, and those who do not complete and return their forms are not counted in the census. In addition, many Kardecists are reluctant to make an official declaration of their religious affiliation for reasons of social disapproval. This contributes as well to underrepresentation in official figures of the numbers of Kardecists.

5. Thus in 1966, the first year in which Kardecism received its own official census category, 760,000 Kardecists were listed (*Anuário Estatístico* 1968:488), but three years later in 1969, despite improved methods of census taking, only 633,000 were listed (*Annúrio Estatístico* 1972:672).

6. The indignation of leading Kardecists, who provided him with ample evidence of his error, led him to correct this statement in a later (1964) revised edition of his book (Amorim 1965:164).

7. For documentation of the manner in which this came about see Brown 1974, chapter 2.

8. See Lavigne and Prado, 1955. On parapsychology see Pires 1964b; on Criminology see Amorim 1957; on education see Renshaw 1969:141; on politics see Noronha Filho 1967.

9. Since Portugal was geographically and politically isolated from the effects of the Renaissance, medieval religious beliefs in spirits and witchcraft survived longer there among all levels of the population than elsewhere in Europe (see Warren 1968a). This form of Catholicism was carried to Brazil, where it has continued to survive, due to the Church's isolation from Rome, its economic weakness, and the extreme dearth of clergy. For example, a 1962 study of the Brazilian clergy revealed an average of one priest for every 15,800 individuals, with the worst ratio found in the large cities (1:17,400) (Gregory, quoted in DeKadt 1967).

10. More detailed descriptions of Kardecist ritual are available in Camargo 1961:17-22; Renshaw 1969:82-89; and Warren 1968:398-44.

11. According to what might be called a law of spiritual affinity, spirits are thought to choose mediums whose level of evolution is similar to their own. The evolutionary level of a particular spirit is judged by its social and cultural identity, but this must be sustained by the quality of the messages (i.e., their moral and intellectual content, the manner of their delivery, choice of words, and nobility and dignity of expression) transmitted through the medium who receives this spirit (Kloppenburg 1964: 327).

12. Arigó's activities are still hotly debated. He is reported to have treated over three million people, many foreigners and many famous. Although often accused of fraud by non-Spiritists and several times jailed under pressure from leading Catholics for the practice of *curandeirismo* (curing by extra-medical methods and without a medical degree), which in the 1940 Brazilian Penal Code is specifically defined as illegal, he nevertheless impressed many Brazilians and inspired the visits of teams of foreign surgeons with his curative abilities.

13. Homeopathy is a form of curing that treats illnesses with infinitesimal dosages of drugs which would produce results similar to the illness in healthy patients.

14. The relationship between Kardecism and Positivism is treated in more detail in Brown 1974.

15. Ardäo notes that Brazil was the only country in Latin America where Positivism received a specifically religious emphasis (1971:15-16).

16. Both Nina Rodrigues, working in Salvador (1945), and Bastide in São Paulo (1959) have found rich and useful material on Afro-Brazilian religous practices in police records.

17. Among the major slave "nations" known in Brazil were the Angola, Congo, Cambinda, Arda, Yoruba (often subdivided into the Oyo, Ketu, Nàgó), and Dahomey or Gêgê (Ewe) nations.

18. Salvador, the capital of Bahia, is a possible exception. Intellectuals and the upper classes participate in and have had a strong influence over Candomblé. However, their status in this religion is mainly honorary, and they do not generally take active possession roles (see Hamilton 1970; Landes 1947: 72-75: Herskovits 1954:518).

19. Major difficulties in ascertaining with precision the provenience of Brazilian slave populations is a result of the imprecise and varied manner in which slave "origins" were recorded. For example, the port of embarkation listed was often distant, culturally as well as geographically, from slaves' actual homelands. This problem is widely recognized by researchers on this topic.

20. These categories became an accepted convention among Brazilian historians by at least the nineteenth century and have since been used uncritically by many students of Afro-Brazilian religions.

21. The belief in the physical, cultural, and moral superiority of "Sudanese" over "Bantu" slaves was widely held by the dominant sectors of Brazilian society, and is also found in some form in almost all major treatments of Afro-Brazilian religions, beginning with those of Nina Rodrigues.

22. Most writers have focused on collective religious practices and have not inquired into the activities of individual sorcerers. One exception to this, Landes' (1957) description of Bahian Candomblé, contains much suggestive material on the activities of such figures. This raises the possibility that at least in Salvador, the numbers and activities of sorcerers may not have been as unlike those of Rio as has been portrayed by researchers, who have tended to contrast the prevalence of individual sorcerers in Rio with that of a collective religious orientation in Bahian Candomblé (see for example Bastide 1960; Peirson 1942; Ramos 1934).

Chapter 3

1. A slightly different version of this story appears in McGregor (1967:167-69). The story is not widely known, for reasons to be discussed.

2. This photograph, apparently taken at the First Congress of Umbanda, was published in the Congress Proceedings (Anon. 1942). Granting that the assignment of racial categories in Brazil can be a very individual matter, nevertheless the agreement among my informants as to the great preponderance of whites is significant.

3. See Chatelain, quoted in Matta e Silva 1969:33, and Ramos 1934:102. Ramos had noted various meanings given to the term and confusion among practitioners as to what it meant. Ramos' book, first published in English in 1934, came out in 1939 in Portuguese and was immediately popular. The citation within the Congress Proceedings of various scholarly works on Afro-Brazilian religions of the period indicates that such sources were both familiar and of interest to Congress participants.

4. Lemuria was invented by Ernest Haeckel during the mid-nineteenth century to account for similarities perceived in rocks, fossils, and especially in the distribution of lemurs in South Africa and India. Haeckel maintained that its inhabitants represented an early stage in human evolution, a hermaphroditic stage that preceded the development of sexual dimorphism. These theories were securely bound into the occult tradition by their inclusion in Mme. Blavatsky's *The Secret Doctrine* (see de Camp 1970:51-55) and the writings of the Rosecrucians (Wauchope 1962:42).

5. The term "Quimbanda" is recorded by Chatelain at the end of the nineteenth century as meaning *"sacerdote, curandeiro, adivinho, invocador de espíritos"* (quoted in Matta e Silva 1969:33) and is reported for the same period by Stein in the state of Rio to mean "curer" (Stein 1957:199). The term "Umbanda" was identified alternatively as meaning "the faculty of healing . . . of divining the unknown (Chatelain, quoted in Matta e Silva 1969:33; see also Bandeira 1961:39-40) and as a term for religious leader (see Nery, quoted in Nina Rodrigues 1945:404; Ramos 1934:102; 1939:100-103; and Carneiro 1936:96).

6. Examples of current Umbandista writers who have perpetuated this theory include Matta e Silva (1969); Freitas (1965); Fontanelle (1961); Figueiredo (1954).

Chapter 4

1. He may also have an African as well as a western, Christian identity and be known by his Yoruba name (Obatalá) or by his Bantu one (Zambi). See figure 1.

2. The correspondences between Orixás and saints are somewhat different in different cities in Brazil (see Bastide 1971).

3. The Oriental Line is led by John the Baptist and is made up principally of spirits derived from Kardecism, which represent various "high" civilizations: Egyptian, Hindu, Chinese, Japanese, Aztec, Inca. The Children's Line *(Linha das Crianças)* is headed by the Catholic saints, Cosmos and Damian.

4. Male Caboclo spirits belong to the lines of the male Orixás, females, generally less prominent, to the lines of the female Orixás, and Caboclo children, called *Caboclinhos*, are apportioned to the various lines according to sex, or if a Children's Line is recognized, they will belong to that. However, Caboclos are undergoing another process of assimilation, and through their association with the forest and with hunting, are merging with the African Orixá Oxôssi, the Yoruba deity of hunting and agriculture, and his Catholic counterpart, St. Sebastian. They may thus become concentrated within the line of Oxôssi. Reflexively, many Umbandistas now deny that Oxôssi is an African deity and insist that he is a Caboclo.

5. Although this line has a Catholic saint, St. Michael, as its leader, he is not associated with an Orixá, it is often said, because this line does not derive from the pantheon of Candomblé.

6. While the most common usage of the term "Caboclo" denotes a physical type with "Indian" features, or a rural "hick," Umbanda employs a specialized usage of the term to refer to unacculturated Indian populations in a way similar to that used by the lower classes in the Amazon region (see Wagley 1952:118-19).

7. Pressel (1970:9) has suggested that Umbanda spirits are modeled on familial roles, and that Caboclos are father figures. My own impression is that they might be better seen as embodiments of *machismo* (male sexual vitality). It is interesting that this role is attributed to spirits of both sexes, who may in turn possess Umbandistas of either sex. For both sexes fulfilling an ideal of proud independence is projected onto the Indian.

8. *Jurema* is a fruit grown in Northeast Brazil and used in an alcoholic drink and as a hallucinogenic drug in *Catimbó*, an Afro-Indian sect reported to have originated in Paraiba (see Bastide 1960).

9. This form of address was commonly used toward house slaves, particularly those who were on close terms with their owners' families. One researcher has identified these spirits as modeled on grandparental figures (Pressel 1970).

10. Descriptions of these terms may be found in diverse accounts of Bahian Candomblé (see for example Bastide 1961).

11. Pomba Gira is said to be a Bantu derivative of *Bombonjira,* a Congolese deity (Bastide 1971:109).

12. See for example Matta e Silva (1969:273-74), who characterizes the Exús as *ignorante, atrasado,* and of "a low level of spiritual development," with "low thoughts" that they impulsively carry out, thus often causing evil without explicit intention. Fontanelle (1961:192-93), on the other hand, characterizes them as evil.

13. Thus, *Orixás* (deities) may be reinterpreted under Kardecist influence as highly evolved spirits—*espíritos de luz* (spirits of light) (see for example Fontanelle 1961:128-29).

Chapter 5

1. The one described above is that recommended by the codifers of Umbanda (Anon. 1942) and by many more recent writers on Umbanda (see for example Freitas 1939; Fontanelle 1961; Braga 1961; Anon. 1944; Zespo 1949, 1951, 1953; Matta e Silva 1969; Magno 1953).

2. Descriptions of Umbanda religious services are also available in Brody (1973:391-426); Camargo (1961:44-48); Levy (1968:39-46); and Pressel (1968a).

3. Members of the "ritual corps" include all mediums, from full initiates to novices, and a few individuals who are not mediums and have nonpossession roles.

4. Each week one session is customarily devoted to Caboclos, one to Pretos Velhos, and one to *desenvolvimento* (development), which in this case refers to the training of new mediums.

5. It is believed that the mediums' own spirits leave their bodies during the period of possession, and the visiting spirits enter.

6. This practice of healing through applications of smoke is said to be derived from Amazonian Indian shamanism, known as *pagé* (see Bastide 1960).

7. This includes by definition members of the ritual corps who are not mediums and those who are still in the early stages of initiation. For other mediums, possession may be considered to be taboo on this particular evening due to ritual impurity from menstruation or recent sexual intercourse.

8. *Umbanda Culto de Nação* (Umbanda of the cult of nations) refers to the African "nations" formed during the slave period, which were mentioned in the discussion of "Macumba." The nations most mentioned in this African-style Umbanda are those of *Angola, Congo, Ketu,* and *"Omolocô,"* which appears to be a new syncretic "nation" that developed in Rio during the early twentieth century.

9. I visited one centro that had only recently converted from Kardecism to Umbanda. While its leader and most of the initiates agreed that the centro was now practicing Umbanda, a few firmly insisted that it was a Kardecist and not an Umbanda centro.

Chapter 6

1. This is based on the calculation made from the ceremonies described, and from other observations, that 60 is an average number of consultas per evening. An average consulta lasts some 10 to 15 minutes (though they may range from 2 or 3 minutes to well over 2 hours). With an average of 60 clients twice a week (and many centros have 3 or more ceremonies), an

average centro would give well over 6,000 consultas per year. Using an extremely conservative estimate that only 5,000 of the estimated 20,000 in Rio practice Umbanda Pura, and thus have consultas of this type within the public ceremony, simple multiplication produces the staggering sum of some 30 million consultas per year of Umbanda Pura in Rio alone. And to this must be added millions of other private consultas for which figures are much harder to estimate.

2. This is a good example of what Goffman has called the "standardization of social fronts," where expressive equipment (in this case hospital attire) used in the performance of one activity (medicine) has acquired a level of generality that enables it to convey the same meaning when transferred to another activity (in this case religious ritual) (see Goffman 1959:24-27).

3. The presence of affluent individuals as clients in Umbanda centros has also been noted by Camargo (1961:94-95).

Chapter 7

1. The use of familial terms for leaders appears to derive from Bahian Candomblé and is associated with more Afro-Brazilian practices. They may also be known by the Yoruba terms *Babalorixá* (male head) or *Ialorixá* (female head). The term *chefe*, which shows the influence of Kardecism, is also commonly employed in Brazilian secular bureaucratic life. *Chefe de secção*, for example, is the term for department head or manager.

2. The chefe may, for example, receive a spirit who is a "Legion Leader" while other initiates only receive spirits with the rank of "Phalanx Leader" or below (see also Camargo 1961:39). It is neither necessary nor customary for the full hierarchy of statuses in the Umbanda pantheon to be represented among the supernaturals at a particular centro.

3. The term *médiun* is taken from Kardecism; *cambono* is said to derive from a Bantu language (Ramos 1934), and, like the kinship references to the leader a "mother" or "father" of the saints, the terms *filha* (daughter) and *filho* (son) *de santo* are also associated with Candomblé.

4. Usually the mediums are themselves possessed and induce possession among novices by putting their hands on the novices' foreheads or by pressing their own foreheads to those of the novices and gently rotating their entire bodies. This same technique is used on clients at consultas, to identify and exorcise the spirits persecuting them.

5. The personality as well as the sex of the visiting spirit may differ quite dramatically from that of the medium who receives it.

6. For example, the Leacocks (1972:182) report that in the Batuque, where, unlike Umbanda, mediums often receive their spirits in their homes, children who have grown up in the homes of mediums are generally much faster learners and often ultimately more successful performers as mediums than those who have not.

7. While chefes admit that mediums sometimes attempt to simulate possession states, experienced chefes claim they can spot such frauds and that offending mediums are expelled from the centro. The frequency and demands of trance performances on mediums would make any consistent effort to simulate trance a taxing job indeed.

8. Civil registration is an inexpensive formality, which affords some degree of protection against police harassment (see also chapter 9). While some of the older centros in Rio remain suspicious of registering because of previous harassment, almost all of the newer ones do so as a matter of course.

9. In 1970, this averaged between 25¢ and 50¢ per month. In centros with a wide socio-economic range of members, dues may be *como pode* (whatever you can afford). I observed wealthier members of such centros contributing the equivalent of 5 or even 10 U.S. dollars per month.

10. In centros of Umbanda Pura, in 1970, the sum charged for a consulta averaged 25 to 50 cents.

11. At the time of my research, the city of Rio formed the State of Guanabara, and the surrounding area of the State of Rio. These have now been joined into the State of Rio de Janeiro.

12. It has been shown that the inhabitants of favelas, particularly of the larger ones such as I lived in, do not come exclusively from the lower sectors (see Leeds and Leeds 1970:240-41). Nevertheless, the great majority of their inhabitants are from the lower sectors.

Chapter 8

1. Despite my intentions to provide a greater balance between middle sector socio-economically heterogeneous centros and lower sector ones, the survey data revealed that more of the centros and their chefes came from the middle sectors than I had expected. See table 7.

2. This same criticism does not obtain for women possessed by male spirits who show "masculine" behavior.

3. I do not mean to include all religions practiced in Brazil. I believe that this pattern of predominantly female participation would not apply in the same degree, for example, to the various forms of Brazilian Protestantism.

4. Salaries were in many cases unobtainable. Many women claimed not to know their husbands' incomes, and many of those employed wished to conceal their earnings, fearing any statements to me might be used against them by tax collectors.

5. Racial identifications run the common risks of being based on the interviewers' perceptions of the Brazilian racial category of the respondents' race. The classification is thus approximate.

6. Such visits provide a mechanism for the diffusion of new ritual techniques and the new *pontos* (sacred songs).

Chapter 9

1. A few centros maintained close ties with the nationalist and Communist oriented *Irgreja Católica Brasileira* (Brazilian Catholic Church), a secessionist movement from within Roman Catholicism which began in 1942 and was active mainly in Rio and São Paulo. Priests of the ICB sometimes said masses in Afro-Brazilian terreiros or Umbanda centros and marched with these groups in religious processions.

2. According to Skidmore, "historical accounts of the Estado Nôvo have tended to minimize the police terrorism of the era (1937-45), perhaps because Vargas later succeeded in replacing his image as a dictator by his democratic phase after 1945" (1967:341 note).

3. Umbanda was reportedly brought to Rio Grande do Sul in the late 1920s, shortly after its founding in Rio, by an army officer transferred from Rio to Porto Alegre. In fact, the

military have been very active in the diffusion of Umbanda, for example, an Umbanda association in the Paraiba Valley (São Paulo), which now affiliates several hundred centros from several different cities, was begun by an army lieutenant who first introduced Umbanda into the area in 1960.

4. Attila Nunes' career is discussed in greater detail in chapter 10.

5. In the ensuing political reorganization, all offices below the rank of state deputy were appointed by the governor.

6. This concerns particularly the "Law of Silence" and the law prohibiting the practice of *curandeirismo* (curing practices outside of orthodox medicine).

7. *Integralismo* was a strongly nationalistic and fascist-influenced right wing political movement of the 1930s.

8. Political issues were somewhat more overtly discussed in Umbanda in Rio Grande do Sul than elsewhere.

9. A comparison of census data for the years 1940 and 1950 showed a general population increase during the decade of 26 percent. Catholic Church membership increased by only 24 percent, below the population growth, while the Protestant population increased by 62 percent and the Spiritists by 78 percent (IBGE, quoted in Kloppenburg 1964:26).

10. I found that the personnel at a number of Umbanda centros did advocate the practice of birth control.

11. In 1956 the official census first began an annual survey of non-Catholic religions with a survey of Brazil's Protestant population. In 1959, the survey was extended to include "Espíritas," that is, Kardecists, and in 1965, Umbandistas finally succeeded in adding their own census category to the national yearly religious survey.

12. Her feast day is celebrated in Bahia on February 2 and in São Paulo on August 15, dates that correspond to the different saints with which she is identified in these cities.

Chapter 10   ·

1. "Clientelist" states, described by Powell in Venezuela and Italy, are similar to the "patron-client democracies" widespread in Southeast Asia, as described by Scott (1972), and to the "Cartorial State" described in Brazil by Jaguaribe (1968:144).

2. Scott (1972:106) suggests that "contemporary" patron-client relations are less durable, lower in affect, less comprehensive in the range of services exchanged, and less monopolistic from the point of view of the patron.

3. These may be either supplements to a Catholic ceremony, or replacements for them.

4. This, perhaps, helps to account for the fact that women appear to require greater age to achieve the position of chefe. These relationships are also independent of the personal relationships between members and chefes that may obtain outside the centro. Even spouses, close friends, and business associates of the chefes assume respectful, subordinate attitudes toward them in the context of the centro.

5. Singer lists community groups such as favela organizations, social clubs, and religious groups (1965:74-75).

6. Candidates for state deputy are elected from an open slate, without previous selection by their respective parties. This often results in literally dozens of candidates for a few positions.

7. In this respect, it is significant that 72 percent of the respondents to the questionnaire who were of voting age reported they were voters and had voted in the last election. This compares to only 42 percent of the Guanabara voters who reported voting in the last election in the 1970 census (I.B.G.E. 1970:817).

8. Verbas are made available to deputies to distribute to qualified worthy causes among their constituents and are commonly used in the establishment of patronage relations.

9. I heard of a number of centros whose chefes had been promised verbas by politicians, so I was surprised to learn from an official at the Legislative Assembly that the distribution of such verbas to any but tax exempt institutions (which includes only a handful of the largest Umbanda centros) has been formally prohibited since 1954.

10. Even a small centro in a local community, such as a favela, may be a source of such prestige and influence; however, even a large and successful centro will not provide it in a location such as a downtown business district.

11. Another of the techniques used by Lacerda in this election was the attempt to divide the lower sector vote between competing candidates. Thus he persuaded Alziro Zarur, president of the *Legião da Boa Vontade* (Legion of Good Will), a mystical, reincarnationist, religio-charitable organization with an extensive following among Rio's lower sectors, to run for governor in competition with the popular lower sector candidate. Zarur's entry into politics was a fiasco which cost him most of his following. His organization appears to offer interesting parallels with Umbanda in its religious, social, and political patronage aspects.

12. Guanabara at this time had the highest rate of urbanization (97 percent) and literacy (85 percent) of any state in Brazil (Brasileiro 1967-68:153-54).

13. Since he was seriously ill and finally died during the time of my fieldwork, I was unable to interview him personally. This account is a reconstruction of his career from other Umbanda leaders with whom he worked and from Umbanda publications.

14. He began in 1958 with the PSP (a heavily populist-oriented party dominated by Adhemar de Barros). In 1962, he shifted to the PTM (another populist-oriented splinter party), and in 1966, after the reorganization of political parties following the 1964 coup, he ran in the MDB, the official Government Opposition Party.

15. He had begun in 1958 with the PSD. In 1962, he switched to the PTB (the party created by Vargas and very strong in Rio Grande do Sul, Vargas' home state). By the early 1960s the PTB had become dominated by leftists Goulart and Brizola, whose successes with the lower sector voters helped to precipitate the 1964 military coup. Moab Caldas was an open supporter of their policies and was thus caught in the post-1964 political purges.

16. After the 1964 military coup, the existing multi-party system was abolished and reformulated into a two-party system consisting of the Government Party (ARENA) and the Opposition Party (MDB).

17. The Leacocks regard only the relationship between mediums and the spirits they receive to be patron-client relationships. They argue that consultas are not patron-client dyads because the medium intrudes into the relationship between the client and the spirit patron (Leacock and Leacock 1972:59-60). However, I did not find this to be true of Umbanda. Umbandistas tend to interpret all behavior of meduims possessed by spirits as emanating from the spirits themselves. Thus the behavior of the medium who receives the spirit patron is not seen as interfering with the dyadic relationship between spirit patron and client.

Bibliography

Adams, Richard N.
  1967 Political Power and Social Structures. *In* The Politics of Conformity in Latin America. Claudio Veliz, Ed. New York: Oxford University Press.
Amorim, Deolindo
  1947 Africanismo e Espiritismo. Rio: Gráfica Mundo Espírita S.A.
  1957 Espiritismo e Criminologia. Curitiba (Paraná): Federação Espírita do Paraná.
  1965 Caraterísticas da Doutrina Espírita. Anais do Instituto de Cultura Espírita do Brasil 2:69-81.
Anonymous
  1942 Primeiro Congresso Brasileiro do Espiritismo de Umbanda. Rio.
  1944 O Culto de Umbanda em Face de Lei. Rio.
  1969 600 Pontos Riscados e Cantados na Umbanda e Candomblé. 6th Ed. Rio: Editora Eco.
Antonio, João
  1969 Quem São os Espíritas? Rio: Manchete. October 19. pp. 108-11.
Ardão, Arturo
  1971 Assimilation and Transformation of Positivism in Latin America. *In* Positivism in Latin America, 1850-1900. Ralph Lee Woodward, Ed. Lexington (Mass.): D.C. Heath and Co.
Augras, Monique
  1983 O Duplo e a Metamórfose: A identidade mítica em comunidades Nagô. Petrópolis: Editora Vozes Ltda.
Azevedo, Fernando de
  1943 A Cultura Brasileira. 1st Ed. Rio: Edição de I.B.G.E.
  1964 A Cultura Brasileira. 4th Ed. São Paulo: Edições Melhoramentos.
Azevedo, Thales de
  1955 As Elites de Côr: Um Estudo de Ascenção Social. São Paulo: Companhia Editora Nacional.
  1963 Social Change in Brazil. Latin American Monograph, No. 22. Gainesville: University of Florida Press.
  1968 Popular Catholicism in Brazil: Typology and Functions. *In* Portugal and Brazil in Transition. Raymond Sayers, Ed. Minneapolis: University of Minnesota Press. pp. 175-78.
Bandeira, Armando Cavalcanti
  1961 Umbanda: Evolução Histórico-Religiosa. Rio.
Bastide, Roger
  1951 Religion and the Church in Brazil. *In* Brazil: Portrait of Half a Continent. T. Lynn Smith, Ed. New York: The Dryden Press, pp. 334-55.

240   *Bibliography*

1958   Le Candomblé da Bahia. The Hague: Mouton and Co.
1959   Sociologia do Folclore Brasileiro. São Paulo: ANHEMBI.
1960   Les Religions Africaines au Brésil. Paris: Presses Universitaires de France.
1971   African Civilizations in the New World. New York: Harper and Row.
1974   The Present Status of Afro-American Research in Latin America. Daedalus 103 (2): 111-23.
1978   The African Religions of Brazil. Tr. by Helen Sebba. Baltimore: The Johns Hopkins University Press.
Bastide, Roger and Florestan Fernandes
1955   Relações Raciais entre Pretos e Brancos em São Paulo. São Paulo: Editora Anhembi.
Bastos, Tocary Assis
1965   O Positivismo e a Realidade Brasileira. Revista Brasileira de Estudos Políticos.
Binon-Cossard, Giselle
1970   Contribution à l'étude des Candomblés au Brésil: le Candomblé Angola. Thèse 3ieme Cycle. Paris: Faculté des Lettres et Sciences Humaines.
Birman, Patricia
1980   Feitiço, Carreco e Olho Grande, Os Males do Brasil São: Estudo de um centro umbandista numa favela do Rio de Janeiro. Masters Thesis, Department of Anthropology, Museu Nacional, Rio de Janeiro.
1982   Laços que unem: ritual, família e poder na Umbanda. Religião e Sociedade 8:21-28.
1983   O Que é a Umbanda. São Paulo: Editora Brasiliense, Coleção Primeiros Passos.
Boff, Clodovis
1979   Comunidade Eclesial, Comunidade Política. Petrópolis: Editora Vozes.
Braga, Lourenço
1961   Umbanda e Quimbanda. 12th Ed. (first published in 1951). Rio: Edições Spiker.
Bram, Joseph
1958   Spirits, Mediums and Believers in Contemporary Puerto Rico. Transactions of the New York Academy of Sciences. Series II, Vol. 20:340-47.
Brandão, Carlos
1980   Os Deuses do Pôvo: Um Estudo Sobre a Religião Popular. São Paulo: Brasiliense.
Brasileiro, Ana Maria
1967-68   As Eleições de 15 novembre de 1966 no Estado do Guanabara. Revista Brasileira de Estudos Políticos 23-24: 151-81.
Brody, Eugene
1973   The Lost Ones: Social Forces and Mental Illness in Rio de Janeiro. New York: International Universities Presses, Inc.
Brown, Diana
1971   Umbanda: Patron-Client Relations in an Urban Religious Movement. Paper presented at the 70th Annual Meeting of the American Anthropological Association, New York, Nov. 17-20.
1974   Umbanda: Politics of an Urban Religious Movement. Unpublished Ph.D. dissertation, Department of Anthropology, Columbia University. Ann Arbor: University Microfilms.
1976   Mulheres e Religião no Brasil: Participação em Papeis de Liderança. Paper presented at the meeting of the Sociedade Brasileira Para o Progresso da Ciência, Brasilia, July 7-14.
1977   Umbanda e classes sociais. Religião e Sociedade 1:31-42.
1979   Umbanda and Class Relations in Brazil. In Brazil: Anthropological Perspectives. Maxine Margolis and William Carter, Eds. New York: Columbia University Press.
1980   Umbanda in Newark: Alternative Healing in the Brazilian and Portuguese Communities. Working Paper No. 24, Resource Center for Multicultural Care and Prevention, College of Medicine and Dentistry of New Jersey, New Jersey Medical School, Newark.

Bruneau, Thomas
1974 The Political Transformation of the Brazilian Catholic Church. London and New York: Cambridge University Press.
1982 The Church in Brazil: The Politics of Religion. Austin: University of Texas Press.
Burns, E. Bradford
1968 Nationalism in Brazil: A Historical Survey. New York: Frederick A. Praeger.
Camargo, Cândido Procôpio Ferreira de
1961 Kardecismo e Umbanda. São Paulo: Livraria Pioneira Editora.
Cardoso, Fernando Henrique
1962 Capitalismo e Escravidão. São Paulo: Difusão Europeia do Livro.
Cardoso, F.H. and Octávio Ianni
1960 Côr e Mobilidade Social em Florianopolis. São Paulo: Companhia Editora Nacional.
Cardozo, Manoel S.
1947 The Lay Brotherhoods of Colonial Bahia. Catholic Historical Review 33:12-30.
Carneiro, Edison
1936 Religões Negras. Rio: Editora Civilização Brasileira S.A.
1937 Negros Bantus. Rio: Editora Civilização Brasileira S.A.
1940 The Structure of African Cults in Bahia. Journal of American Folklore 53:271-78.
1961 Candomblés da Bahia. 3rd Ed. Rio: Editora Conquista.
1964 Os Caboclos de Aruanda. *In* Ladinos e Crioulos: Estudos Sobre o Negro no Brasil. Edison Carneiro, Ed. Rio: Editora Civilização Brasileira, S.A. pp. 143-58.
Carneiro da Cunha, Manuela
1977 Religião, Comércio e Etnicidade: uma interpretação preliminar do Catolicismo brasileiro em Lagos, no século XIX. Religião e Sociedade 1:51-60.
Chauí, Marilena
1978 Apontamentos para uma Crítica da Ação Integralista Brasileiro. *In* Ideologia e Mobilização Popular. Marilena Chauí and Maria Sylvia Carvalho Franco, Eds. Rio: Co-edições CEDEC/Paz e Terra.
Concone, Maria Helena
1981 Ideologia Umbandista e Integralismo. *In* Trabalho e Cultura no Brasil. Leóncio Martins Rodrigues et al., Eds. Vol. I: 379-95. Recife/Brasília: ANPPCS/CNPq.
Conrad, Robert
1967 The Struggle for the Abolition of the Brazilian Slave Trade 1808-1853. Unpublished Ph.D. dissertation, Department of History, Columbia University.
Correa, Mariza
1982 As ilusões da liberdade: A Escola Nina Rodrigues e a Antropologia no Brasil. Unpublished Ph.D. dissertation, Department of Anthropology, Universidade de São Paulo.
Costa, Luciano
1944 Kardec e Não Roustaing. Rio: Gráfica Mundo Espirita S.A.
Costa Eduardo, Octávio da
1948 The Negro in Northern Brazil. Monographs of the American Ethnological Society No. 15.
Costa Lima, Vivaldo
1976 O Conceito de 'Nação' nos Candomblés da Bahia. Afro-Asia (Centro de Estudos Afro-Orientais) 12:65-90.
1977 A Família-de-Santo nos Candomblés Jeje-Nagôs da Bahia: Um Estudo de Relações Intra-grupais. Masters Thesis, Universidade Federal da Bahia.
Costa Pinto, Luis A.
1952 O Negro no Rio de Janeiro. São Paulo: Companhia Editora Nacional.
Coutto, Francisco Pedro do
1966 O Voto e o Pôvo. Rio: Civilização Brasileira S.A.

Da Matta, Roberto
1981   The Ethic of Umbanda and the Spirit of Messianism: Reflections on the Brazilian Model. *In* Authoritarian Capitalism: Brazil's Contemporary Economic and Political Development. Thomas Bruneau and P. Faucher, Eds. Boulder, Colorado: Westview Press, Inc.

Dantas, Beatriz Gois
1979   A Organização Económica de um Terreiro de Xangô. Religião e Sociedade 4:181-94.
1982a   Repensando a pureza nagô. Religião e Sociedade 8:15-20.
1982b   Vovó Nagô e Papai Branco: Usos e abusos da Africa no Brasil. Masters thesis, Department of Anthropology, Universidade Estadual de Campinas (São Paulo).

Darnton, Robert
1968   Mesmerism and the End of the Enlightenment in France. Cambridge: Harvard University Press.

Dean, Warren
1970   The Industrialization of São Paulo. Austin: University of Texas Press.

DeCamp, L. Sprague
1970   Lost Continents. New York: Dover Publications, Inc.

Decelso
1967   Umbanda de Caboclos. Rio: Editora Eco.

Degler, Carl N.
1971   Neither Black Nor White: Slavery and Race Relations in Brazil and the United States. New York: The Macmillan Co.

de Kadt, Emanuel
1967   Religion, the Church and Social Change in Brazil. *In* The Politics of Conformity in Latin America. Claudio Veliz, Ed. New York: Oxford University Press.

Diniz, Eli
1982   Voto e Máquina Política: Patronagem e Clientelismo no Rio de Janeiro. Rio: Paz e Terra.

Elbein dos Santos, Juana
1976   Os Nàgô e a Morte. Petrópolis: Editora Vozes.

Epinay, Christian Lalive d'
1969   Haven of the Masses. Marjorie Sundell, Trans. London: Lutterworth Press.

Erickson, Kenneth P.
1970   Labor in the Political Process in Brazil: Corporatism in a Modernizing Nation. Unpublished Ph.D. dissertation, Department of Political Science, Columbia University.

Estudos Afro-Brasileiros Vol. I
1935   Trabalhos apresentados ao 1° Congresso Afro-Brasileiro reunido no Recife em 1934. Rio: Ariel Editora Ltda.

Fernandes, Gonçalves
1938   O Folclore Mágico do Nordeste. Rio: Civilização Brasileira, S.A.

Fernandes, Florestan
1964   A Integração do Negro a Sociedade de Classes. Ph.D. dissertation, Universidade de São Paulo.

Fernandes, Rubem Cesar
1984   Religiões Populares: uma visão parcial da literatura recente. BIB (Rio de Janeiro) 18:3-26.

Ferreira, Olímpia do Carmo
1983   Prática Médica e Prática Umbandista: duas formas de lidar com o doente mental. Masters thesis, Department of Clinical Psychology, Universidade Pontífica de Campinas (São Paulo).

Figueiredo, Benjamin
1954   Primado de Umbanda. Rio: Artes Gráficas São Jorge Ltda.
1967   Okê Caboclo! Rio: Editora Eco.
Figueiredo, Napoleão
1975   Religioes Mediúnicas na Amazônia: O Batuque. Journal of Latin American Lore 1(2):173-84.
Fontaine, Pierre-Michel
1980   Research in the Political Economy of Afro-Latin America. Latin American Research Review XI (2):111-42.
Fontanelle, Aluísio
1961   Umbanda Através dos Séculos. 3rd Ed. Rio: Editora Aurora.
Foster, George
1963   The Dyadic Contract in Tzintzuntzan II: Patron-Client Relationships. American Anthropologist 65:1280-94.
Franco, Jean
1983   "What's in a name." Popular Culture Theories and their Limitations. Studies in Latin American Popular Culture 1(1):5-14.
Frei Betto
1981   O que comunidade Eclesial de Base. São Paulo: Editora Brasiliense.
Freitas, Byron Torres de, and Tancredo da Silva Pinto
1956   Fundamentos de Umbanda. Rio: Editora Souza.
1957   Camba de Umbanda. Rio: Editora Aurora.
n.d.   As Mirongas da Umbanda. Rio: Editora Souza.
n.d.   As Impressionantes Ceremónias da Umbanda. Rio: Editora Souza.
Freitas, João de
1939   Umbanda. Rio: Editora Moderna.
1965   Oxum-Maré. Rio: Livraria Freitas Bastos S.A.
Freyre, Gilberto
1946   The Masters and the Slaves. Samuel Putnam, trans. New York: Alfred A. Knopf.
Freyre, Gilberto, ed.
1937   Nôvos Estudos Afro-Brasileiros. Biblioteca de Divulgação Científica, Vol. 9. Rio de Janeiro: Editora Civilização Brasileira.
Fry, Peter H.
1974   Reflexões sobre o crecimento da conversão à Umbanda. Cadernos do ISER 1:29-40.
1976   Regional Cult or National Religion: The Predatory Expansion of Umbanda in Urban Brazil. Paper presented at the Annual Conference of the Association of Social Anthropologists, Manchester, March 31-April 3.
1977   Mediunidade e Sexualidade. Religião e Sociedade 1:105-24.
1978   Two Religious Movements: Protestantism and Umbanda. In Manchester and São Paulo: Problems of Rapid Urban Growth. John Wirth and R. Jones, Eds. Stanford: Stanford University Press.
1982a   Para Inglês Ver: Indentidade Política na Cultura Brasileira. Rio: Zahar Editores.
1982b   Feijoada e Soul Food: Notas sobre a manipulação de Símbolos Etnicos e Nacionais. In Para Inglês Ver. Peter Fry, Ed. Rio: Zahar Editores.
Fry, Peter and Gary Howe
1975   Duas Respostas à Aflição: Umbanda e Pentecostalismo. Debate e Crítica 6:75-94.
Fuller, John G.
1974   Arigó: Surgeon of the Rusty Knife. New York: Thomas Y. Crowell Co.
Gabriel, Chester E.
1979   Umbanda and Regional Cults in Manaus, Brazil: The Dynamics of Mediunistic Trance in a Process of Assimilation. Paper presented at the 43rd International Congress of Americanists, Vancouver, Canada, August 10-17.

1980 Communications of the Spirits: Umbanda, Regional Cults in Manaus and the Dynamics of Mediunistic Trance. Ph.D. dissertation, Department of Anthropology, McGill University.

Galeano, Eduardo
1970 La Religion de los Malditos. Marcha (Montevideo).

Gardel, Luis
1967 Escolas de Samba. Rio de Janeiro.

Geertz, Clifford
1960 Religion in Java. Glencoe: The Free Press.
1966 Religion as a Cultural System. *In* Anthropological Approaches to the Study of Religion. Michael Banton, Ed. London and New York: Tavistock Publications.

Goffman, Erving
1959 The Presentation of Self in Everyday Life. Garden City, New York: Doubleday Anchor Books.

Goldwasser, Maria Júlia
1975 O Palácio do Samba: Estudo Antropológico da Escola de Samba Estação Primeira de Mangueira. Rio: Zahar Editores.

Goode, Judith
1970 Latin American Urbanism and Corporate Groups. Anthropological Quarterly 43(3): 146-67.

Gordon, Jacob
1979 Yoruba Cosmology and Culture in Brazil. Journal of Black Studies 10(2): 231-44.

Graham, Lawrence S.
1968 Civil Service Reform in Brazil. Latin American Monographs, No. 13. Austin: University of Texas Press.

Greenfield, Sidney
n.d. Patron-Client Contracts and the Model of the Patronage Network. Unpublished, mimeographed paper.
1984 Spirit healing in Brazil (film). Latin American Center, University of Wisconsin, Milwaukee.

Gross, Daniel
1971 Ritual and Conformity: A Religious Pilgrimage to Northeastern Brazil. Ethnology 10: 129-48.

Guedes, Simoni
1974 Umbanda e Loucura. *In* Desvio e Divergência. Gilberto Velho, Ed. Rio: Zahar Editores.

Hamilton, Russell G. Jr.
1970 The Present State of African Cults in Bahia. Journal of Social History 3-4: 357-73.

Haring, C.H.
1958 Empire in Brazil. Cambridge: Harvard University Press.

Harris, Marvin
1956 Town and Country in Brazil. New York: Columbia University Press.
1964 Patterns of Race in the Americas. New York: Walker and Co.

Hasenbalg, Carlos
1979 Discriminação e Desigualdades Raciais no Brasil. Rio: Editora Graal.
1983 Race and Socioeconomic Inequalities in Brazil. Rio: Instituto Universitario de Pesquisas do Rio de Janeiro, Serie Estudos No. 13.

Henfry, Colin
1981 The Hungry Imagination: Social Formation, Popular Culture and Ideology in Bahia. *In* The Logic of Poverty: The Case of the Brazilian Northeast. Simon Mitchell, Ed. Boston: Routledge and Kegan Paul.

Herskovits, Melville
1937 African Gods and Catholic Saints in New World Negro Belief. American Anthropologist 39: 635-43.
1943 The Southernmost Outposts of New World Africanisms. American Anthropologist 45: 495-510.
1954 The Social Organization of Candomblé. Congresso Internacional de Americanistas 31: 505-32.
Hess, David
1983 Spiritists, Catholics and Doctors in Brazil: A Study of Religious and Scientific Values in a Modern Society. Project proposal submitted to Social Science Research Council, New York.
Hutchinson, Harry William
1957 Village and Plantation Life in Northeastern Brazil. Seattle: University of Washington Press.
Ianni, Octávio
1962 As Metamórfoses do Escravo. São Paulo: Difusão Européia do Livro.
1963 Industrialização e Desenvolvimento no Brasil. São Paulo.
1966 Raças e Classes Sociais no Brasil. Rio: Editora Civilização Brasileira S.A.
I.B.G.E. (Instituto Brasileiro de Geografia e Estatística)
1960 Censo Demográfico de 1960: Guanabara. Vol. I, No. 12, Part II. Rio.
1968 Anuário Estatístico do Brasil 1968. Rio.
1969 Anuário Estatístico do Brasil 1969. Rio.
1972 Anuário Estatístico do Brasil 1972. Rio.
Ireland, Rowan
1983 Catholic Base Communities, Spiritist Groups, and the Deepening of Democracy in Brazil. Washington, D.C.: The Wilson Center, Working Paper No. 131.
Isto E
1983 O Peso do terreiro. June 1, No. 336: 40-41.
Jaguaribe, Hélio
1968 Economic and Political Development: a Theoretical Approach and a Brazilian Case Study. Cambridge: Harvard University Press.
Jilek, Wolfgang G.
1976 Review of Geisterkult Besessenheit und Magie in Der Umbanda Religion Brasiliens, by Horst H. Figge. Freiburg/Muenchen: Karl Alber, 1973. In Transcultural Psychiatric Research Review, April, Vol. VIII: 79-82.
Johnson, Allen W.
1971 Sharecroppers of the Sertão: Economics and Dependence on a Brazilian Plantation. Stanford: Stanford University Press.
Kardec, Allan (Léon Rivail)
1857 Livro dos Espíritos. Rio: Federação Espírita Brasileira.
1861 Livro dos Médiuns. Rio: Federação Espírita Brasileira.
1864 Evangelho Segundo o Espiritismo. Rio: Federação Espírita Brasileira.
1865 O Céu e o Inferno. Rio: Federação Espírita Brasileira.
1868 A Gênese. Rio: Federação Espírita Brasileira.
1890 Obras Pósthumas. Rio: Federação Espírita Brasileira.
Keefe, David L.
1976 Interaction of Spiritualism and Western Medicine in Rio de Janeiro, Brazil. Unpublished Masters thesis, Harvard University.
Keller, Frei Alfredo O.F.M.
1969 Sugestões para a Reflexão em Círculos de Estudo. In Saravá: Os Cultos Afro-Brasileiros. Boaventura Kloppenburg and Alfredo Keller, Eds. Rio: Sóno-Víso do Brasil.

Kerri, James
  1976   Studying Voluntary Associations as Adaptive Mechanisms: A review of anthropological perspectives. Current Anthropology 17(1): 23-47.
Kloppenburg, Boaventura O.F.M.
  1961a   Umbanda: Orientação Para os Católicos. Rio: Editora Vozes.
  1961b   Ação Pastoral Perante o Espiritismo: Orientação para Sacerdotes. Rio: Editora Vozes.
  1964   O Espiritismo no Brasil: Orientação Para os Católicos. Rio: Editora Vozes.
  1969   Posição Católica Perante a Umbanda. In Saravá: Os Cultos Afro-Brasileiros. Boaventura Kloppenburg and Alfredo Keller, Eds. Rio: Sóno-Víso do Brasil.
Koss, Joan
  n.d.   Why Cults are Born: the Case of Espiritismo in Puerto Rico. Unpublished mimeographed paper.
Krischke, Paulo
  1983   Utopia e Cidadania na Crise do Autoritarismo: Igreja, motivações e orientações políticas dos moradores em loteamentos clandestinos em São Paulo. Notre Dame: Kellog Institute, mimeo.
Landes, Ruth
  1947   City of Women. New York: The Macmillan Co.
Lanternari, Vittorio
  1963   Religions of the Oppressed. Tr. by Lisa Sergio. New York: Alfred Knopf.
Lavigne, Eusinio and Sousa do Prado
  1955   Os Espíritas e as Questões Sociais. Niteroi: Editora Renovação Ltda.
Leacock, Seth and Barbara Leacock
  1972   Spirits of the Deep: A Study of an Afro-Brazilian Cult. New York: Doubleday Natural History Press.
Leeds, Anthony
  1965   Brazilian Careers and Social Structure: A Case History and Model. In Contemporary Cultures and Societies of Latin America. Dwight Heath and Richard Adams, Eds. New York: Random House, pp. 379-404.
Leeds, Anthony and Elizabeth Leeds
  1970   Brazil and the Myth of Urban Rurality: Urban Experience, Work, and Values in "Squatments" of Rio de Janeiro and Lima. In City and Country in the Third World. Arthur J. Field, Ed. Cambridge: Schenckman Publishing Company, Inc.
Lerch, Patricia
  1972   The Role of Women in Possession-Trance Cults in Brazil. Masters thesis, Ohio State University.
  1980   Spirit Mediums in Umbanda Evangelada of Porto Alegre, Brazil: Dimensions of Power and Authority. In A World of Men. E. Bourguignon, Ed. New York: Praeger.
Levy, Maria Stella Ferreira
  1968   The Umbanda is for all of us: An Alternative Dimension of Socialization. Unpublished Masters Essay, Department of Anthropology, University of Wisconsin.
Lewis, I.M.
  1971   Ecstatic Religion: An Anthropological Study of Spirit Possession and Shamanism. Baltimore: Penguin Books.
Lins do Rêgo, José
  1932   Menino do Engenho. Rio.
Little, Kenneth
  1957   The Role of Voluntary Organizations in West African Urbanization. American Anthropologist 59: 379-96.

Lopes, Juarez Brandão
1967   Some Basic Developments in Brazilian Politics and Society. *In* New Perspectives of Brazil. Eric Baklanoff, Ed. Nashville: Vanderbilt University Press. pp. 59-77.

Love, Joseph
1970   Political Participation in Brazil, 1881-1969. Luso-Brazilian Review 7(2): 1-24.

Luz, Marco Aurélio and Georges Lapassade
1972   O Segredo da Macumba. Rio: Editora Paz e Terra.

Macáia
1966-   Mimeographed monthly newsletter published by TULEF (Tenda de Umbanda Luz, Esperança, Fraternidade). Rio.

Maes, Hercílio (under the guidance of the spirit Rámatis)
1965   A Vida no Planeta Marte. Rio: Livraria Freitas Bastos.

Magno, Oliveira
1952   Prática de Umbanda. Rio.

Mainwaring, Scott
1983   The Catholic Youth Workers' Movement (JOC) and the Emergence of the Popular Church in Brazil. Notre Dame: Kellog Institute, Working Paper No. 6.

in press   Brazil: The Catholic Church and the Popular Movement in Nova Iguaçu, 1974-1982. *In* Popular Religion, the Churches and Political Conflict in Latin America. Daniel Levine, Ed. Chapel Hill: University of North Carolina Press.

Marcondes, Carlos Eugênio, ed.
1982   Bandeira de Alairá: Outros escritos sobre a religião dos Orixás. São Paulo: Nobel.

Martz, John D.
1971   Characteristics of Latin American Political Thought. *In* Positivism in Latin America 1850-1900. Ralph Lee Woodward Jr., Ed. Lexington (Mass.): D.C. Heath and Company.

Matta e Silva, W.W.
1969   Umbanda de Todos Nós. 3rd Ed. (Originally published 1957). Rio: Livraria Freitas Bastos S.A.

Maybury-Lewis, David
1968   Growth and Change in Brazil since 1930. *In* Portugal and Brazil in Transition. Raymond Sayers, Ed. Minneapolis: University of Minnesota Press. pp. 159-72.

Mayer, Adrian C.
1968   The Significance of Quasi-Groups in the Study of Complex Societies. *In* The Social Anthropology of Complex Societies. Michael Banton, Ed. London and New York: Tavistock Publications.

McGregor, Pedro
1967   Jesus of the Spirits. (Also published in England under the title The Moon and Two Mountains.) New York: Stein and Day.

Messing, Simon
1958   Group Therapy and Social Status in the Zar Cult of Ethiopia. American Anthropologist 60.

Milan, Betty
1979   Manhas do Poder: Umbanda, Asilo e Iniciação. São Paulo: Editora Atica.

Mintz, Sidney and Richard Price
1976   An Anthropological Approach to the Afro-American Past: A Caribbean Perspective. Philadelphia: ISHI, Occasional Paper No. 2.

Mironga
1969   Rio.

Montero, Paula
1979   Umbanda: A doença e o corpo. Ciência e Cultura 31(1): 25-31.
1983   Da Doença à Desordem: as práticas mâgico-terapeutas na Umbanda. Ph.D. dissertation, Department de Ciências Sociais, Universidade de São Paulo.
Montero, P. and Renato Ortiz
1976   Contribuição para um estudo quantitativo da religião Umbandista. Ciência e Cultura 28(4): 407-16.
Moro, America and Mercedes Ramirez
1981   La Macumba y otros cultos Afro-Brasileños en Montevideo. Montevideo: Editora Oriental.
Morse, Richard
1965   Recent Research on Latin American Urbanization: A Selective Survey with Commentary. Latin American Research Review 1(1): 35-74.
Mott, Yoshiko Tanabe
1976   Caridade e Demanda: um estudo de acusação e conflito na Umbanda em Marília. Masters thesis, Departamento de Antropologia, Universidade Estadual de Campinas (São Paulo).
1978   Umbanda e Doença. Marília. Ensaios No. 1: 1-31.
Motta, Eunice Seroa da (under the guidance of the spirit M. Penalva)
1957   Yvone, a Menina dos Olhos Escuros (Romance Mediúnico). Rio.
Motta, Roberto
1982   Bandeira de Alairá: A festa de Xangô-São João e problemas do sincretismo. In Bandeira de Alairá. Carlos Eugênio Marcondes, Ed. São Paulo: Livraria Nobel S.A.
1983   The Xangô Religion in Recife, Brazil. Ph.D. dissertation, Department of Anthropology, Columbia University.
Myers, Lora
1983   Capoeira of Brazil: An Ethnographic Portrait. Mimeo.
Nascimento, Abdias
1978   O Genocídio do Negro Brasileiro. Rio: Editora Paz e Terra.
Nina Rodrigues, Raimundo
1935   O Animismo Fetichista dos Negros Baianos. (Originally published 1900, in French.) Rio: Civilização Brasileira.
1945   Os Africanos no Brasil. (Originally published 1906.) São Paulo: Companhia Editora Nacional.
Nogueira, Oracy
1962   Família e Comunidade: Um Estudo Sociologico de Itapetininga, São Paulo. Rio: Centro Brasileiro de Pesquisas Educacionais.
Noronha Filho, Oscar
1967   Espiritismo e Participação. Paz e Terra 1(4): 192-208.
Novaes, Regina
1980   Os Pentecostais e a organização dos trabalhadores. Religião e Sociedade 5: 65-93.
O Globo
1968   Atila Nunes foi sepultado ontem. October 28. p. 10.
1969   Sambas e Toadas substituirão na Missa as Músicas Sacras. October 13. p. 12.
Oliveiro, Agamemnon
1978   Candomblé Sergipano, subsídios para sua história. Cadernos de folclore Sergipano No. 4, Aracajú.
Ortiz, Renato
1978   A Morte Branca do Feitiçeiro Negro. Petrópolis: Editora Vozes.
O Semanário
1959-62   Published by ISEB (Instituto Superior de Estudos Brasileiros). Rio.

Ott, Carlos
1953   O Negro Baiano. *In* Les Afro-Americaines. Memoires de L'institut Français d'Afrique Noire. IFAN-DAKAR.
Page, John
1984   Brasil Para Cristo: The Cultural Construction of Pentecostal Networks in Brazil. Ph.D. dissertation, Department of Anthropology, New York University.
Pechman, Tema
1982a   Umbanda e Política no Rio de Janeiro. Religião e Sociedade 8:37-45.
1982b   Umbanda e Política na Conjuntura Eleitoral de 1982: uma análise preliminar. Mimeo.
1983   Líderes Religiosos e as Eleições de 1982. Mimeo.
Peirson, Donald
1942   Negros in Brazil. Chicago: University of Chicago Press.
Perelberg, Rosine
1980   Umbanda and psychoanalysis as different ways of interpreting mental illness. British Journal of Medical Psychiatry 53: 323-32.
Perreira Barreto, Maria Amália
1977   Os Voduns do Maranhão. São Luis: Fundação Cultural do Maranhão.
Pinto, Tancredo da Silva
        see Freitas, Byron Torres de
Pinto, Tancredo da Silva and Ernesto Lourenço da Silva
1968   Umbanda: Preto Velho. Rio. O Dia. December 1-2. p. 20.
Pires, Herculano
1964a   O Espírito e o Tempo: Introdução Histórica ao Espiritismo. São Paulo: Editora Pensamento.
1964b   Parapsicologia e Suas Perspectivas. São Paulo: EDICEL.
Powell, John Duncan
1970   Peasant Society and Clientelist Politics. American Political Science Review 64(2): 411-25.
Pressel, Esther J.
1968a   Structure, Beliefs and Ritual Behavior in Umbanda. Cross-Cultural Study of Dissociational States. Working Paper No. 18. Ohio State University. Mimeo.
1968b   Some Aspects of Spiritual Psychotherapy in Umbanda. Cross-Cultural Study of Dissociational States, Working Paper No. 28. Ohio State University. Mimeo.
1970   Symbolic and Practical Aspects of Spirit Types in Umbanda. Paper read at the 69th Annual Meeting of the American Anthropological Association, San Diego, California.
1973   Umbanda in São Paulo: Religious Innovation in a Developing Society. *In* Religion, Altered States of Consciousness and Social Change. E. Bourguignon, Ed. Columbus, Ohio: Ohio State University Press.
1974   Umbanda Trance and Possession in São Paulo, Brazil. *In* Trance, Healing and Hallucination. F. Goodman, J. Henney and E. Pressel, Eds. New York: John Wiley & Sons.
1977   Negative Spiritism in Experienced Brazilian Umbanda Mediums. *In* Case Studies in Spirit Possession. V. Crapanzano and V. Garrison, Eds. New York: John Wiley & Sons.
1980   Spirit Magic in the Social Relations between Men and Women (São Paulo, Brazil). *In* A World of Men. E. Bourguignon, Ed. New York: Praeger.
Ramos, Artur
1934   O Negro Brasileiro. Rio: Editora Civilização Brasileira.
1935   O Folk-lore Negro do Brasil. Rio: Civilização Brasileira.
1939   The Negro in Brazil. Washington, D.C.: The Associated Publishers, Inc.
1951   The Negro in Brazil. *In* Brazil, Portrait of Half a Continent. T. Lynn Smith, Ed. New York: The Dryden Press.

Raphael, Alison
1975   Miracles in Brazil: A Study of the Pentecostal Movement "O Brasil Para Cristo." Masters thesis, Department of History, Columbia University.

Reformador: Deus, Cristo e Caridade, Mensário Religioso de Espiritismo Cristão
1883-   Rio: Federação Espírita Brasileira.

Rêgo, Waldeloir
1968   Capoeira Angola: Ensaio socio-etnográfico. Salvador: Editora Itapũa.

Renshaw, J. Parke
1969   A Sociological Analysis of Spiritism in Brazil. Ph.D. dissertation, University of Florida, Gainesville.

Ribeiro, René
1952   Cultos Afrobrasileiros do Recife. Recife: Boletim do Instituto Joaquim Nabuco.

Rio, João do (Paulo Barreto)
1951   As Religiões no Rio. (Originally published 1904.) Rio: Edições da Organização Simões.

Risério, Antonio
1981   Carnaval Ijexá: notas sobre afoxés e blocos do novo carnaval afrobaiano. Salvador: Corrúpio.

Roberts, Bryan R.
1968   Protestant Groups and Coping with Urban Life in Guatemala City. American Journal of Sociology 73(6): 753-67.

Rodrigues, José Honorio
1965   Brazil and Africa. R.A. Mazzara and Sam Hileman, Trans. Berkeley: University of California Press.

Roustaing, Jean Baptiste
1900   Os Quatro Evangelhos (also known as Revelação da Revelação). Ewerton Quadros, Trans. Rio: Federação Espírita Brasileira.

Sahlins, Marshall
1963   Poor Man, Rich Man, Big-Man, Chief: Political Types in Melanesia and Polynesia. Comparative Studies in Society and History 5(3): 285-303.
1968   Tribesmen. Englewood Cliffs, N.J.: Prentice-Hall.

Sayers, Raymond S.
1956   The Negro in Brazilian Literature. New York: Hispanic Institute in the United States.

Scott, James C.
1972   Patron-Client Politics and Political Change in Southeast Asia. American Political Science Review 66(1): 91-113.

Seiblitz, Zélia Milanez
1979   Dentro de um ponto riscado: Estudo de um centro espírita na Zona Norte do Rio de Janeiro. Masters thesis, Departamento de Antropologia, Museu Nacional, Rio de Janeiro.

Serra, José Ordep (see also Trindade-Serra)
1976   Um Caso de Psicoterapia num candomblé baiano. Brasília: Pesquisa Antropológica, No. 11. Mimeo.

Silva, Nelson
1978   Black-White Income Differentials in Brazil 1960. Ph.D. dissertation, University of Michigan.
1979   As Duas Faces da Mobilidade. Dados 21: 41-67.

Silverstein, Leni
1976   The Ideology of Harmony: the Power of Women in an Angolan Candomblé Terreiro. Mimeo.
1979   Mãe de Todo Mundo—Modos de Sobrevivência nas Comunidades de Candomblé da Bahia. Religião e Sociedade 4: 143-70.

Silverstein, Leni, P. Birman and Z. Seiblitz
1982 Os Saravás da Umbanda: Um Estudo das Federações Umbandistas no Grande Rio. Report prepared for the Ford Foundation. Mimeo.
Singer, Paulo
1965 A Política das Classes Dominantes. *In* Politica e Revolução Social no Brasil. Octávio Ianni et al., Eds. Rio: Editora Civilização Brasileira, pp. 65-125.
Skidmore, Thomas E.
1967 Politics in Brazil. New York: Oxford University Press.
1968 Brazil's Search for Identity in the Old Republic. *In* Portugal and Brazil in Transition. Raymond Sayers, Ed. Minneapolis: University of Minnesota Press. pp. 127-41.
Soares, Gláucio Dillon
1966 Economic Development and Class Structure. *In* Class, Status and Power. 2nd Ed. Reinhard Bendix and Seymour Lipset, Eds. New York: Free Press. pp. 190-99.
1968 The New Industrialization and the Brazilian Political System. *In* Latin America: Revolution or Reform? James Petras and Maurice Zeitlin, Eds. Greenwich, Conn.: Fawcett Publications, Inc.
Souza, Amaury
1971 Raça e Política no Brasil Urbano. Revista de Administração de Empresas 11(4): 61-70.
Squeff, Enio and Jose Miguel Wisnik
1982 Música. Coleção O Nacional e o Popular na cultura brasileira. São Paulo: Editora Brasiliense.
Stein, Stanley
1957 Vassouras. Cambridge: Harvard University Press.
Stepan, Alfred C.
1969 The Military in Politics: Patterns of Civil-Military Relations in the Brazilian Political System. Unpublished Ph.D. dissertation, Department of Political Science, Columbia, University.
Taussig, Michael
1979 Black Religion and Resistance in Colombia: Three Centuries of Social Struggle in the Cauca Valley. Marxist Perspectives 2(2): 84-116.
1980a Folk Healing and the Structure of Conquest in the Southwest of Colombia. Journal of Latin American Lore 6(2): 217-78.
1980b The Devil and Commodity Fetishism in South America. Chapel Hill: University of North Carolina Press.
Teixeira Monteiro, Duglas
1954 A Macumba de Vitória. Congresso Internacional de Americanistas 31: 463-72.
Thompson, E.P.
1963 · The Making of the English Working Class. New York: Random House.
Thornton, Mary
1948 The Church and Freemasonry in Brazil, 1872-1875, a Study of Regalism. Washington, D.C.: The Catholic University Press of America.
Toop, Walter
1972 Organized Religious Groups in a Village of Northeastern Brazil. Luso-Brazilian Review 9(2): 58-77.
Torres, João Camilo de Oliveira
1968 Historia das Ideas Religiosas no Brasil. São Paulo: Editora Grijalbo Ltda.
Trindade, Liana
1982 Exú: reinterpretações individualizados de um mito. Religião e Sociedade 8: 29-36.
Trindade-Serra, Ordep
1978 Na trilha das Crianças—os erês num terreiro de angola. Masters thesis, Universidade de Brasilia.

Ubaldi, Pietro
    c.1935   O Grande Síntese. Rio: Federação Espírita Brasileira.
Vallier, Ivan
    1967   Religious Elites: Differentiations and Developments in Roman Catholicism. *In* Elites in Latin America. Seymour Lipset and Aldo Solari, Eds. New York: Oxford University Press.
Vandezande, René
    1975   Catimbó—Pesquisa exploratória sobre a forma nordestina de religião mediúnica. Masters thesis, Instituto de Filosofia e Ciências Humanas, Universidade Federal de Pernambuco, Recife.
Various authors
    1982/83   Religões e Eleições. Comunicações do ISER, Nos. 2, 3, 4, and 5.
Veja
    1983   Festa nagô: Santos de todo o mundo baixam em Salvador. July 27, No. 777: 49-50.
Velho, Yvonne Maggie
    1975   Guerra de Orixá: Um estudo de Ritual e Conflito. Rio: Zahar Editores.
Verger, Pierre
    1964   Bahia and the West Coast Trade: 1549-1851. Ibadan: Ibadan University Press.
Vergolino e Silva, Anaïsa
    1976   O Tambor das flores: Uma análise da Federação Espírita Umbandista e dos cultos afro-brasileiros do Pará (1965-1975). Masters thesis, Departamento de Antropologia, Universidade Estadual de Campinas. (São Paulo).
Viera, Waldo, and Francisco Cândido Xavier (under the guidance of the spirit André Luiz)
    1958   Evolução em Dois Mundos. Rio: Federação Espírita Brasileira.
Viveiros de Castro Cavalcanti, Maria Laura
    1983   O Mundo Invisivel: Cosmologia, Sistema Ritual e Noção de Pessoa no Espiritismo. Rio: Zahar Editores Ltda.
Wagley, Charles
    1952   Race and Class in Rural Brazil. Paris: UNESCO.
    1963   An Introduction to Brazil. New York: Columbia University Press.
    1964a   Amazon Town: A Study of Man in the Tropics. New York: Alfred A. Knopf.
    1964b   Luso-Brazilian Kinship Patterns: The Persistence of a Cultural Tradition. *In* Politics of Change in Latin America, J. Maier and P. Weatherford, Eds. New York: Frederick A. Praeger.
Wagley, Charles and Eduardo Galvão
    1949   The Tenetehara Indians of Brazil. New York: Columbia University Press.
Warren, Donald
    1965·   The Negro and Religion in Brazil. Race. January. pp. 199-216.
    1968a   Portuguese Roots of Brazilian Spiritism. Luso-Brazilian Review 5(2): 3-33.
    1968b   Spiritism in Brazil. Journal of Inter-American Studies 10: 393-405.
Wauchope, Robert
    1962   Lost Tribes and Sunken Continents. Chicago: University of Chicago Press.
Weffort, Francisco C.
    1970   State and Mass in Brazil. *In* Masses in Latin America. Irving Horowitz, Ed. New York: Oxford University Press.
Weingrod, Alex
    1968   Patrons, Patronage and Political Parties. Comparative Studies in Society and History 10(4): 377-400.

Bibliography *253*

Willems, Emílio
1966 Religious Mass Movements and Social Change in Brazil. *In* New Perspectives of Brazil. Eric Baklanoff, Ed. Nashville: Vanderbilt University Press.
1967 Followers of the New Faith: Culture Change and the Rise of Protestantism in Brazil and Chile. Nashville: Vanderbilt University Press.
1969 Religious Pluralism and Class Structure: Brazil and Chile. *In* Sociology of Religion. Roland Robertson, Ed. Baltimore: Penguin Books.
Wilson, Bryan
1959 Analysis of Sect Development. American Sociological Review 24: 3-15.
1973 Magic and the Millenium: A Sociological Study of Religious Movements of Protest among Tribal and Third-World Peoples. New York: Harper and Row.
Wolf, Eric
1965 Aspects of Group Relations in a Complex Society: Mexico. *In* Contemporary Cultures and Societies of Latin America. Dwight Heath and Richard Adams, Eds. New York: Random House. pp. 85-101.
1968 Kinship, Friendship and Patron-Client Relations in Complex Societies. *In* The Social Anthropology of Complex Societies. Michael Banton, Ed. London and New York: Tavistock Publications.
Worsley, Peter
1957 The Trumpet Shall Sound. London: MacGibbon and Kee.
Xavier, Francisco Cândido (see also Viera, Waldo)
1965 Brasil, Coração do Mundo, Pátria do Evangelho, pelo Espirito de Humberto de Campos. 7th Edition. Rio: Federação Espírita Brasileira.
Xavier, Francisco Cândido and Waldo Viera
1961 Juca Lambisca. Rio: Federação Espírita Brasileira.
Zeigler, J.
1972 O Poder Africano—Elementos de uma Sociologia Política da Africa Negra e de sua Diaspora nas Américas. São Paulo: Difusão Européia do Livro.
1977 Os Vivos e a Morte—Uma "Sociologia da Morte" no Ocidente e na Diaspora Africana no Brasil e seus mecanismos culturais. Rio de Janeiro: Zahar Editores.
Zespo, Emanuel
1949 O Que é a Umbanda. Rio.
1951 Codificação da Lei de Umbanda: Parte Ciêntífica. Rio.
1953 Codificação da Lei de Umbanda: Parte Pragmática. Rio.

Index